a pictorial history of the
THEATRE GUILD

One of the Theatre Guild's memorable productions. Alice Brady and Alla Nazimova on the Robert Edmund Jones set for *Mourning Becomes Electra*. *Vandamm
photograph*

a pictorial history of the

THEATRE GUILD

by Norman Nadel

special material
by Lawrence Langner and Armina Marshall

introduction by Brooks Atkinson

CROWN PUBLISHERS, INC. 419 Park Avenue South New York, N.Y. 10016

Dedication

To Theresa Helburn and Lawrence Langner, who guided the Theatre Guild for the greater part of its fifty years; to Philip Moeller, Helen Westley, Lee Simonson, and Maurice Wertheim, who, with Miss Helburn and Mr. Langner, founded the Theatre Guild and co-directed it for the first twenty years; and to John Gassner who, as play-reader and *dramaturg,* significantly shaped its artistic development

116840

Contents

Preface   vi

Introduction by Brooks Atkinson   vii

   I   The Beginnings   1

  II   The Plays: 1919–1926   6

 III   George Bernard Shaw by Lawrence Langner   44

 IV   1926–1929   62

  V   Eugene O'Neill by Lawrence Langner   86

 VI   1929–1939   100

VII   1939–1948   164

VIII   The Theatre Guild on Radio and Television by
      Armina Marshall   211

 IX   1948–1958   216

  X   1958–1968   249

 XI   The Guild in Films: 1968–1969   273

XII   Today and Tomorrow   276

Appendixes

   I   List of Theatre Guild Plays   278

  II   List of Theatre Guild Productions on Radio   287

 III   List of Theatre Guild Productions on Television   296

Index   304

Preface

There is an apocryphal story about the reporter working against a deadline who rushes up to his city editor with his copy and apologizes: "I'm sorry this piece is so long, but I didn't have time to write a short one." This doesn't have to be explained to any professional journalist—or, in fact, any other serious writer—who knows it is far easier to go on at length than to write concisely. Similarly, the temptation in preparing a 50th anniversary history of the Theatre Guild was to use all the source material available, in which case it would have run to a dozen or more large volumes. Today it is not uncommon for a playwright to do a book about his own play and his troubles in getting it produced; several such have been done in recent seasons. A book probably could have been written about each of the 220 productions discussed in the following pages.

But the intention here was not to be encyclopedic; rather, to tell the Theatre Guild story directly, and with the emphasis on the plays and productions themselves. A pictorial treatment also was indicated, because it is as useful to recall faces as to recall names. What could not be included were the myriad details of searching for and selecting plays, of the writing, rewriting, and production of them. Nor was it possible to encompass all facets of the critical and popular reaction to each Theatre Guild enterprise. Yet all that information was and is available, mostly in the Theatre Guild collection at the Beinecke Rare Book Library at Yale University in New Haven, Connecticut.

This book is full of opinions—those of critics who reviewed these plays as they opened, and of critics who have evaluated them retrospectively. My opinions and evaluations, in both categories, also are included. Yet none of this has been done with the intent of imposing a point of view on the reader, either about a particular production or about the sum of the Theatre Guild's contribution to the theatre in America. For one thing, the critical reaction to, say, a 1937 play might seem dated in terms of altered attitudes and events since. But there is no assurance that a 1969 opinion is any more nearly "right" (if any critical evaluation in the arts ever can be right or wrong) than an earlier one. Nor can we be sure that today's assessment of these plays will not change again in the next few years or decades. So, hopefully, there is enough here to guide a reader toward his own judgment, which will be of greater value to him if he also has read or—even better—seen these plays.

Grateful acknowledgment is due the staff of the Beinecke Library for its help in the preparation of this book. The librarians at the New York Public Library's Theatre Collection at Lincoln Center proved to be enthusiastic collaborators. The Museum of the City of New York made its collection of theatre photographs available, augmenting those in the Beinecke and Lincoln Center collections.

Armina Marshall's ardent involvement has given the book an immediacy, a firsthand aspect, it could not have had otherwise. She was there, as Lawrence Langner's wife, as an actress, and as a director of the Guild. Philip Langner has contributed in a number of ways, as have Julie Morgan and others of the Theatre Guild staff, along with Warren Munsell and Warren Caro, who were key men in the organization for a number of years. Mollie Gassner offered valuable advice and information. Romney Brent proved an amiable aid, remembering much of interest and supplying photographs and clippings from his own archives. Stanley Trachtenberg, senior editor for Crown, made literally hundreds of suggestions which have made this book more readable and informative.

Thanks also are due Arlene Nadel and Leslie West, two professional actresses who not only retyped the manuscript but checked and corrected a wealth of detail while doing it. Finally, no one worked harder or more devotedly on the book than my wife, Martha, who was able to contribute not only her industry, time, and intelligence, but her experience as a professional librarian and accomplished researcher.

Introduction

The modern American theatre began with the appearance of one dramatist and one producing organization. The dramatist was Eugene O'Neill. The producing organization was the Theatre Guild. They made deep impressions on Broadway after World War I at about the same time. In the beginning they had no connection. O'Neill's first Broadway play, *Beyond the Horizon,* was produced by a commercial manager. The Theatre Guild's first production was Jacinto Benavente's *The Bonds of Interest* from the Spanish. Its second play, *John Ferguson,* was by St. John Ervine, an Irish dramatist. It was the popular success of *John Ferguson* that established the Theatre Guild as an enterprising and talented organization.

O'Neill's early plays—*The Emperor Jones, The Hairy Ape,* and *Desire Under the Elms*—were produced in Greenwich Village, and *Anna Christie* was produced on Broadway by Arthur Hopkins. The Guild and O'Neill did not get together until it produced his *Marco Millions* in 1928. After that the association of the two primary forces in the development of the modern American theatre was close. The Guild productions of *Strange Interlude, Ah, Wilderness!, Mourning Becomes Electra,* and *The Iceman Cometh* were milestones—powerful plays produced with great skill and vitality.

There were two peripheral similarities in the experiences of O'Neill and the Guild. Before they established themselves on Broadway they were both contemptuous of the provinciality of the American theatre. Strindberg was the primary source of O'Neill's point of view, and could hardly have been more alien to the tone of the American theatre before World War I. In its early days the Guild was preoccupied with foreign dramatists quite outside the experience of America—Molnár, Andreyev, Werfel, Toller, Zweig, Lenormand, Claudel, Ćapek, Kaiser, Milne, and, of course, Shaw. Until the mid-twenties the foreign influence was greater than the domestic. Both O'Neill and the Guild were criticized as being un-American.

People complained that O'Neill's tragic style was unfair to America; they resented his preoccupation with misery and failure. And so with the Guild: many people suspected that it was subversive because it imported so much immorality and brooding from abroad. As late as 1933 the Guild was denounced as being consistently corrosive and vitriolic and as lacking in the faith, hope, and charity of the old America.

Those were exciting years; so much that was new was appearing on Broadway, and the standards of production were rising so fast. The scenery and lighting of Lee Simonson, a member of the Guild board, made an art out of a craft, as Robert Edmond Jones was doing for Arthur Hopkins. Jo Mielziner, one of Broadway's most creative designers, began his career with the Guild's production of *The Guardsman.* Philip Moeller was one of the early directors who had style. Alfred Lunt and Lynn Fontanne were the stars of the Guild's acting company, though it was thought not to be in good taste to say so because the acting company was supposed to be composed of equals. After civilizing audiences with startling plays from abroad, the Guild soon attracted a number of young American dramatists who had stimulating things to say—S. N. Behrman, Robert E. Sherwood, Sidney Howard, Elmer Rice, Maxwell Anderson, Philip Barry, John Howard Lawson, Dorothy and Du Bose Heyward.

Founded in 1918, the Guild conducted a revolution that helped to liberate the American theatre from hackneyed formulas. In this book Mr. Nadel points out that the revolution was over by 1931 because by that time all reputable producers had adopted the standards that the Guild had set up. Other producers were putting on notable dramas that were equally modern. So, the Guild was vindicated. But while the revolution was going on many people resented the Guild. They regarded the revolution as intellectually snobbish and pretentious; and the Guild's many failures were denounced with a kind of righteous violence as if they were proof that the Guild was a hoax.

Mr. Nadel's comprehensive book with its wealth of information and its thoughtful judgments accounts for the stature of the Guild. The Guild was a primary influence on bringing a childish theatre to maturity. Without the broad views and the tenacity of the original board members, the Theatre Guild would have succumbed to the pleasant superficiality of the old theatre.

BROOKS ATKINSON

I

The Beginnings

A BEGINNING—a true beginning—rarely can be nailed down with anything as convenient or tidy as a date and a place. The temptation is to say that the Theatre Guild was born on a Thursday evening, December 18, 1918, when Lawrence Langner encountered Philip Moeller and Helen Westley having a drink in the basement of the Brevoort Hotel on lower Fifth Avenue in New York City, and broached the idea to them. Or that it started a few nights later at the home of the ailing Josephine A. Meyer, during the first meeting explicitly called to discuss and formulate a new theatre project. Both these events did indeed occur and were unquestionably pivotal, or even epochal. If there was a specific moment when the theatre in America abruptly altered course, it could have been either or both of these.

But a wealth of evidence indicates that these two gatherings were as much a culmination as a beginning. In his play *Who's Afraid of Virginia Woolf?* Edward Albee turns the phrase, "historical inevitability," into a goad, a jibe, and a weapon of derision; people have been intimidated by it ever since. Nevertheless, the Theatre Guild probably was a historical inevitability, insofar as both the need for such an enterprise and the enthusiasms, skills, and personalities needed to implement it were at hand. It would be wrong to say that the need alone made it inevitable; the world—and the arts in particular—is full of needs which all too often go unfulfilled because of the lack of leadership, vision, and ingenuity. The American theatre had suffered the indignities of an almost entirely commercial orientation for years before the Guild people decided to try to do something about artistic quality. (They were

After a few personnel changes in the first months of the Theatre Guild, the guiding board of directors consisted of these six: seated—Lawrence Langner, Maurice Wertheim, Helen Westley, Philip Moeller; standing—Theresa Helburn and Lee Simonson. *Vandamm photograph.*

not the first; the Provincetown Players and the Washington Square Players, along with some dedicated individuals, had tried valiantly if less enduringly to improve the level of theatre taste.) What might be termed a blessed accident was the coming together a half-century ago of Langner, Moeller, Miss Westley, Theresa Helburn, Lee Simonson, and Maurice Wertheim—who became the managing directors—along with others whose contributions helped to make the Guild a reality. The six represented a peculiarly effective union of talents. Much of the time they didn't get along.

1

Some of their battles were Olympian. But out of wrath, connivance, pleading, dealing, and perhaps an amiable touch of double-dealing, they managed to make artistic decisions which seemed right then and—in some but not all cases—seem right and admirable today. The sum of their individual and collective ardor can be read not just in the 230 plays produced by the Guild to date, or even in the millions of people who were reached as the Guild spread its activities to a number of American cities. It is the undeniable fact that today's theatre is more vital, imaginative, and daring, also less provincial and prosaic, that testifies to the impact of these people on the theatre arts.

So somewhere among two needs and several personalities can be found the most subtle and meaningful beginnings of the Theatre Guild. One need was for a kind of stage fare which would be determined by something more lofty than box office—catering to the lowest common denominator among entertainment-seekers. Ideas such as educating an audience or enriching the literature of the stage were seldom mentioned around Broadway, except with indulgent amusement. The professional stage was dominated by two factions, Klaw and Erlanger, and the brothers Shubert. They were out to make money, and they did; they could afford to ignore a minority who believed that going to the theatre could be not only entertaining but an enlightening or even exalting experience. Nevertheless the need for better plays was there, even if it was not being met.

The second need, which actually is closely interwoven with the first, was for a place where young people trained in theatre at colleges and universities, such as the graduates of George Pierce Baker's '47 Workshop at Harvard, could put their abilities to professional use at a level commensurate with their training. They were openly wondering why the contemporary theatre should have been so arid, if not trashy, when the stage in other times and places had turned out writers such as Shakespeare, Molière, Ibsen, and the indestructible Greeks. Miss Helburn, Simonson, and Wertheim all had studied with Baker. Miss Westley was a graduate of the American Academy of Dramatic Arts, and Philip Moeller had been graduated from Columbia, continuing to study with Brander Matthews for several years thereafter. Langner, whose formal education had terminated when he was about thirteen but whose self-learn-

ing and scholarship in theatre were prodigious, had come by a different route to the same conclusion about the deficiencies of the American stage.

Of the six, only Lawrence Langner was not a native American. Born in Swansea, in South Wales, on May 30, 1890, he had endured a childhood which was something less than idyllic. His parents were divorced when he was small (divorce inflicted even crueler punishment on children then, when the whole business was considered a disgrace, than now, when society is considerably more tolerant—or indifferent). Still, he was an adaptable lad, who found not only escape but a deep enjoyment in a large toy theatre, with cutout scenery and actors, which his father had given him. He was able to stage *The Corsican Brothers, The Sleeping Beauty, Cox and Box,* and other Victorian theatre pieces. Though he might not have realized it then, at the age of ten he was hooked. He read a great deal, then and throughout his life, more than compensating for the lack of formal schooling. Subsequently he worked very briefly as a junior clerk for a theatrical agency, then as a novice for a patent office. Equally talented in engineering and the arts, he rose rapidly in patent work, coming to New York at the age of twenty as technical assistant for his English firm specializing in American patents. That side of his career is a story in itself; briefly, he did very well as a young man and all through his life in patent law, working with inventors such as Charles F. Kettering who, when they met, had just designed the automobile self-starter.

He was fortunate in meeting other stimulating young people right from the time he came to this country. Through his friends Alice and Claire Raphael he became acquainted with Theresa Helburn and Philip Moeller, the latter already launched as a playwright and stage director. Other new friends included Edward Goodman, who was to become director of the Washington Square Players, political writer Walter Lippmann, novelist Waldo Frank, painter Robert Henri, and Robert Edmond Jones, then an assistant art instructor at Harvard, who was to emerge as one of the most creative scenic and costume designers of the American stage. Moeller introduced Langner to his cousin, Josephine A. Meyer, a physically frail but spiritually luminous girl whose idealism and good sense proved invaluable to Langner and the rest of that group during the few years she had yet to live. It was at her home, not long before her death, that the first Guild organizational meeting was held.

During the winter of 1914, the Liberal Club formed a dramatic branch to produce plays, but Langner and a few others didn't care for the idea and decided to start a theatre of their own. The next evening, at the home of Max Eastman, then editor of *The Masses,* Langner and Mrs. Eastman (Ida Rauh, an actress) plotted to bring into their venture such theatrically inclined individuals as Robert Edmond Jones, Sam Eliot, Edward Goodman, Moeller, Miss Meyer, George Cram Cook, Susan Glaspell, Lucy Huffaker, Helen Westley, Ralph Roeder, Daisy Thompson, and Dudley Tucker. The new group took the name of the Washington Square Players. Its manifesto focused on artistic merit, with a subscription system designed to keep the price of tickets at fifty cents. These were to be two of the legacies to the Theatre Guild—play quality as a primary determinant and the subscription plan. A third was the revolutionary concept of committee directorship, with all the checks, cross-checks, and frustrations involved. It was democratic but bloody, still achieving its end of avoiding the usual autocratic guidance of a theatre project by one man or woman. The fact that some of the plays were, frankly, ghastly doesn't invalidate the project or lessen its value in developing a new concept of theatre. They experimented; they made grand, brash mistakes, and they developed some of the best actors, actresses, and technicians to dominate the stage in the next twenty or thirty years. In four years (closing in May, 1918) the Washington Square Players produced sixty-two one-act plays and pantomimes and six full-length dramas. Thirty-eight of these plays were American—over 50 percent—which, at that time, was unprecedented. Some of its people helped to organize the Provincetown Players, best remembered for having introduced the dramas of Eugene O'Neill.

So what Langner brought to the Guild was this earlier seasoning in experimental theatre, a sound knowledge of who the most daring, inventive, and talented of the young theatre people were, and his own drive and uncanny acumen. Married for a few years to Estelle Roege, he later wed Armina Marshall, who both admired his powers of concentration and found them irritating. "When I wanted to tell him something I'd yell and stamp my feet," she recalled years later, "but nothing would penetrate when he was deep in thought or work on a project. Finally, when he was finished, he'd look up and ask: 'What did you say?' He had learned to concentrate when studying patent law while working as a novice in England. He could shut off everything else from his consciousness."

A natural conciliator, he usually resolved differences productively after his colleagues on the Guild's Board of Managers had argued themselves into exhaustion. Still, it frustrated even him not to have his own way, as was bound to happen much of the time with six directors making the decisions, which is why he and Armina eventually started the Westport (Connecticut) Country Playhouse; there he could stage any play any way he wanted.

Philip Moeller was an utter realist about the theatre, who nonetheless directed by instinct—and in his case these two qualities were not contradictory. Whenever he discussed his profession he would refer to "work in the theatre" rather than "the art of the theatre," which was a currently popular phrase. In so doing he had no intention of denying the esthetics of the drama, but he wanted his listeners to understand that the preparation of a play was first and foremost an exercise in communication; that the director, no matter how lofty his concepts, had no value unless he could transmit every subtlety of his and the playwright's ideas and feelings to the people out front.

He rarely, if ever, approached a play with a rigid plan laid out, though naturally he had a pretty clear idea in his own mind of the eventual effect he hoped to achieve. But his technique was to find out what each player could do, then turn that ability to the uses of the play. Whereas some directors have been psychically blind to the cast (or so actors and actresses are apt to claim), Moeller really perceived the play through them. He was acutely aware of the person on stage—of body, movement, gesture. He directed with that in mind, going more by what they could do than by demanding that they implement his preconceived ideas. Consequently the rehearsal of a play seemed —and probably was—spontaneous. He knew when to toss his players an idea, and when to let them develop their own means of dealing with a situation. Naturally, when he worked repeatedly with performers such as the Lunts, Ina Claire, or Clare Eames, he understood at the start just what talents he had at hand, and what he could do with them.

He did have his idiosyncrasies. Once he had directed a play, and stood in the back of the house watching it on opening night, he never looked at it again. He wouldn't re-rehearse a company, or prepare a second production for the road; the Guild would have to find someone else to do that. In dress he permitted himself the affectation of wearing his overcoat, or sometimes a cape, thrown over his shoulders in winter, with a thick woolen scarf around his neck. Quite apart from the sensible purpose of keeping him warm, this did give him a casual elegance which certainly didn't hurt the director image.

Moeller was deeply, though apparently not romantically, devoted to the actress Helen Westley, one of his colleagues on the Guild board, as she was to him. They ate together regularly, splitting the bill to the exact penny. Even when they argued, it was with that fine, florid vehemence of two people who are very close to each other.

She was very much an individual, including dress; even in the flapper era of the 1920's Helen wore skirts that cleared the floor by a scant six inches. She carried not only her cash but her several bankbooks in her stockings—nine of them on one occasion—which, when she was seated, showed beneath her slightly raised skirt. She liked to have several young men around her, and was as direct and forthright in her speech as Tallulah Bankhead became some years later. She lived in Brooklyn, had been married and had a daughter, but had left her husband. In *The Theatre Guild: The First Ten Years,* Walter Prichard Eaton writes:

> Besides her special gifts as an actress, Miss Westley contributed to the organization an original personality, with a mind unusually free from social or conventional prejudices. Her catholicity of taste in the selection of plays and her uncompromising devotion to the ideals of the art theatre have made her a collaborator whose sincerity has always been respected by her associates, even when there have been wide variations of opinion between her and them on matters of policy and play selection.

Theresa Helburn had started with the Guild as play representative, or play-reader, but after the first few meetings she was engaged as executive director and a member of the board, and stayed for more than thirty years. Like the others, she had not just one but a number of qual-

ities which were of value. First of all, Theresa—or Terry—was charming, with little-girl qualities that never seemed the least bit affected. She had a brilliant mind, was beautifully educated (Bryn Mawr and Baker's '47 Workshop at Harvard), and responded among friends with a great deal of warmth, though that quality never descended into sentimentality. She was a shrewd business manager, able to get people cheap without hurting their feelings, and she had good taste. She was the first and the most insistent to propose making Lynn Riggs's *Green Grow the Lilacs* into the musical which eventually emerged as *Oklahoma!* Before joining the Guild she had been drama critic for *The Nation,* which provided one more point of vantage for the development of her taste in theatre. The time was to come when her efficiency as executive director led to grumblings about the extent of her authority by the other five directors, with Lee Simonson charging that she had established a "dictatorship of the executariat." She weathered that, but soon after resigned the executive post, remaining, however, a member of the board.

Lee Simonson, like Robert Edmond Jones, was a painter before he was infected with the living theatre and turned to scenic and costume design, but even then he continued to express himself in several fields; he edited *Creative Art* for a while, designed furniture, and did interior decorating. From the Guild's beginning he was the technical expert in design, but his participation went far beyond that. He had come into the picture directly after his discharge from the Army at the close of World War I, bringing what Langner described as "the most intensely logical mind I have ever encountered anywhere," adding: "but once it was made up, it was a Herculean task to get him to change it." In the Guild meetings, Lee usually was the noisiest and most vituperative, but these characteristics stemmed not from malice or conceit as much as from the assurance that his ideas were the right ones and should be followed. As a rule at Guild sessions, Terry and Lawrence would tend to agree, and Helen and Philip would team up on their own preference concerning which play they'd do next. Lee wouldn't like either, and Maurice Wertheim usually would cast the deciding vote.

Langner had known Wertheim well before the Theatre Guild days; in fact, he and his first wife had been married on Thanksgiving Day,

1915, at Maurice's estate in Greenwich, Connecticut. The two men were the only members of the Guild's board of managers who followed careers outside the theatre; Wertheim's ability to handle money, and to earn it (he was a millionaire) was invaluable to the struggling young theatre organization. His judgment was considered, rather than impassioned, and, like the others, he was blessed with good taste.

Back to the night of December 18, 1918. The Washington Square Players had come to an end the preceding spring, which meant that a number of its members were at loose ends, still driven by the conviction that they—or somebody— should be providing better theatre than was being made available by the Broadway commercial managements. While there is no record to bear this out, it is quite likely that several plans were being discussed, though it is impossible to say if another would have been implemented if the Guild hadn't shaped up first.

At any event, Langner encountered Moeller and Miss Westley in the basement of the Brevoort, where they enjoyed a bottle of wine, each other's company, and their collective exuberance for theatre. Lawrence's announcement that he intended to start a new company to succeed the Washington Square troupe delighted Helen, who enthused, "Why of course; I want to act again!" Philip was all set to start work immediately. So Lawrence, whose good attributes included an orderly mind, said he'd call a meeting.

Attending that first session were Langner, Moeller, Miss Westley, Rollo Peters, Edna Kenton, and Josephine Meyer, at whose home it was held. These decisions were reached:

1—That we will form a group to carry out the idea of an expert theatre; that is, a theatre which will be entirely different from the little theatre or Provincetown Players type of theatre, but would be made up only of artists of the theatre who are experts in their work.

2—That we will either lease or secure the building of a theatre seating a considerable number of people, and certainly larger than the usual little theatre (between 500 and 600 seating capacity), in some place where the rents are sufficiently low not to make rentals a burden.

3—To govern absolutely by a committee which will delegate its executive and administrative powers to members thereof.

The organizational name was suggested by Langner, who remembered the medieval guildhouses in Brussels. A bit later the group's fundamental aim was edited down to a sentence: "To produce plays of artistic merit not ordinarily produced by the commercial managers." A measure of the Guild's success is the fact that in time this declaration no longer worked; the "commercial managers" followed their lead in finding and staging plays of artistic merit. Also, the Guild, by virtue of its own success in attracting audiences and making money at least part of the time, became "commercial managers" themselves.

Rollo Peters, an accomplished actor and scenic artist, helped make many of the pivotal decisions at the start, as well as holding out staunchly for professionalism in the Guild against the proponents of amateur participation. He went with Langner to see the wealthy Otto Kahn, who held a lease on the old Garrick Theatre, which the two young men coveted for their group's purpose. They explained that their finances were almost nil, whereupon the old gentleman decided: "Very well. When you make the rent, you will pay the rent. When you do not make it, you need not pay it."

As the organizational meetings continued, they attracted such talent as Dudley Digges, Augustin Duncan, Edna St. Vincent Millay, Henry Herbert, Justus Sheffield, Helen Freeman, and others, along with those previously named. Peters was the first director, with Miss Meyer as playreader. As might have been expected, there was a natural sorting-out process which had to occur; it included disputes over casting, operation, and other matters. In time some of these people separated themselves from the group, either over differences that were administrative or artistic in nature, or simply because their other activities or interests interfered. So it was not until several plays had been produced that the board of managers evolved with the six who were to stay with the Guild for many years to come—Lawrence Langner, Theresa Helburn, Lee Simonson, Philip Moeller, Maurice Wertheim, and Helen Westley.

II

The Plays: 1919-1926

TRUE TO THEIR HIGH IDEALS, the directors of the newly formed Theatre Guild selected *The Bonds of Interest,* written in 1907 by the Nobel Prize winner, Jacinto Benavente, to launch their enterprise. A puppet play performed by living actors, it probably is the best of Benavente's more than 100 plays, and provides a commedia dell'arte atmosphere for a satiric comment on human behavior. The servant Crispin establishes credit for his master, Leander, so the latter can woo Silvia, but the creditors catch up with Leander. Crispin points out that they can be paid only if Leander marries Silvia. So the play ends happily, but with the warning that "the bonds of love are as nothing to the bonds of interest."

Helen Westley, Dudley Digges, Rollo Peters, and Augustin Duncan were cast in principal roles, and Edna St. Vincent Millay made a delicate Columbine. Peters also directed. One hundred thirty-five loyal Guild subscribers were in their seats at the Garrick for the opening performance on Monday evening, April 14, 1919; though their applause was generous, the critical reviews the following day were not favorable. For three weeks Langner met the operating losses of about $500 a week—he'd been saving the money to buy a car—and was nearing the point of despair when Maurice Wertheim attended a performance. He offered to meet some of the losses and thus became a partner in the Guild.

A combination of fortuitous circumstances changed things dramatically for the Guild with its second play, *John Ferguson.* Langner had found a copy of it at Brentano's bookstore on Fifth Avenue one afternoon, and, having met the author, St. John Ervine, in England some years be-

The Bonds of Interest—Jacinto Benavente's rueful comment on human nature was the first Theatre Guild production. Above, Rollo Peters and C. Hooper Trask.

Bonds of Interest—The petite girl in the center soon abandoned acting in favor of poetry. She was Edna St. Vincent Millay. At left, Guild director and co-founder Helen Westley.

fore, eventually managed to secure production rights without having to make an advance payment. That would have been impossible anyway, as the Guild was broke, following the losses incurred by *The Bonds of Interest.*

Opening on May 12, 1919, this tragic drama of pyramiding misfortune was an immediate success, with critics as well as audiences. The play, premiered in Dublin in 1915, is set in County Down, Ireland, where the title character, a crippled farmer, waits for God and his rich brother in America to prevent foreclosure of the mortgage. Ere long his daughter is seduced ("ruined," in the vernacular of the time) by the man who holds the mortgage, who in turn is murdered. To make this all the more ironic, the money from Andrew in America finally arrives; he had forgotten to post the letter. Though *John Ferguson* has all the earmarks of the most blatant melodrama, it is told with simplicity and directness, and enjoyed a number of revivals as Ervine's most popular and possibly most skillfully wrought drama.

It was during the run of this play that actors finally organized to secure basic rights of income and working hours, and went on strike to enforce their demands. The Theatre Guild was the first organization to recognize Actors Equity Association. As a result, *John Ferguson* was the only play running in New York for several months. It put the young Guild on its feet and permitted the move from the Garrick to the Fulton Theatre, where the play enjoyed a long and highly profitable stay.

The 1919–1920 season began on October 13 with John Masefield's *The Faithful,* based on a Japanese legend dating from the fourteenth century B.C. An expensive play to stage and costume, it lost a lot of the money which had been earned by *John Ferguson,* and also caused the first split in the Guild ranks. Rollo Peters, the Guild's director, and Augustin Duncan, who produced *The Faithful,* had insisted on doing Masefield's long script without cuts, which was protested by some of the backers. Also, portions of the dialogue held the rich up to scorn for their treatment of the poor. One of the backers pointed out that wealthy persons had made possible the artistic success of the Guild, and that such an attack on persons of fortune was unjustifiable. When Guild sentiment appeared to favor dropping those passages, both Peters and Duncan resigned; Lee Simonson replaced Peters as director. However,

John Ferguson—Helen Westley and Augustin Duncan depicted benign old age in the Guild's second play and first box-office success.

John Ferguson—Barry McCollum.

The Faithful—sets and costumes were designed by Lee Simonson, who became a Guild director at this time.

the two dissenters, both with principal roles, remained in the cast. Later Simonson denied that the Guild had any rich backers, and said the text had been cut at Masefield's suggestion, because of its length.

For the first time, and contrary to its avowed policy of "starring" the play rather than a particular actor or actress, the Guild employed James K. Hackett to do the title role in Lillian Sabine's adaptation of the William Dean Howells novel, *The Rise of Silas Lapham.* A costly production, it was the first of many over the ensuing years to almost kill the Theatre Guild through financial disaster. Fortunately, the Guild always survived. *Silas Lapham* drew a mixed press. The *New York Herald,* in a burst of patriotic fervor, enthused: "The play was blessed by being so entirely and worthily American. One of the most fortunate dramatic events of the dramatic season." However, the opposition was well voiced by the *Tribune*'s comment that "The only thing more conventional than the play itself was the performance of James K. Hackett in the leading role." Hackett retreated to London, to appear opposite Mrs. Pat Campbell in a Shaw play, and the Guild decided its brief experiment with the star system had been a failure. It returned to "starring" the play and "featuring" the players for the next 20 or more years, until a playwright insisted on listing Alfred Lunt and Lynn Fontanne as stars.

Moral preachment proved ineffectual at the box office with the production of Leo Tolstoy's *The Power of Darkness* opening January 19, 1920. It is a dark and brooding play, somewhat in the mood of Ervine's *John Ferguson,* though lifted at the end by the hope of redemption through prayer. Tolstoy had written it in 1866, following his own turn toward a deeper belief in Christianity. A young farm wife, encouraged by her mother, poisons her old husband so she can go to bed with the farmhand, Nikita, who has seduced and killed an orphan girl. After she weds Nikita, he seduces her half-witted stepdaughter, then kills the child of that illicit union. "The point of the play," observed a *Christian Science Monitor* writer when it was revived in 1949, "lies in its climax, when the laborer falls on his knees in repentance and begs pardon of God." Writing about the play, Dr. Joseph Shipley notes that Shaw had said of it: "I remember nothing in the whole range of drama that fascinated me more"; and Zola had cried out in the theatre when it was done in Europe: "Don't change a single word." Nevertheless, it failed to stir or even attract audiences when the Guild staged its American premiere, and the venture left the young producing organization with less than $200 in the bank.

Once again, a St. John Ervine drama saved the day. It was *Jane Clegg,* suggested by Emmanuel Reicher, who had directed *The Power of Darkness.*

The Rise of Silas Lapham—use of a "star" name—James K. Hackett—in the title role failed to draw audiences to this dramatization of the William Dean Howells' novel. *Vandamm photograph.*

The Power of Darkness—a moralizing Leo Tolstoy had written this brooding tragedy with its message of redemption through prayer. It did not prove popular.

Jane Clegg—Margaret Wycherly, Dudley Digges, and Helen Westley in the Theatre Guild's second St. John Ervine play which, like his *John Ferguson,* was cordially received.

Margaret Wycherly portrayed the title character, a lower-middle-class wife burdened by a husband who is not faithful, nor honest, nor dependable. She tries to leave him, but when he cashes a check belonging to his employer, she uses money set aside for the children's education to keep their father out of jail. Eventually she does get rid of him, but moves in with her mother-in-law, who shows every prospect of spoiling Jane's three children as she had spoiled her own son. The strength of the play lies in the way Ervine has provided insights to make even the most sordid or senseless actions of its people seem reasonable in terms of their own background and circumstance. Critical reviews noted this quality of honesty and realism. Heywood Broun in the *Tribune* keynoted the prevailing admiration when he described *Jane Clegg* as the finest achievement of the Theatre Guild. And George Jean Nathan wrote that "the Theatre Guild, which seemed to be tottering, has brilliantly redeemed itself and again found its feet."

The Guild was one of the first producing organizations in the United States to recognize the status and significance of the late Swedish dramatist August Strindberg. Solidly bankrolled again by *Jane Clegg,* it prepared two performances, for subscribers only, of *The Dance of Death* on successive Sunday evenings in May of 1920. If ever there was evidence of the Guild's enlightened and noncommercial outlook, this was it. Doing Strindberg then was as avant-garde as the staging of Genet, Ionesco, Albee, and de Ghelderode were only a few years ago. In fact, the climate today is far more cordial toward experimental theatre than it was in 1920. And whatever charges of commercialism might be leveled against the theatre in the late 1960's, it is considerably more artistically oriented than it had been forty or fifty

The Dance of Death—Albert Parry, Dudley Digges, and Helen Westley performed in one of the pioneer American productions of this avant-garde drama by Sweden's August Strindberg.

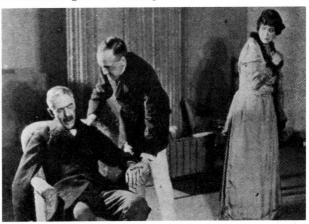

years earlier. Today an audience is apt to be intrigued by a new play in an unfamiliar style, but audiences were not nearly as adventurous when the Guild was getting started. Nevertheless, the name of the game was dramatic quality, from the very inception of the group, and they were right in doing Strindberg's heavy and pessimistic drama about the never-ending battle between man and woman, because its psychological probings foreshadowed much of significance about the theatre to come when he wrote it in 1901.

Once again the Guild turned to rural tragedy in *Nightshade,* by Henry Stillman, who produced four special matinees of his drama to finish the first season; it ran concurrently with *Jane Clegg* and apparently was a fairly ghastly play.

Launching the season of 1921–1922 was *The Treasure,* by David Pinski. A Jewish story, it was cast almost entirely by Irish or Irish-American players, which certainly didn't help. Despite a sympathetic production by Emmanuel Reicher, who was a friend of the playwright, and some critical approval of the play itself, it didn't do well, though it had been produced more successfully during the previous ten years in the Yiddish theatre. Yudke, half-witted son of Chone the gravedigger (Dudley Digges), unearths a few gold coins in the graveyard. Eventually Chone's family and the entire village believe that Yudke has discovered a fortune and react accordingly. Irony and bitterness set the tone of the play, but the ending is not as grim; Chone gets to keep his job, his daughter gets to keep the new clothes she bought with the money, and there is hope that she'll land a husband.

The second adventure that second season was *Heartbreak House,* beginning a long and colorful association between the Guild and Bernard Shaw that was to include the production of seventeen of his plays in the years to come. It followed a long hiatus in Shaw's career during World War I and, in the playwright's own words, " . . . saved me from bankruptcy." Not only did it achieve a welcome success with audiences but it added immeasurably to the prestige of the young Guild. When Lawrence Langner cabled Shaw for permission to stage the play, Shaw telegraphed his friend St. John Ervine, "Who on earth is Langner?" Ervine, having had two of his works done by the Guild, assured the Irish writer that Langner and the Guild could be trusted to do

The Treasure—Helen Westley and Fred Eric in a play which had been done ten years earlier in the Yiddish theatre.

the job properly. Later Shaw cabled to order that the opening be delayed until after the Presidential election, so it was held until November 10, by which time Warren G. Harding had been chosen to lead the country back to "normalcy." The details of Langner's wonderfully warm relationship with GBS are described by Langner in a following section of this book.

Shaw showed uncanny foresight in his preface to *Heartbreak House,* which predicts that only one generation would pass before another great war, in which Germany and Russia would again be major world powers. Like Chekhov's *The Cherry Orchard,* it uses the setting of a country house of upper-class people to depict the deterioration of a segment of society. This "fantasia in the Russian manner upon English themes" describes cultured, leisured Europe before the war. "Heartbreak House in short, did not know how to live," wrote Shaw, "'at which point all that was left to it was the boast that at least it knew how to die; a melancholy accomplishment which the outbreak of war presently gave it practically unlimited opportunities of displaying." The Guild pressured him to permit cuts in a long and discursive script, but the playwright curtly cabled back: "Abandon play, cancel contract." So no cuts were made, and while some of the critics complained of its length, theatre opinion since has tended to vindicate Shaw for holding on to every word. Nevertheless, the cleverly metaphorical Heywood Broun said it well when he wrote fol-

Heartbreak House—suggesting the great cabin of an old square rigger was Lee Simonson's set for the Guild's first bout with Shaw. The players: Erskine Sanford, Elizabeth Risdon, Ralph Roeder, Fred Eric, Lucile Watson, and Albert Parry.

lowing the opening: "We like the needle but we could dispense with the haystack."

During the 129-performance run of *Heartbreak House,* the Guild put on six matinees of *John Hawthorne,* by David Liebovitz, an enterprise notable only as the first American play to be done by the Guild. According to the Boston *Transcript,* it was laughed off the stage. Said Gilbert Seldes: "It has been universally panned. I have yet to find the person or persons who can understand the why and wherefore of this production at the hands of the Guild." The action is set in the Kentucky hills, and describes a pious young woman's struggle between her conscience and her awakening love for her husband's young farmhand.

The comedienne Laura Hope Crews had been in retirement when, at the suggestion of Theresa Helburn, the Guild invited her to play Olivia in A. A. Milne's English comedy, *Mr. Pim Passes By,* in which Erskine Sanford did the title role. At the time, Milne's dramatic work was al-

most unknown in America, his *Belinda* being the only one which had been done here, and he was having a tough time finding producers. After *Mr. Pim,* which ran for 232 performances first at the Garrick and then uptown at Henry Miller's before going on tour under a commercial management, Milne was much in demand. The title character upsets a proper English household when he comes from Australia to mention casually that he had met a man with the name of the wife's first husband (previously believed dead) on the ship. Later he decided he had the name wrong, but by that time the sinews of affection between his hostess and host have been properly tested.

Ferenc Molnár's *Liliom* was written in 1908 but didn't reach New York until the Guild premiered it on April 20, 1921, with Dudley Digges, Eva Le Gallienne, Helen Westley, and Joseph Schildkraut heading the cast. Twenty-four years later it was to achieve another kind of triumph rewritten and set to music by Richard

Mr. Pim Passes By—Erskine Sanford, Dudley Digges, and Laura Hope Crews in A. A. Milne's comedy. *Vandamm photograph.*

Mr. Pim Passes By—Laura Hope Crews came out of retirement to help this play run for 232 performances. With her is Dudley Digges.

Lee Simonson, who served on the Theatre Guild's board, designed sets and costumes for many of its plays, including *Liliom, He Who Gets Slapped, The Tidings Brought to Mary,* and *Goat Song. Pinchot photograph.*

Rodgers and Oscar Hammerstein II as the musical *Carousel.* In 1921 it benefited from some of Lee Simonson's most ingenious sets, which were charming and pictorial without the sacrifice of their apparent simplicity. While *Liliom* had been done before abroad, it had failed in its Budapest world premiere, but the New York triumph began another round of productions overseas. The thought of making this fantasy about a carousel barker into a musical had occurred to many people over the years, but Molnár had steadfastly refused permission to anyone, even the Italian operatic composer Puccini. Out of gratitude and faith, he did extend permission when the Guild requested that the play be done as a musical by Rodgers and Hammerstein. Today it is considered a masterpiece in both forms. *Liliom* ran for 311 performances, before being released for tour.

In May of 1921 a revival of *John Ferguson* was attempted, but the original cast could not

Liliom—Eva Le Gallienne, Joseph Schildkraut, and Helen Westley were featured in the American premiere of Molnár's play about a carousel barker.

be reassembled and the good effect of the initial production was lost. The theatre year concluded with two performances of Emile Verhaeren's *The Cloister,* translated in blank verse and rhyming couplets by Osborne Edwards. One review remarked that "It is perhaps most important to note that the Guild does not slight its private performances," going on to describe beautiful scenic design (by Sheldon K. Viele) and good acting, and concluding: "Again the Guild has demonstrated that membership in it, far from being a charity, is a privilege." Verhaeren (1855–1916) was a poet of the "Young Belgium" group whose motto was "Let us be ourselves." Within the monastic calm of the cloister seethes a struggle between the well-born monks who traditionally have guided the colony and the more ambitious and plebeian younger men who have embraced the cloistered life. The play examines the kind of humility, if it is that, which would make a brother confess a crime not just to his church but to the whole village.

An American play—second to be done by the Guild—began the fourth season on October 10, 1921. With a Jersey City locale, Arthur Kickman's *Ambush* describes the plight of a well-intentioned father who learns that his daughter, wanting more of the nice things of life than his small income can provide, has turned to commercializing her good looks. Florence Eldridge portrayed the girl who takes the short cut to what she wants, and Frank Reicher played the father, with Jane

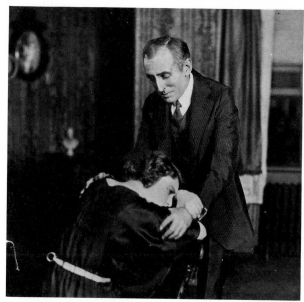

Ambush—Florence Eldridge and Frank Reicher as daughter and father.

Wheatley as the mother who not only condones but assists her daughter's saunter down the primrose path. Milton himself was neither poor nor trapped in Jersey City. He belonged to the country club set, and used to speculate on the lives of the people in dingy Jersey City houses while riding through there on the way into Manhattan. While the play is not outstanding, it does offer the innovation, for that time, of having the story told entirely from the point of view of a single character—the father.

Two French plays made up an interim double bill while the Guild was preparing for its second bout with Shaw. Georges Courteline's farce, *Bourbouroche,* was enjoyed by critic Francis Hackett of *The New Republic,* who observed that the playwright applies farce "not to the physical conduct of his people, which is quite restrained, but to the human folly they illustrate." The play makes the reasonable point, by French standards, that a girl might have two lovers and, in a sense, two lives, if she keeps them free of conflict. Hackett cared much less for the Denys Amiel–André Obey tragi-comedy, *The Wife with a Smile,* in which Blanche Yurka portrayed the suffering wife of a businessman.

Greater interest was stirred by the first American professional staging of Leonid Andreyev's *He Who Gets Slapped,* which had been done previously by students of Alexander Dean at the University of Montana. Through the use of two stage levels connected by stairs, designer

The Cloister—a scene from Emile Verhaeren's poetic drama.

He Who Gets Slapped—Margalo Gillmore as Consuelo and Richard Bennett as "He." *Vandamm photograph.*

Simonson was able to accommodate a large cast without crowding the set. A fantasy. which bewildered many of the audience, the drama depicts a sensitive, cultured man who is slapped in the face by circumstance. "He" sees the irony of it and realizes the added irony of taking a job in a circus as the man who gets slapped by the rest of the company in front of the audience. He joins in the laughter at himself. But slapping "He" doesn't make the circus people happy. Consuelo, the bareback rider, is to be sold by her father to a wealthy baron. Rather than face that, she takes poison with "He," who loves her. When the baron hears she is dead, he commits suicide. Richard Bennett appeared in the Guild production as "He," and Margalo Gillmore was the lovely Consuelo. Andreyev wrote *He Who Gets Slapped* in 1916, and he died three years later.

After a month at the Garrick, where it opened on January 9, 1922, the Andreyev play was moved to the Fulton, later back to the Garrick, chalking up a gratifying total of 274 performances in New York. That made it far more successful than Shaw's *Back to Methuselah,* which followed, surviving either twenty-five or seventy-five performances, depending on how you look at it. The complete play was done twenty-five times, but that entailed seventy-five evenings in the theatre. Nevertheless, the Shavian undertaking is more fondly remembered as an example of the Guild's daring, tenacity of purpose, and perhaps sheer recklessness. Also, Shaw is Shaw, and his "Gospel of Creation," as he also called this dramatic marathon, is something to experience. The playwright was realistic about it; when the Guild asked him for a contract he had replied: "A contract is unnecessary. It isn't likely that any other lunatics will want to produce it." That reply provided the title for Lawrence Langner's posthumously published *GBS and the Lunatic.*

Back to Methuselah articulates Shaw's theory of creative evolution—the idea that if men can live long enough to really mature (about 300 years), there is hope for civilization to endure. The preface alone runs over 30,000 words, and there are 90,000 in the play proper, a "metabiological pentateuch" whose five parts were spread over three evenings of performances in the Guild's production which opened February 27 at the Garrick.

The "philosophic fantasy" begins in the Garden of Eden, where Eve's scanty costume (Ernita Lascelles in the role) occasioned as much com-

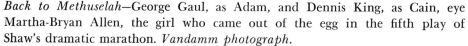

Back to Methuselah—George Gaul, as Adam, and Dennis King, as Cain, eye Martha-Bryan Allen, the girl who came out of the egg in the fifth play of Shaw's dramatic marathon. *Vandamm photograph.*

Back to Methuselah—Lee Simonson's stark set for this scene suggested stage designs of the future. The actor is George Gaul. *Vandamm photograph.*

Back to Methuselah—George Gaul and Ernita Lascelles depict biblical characters in this early part of the five-play series. *Vandamm photograph.*

ment among some of the reviewers as the play itself. Here Lilith has divided herself to create Adam and Eve, and Eve's persistent question "Why?" is answered reasonably by the serpent with "Why not?" A few hundred years later Eve is still looking for some way to make life worth living, but Adam is waiting for death. Part II is political and contemporary, as of the time when Shaw was writing it (1918–1920). By Part III time has moved ahead to the year 2170, and the idea of long life is being pursued keenly by the President of the British Isles, who is interested in an American device by which people can breathe underwater. By this time some of the principal characters are approaching 300 years of age. By Part IV, in A.D. 3000, the world is run by the people who have discovered long life, and the capital of the British Empire has moved to Baghdad. "As Far As Thought Can Reach" is the title for Part V, set in A.D. 31,920, when children are hatched from eggs when they reach adolescence, are permitted to devote the next four years to love and play, then are turned into "Ancients," who live forever if they can avoid accidents. The ghosts of Adam, Eve, and Cain, and the voice of the serpent are heard as the play finally is brought to its conclusion.

Staging *Back to Methuselah* required more time than director Philip Moeller possibly could give it, so the Guild asked the Neighborhood Playhouse, a function of the Henry Street Settlement, to assist; its directors, Alice Lewisohn and Agnes Morgan, prepared the first part, "In the Beginning." After the run had started, Lawrence Langner visited Shaw in England and, with the connivance of Mrs. Shaw, got the playwright to agree to some cuts. That helped, but not enough to overcome public and critical resistance to a drama so lengthy and discursive; it closed after a nine-week run at a loss of $20,000. Some years later Shaw claimed that the Guild had made $10,-000 on his name because they had expected to lose $30,000.

According to the critic Joseph T. Shipley, the play:

. . . represents Shaw's fullest and most deeply pondered study of the problems of mankind. It is, however, scintillant and searching, satiric and expository, rather than dramatic: a thesis in the theatre. The basic problem man faces, as Shaw presents it, is to grow strong enough to surmount the destructive forces that man's own development has loosed within the world. He can achieve this through the creative evolution of the self-conscious mind, achieving indefinite longevity. This leaves him free for the ecstatic contemplation of the free intelligence, which Shaw, in a measure, equates with God.

All that was proved by Arnold Bennett's comedy, *What the Public Wants,* when it opened at the Garrick on May 1, 1922, was that this wasn't it. The Guild might well have noted one line toward the end of this satire on yellow journalism in England, when a character—a drama critic of all people—warns: "Take care that the day doesn't come when the public will want something better than you have to give." The public did want something better than *What the Public Wants,* but to the everlasting credit of the Guild's guiding minds, they more often than not displayed a level of taste far ahead of that which prevailed at the time.

Georg Kaiser's *From Morn to Midnight,* which bowed on May 21, 1922, was the first expressionistic play to be given in the United States; it not only aroused considerable interest but also influenced a form of playwriting exemplified by Elmer Rice's *The Adding Machine* and John

From Morn to Midnight—Frank Reicher as the cashier in the Guild's first Expressionist play.

Howard Lawson's *Processional*. Originally staged for Guild subscribers only, it gathered momentum and eventually was moved into the Frazee Theatre for a run. Kaiser (1878–1945) was the outstanding figure in the German dramatic expressionist movement, which was most vigorous from about 1914 to 1924, during which time *From Morn to Midnight* was premiered in Berlin by Max Reinhardt. It is a monodrama, in which everyone and everything is seen through the mind of one person, and it deals more with states of mind than with behavior as it previously had been encountered on stage. The play's central character is a bank cashier whose long-simmering passions are loosed by the scent of a customer's perfume. Before the day and night are spent he has stolen 60,000 marks, chased the sweet-smelling client, gone to the bicycle races, and even looked in at the Salvation Army. But oppressed by guilt and the fear of retribution, he finally shoots himself. The play's mood is threatening largely because it deals with dream-fantasies, which we all have, and which can prove so destructive when—as in this case—they come true. One critic noted how designer Simonson was starting to move away from the heavily detailed set, and another lauded the bicycle races, which are not depicted on stage but which are vividly suggested through staging and dialogue. Heywood Broun wrote: "In bringing Georg Kaiser's play to the stage for the Theatre Guild, Lee Simonson has been lavish with elimination. He gives the audience the scene cue for every picture and then allows us to go on with the story. After all, there is such a thing as imagination and there is no reason why it should be pauperized."

Already the Guild was starting to assemble the men and women whose ability and loyalty were to keep it a tightly knit organization for so many years. In 1922 Warren Munsell came into the office to handle a number of details. Following service in World War I he had gone into acting for a career, and had marched in the Actors Equity parade at the time of its strike against the New York theatre managements in 1919. He was to spend twenty years with the organization, finally leaving it in 1942 to return to military service, this time in World War II; he served in the Air Force.

Munsell's eventual title was general manager; his ability at watching over costs, and working out favorable business deals, had much to do with the Guild's good fiscal position when it was making money, and its economic survival when it wasn't. "Warren wouldn't take any nonsense from the Shuberts," recalled Armina Marshall with pride and satisfaction many years later. But to Munsell, the Shuberts—admittedly a tough competition as well as a tough landlord (many Guild productions were staged in Shubert theatres)—were not difficult to get along with:

> My dealings with the Shuberts were very pleasant. We always got good terms, not so much in rental fees themselves, which were fairly fixed, but in fringe benefits. They often would assume box office costs and work out arrangements with the stage hands that would be beneficial to us.

It was after Munsell became part of the operation that the Guild started getting its plays published, with Walter Prichard Eaton as its editor, and Munsell also had a large part in launching touring companies starting about 1926.

Long before the computer threatened to usurp most of thinking man's prerogatives, writers were concerned that man might become the slave of the machine. This certainly was in the mind of Czechoslovakian playwright Karel Čapek when he wrote *R.U.R.*, with which the Theatre Guild opened its fifth season on October 9, 1922; it had been premiered in Prague the previous year. The title refers to Rossum's Universal Robots, mechanical creatures that can work in factory or farm or fight battles, while the female of this machine species are fine as clerks, typists, and housemaids. When the well-meaning president of the Humanitarian League persuades their maker to give them nerves and feelings, the first feeling they respond to is hate, and they wipe out the human race, except for one man. When he discovers that they can love too, he decides that there still is hope for the world.

Described as a "murderous social satire" by Alexander Woollcott and praised in the *New York Sun* as "a supermelodrama of action plus ideas," *R.U.R.* was attacked in the *Philadelphia Public Ledger* as Soviet propaganda which could just as well have been written by Lenin or Trotsky. Raymond G. Carroll, who loosed this diatribe, offered as antidote the sterling career of Gerard Swope, president of General Electric. "In the American-plan career of Mr. Swope is offered the best answer to the purveyors of such ideas as have their expression in plays like *R.U.R.*"

R.U.R.—Dudley Digges cowers before a robot attack. *Vandamm photograph.*

R.U.R.—Sylvia Field tries to reason with an angry robot—Albert Van Dekker, who later dropped the "Van." *Vandamm photograph.*

Either despite or because of the controversy it stirred, the play was good for 184 performances in this Guild production which featured Basil Sydney, Helen Westley, and Louis Calvert. The following spring it was done in London with comparable success, and has been popular in professional and university theatre ever since.

A. A. Milne once wrote that he had little hope of ever seeing his play, *The Lucky One*, performed, which might have been why the Guild decided to do it. Mildly praised by some critics and as mildly panned by others, it made its moral point by scrutinizing the two sons of Lord Farrington each of whom reponds differently to life. Young Dennis King played the feckless, charming Gerald, and Violet Heming was the girl who finally leaves him for hard-working, silent-suffering brother Bob (Percy Waram) who goes to prison for his business partner's crime.

It was followed on Christmas night of 1922 by Paul Claudel's delicate drama, *The Tidings Brought to Mary*, in a somewhat trimmed translation of the French inspirational play. Jeanne de Casalis portrayed the saintly Violaine, whose compassionate kiss of a leper infects her with the disease. Her sister marries Violaine's fiancé, and they have a child, who dies. On Christmas Day Violaine restores the infant to life. Some observers found the play obscure and undramatic, which might have stemmed partly from its subtlety and partly from a less than ideal set of performances. Nevertheless, Simonson's settings and Theodore Komisarjevsky's direction were credited with realizing the miraculous quality of some of its best moments.

Komisarjevsky also staged Henrik Ibsen's *Peer Gynt*, which presented Joseph Schildkraut in the title role and one of the largest casts assembled

Peer Gynt—Joseph Schildkraut in the title role, with Louise Closser Hale as his aged mother, Aase.

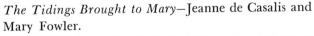

The Tidings Brought to Mary—Jeanne de Casalis and Mary Fowler.

for a Guild production in those early years; it began its run on February 5, 1923. Ibsen had been thirty-nine when he had written it, and had been only recently recognized as a playwright of genius, following the publication of his dramatic poem, "Brand." It was in the exhilaration of his success with "Brand" that he took off on a diametrically opposite tack to write *Peer Gynt*.

According to William Archer, who translated the play from the Norwegian, Ibsen conceived Peer Gynt:

> . . . as the antithesis of Brand, the embodiment of all the vices which that fanatical idealist denounced and scourged. Brand's whole soul was devoted to fighting the spirit of compromise, which Ibsen believed to be the besetting sin of the Norwegian national character; where Peer Gynt made compromise his rule of life, shrank from any decisive, irrevocable resolution, and lived in dreams, while he let reality slip through his fingers. There is no direct reference in the one poem to the other; but the scene in which Peer Gynt drives his dying mother to a fantastic, fairy-tale heaven is an unmistakable counterpart to

Peer Gynt—Peer (Joseph Schildkraut), now old, kneels beseechingly beside Selena Royle. The lad at left is Edward G. Robinson.

the scene in which Brand, full of priestly austerity, proclaims the wrath of God beside his unrepentant mother's deathbed.

The boastful, opportunistic Peer begins his adventures by abducting the bride at a wedding party, spending the night with her, then abandoning her. Subsequently he experiences the temporal rewards and the spiritual anguish which derive from his way of life. Early in his wanderings he had come upon the mountain trolls, and abandoning Man's motto of "Be thyself," he accepts the trolls'—"Exist for thyself." Only at the end, after an encounter with the button-molder Death (Edward G. Robinson), does he find himself in the heart of Solveig, the virgin who had died for him

in his young manhood. At Ibsen's request, Edvard Grieg had written a musical suite for *Peer Gynt*, which has been done far more often than the play itself. The fantasy-drama is too long for theatrical presentation, and was cut by translator Archer.

Schildkraut, who had made a fine Liliom, was deemed less effective in the role than Richard Mansfield had been in the American premiere production in 1906 in Chicago and later in New York. The Guild directors were quite satisfied with their production until the great Russian director Constantin Stanislavsky, then in New York with the Moscow Art Theatre, sat through a performance and then told them that their production had only "surface." Reviews of the play are difficult to assess, because the play can be approached from so many different critical points of view. Certainly the cutting could have been done better, with a telling succession of scenes in the last act restored. Also, apparently not all the Guild players were yet equipped to do this kind of theatre. However, the setting and many details of production were praised, and the Guild gained further prestige from having tackled this massive and unique stage masterpiece. Its run of 121 performances probably was its longest anywhere.

Elmer Rice's expressionistic drama, *The Adding Machine,* moved the Guild one significant step forward in its aim of presenting American plays as well as those which were unconventional and forward-looking. It featured Dudley Digges as Mr. Zero, the bookkeeper, who expects a raise after twenty-five years of faithful service but is fired instead and replaced by an adding machine. Condemned to death for stabbing his boss, he finds himself in one of the next worlds with the fair Daisy Diana Dorothea Devore, whom he had admired when she was his office assistant on earth. But this utopian existence doesn't overcome his own leaden conventionality, and not until he is back at bookkeeping—a comforting drudgery for him—does he feel alive again.

While *The New York Times* described this as "the best and fairest example of the newer expressionism in the theatre that New York has ever experienced," other opinion was not so ready to commend the Guild for its innovation. The comment of H. Z. Torres in the *New York Commercial* was typical:

The Adding Machine is another integral added to that speedily growing number of morbid plays, possessing neither dramatic form nor literary merit, singularly devoid of beauty, debasing in context and repellent in language, destructive of national sanity and which must inevitably corrode the moral fiber. If this so-called "expressionism," with its profanation of the dead, its profanity, its mockery of patriotism, and its intimate revelation of the tactics of a prostitute which are vouchsafed us in *Roger Bloomer* and *The Adding Machine* are really as claimed "the theatre of tomorrow," then let those of us who respect dramatic literature and who love the beauty of the theatre clamor for a censorship which will save to posterity the "theatre of yesterday."

The Wall Street Journal, in a story headed "Trying to Make the Unpleasant Popular," took a dim view of building a theatre for the Guild, which was then in a fund-raising campaign, to house the "new art." For all its righteousness, the *Journal* piece was explicit in calling attention to a scene depicting "the intimate toilet details of a lower-class woman undressing and going to bed,"

The Adding Machine—Elmer Rice wrote one of the Theatre Guild's most significant early plays. The angular set is by Lee Simonson.

The Adding Machine—Simonson's giant machine heightened the symbolism. Dudley Digges was Mr. Zero, the faithful bookkeeper who is replaced by the instrument.

without noting if an upper-class woman might have been more acceptable. It also described the use of slang and profanity, and the effort of a prostitute to seduce a young man in a cemetery. All of which probably proved stimulating for the box office, once *The Wall Street Journal* story got around.

Reviewing the play for *The Nation*, Ludwig Lewisohn wrote:

> Examine this play scene by scene, symbol by symbol. The structure stands. There are no holes in its roof. It gives you the pleasure of both poetry and science, the warm beauty of life and love, the icy delight of mathematics. . . . Here is an American drama with no loose ends or ragged edges of silly last-act compromises, retractions, reconciliations. The work, on its own ground, in its own mood, is honest, finished, sound.

The fifth season concluded with Shaw's *The Devil's Disciple*, written in 1897 as the first of his "Three Plays for Puritans." Shaw claims he wrote it, following a three-year stint of reviewing bad plays, to show that better ones could be done. The satire on puritan attitudes is set in New England during the Revolutionary War and wittily devastates self-righteous morality. Critic Kenneth MacGowan took director Philip Moeller sharply to task for changes he had made, such as converting Dick Dudgeon's cruel and crusty old mother into a somberly heroic figure. He found the production "surprisingly tame" for about half its length, revived only with the entrance of Roland Young as General Burgoyne. Basil Sydney played Dudgeon, who declares himself a diabolonian, and is rejected by the over-righteous townspeople.

Windows, described by some reviewers as minor Galsworthy, began the sixth season on October 8, 1923. A comedy about an English family which has employed a housemaid with a past, it winds up by advising that we should clean our windows and see people as they really are. The play lasted only until the subscribers—now numbering 12,000—had seen it.

The Devil's Disciple—Basil Sydney as Dick Dudgeon in this first of Shaw's *Three Plays for Puritans.*

The Devil's Disciple—a taut moment of anticipated confrontation in the American colonies.

Windows—Phyllis Povah, Kenneth McKenna, and Frieda Inescort in the Galsworthy drama which opened the sixth season.

Drama critic Stark Young directed *Les Ratés (The Failures)*, by H. R. Lenormand, which details the steady degradation of an aspiring playwright and a young actress. Tragic, hopeless, and neurotic, it benefited from swift pacing and from the stark economy of Simonson's settings. Jacob Ben-Ami as the young man and Winifred Lenihan as the girl earned warm praise for their performances. Less than a month after it opened, a short matinee run of Wilhelm von Scholz's *The Race with the Shadow* occupied the Garrick stage. A psychological melodrama, it deals with a writer whose novel is discovered to be fact, with the characters himself, his wife, and the friend to whom he is reading the manuscript.

To some of us, *Saint Joan* will stand everlastingly as one of the half-dozen great plays of the twentieth century as well as one of the most intellectually and passionately exalting experiences of a theatre-going lifetime. It has been called the finest English play since Shakespeare and is generally conceded to be the supreme drama to come from the pen of G. B. Shaw. If it is treated more briefly here than such an introduction might seem to warant, that is only because the play has been written about and analyzed at considerable length since the Guild staged its world premiere on December 28, 1923.

At first, not everyone was in agreement with the high esteem later accorded *Saint Joan*. For that matter, theatre people are far from unanimous about it now, even though the prevailing opinion is highly favorable. But the morning after the premiere, Percy Hammond wrote in the *Tribune:*

> Mr. Shaw's chronicle of Joan of Arc makes the life and works of that sainted maiden duller though more probable than the legends have taught us to believe. . . . The play as produced at the Garrick last night seems just another example of Mr. Shaw's gift for interminable rag-chewing, and it is over, so far as entertainment is concerned, long before the final curtain falls.

It is entirely possible that this was not the ultimate production or anywhere near it. I would hold up Uta Hagen's Joan a couple of decades later as the ideal portrayal, or close to it. Winifred Lenihan, who originated the role, was not as impassioned or dynamic as Shaw wanted his Joan to be; a number of critics found her wanting in "inspiration." A London critic covering the New York premiere found her "uniformly soft and feminine, perpetually smiling, with her voice rarely ascending above a demure and almost colorless monotone." Shaw, who didn't see the play, wrote on the basis of production photographs: "In the second act Joan's hair should be bobbed; and she should be dressed as a soldier, quite definitely masculine in contrast to her girlish appearance in the first act. And at the end of the act she should be in front of all the rest, in command of the stage in the good old-fashioned way from the point of view

The Failures—Jacob Ben-Ami looking every inch of the title.

The Failures—Winifred Lenihan matched Jacob Ben-Ami in utter despondency.

Saint Joan—Winifred Lenihan created one of the most stirring roles in twentieth-century drama in the world premiere of the Shaw masterpiece.

Saint Joan—Winifred Lenihan as Joan and Philip Leigh as the Dauphin. *Vandamm photograph.*

Saint Joan—Gaston Liebert, Minister Plenipotentiary of France, presents the gold medal of Joan of Arc to Winifred Lenihan. *Kadel & Herbert photograph.*

of the audience, and not beautifully composed in the middle of the picture with all the other people turning their backs on the spectators. Why don't you carry out my directions and get my effects instead of working for pictorial effects?" He concludes his note: "The drag toward the conventional is very evident, and is the last word in operatic artificiality; but still, it is all very pretty in the American way, and might have been worse."

Philip Moeller's staging of the play might have been at least partly responsible for Miss Lenihan's conventional stage-heroine interpretation. Successive productions over the years tended to better realize the Shavian concept of Joan as a blaze of a girl in her scenes of inspiration and fervor, contrasted with a quite confused and terrified teen-ager when she is being threatened and browbeaten. Miss Lenihan admitted in an interview that she wasn't happy with her performance, nor was she consoled by the accolade from critics who found her ideal as Joan.

In sum, however, December 28 was a memorable night for the Guild and for the English-speaking theatre. By this time the Guild had exclusive first rights to Shaw's plays, which it con-

tinued to present in America for a number of years. It already had affirmed repeatedly its function as a freshener of the living theatre in America, which had not been the same ever since Langner, Simonson, Moeller, Theresa Helburn, and the others had launched their venture less than five years before. So *Saint Joan* crowned one segment of Guild history and keynoted a new and even more resourceful and rewarding era. The twenty years to follow were to assault and awe the American audience with the eloquence of Shaw, the brooding force of O'Neill, and the vitality of a new and socially conscious American theatre of the 1930's.

Ernest Vajda's *Fata Morgana* was the fifth production of the sixth season. George Jean Nathan described it as the best comedy of sex to come out of Hungary in the last ten years, which makes you wonder just what other Hungarian sex comedies of that decade he was comparing it with. As opposed to today's play-by-play treatment of sex on stage and screen, Vajda depended on scenes which implied rather than depicted—still an admirable trait. The theatre year concluded with Ernst Toller's *Man and the Masses,* a play about the Russian

Fata Morgana—this Hungarian sex comedy featured Emily Stevens, who was the niece of the distinguished English actress, Mrs. Fiske. *Genthe photograph.*

Fata Morgana—Morgan Farley and Josephine Hull. *Vandamm photograph.*

Fata Morgana—Helen Westley and Josephine Hull flank two very young actresses. *Vandamm photograph.*

Revolution. Though written by an ardent communist, it questions revolution, from a poet's point of view. Its theme is the inevitably tragic nature of the conflict between man the individual and the needs of the masses. *Fata Morgana* had been a box-office success, running 249 performances, but *Man and the Masses* survived for only thirty-two. Opinion was that Toller might have been a good communist but he was a poor playwright.

They [Lunt and Fontanne] have youth and great gifts and the unmistakable attitude of ascent, and those who saw them last night bowing hand-in-hand for the first time may well have been witnessing a moment in theatrical history. It is among the possibilities that we were seeing the first chapter in a partnership destined to be as distinguished as that of Henry Irving and Ellen Terry. Our respective grandchildren will be able to tell.

The critic who wrote these words in the small hours of the night of October 13, 1924, had the gift of prophecy. He was not alone, however, in recognizing Alfred Lunt and Lynn Fontanne as a superlative acting pair, and Ferenc Molnár's comedy, *The Guardsman,* as quite possibly the first of many vehicles ideally suited to their bright and flexible talents. This, in some critical opinion, was the most fortuitous opening in the Guild's history so far, at least in terms of exhilarating an audience. No one was apt to claim that this story of a jealous husband—an actor—who poses as a Russian count to test his wife's fidelity was in the least profound or important. It was, however, cleverly written, skillfully directed by Philip Moeller, and stunningly played not only by Mr. and Mrs. Lunt but by such Guild regulars as Dudley

Fata Morgana—the shy couple are Edith Meiser and Sterling Holloway. *Vandamm photograph.*

Man and the Masses—Blanche Yurka is the woman in Ernst Toller's drama of the Russian Revolution. *Muray photograph.*

The Guardsman—this was the first of many plays to enjoy the grand talents of Lynn Fontanne and Alfred Lunt under the Theatre Guild banner.

Man and the Masses—capitalism at its worst is depicted in this imposingly symmetrical scene.

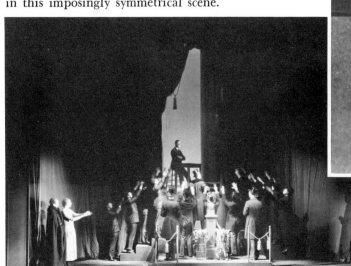

The Guardsman—Lynn Fontanne portrayed an actress tired of her actor-husband. Alfred Lunt was the spouse who masquerades as a Cossack soldier in order to woo her anew, and, in so doing, to test her fidelity to his real self.

Digges, Helen Westley, Edith Meiser, Philip Loeb, and Kathryn Wilson.

As a child in her native England, Lynn Fontanne had had the good fortune to meet Ellen Terry, who accepted her as an acting student. Miss Fontanne acted on the English stage in *Milestones* and *Milady's Dress* before she came to this country with Laurette Taylor for roles in *The Harp of Life, Out There,* and *Happiness.* But it was in *Dulcy* that the young actress earned both fame and a choice of roles from almost every manager in town.

Meanwhile, Alfred Lunt had come east from his native Wisconsin to attend Harvard, barely pausing long enough to enroll before getting a five-dollar-a-week job at the Castle Square Theatre in Boston, where he quickly rose to stage manager, meanwhile playing all the "heavy" roles in the productions. Two years later he was touring with Margaret Anglin, Laura Hope Crews, and Mrs. Langtry, successively. Booth Tarkington saw him in New York in *The Country Cousin* and wrote *Clarence* for him, which did for Lunt what

Dulcy had accomplished for Miss Fontanne. The two met one summer when both were engaged for a stock company in Washington, D.C. *The Guardsman* was indeed the first of many appearances together, and today there is no question but that they have fulfilled that opening-night prophecy. Nominally retired as this is written, and living on their farm in Wisconsin, they admit that, given the right role, they might go back to work.

It is worth noting that *The Guardsman* had been a failure when first produced in New York. The inspiration for casting Lunt and Fontanne in it was Theresa Helburn's. The play eventually toured the United States and was made into a successful motion picture, with the Lunts.

They Knew What They Wanted, by Sidney Howard, was the first Theatre Guild play to win a Pulitzer Prize. It followed *The Guardsman,* opening November 24, 1924, at the Garrick for a long run which necessitated moving it to another theatre. *The Guardsman* also was continuing, so that when John Howard Lawson's *Processional* started its engagement at the Garrick on January 12, 1925, the Guild simultaneously was operating productions in three New York theatres.

American morality of the 1920's being what it was, there were rumblings of disapproval about a drama in which a girl is seduced, much as that had happened before not only in life but in the theatre. Infidelity, apparently, was one thing, but an act of infidelity on a girl's wedding night was a bit too much. Also, the husband finally forgives her, which some moralists found objectionable. None of this hurt the play's popularity, either before or after a play jury cleared it on April 26, 1925—the same day it was announced winner of the Pulitzer Prize "for raising the standard of good morals, good taste, and good manners."

Pauline Lord was the San Francisco waitress who accepts a mail-order proposal from a wealthy Italian grape-grower (Richard Bennett) but submits to his young and handsome foreman (Glenn Anders) after the older man wrecks his truck and injures himself driving to meet the girl's train. When she becomes pregnant she feels she must tell her husband who, eventually, forgives her and looks forward to bringing up the child as his own. Meanwhile, the foreman, a restless type, has left. *They Knew What They Wanted* proved that an American author and an American situation could provide a drama of universal interest and enduring validity—this at a time

They Knew What They Wanted—Richard Bennett as the grape-grower and Pauline Lord as his mail-order bride in Sidney Howard's Pulitzer Prize winner.

They Knew What They Wanted—Pauline Lord, Richard Bennett, and Glenn Anders.

when most American plays were fairly parochial, insignificant, and escapist.

Lawson's *Processional,* which he subtitled "A Jazz Symphony of American Life," depicted a strike in a West Virginia mining town by using burlesque and vaudeville entertainers as the players. While the treatment was comic on the surface, the implications were serious, touching on racial prejudice, cruelty, and the Ku Klux Klan. It probably could be called a prototype for a whole school of intentionally theatrical and symbolic drama to come; its spirit of revolt against conventional theatre naturalism and some of our national in-justices and indecencies is not far removed from that of many theatre experiments today. With George Abbott (later to become famous as a producer) and June Walker in leading roles, and staged by Moeller, it proved moderately popular, running for ninety-five performances.

According to Burns Mantle, A. A. Milne's comedy *Ariadne* was ". . . one of those bright and light affairs that plays for two hours with practically nothing to say after the first 30 minutes." Fortunately, it was the only weak entry in what turned out to be a spectacularly successful season, which the Guild concluded impressively with

Processional—the young actor was to become a famous director of comedies. He is George Abbott. The girl, also on the threshold of a bright career, June Walker. *Bruguiere photograph.*

Processional—a moment of romantic levity. That's Ben Grauer hawking *The Washington Post,* with June Walker.

Ariadne—Lee Baker, Catherine Proctor, Laura Hope Crews, and Orlando Daly. *Vandamm photograph.*

Shaw's *Caesar and Cleopatra*. The Shavian play opened the new Guild Theatre (now the ANTA), just as it had opened the Shubert earlier on its first presentation in New York. The auditorium was decorated with fine Gobelin tapestries, which occasioned Alexander Woollcott's aside: "The Gobelins will get you if you don't watch out." Pressing an electric button, President Calvin Coolidge in Washington gave the signal for raising the curtain on the opening scene which showed Caesar (Lionel Atwill) meditating by a small sphinx on which Cleopatra (Helen Hayes) was hiding.

What Shaw set out to do in *Caesar and Cleopatra* was to set Shakespeare straight. Not that Shaw wrote a literal play by any means; he used the situation in Egypt's capital to illustrate some of his own points about public and private responsibility; in fact, this was another of his "Three Plays for Puritans," and the playwright didn't hesitate about writing the characters as people he or his audiences might know personally. Nevertheless, he believed that Shakespeare had romanti-

Caesar and Cleopatra—Helen Hayes as Egypt's teen-age queen. *Muray photograph.*

Caesar and Cleopatra—dinner at home, with Helen Hayes and Lionel Atwill in the title roles. *Bruguiere photograph.*

Caesar and Cleopatra—Lionel Atwill (Caesar) in mufti.

Caesar and Cleopatra—Lionel Atwill and Helen Hayes.

cized and thus distorted the relationships of Caesar, Cleopatra, and Antony, so he also took the liberty to view the situations in his own light. Over the years a number of critics have compared Shaw and Shakespeare in this area of their work. In 1935 Brooks Atkinson of the *Times* wrote: "*Caesar and Cleopatra* is superior to *Julius Caesar* and *Antony and Cleopatra* in thinking and form, being inferior only in passion, which is perhaps the whole thing." In wit, Shaw has it, hands down.

Along with producing plays for its subscription audiences and the general public, the Guild was beginning to branch out in several related areas. One was a kind of experimental theatre group, encouraged by Theresa Helburn and made up of some of the company's young actors and actresses. They would rehearse on the Garrick stage at night, following the regular performance, and would stage their plays for the Guild Board when they were sufficiently rehearsed. One of those was *Fata Morgana*, which subsequently was done on subscription.

Meanwhile, a young composer named Richard Rodgers and a lyricist, Lorenz Hart, had been writing musical shows at Columbia University. Ben Kaye, an attorney, and Paul Moss, who became New York City's commissioner of licenses, introduced the two young men to Miss Helburn with the proposal that they might prepare a show to exploit the talents of the Guild's junior troupe. It was prepared for a single Sunday night, June 8,

Caesar and Cleopatra—Helen Westley (right) made a fearsome Ftatateeta.

1925, but lasted a season. *The Garrick Gaieties* introduced such durable tunes as "Manhattan" and "Mountain Greenery," while announcing to the theatre world the discovery of a major pair of talents. The cast of the Guild's first musical included such able players as Lee Strasberg, Peggy Conway, House Jameson, Romney Brent, Sanford Meisner, and Sterling Holloway. Harold Clurman was stage manager.

Although Shaw's *Arms and the Man* opened September 14, 1925, and thus would seem to start the eighth season, it is listed in the Guild's records as one of the seventh season attractions. An immediate hit in New York when it was first done with Richard Mansfield and Lillah McCarthy thirty years earlier, it also was already familiar to audiences through its musical adaptation, *The Chocolate Soldier,* with music by Oscar Straus. The operetta had run for 296 performances starting in the fall of 1909, and had made immortal hit tunes of "Falling in Love" and "My Hero."

In *Arms and the Man* Shaw puts down the absurd romanticism and deceptive glory of the traditions of war. Raina (Lynn Fontanne), fiancée of a Bulgarian hero, shelters the enemy Serbian Captain Bluntschli (Alfred Lunt) when he takes refuge in her bedroom, much as she disapproves of his matter-of-fact and businesslike attitude toward his military career. War was indeed romanticized when GBS wrote the play toward the end of the nineteenth century, though much less so when the Guild staged it following the grim realities and futilities of World War I. If anything, the change in public thinking about warfare worked to the advantage of the play; audiences were more predisposed to see the aptness and irony within the witty dialogue of this charming and comic satire.

As might be expected, the work the Guild was doing, and its selection of plays and writers, was generating comment in many quarters. One of the most pertinent observations came from a London producer, Basil Dean, writing in *The Theatre Magazine.* Referring to the "tremendous vitality of the American theatre," he goes on to say:

> The most considerable achievement of the American theatre to date I hold to be the work of the Theatre Guild. . . . Here, in its realization of policy definitely applied to workaday practise, the American theatre triumphantly redeems itself. I consider policy in the theatre more important than the high-

The Garrick Gaieties—introduced composer Richard Rodgers and lyricist Lorenz Hart. *Muray photograph.*

The Garrick Gaieties—Sterling Holloway and June Cochrane singing an appealing new Rodgers and Hart melody, "Manhattan."

The Garrick Gaieties—Betty Starbuck and boyish Romney Brent were two more of the talented young Theatre Guild performers. Brent appeared in a number of subsequent productions as well.

Arms and the Man—Lynn Fontanne, Ernest Cossart, Pedro de Cordoba, and Jane Wheatley in Shaw's comic attack on the romanticizing of war.

Arms and the Man—another in what was to become a long list of successes for Lynn Fontanne and Alfred Lunt.

Arms and the Man—Pedro de Cordoba as Sergius, Lynn Fontanne as Raina, Alfred Lunt as Bluntschli, the Swiss mercenary who carries chocolates in his cartridge belt (that's right; he's also the hero of the Oscar Straus comic opera, *The Chocolate Soldier*).

est individual artistic accomplishment; that is why I mention it first.

In England we should probably call the work of the Theatre Guild "highbrow" and curtail its influence by relegating the performances to the doubtful dignity of what is popularly termed across the water the "Sunday show." Here in the U.S. you honor it; you patronize it; you even build a theatre for it. Small wonder then that the workmen of the British theatre look with longing eyes at the possibilities which their more fortunate cousins have before them. The Theatre Guild has proved that it is possible to persist in policy of the best and only the best and to make that policy pay. It has probably had more influence on the modern American stage than all other influences put together.

Ferenc Molnár's *The Glass Slipper* wasn't much of a play; R. Dana Skinner of *The Commonweal* wrote of passages in it "as vulgar, as trite and as cynically affected as anything yet imported from the Hungarian stage." But he, along with others, admitted that it has one beautifully conceived character in Irma Szabo, a boardinghouse drudge with the spirit of a poetess, and that June Walker realized the part sensitively. Skinner described her performance as "a portrait of astonishing honesty, elusiveness and tender beauty."

Shaw was welcomed back to a Guild stage (at the Klaw Theatre this time) with the double bill of *The Man of Destiny* and *Androcles and the Lion* on November 23, 1925. The former—distinctly lesser Shaw—apparently suffered as well from quite inadequate performances, including that of Tom Powers as the title character, Napoleon. *Androcles,* however, proved a delight in Philip Moeller's production with properly evocative costumes and setting by Miguel Covarrubias;

The Glass Slipper—June Walker appeared as Irma in the third Molnár play to be done by the Theatre Guild.

The Glass Slipper—Lee Baker and June Walker. *Vandamm photograph.*

The Man of Destiny—Tom Powers wrestled with Shaw's concept of Napoleon, whom Clare Eames seems to be imitating. *Vandamm photograph.*

Romney Brent as the Lion and Henry Travers as Androcles. GBS fashioned the comedy from a tale in the *Attic Nights* of Aulus Gellius (around A.D. 150), about the Christian who withdraws a thorn from a suffering lion's paw and later, thrown to his intended death in a Roman arena, he is recognized and befriended in return by the animal. First done in New York in 1915, it has been popular since, and is one Shavian play which is a perennial favorite with children.

Somewhat after the fashion of *Arms and the Man* and *What Price Glory?*, *Merchants of Glory*, by Marcel Pagnol and Paul Nivoix, attempted to look realistically at war, achieving something of grim and sardonic humor. Burns Mantle found it "a good play and interesting, though overwritten," and most reviewers approved its attack on stay-at-homes who profit from the sufferings of others in war. If it was good it certainly didn't make any lasting impression on the theatre, and apparently was soon forgotten by American producers, though it might have had some continuing interest in France, where it was written and set.

Goat Song, by contrast, has proved enduring as theatre and resourceful for its audiences and the people who produce it. Written in 1920 and given its American premiere by the Guild on January 25, 1926, it is conceded to be Franz Werfel's finest and most meaningful play, with a message about violence let loose on the world that is as pertinent now as ever, if not more pertinent. "I am especially glad that my *Bocksgesang* is to be played in America," Werfel wrote. "For there you have a real youth, and this play was written for youth—by youth, I might say. It is a protest against the degeneration of the past, and although the scene is laid in remote Serbia, the protest is the same the world around. I believe that America will understand this play."

Jacob Ben-Ami's direction and Simonson's settings provided the requisite power, sweep, and dark imagination for Werfel's alarmingly realistic fantasy about a monster—half man, half goat—born to a farm couple. Fully grown, it escapes from the prison where its parents had kept it hidden, to loose revolution, devastation, and death upon the world. The monster is not so much the destroyer as a symbol of the forces within men which periodically prompt them to acts of violence. Eventually the monster is destroyed, but already its child is stirring with life within Stanja, betrothed of the creature's normal brother, who had been sacrificed to it. *Goat Song*, incidentally, is a literal translation of the Greek *tragoidia,* from which comes the word tragedy. The title was also an allusion to the biblical account of the scapegoat in Werfel's fearsome and foreboding drama. The play earned acclaim from some Theatre Guild subscribers, and caused a number of others to cancel their memberships.

Lawrence and Armina Langner were honeymooning in Rome some time earlier when they saw and were intrigued by *The Chief Thing*, a symbolic drama by the Russian playwright Nicolai Nikolayevitch Evreinov. When the Guild staged it in March of 1926 it proved to be a resounding failure. The play is a dramatic parable of man's search for happiness, which Evreinov implied was more easily found in our illusions than in reality. C. K. Munro's *At Mrs. Beam's,* which closed the eighth season, had been a comic success in London starring Jean Cadell, who was brought to New York to repeat her role for the Guild. The Lunts, who were members of the permanent acting company, had supporting roles—he as an English adventurer and she as a tempestuous lady from Argentina. It is of perhaps minor historical significance that the Lunts had their first stage fight in this play. It worked so well that exhilarating stage tussles were incorporated in many of their plays, such as *The Taming of the Shrew.*

Androcles and the Lion—Henry Travers and Romney Brent in the far more lasting half of a Shavian double bill which also included *The Man of Destiny. Vandamm photograph.*

Androcles and the Lion—Miguel Covarrubias designed set and costumes.

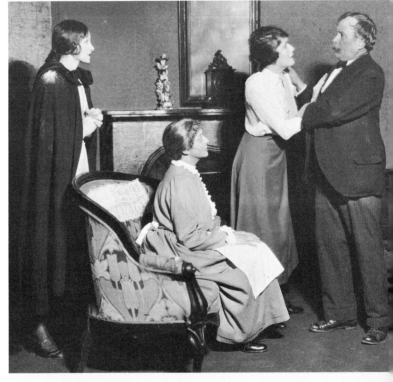

Merchants of Glory—Betty Linley, Helen Westley, Armina Marshall, and Augustin Duncan.

Goat Song—director Jacob Ben-Ami instructs his cast. Seated: Edward G. Robinson, Albert Bruning, Blanche Yurka, Lynn Fontanne, Helen Westley, and Herbert Yost. Standing: George Gaul, Dwight Frye, and Alfred Lunt.

Goat Song—one of Lee Simonson's sets.

Goat Song—playwright Franz Werfel.

Goat Song—Blanche Yurka as Mirko's mother. *Muray photograph.*

Goat Song—Blanche Yurka, Lynn Fontanne, and Edward G. Robinson.

The Chief Thing—man's search for happiness, the theme of this Russian drama, failed to captivate Americans. Above, McKay Morris and Estelle Winwood. *Leonetti photograph.*

At Mrs. Beam's—Alfred Lunt and Lynn Fontanne staged another of their entertaining brawls. At ringside, Jean Cadell. *Vandamm photograph.*

At Mrs. Beam's—Jean Cadell was brought from London to play Miss Shoe, the role she had created in her native England.

III

George Bernard Shaw

by Lawrence Langner

THE SHOCK created by Shaw on the modern world was that of an alert, intelligent mind intent on smashing up the shibboleths of Victorian morality, and armed with the weapons of rapier-like wit and bludgeoning horseplay whose thrusts delighted the younger generation that followed him. He was not the first to use the theatre for the explosion of social ideas. Ibsen had done the same thing before him. But where Ibsen was solemn and dour, Shaw was humorous and gay. He destroyed with laughter where Ibsen had destroyed with tragedy. Shaw's major contribution was to provide a galaxy of brilliant theatrical experiences which both entertained and stimulated his audiences. His ideas flowed in an ebullient stream out of the theatre into the lives of the intelligent public of his day. Before his advent, the theatre of ideas was like a dreary church in which the congregation took itself so seriously that its influence was confined to a coterie which regarded itself as the custodian of modern thought. Shaw himself in *The Philanderer* satirized these heavy-going intellectuals as members of what he called the Ibsen Club.

At the time when I first visited Shaw, his major writing of plays was done. We had already produced *Mrs. Warren's Profession* in the days of the Washington Square Players. Its original crusading zest on the subject of prostitution had already become dimmed in the years which followed its first presentation in New York, at which time it was closed by the police. *Heartbreak House* which was the Theatre Guild's first production of a Shaw play, sounded a tocsin of warning against the possible world destruction which would ensue if mankind continued to fail to find a remedy for

disputes other than war. Alas, it seems that we of this century must always live under the dread of airplanes or rockets droning in the skies which threaten to bring down the rain of destruction on our civilization. Three times in my own life I have witnessed periods when this play was topical. *Heartbreak House,* unlike so many of Shaw's plays, did not demolish the target at which it was aimed, and so it continues to be of current interest.

No writer for the theatre has affected his times as much as Shaw has done, and for this very reason, many of his plays have become obsolete because the social customs against which they were directed also have become obsolete. Once when I discussed with Shaw the revival of his play *Man and Superman,* I mentioned that the idea of women pursuing men, on which it was based, had now lost its novelty, and that the play would be affected as a result. "Nonsense!" said G. B. S. "When the play was first done, the audiences were so shocked that they were unable to laugh. Now that they are no longer shocked, they laugh heartily at the play itself. Indeed, it is actually now possible to appreciate my play as a comedy and not as a social document." However, much as this may be true of some of Shaw's plays, there are several, such as *John Bull's Other Island,* which deal with situations that no longer exist. Though the same is true of almost all of Shakespeare's plays, the latter are always topical as compared to many of Shaw's, because Shakespeare was not attempting to change the social customs of his day. Shaw, however, was nearly always intent on demolishing some current injustice or folly, and when he succeeded, as he often did, the plays which accomplished this lost much of their topical interest.

But this interest may easily return in the years to come.

Having worked on so many plays of O'Neill and Shaw, the two outstanding theatre geniuses of our time, I was interested in learning their opinions of each other and in comparing their attitudes toward each other's work. I once asked O'Neill to what extent Shaw had influenced his own writing. Gene said he had been more influenced by Shaw as a man and as a writer than as a playwright. When he went to school in Stamford, Connecticut, he was wildly excited about Shaw's *Quintessence of Ibsenism*. It was his favorite reading during his last year at school, and he kept underlining the points with which he agreed with Shaw in red ink to such an extent that the book was almost entirely underlined. Whenever Gene indulged in an argument, he would slap his opponents by quoting from Shaw, and indeed, he gained a reputation for being almost Mephistophelian among the other boys by his apt quotations.

Gene remarked that he had never been unwilling to admit that he had been influenced not only by Shaw but even to a great extent by Strindberg. Notwithstanding the fact that Shaw's *Quintessence of Ibsenism* had greatly predisposed him in favor of Ibsen, he drew a sharp line of distinction between his own plays and those of Ibsen, stating that he had sometimes been referred to as a "naturalistic" or "realistic" writer whereas he had never actually written along these lines except on a few occasions. Notwithstanding O'Neill's interest in Ibsen, he was no disciple of the gloomy Norwegian dramatist. On one occasion he stated to me, "Ibsen has set back the theatre for many years by his very success in developing a so-called 'naturalistic' method which in reality is not naturalistic at all. Ibsen's realism in the theatre is just as much manufactured as the theatre of Sardou which preceded it." Throughout his writing career, O'Neill constantly attempted to break down the realism or naturalism of Ibsen and to add to the dimensions of the theatre by the use of masks as in *The Great God Brown* and *Lazarus Laughs,* asides as in *Strange Interlude* and *Dynamo,* and sheer fantasy as in the case of *Days Without End.*

Shaw greatly admired O'Neill's work as a dramatist, but with his old-maidish temperance attitude he could never quite get over being shocked at Gene's early drinking. When I told him at Stresa that Gene had not touched a drop of liquor for years, and had "sworn off" it for life Shaw replied, "He'll probably never write a good play again." I explained that Gene had already written many good plays since he had stopped drinking, which seemed to make very little impression on G. B. S., for a few years later he asked me the same question again.

"How is O'Neill feeling?" asked Shaw when I was in England in 1947. I stated that he was well, but that he took a pessimistic view about the state of the world, and was of the opinion that our present civilization was on its way downhill, and headed for ultimate disaster. "Tell him not to worry about that," said Shaw cheerily. "If mankind turns out, as I suspect, to be a failure, it will destroy itself and be replaced by some other creature." Their outlooks appeared to be the same, but O'Neill, the writer of tragedy, was tragic about it, while Shaw, the writer of comedy, was cheerful, and this difference in attitudes existed notwithstanding the difference in their ages, Shaw being the older man by over thirty years.

My first contact with Bernard Shaw began when I was fifteen, and working in the office of Wallace Cranston Fairweather in London. He gave me a ticket to a lecture by Shaw at the Fabian Society, with the intriguing title "The Position of the Artist under Socialism." Shaw, aflame with his red beard and his subject, made a profound impression on me. The position of the musician, author, or actor under socialism, according to Shaw, would be that of a capitalist millionaire. "My income," said Shaw, "as a state dramatist would be enormous!" "And serve you right!" cried someone in the audience. Shaw was not entirely mistaken in his prophecy, for years later Stanislavsky told me that Chaliapin, a national hero in Soviet Russia, was paid handsomely for each appearance. One day he was set upon by robbers in a remote village. "I'm Chaliapin!" he announced imperiously to the footpads. They apologized profusely, gave him a handsome present, and escorted him on his way to safety.

At the time we produced *Heartbreak House,* Bernard Shaw was anathema to the public because of his attitude toward World War I. Instead of being purged or shot, as would undoubtedly have been the case with this particular artist at such a time under communism, he had retired to his home in the country to work in peace and quiet.

After Shaw gave us permission to produce

Heartbreak House, I was informed by him that I was to communicate with his lawyer, Benjamin Stern, a charming and urbane gentleman who had represented Shaw's interests in this country for generations without showing any appreciable signs of accompanying wear and tear. Whether instructed to do so by Shaw, or as a personal favor to me, Stern in a fatherly manner did his best to frighten me into a panic. "I must warn you," he said, "that Shaw will not permit you to alter as much as one single word in his play. He once closed Favershams' production of *Getting Married* because the actor dared to cut it without his permission. And lest you think," he proceeded, fixing me with his penetrating eyes, "that you can tamper with the play without Shaw knowing about it, let me also warn you that he has the most uncanny way of knowing exactly what you are doing. Once Arnold Daly wanted to present one of Shaw's plays at the Maxine Elliott Theatre on Fortieth Street. Shaw cabled his refusal because the street was being repaired!"

I learned later from Shaw that a lady, one of his early admirers, had been in the habit of attending the performances of all his plays in New York with the book in her lap, and wrote Shaw instantly if anyone deviated from the printed word. She undoubtedly also kept him informed of the condition of the New York streets.

Armed with Shaw's ferocious contract, which no lawyer has ever dared to interpret, we proceeded to make the first production of *Heartbreak House.* The world premiere took place on November 10, 1920, and brought this playwright back to the living theatre after an absence of several years. But at the outset we were faced with a difficulty, for after engaging the beguiling blonde-haired Effie Shannon for the part of Hesione Hushabye, we noticed she was described by Shaw as having "magnificent black hair." In the text of the play, Ellie, another character, says to her, "Oh, you don't mean to say, Hesione, that your beautiful black hair is false." Effie was requested either to dye her hair black or wear a black wig, but her reaction to both proposals turned the approach into a retreat, if not a rout. The six Guild directors put their heads together and hit upon the ingenious plan of having the line slurred in the reading.

I had corresponded with Shaw regarding *The Devil's Disciple,* and he had invited me to communicate with him when I arrived in London,

although he expressed the belief that Richard Mansfield had "squeezed the last farthing out of the *D's D* and that the play was essentially a "star melodrama and, as such, not so much the Theatre Guild's business as, say, Barrymore's."

Arriving in London in the winter of 1921 I called on St. John Ervine, who gave me some advice as to how to achieve my objective. "He's really a very kind man," said St. John. "When I lost my leg in the war, he sent me a postcard saying every tree is better off for a little pruning. This was his way of telling me not to dwell too much on my troubles."

This did not sound very reassuring, and I left Ervine with the impression that a difficult task lay ahead of me. The morning arrived when I was instructed to call at 10 Adelphi Terrace, and I walked up the stairs to the entrance of Shaw's apartment. A low fan-shaped grill of sharp iron spikes separated the staircase landing from the lower floor of the building, and I speculated on how easily a precipitous retreat might result in one's being impaled on this formidable barricade. The door opened, and I was shown into the study, a comfortable Georgian room, crowded with photographs and busts of Shaw himself, and dominated by a cheerful fireplace on the white mantel of which was carved the words, "They say—what say they—let them say!" I innocently supposed that this was Shaw's own personal formula for iconoclasm, but learned from him years later that this legend was on the mantelpiece before Shaw moved into the apartment. Paraphrasing the motto, I said to myself, "Shaw says—what says he—let him say!" and I waited with a little more courage as a result.

After a few minutes, Shaw came in, lean, white-bearded, and erect, looking rather like Father Christmas on a hunger strike, minus only the red cloak and the bell. His face was pink and red, his eyes alive and keen, and his manner very cheerful and sprightly. He greeted me warmly, put me at my ease, and after discussing the production of the play, asked to see the photographs I had brought with me. His sharp blue eyes scanned the very handsome sets Lee Simonson had provided. "Quite good," he said, rather severely, in the manner of a schoolmaster appraising an examination paper, "only the room should look like a ship's cabin, and Simonson has made the tops of the doors rounded instead of flat. Doors on ships are never rounded." I mur-

mured apologies, and said that it hadn't hurt the play—no one had noticed the tops of the doors anyway, they were so engrossed in his dialogue! His severity relaxed until he came across a picture of Effie Shannon. "Isn't she playing the part of Hesione?" he asked sharply. My heart momentarily stopped beating. The vision of being permitted to produce more Shaw plays began to fade. I nodded, and the sharp blue eyes regarded me angrily. "But she has fair hair—you must have cut one of the lines!" "Well, not exactly," I replied. "We just mumbled it—what would you have done?" The fate of my mission hung in the balance. Shaw smiled. "That's all right," he said, and the crisis was passed.

I broached the subject of producing more of his plays. He evaded me—plunging into an account of his latest work, *Back to Methuselah,* which he had been writing during the war, and which he assured me was probably the longest and best play ever written. It was based on the theory that mankind could extend the span of human life from the biblical threescore and ten to many thousands of years, by leading a Shavian existence on lines laid down by Shaw himself, and which succeeded to the extent of carrying him into his nineties with no mental idiosyncrasies other than those which have been habitually associated with him. The play itself was in five separate parts, and since it began with Adam and Eve and stretched over millions of years, it seemed that no member of our Theatre Guild audience was likely to live long enough to be able to disprove any of Shaw's prophetic conclusions. My interest was excited, and I asked for a copy. "On your way back from the Continent, drop in to see me again, and I'll have the plays ready by that time."

Returning to London a month or so later, I called again on the Shaws. We talked about *Back to Methuselah,* and the best way to present it. Shaw's idea was to have all five plays produced consecutively, so that the audience would have to take the entire dose in one helping. On leaving, he said he would send me the printed proof sheets, and I asked for a contract. "Don't bother about a contract," he said, as I stood at the door taking my leave, "it isn't likely that any other lunatic will want to produce *Back to Methuselah!*"

And he was right, as usual.

Shaw had evolved the idea of certain individuals living for several hundred or even thou-

sands of years from studying some of the experiments made in Austria by Dr. E. Steinach, and this was the main theme of the play. In due course, the proof sheets arrived at my hotel together with a letter dated March 9, 1921, reading:

At last I have got a complete set of proofs of the forthcoming volume.

You will understand that I am breaking faith with my publishers in letting them out of my own hands for export and that I must place you under the most blood-drinkingly sacred obligation not to show them to a soul except in confidence to your colleagues in the T. G. of America. If any account of them or quotations from them reach the press in either country there would be the devil to pay for me. Further, as they are not finally corrected for press will you send them back to me when the book is published or else write me an assurance that you have destroyed them with your own hands. If you once let an imperfect text loose, you can never overtake it and I always have to destroy my unused proofs with the greatest care. Bon Voyage!

His postscript read:

The final corrections will not involve any change that you need take into account. Also you may regard the dialogue as drastically cut, so the producer has nothing more to hope in that direction.

My heart fell as I read the postscript. I was to regard these plays, running into thousands upon thousands of words, "as drastically cut!" I studied the proof sheets on shipboard, and whether due to a bad storm which lasted for several days, or to the plays themselves, no Atlantic crossing ever seemed longer. Nevertheless, I was highly excited by the adventure of producing so imaginative a work, and I wrote him en route telling him so, and also calmly suggesting that he rewrite the second play of the series, which struck me as too local. My first task on arrival in New York was to ensure the secrecy which Shaw had imposed on me as a "blood-drinkingly sacred obligation," whatever that might mean.

On arriving in New York, I swore my colleagues to secrecy and then let them read *Back to Methuselah.* They did, and realizing the length and expense involved, as well as the fact that we were nearing the end of the theatrical season, the decision to produce the play was postponed over the summer. Meanwhile, Shaw wrote me that he wanted the play published in book form, which seemed illogical in view of his earlier admonition to make no mention of the plot before its public performance. I suggested he postpone publication until after the play had opened.

Shaw's reply explained that he was certain that the first part of the play could be tremendously effective on the stage and that to perform it along with the second part at the same performance would be impossible. We would have to resign ourselves to putting on *Back to Methuselah* on three evenings and two matinees. He added:

> You must sell tickets in batches of five, all five tickets on one sheet with perforated card divisions. If people buy them that way they will not throw them away. They may be bothered and disappointed by the first two plays, as you expect; but their bewilderment will not take the form of throwing their tickets in the fire, especially if you charge enough for them. You can warn them that the prologue in the Garden of Eden will last only an hour (or perhaps 50 minutes; you can time it at rehearsal) and that no assumptions must be made as to the duration of each part of the play. The wording of your programmes and announcements must always rub in the fact that what the public is going to see is one play, with sections of various lengths—later on we can see about giving separate performances of the sections; but for the first ten performances (say) it must be impossible to take less than the whole dose. The book will be published on the first of June or thereabouts. I note your calm suggestion that it should be held back until you are ready to produce. I told you you wanted the earth. If you want to produce simultaneously with the publication you must hurry up very smartly, indeed.

In the meantime, the question of the expense of this enormous undertaking was bothering us considerably. Though published in book form as one play, *Back to Methuselah* is in reality five separate and complete plays, calling for quite different sets, actors, and costumes. We had the Garrick Theatre, the seating capacity of which was so small that it was impossible to operate on a profitable basis there, no matter how well the play was attended. While we were debating the matter, I reported to G. B. S.:

> The general consensus is that it is a stupendous piece of work, and the Guild stands awed. The greatest difficulty seems to be the second play. The majority of the Guild are in favor of putting it on next season during a lull, so that we can all work on it, but we are all worried about the second play. I have never heard from you about this, and hope I may do so shortly.

In the meantime, my colleagues and I at the Theatre Guild, who had been holding back a decision because of the artistic and financial problems involved, finally decided to present the series of plays on a "Festival" basis, which I jubilantly reported to G. B. S.:

July 28, 1921

> The lunatic has prevailed. God and yourself willing, the curtain will ring up on *Back to Methuselah* in February or March of the coming year (unless some dire financial calamity happens to the Theatre Guild). We shall, of course, perform the play without any cuts (unless you, yourself, want some), and will endeavor to give the very best possible production.

Back to Methuselah was put into rehearsal early in the year 1922. We decided that the first four plays should be given two at a time, which made a somewhat lengthy evening, and they opened a week apart. As this called for more work than our stage director Philip Moeller could possibly put in, we decided to share the production with the Neighborhood Playhouse, connected with the Henry Street Settlement, and the directors Alice Lewisohn and Agnes Morgan staged the first play *In the Beginning*. The costumes of Adam and Eve presented a problem, since they were in the pre-fig-leaf period of the story, and the difficulty was to find a compromise between stark-naked realism and what the New York Police Department would permit to appear on the stage of a so-called "legitimate" theatre.

Our scenic artist, Lee Simonson, decided to swathe Ernita Lascelles, who played Eve, in heavy pink tights with hair of cloth of gold, while Adam, played by George Gaul, was given a pair of bathing trunks of the same gold material. On the day of the dress rehearsal, the Garrick Theatre was filled with spinsters from the Neighborhood Playhouse, who brought with them an atmosphere of Social Welfare and Higher Morality not usually associated with the theatre. On the stage Margaret Wycherly was trying to hide herself behind a bush out of which her arm, garbed as a serpent, protruded as she moved it in sinuous undulations —it being our intention that Margaret's head should be hidden by the bush, but the bush was not quite large enough. "I can still see your head," cried Theresa Helburn from the rear of the theatre. "Can you see it now?" asked Margaret, shrinking into an impossible position behind the bush. Suddenly George Gaul, resplendent in his gold loincloth, appeared from the wings as Adam. As he walked into the spotlight, nothing was visible on stage but his highly illuminated gold loincloth which sent a gasp through the assembled ladies. "If you think we *can't see it,* you're very much mistaken," shouted Theresa Helburn to Margaret Wycherly. George Gaul, thinking the remark was addressed to him, rushed off the stage in frightened embarrassment, while the Social Welfare and Higher Morality ladies rocked with unashamed laughter for ten minutes before order was restored.

Finally, on February 27, 1922, the first two plays of the cycle opened. They were enthusiastically received by the audience, but not by the press. The second bill included the play, *The Tragedy of the Elderly Gentleman,* which contained one of the most long-winded parts ever written, and the strain on the audience listening to the play was excessive. One day a Guild director asked William, our enthusiastic doorman, how the play was going. "Fine!" said William. "Less and less people walk out on it every night."

After the opening of the third play of the cycle, I left for Europe, and called on G. B. S. with the intention of securing his permission to cut *The Elderly Gentleman* so that the play would have a chance for a New York run. I was met very cordially by Shaw, and also by Mrs. Shaw, who stayed and chatted with us while we looked over the photographs of the production. "Look, Charlotte," he said to Mrs. Shaw, as he examined the picture of Albert Bruning as the Elderly Gentleman, "they've given the actor a make-up so that he looks like me! Why, the Elderly Gentleman was an old duffer. Why on earth did you suggest me?" "Because he talked on and on and on," I replied. "Besides, he said he could not live in a world without truth, by which we of course assumed you had written yourself into the character." This was a bad beginning for an interview in which I wished to persuade him to cut the play, but encouraged by Mrs. Shaw, I persevered. "The reason I object to cutting my plays, is this," said G. B. S. "I write a certain amount of deadly serious dialogue, and

when I have given the audience as much as they can possibly take, I throw in some humor as a reward. Now when my plays are cut, the actor or other person who does the cutting always takes out the serious dialogue, and leaves the funny parts, so that the whole purpose of the play is defeated. Besides," he said, "you can never trust an actor to cut a play." "But I suggest you cut this yourself," I replied, "and I'll cable the changes to New York." "You shouldn't have given the two plays in one evening," was the retort. "But people can't come in the afternoon," I replied, "and it's so long, they really suffer."

Then G. B. S. began to suffer, too. "This goes against all my principles," he said, looking at Mrs. Shaw. "G. B. S.," she said, "perhaps the Americans don't always know what the Elderly Gentleman is talking about. There's that long piece about John Knox and the Leviathan; hardly any English people know about that either." I unashamedly and unscrupulously followed Mrs. Shaw's lead, and suggested that there was a great deal more in the play that wasn't understood by Americans—or by anybody else either. "Besides," I added, "at least half a dozen times the Elderly Gentleman starts to leave the stage. Each time the audience settles back delighted, but each time he turns around and comes back for another ten minutes of monologue."

"After all," said Mrs. Shaw, "you did intend him to be an old duffer, and it *is* hard to listen to an old duffer going on and on." G. B. S. squirmed and twisted, but finally gave in. "Very well," he said. "We'll go over it line by line." "I have some cuts suggested," I said, quickly offering him the printed version on which I had marked my deletions. In a few minutes he grew so interested in cutting the play, that he took out at least half as much again as I had originally hoped for. An hour later I left, trying to stop from looking too pleased with myself; for I had been told in New York that I would be wasting my time, as no one had ever been able to persuade Shaw to cut one of his plays before. And I doubt very much whether I would have succeeded without the help of Mrs. Shaw.

The play was considerably improved by the cutting, but the run of the cycle was not greatly prolonged as a result, and it closed after nine weeks of playing. I returned to New York in August, and wrote G. B. S. as follows:

August 25, 1922

On arriving here I inquired into what loss had been incurred in respect of *Back to Methu-*

selah, and found that it had amounted to about $20,000. It was not announced, but the news leaked out as such news sometimes does leak out. Part of this loss was due to the fact that it ran two weeks longer than it should have run; it is not a total loss because most of the materials, etc., which we used can be used over again, and anyway, the Guild is not the least bit worried about it. In having ventured to tackle so big a job we have made a tremendous number of friends and shall have nearly doubled the number of subscribers for the coming season as we had for this season so it will all come back to us eventually.

Shaw, however, never quite forgave us for not making a financial success of *Back to Methuselah.* I did my best to take the blame on ourselves, feeling that he should not be discouraged (as if that were possible!), and later on in 1924 I wrote him:

> I have been somewhat depressed by your letters, because I think you are angry with the Guild over *Back to Methuselah.* You do not realize that over here it was regarded as a great success, and not as a failure. When you take into consideration that it ran for nine weeks in a small theatre, playing every night, you must appreciate that this was a magnificent achievement. The fact that we lost money was not due to any arrangement of the parts, but because the Garrick Theatre was too small for us to make money out of the play. If we had had a theatre twice the size, there would have been a profit instead of a loss. I hope you will not feel badly any more about this. I am quite certain that if Goethe had seen *Faust* presented in parts one and two every evening for nine successive weeks, he would have stood on his head with amazement.

When Lee Shubert, some years later, financed the production of *Jitta's Atonement,* he wrote a letter to Shaw questioning the royalties. Shaw replied to Mr. Shubert that he underestimated the value of Mr. Shaw's name, which had been proved to be worth at least $10,000 to a play. He explained this by stating that the Guild had expected to lose $30,000 on *Back to Methuselah,* but had lost only $20,000, thus showing that Shaw's name alone was worth $10,000!

On my visit to the Shaws in 1922, I had asked whether there was any new play in the offing. "The trouble is, we haven't been able to find a good subject," said Mrs. Shaw. I must have looked astonished, for she continued, "Yes, I sometimes find ideas for plays for the Genius. If we can find

a good subject for a play, he usually writes it very quickly."

Some months later, Mrs. Shaw found a good subject. She told me about it later. "I had always admired the character of Saint Joan, so I bought as many books about her as I could find, and left them in prominent places all over the house. Whenever the Genius picked up a book on the table or at the side of his bed, it was always on the subject of Saint Joan. One day he came to me and said quite excitedly, "Charlotte, I have a wonderful idea for a new play! It's to be about Saint Joan!" "Really," I replied, "what a *good* idea!" Mrs. Shaw's eyes twinkled as she told me the story.

I first became acquainted with the fact that *Saint Joan* was being written by a letter I received from St. John Ervine in the summer of 1923. I then wrote G. B. S.:

> St. John Ervine has just written me that he has heard you have finished a new play on the subject of Joan of Arc. Provided that this is not the chronicle play in five hundred scenes, I think we shall want to do this, and I hope you will let us see it.

Meanwhile, *Back to Methuselah* was to be produced in England by the Birmingham Repertory Theatre, under the management of Sir Barry Jackson. I had written to St. John Ervine suggesting that we visit Birmingham together, and he had agreed to accompany me. Shaw wrote:

> DEAR L. L.,
> *Saint Joan* is finished except for revising and inserting stage business. It's a star play for one woman and about twenty men. Sybil Thorndike is to play it in London.
> Incidentally, I fell on the rocks in Ireland, and cracked a couple of my ribs, besides tearing one of them nearly out of my spine; and though I have kept going I realize that 67 is too old for such games . . .

Shaw's ribs suggested a "press release," but I was careful to write for permission. This came with the following letter:

> Provided you don't suggest to the insurance companies that I am too much disabled, my rib can bear a little publicity.
> The scenes in *Joan* can all be reduced to extreme simplicity. A single pillar of the Gordon Craig type will make the cathedral. All the Loire needs is a horizon and a few of Simonson's lanterns. The trial scene is as easy as the cathedral. The others present no difficulty.

There should be an interval at the end of the Loire scene and one (very short) after the trial scene, and even that makes an interval too many: the act divisions should be utterly disregarded.

Early in October, St. John Ervine and his wife Nora accompanied me to Birmingham, where *Back to Methuselah* was produced consecutively for five performances, each afternoon and evening for three days. The effect of seeing all these plays one after the other was murderous, but G. B. S. was triumphant. "This," he said, "is the way you should have done it in New York!" I replied that the title should be changed to *Back and Back and Back to Methuselah*.

"Tell us something about *Saint Joan*," said Ervine. Whereupon Shaw, his tall figure standing before the fireplace, head erect, white beard waving, and blue eyes twinkling, launched into the story of Joan, and what he had done with it; his conversations with an Irish priest who had been most helpful; and the impact of his own keen mind upon the original source material. For at least two hours St. John, his wife Nora, myself, and Mrs. Shaw, grouped around the fireplace, listened with rapt attention as G. B. S. told us not only the story of the play, but threw in practically all the contents of the Preface for good measure.

All of us were exhilarated by his lively stories, which happily seemed endless; and while he talked, Mrs. Shaw, seated on a low chair at one corner of the fireplace, appeared to be engrossed in her knitting, pausing only to smile now and again, like a kindly mother whose grown son was distinguishing himself before an appreciative audience. During one of the lulls in the conversation, which were infrequent, and came only when G. B. S. had reached the end of one anecdote and waited for the chorus of "How wonderful!" before going on to the next, Nora Ervine leaned over to Mrs. Shaw, looked at her knitting, and asked with some concern, "Whatever are you making, Mrs. Shaw?" "Nothing," replied Mrs. Shaw in a whisper. "Nothing, really. But I've heard the Genius tell these same stories at least a hundred times, and if I didn't have something to do with my hands, I think I'd go stark raving mad!"

One might imagine from this little story that there was not the greatest understanding and sympathy on Mrs. Shaw's part toward her husband. But that would be wrong. She regarded him with amused admiration, and never lost her sense of humor about him. On one occasion when Alfred Lunt and Lynn Fontanne were lunching with the Shaws, I was seated next to Mrs. Shaw. G. B. S. presided at the other end of the table, and proceeded to entertain Alfred, Lynn, and Philip Moeller with a stream of amusing anecdotes of the theatre. I asked Mrs. Shaw why G. B. S. always refused to visit America. "I'm afraid he's liable to get overexcited, meeting so many people, and getting so much publicity," said Mrs. Shaw. "But we could arrange to protect him," I replied. A particularly loud burst of laughter came from the other end of the table. "I'm sure you'd do *your* best to keep him quiet," she replied, "but you see, there's Mr. Shaw himself!"

Mrs. Shaw's influence was always directed to the more human, emotional side of G. B. S.'s work, and I felt that had it been even stronger, G. B. S. might have written many more plays of the stature of *Saint Joan*.

During the dripping interludes between plays at Birmingham, and later in London, G. B. S. discussed some ideas about casting *Saint Joan*. He had recently seen Alla Nazimova in the moving pictures (they were silent in those days) and thought she might be right for the part, despite her accent. I felt, however, that some quality of the character would be lost if it were not played by a young girl. Eva Le Gallienne had been playing the part of Julie in *Liliom* with a great deal of spiritual quality, and I suggested her as the best possibility for the part.

In due course at my hotel in London there arrived a printed paperbacked copy of *Saint Joan* marked in G. B. S.'s meticulous handwriting, "Private and Confidential, to Lawrence Langner." I took a measure of the play; it was terribly long. "Another long-winded one," I thought; but soon lost myself in admiration as I read it. I mailed the book to New York, and followed soon after. I rushed from the ship to the Garrick Theatre where the play had been read immediately on receipt by the rest of the Guild board. Where *Back to Methuselah* found us hesitant, *Saint Joan* galvanized us all into quick action.

After a debate as to who should play the Saint, which lasted with undiminished violence for many days, the board finally selected Winifred Lenihan for the part—a selection which was excellent, for I have seen five productions of *Saint Joan* in three languages, and I have yet to see a performance to equal hers. This was due to the fact that she possessed in herself the attributes of courage, fervor, and youth which the part called for. The keynote of the Guild's production was its essential simplicity. Simonson's scenery and costumes gave it a stark, hard, masculine quality which I have never seen in any other production, and the English presentation which Shaw raved about, and which I saw later, struck me as very prettified and feminine indeed.

We all felt that the play was far too long, and remembering our unhappy experience with *Methuselah* decided to write Shaw begging him to make some deletions, mentioning the fact that many persons in the audience lived in the suburbs, and would miss the last train home if they waited for the end of the play. Shaw's laconic cable in reply was as follows:

London, November 19, 1923

The old old story begin at eight or run later trains await final revision of play—Shaw.

As we were all set for rehearsals, Shaw's reference to a final revised version of the script dropped like a bombshell in our midst. Cables passed back and forth, resulting in the demand by Shaw that we stop rehearsals immediately and postpone the opening. We protested by cable that to postpone for a week would cost £400, and requested G. B. S. to send the revised draft as soon as possible. Shaw's irate reply arrived a week or so after we received the corrected copy:

December 3, 1923

I enclose a letter just received from my printers. I presume you have had the corrected copy by this time.

The worst part of dealing with you T. G. people is that you are each and all half and half very superior beings and exasperating idiots. When I heard that you were actually rehearsing from a copy which you knew to be an unrevised first proof I tore my hair. I should not have trusted you with it. A man who would play *Methuselah* in three nights is capable of anything. But at least I did tell you very expressly that what you had was not the play in its final form. Only, you never attend to what I say; and if the stoppage of the rehearsals (not that I have any hope that you really stopped them) cost you £400, which is great nonsense, my only regret is that it did not cost you £4000, an all-too-slender penalty for such criminal recklessness. I read the play to Sybil Thorndike from the second set of proofs; and the dialogue occupied exactly 3 hours 3 minutes. Since then I

have made another and more drastic revision which has, I think, got the last bits of dead wood out of the play, and have certainly saved the odd three minutes. I think therefore it should be possible to begin at eight and finish at 11:30. The English edition of *Heartbreak House,* uniform with the proofs just sent you, contains 110 pages, including only two specifications of scenery. *Joan* contains seven different scenes. Compare the number of pages and you will see that your estimate of four hours is far over the mark.

Simonson must not make the scenery fantastic. It may be very simple; but it must suggest perfectly natural scenery. Joan was an extremely real person; and the scenery should be keyed to her reality. Simonson must also be limited to three cigarettes a day.

As can be imagined, I was between two fires; Shaw on the one hand, and the rest of the Guild Board on the other. But lest any of my readers should be under the impression that Shaw had greatly reduced the length of the play, let me add that he had omitted very little from his first copy. *Saint Joan* was, and still is, a long long play.

On December 14 I wrote G. B. S.:

As to never attending to what you say, I can only say that I listened most attentively at Birmingham; in fact, you never gave me an opportunity to do anything but listen, nor anybody else either. Not that I wanted to do anything but listen, but if I forgot something of what you said, please put it down to torrents of rain in Birmingham, torrents of conversation in Birmingham, and fifteen waking hours out of forty-eight spent at the theatre . . . my mental processes must have been paralyzed.

After our first dress rehearsal we decided to make one more attempt to have G. B. S. cut the play, and cabled him as follows:

Joan opens Friday evening, consensus of opinion at first dress rehearsal fatal drop of interest during tent scene and beginning trial scene. Were you here sure you would agree with us. We will not drop one line without your consent but for good of play and turning possible financial loss into assured artistic financial success strongly urge your cabling consent our expense following omissions. . . . Our duty to give you our frank opinion. Final responsibility yours. Play magnificent.

THE GUILD.

My readers will note that we suggested Shaw's cabling at our expense, but even with this inducement, he maintained an obdurate silence. On Friday, December 28, *Saint Joan* made its first appearance on any stage. It was enthusiastically received by its audience. But as usual the critics complained of its length. Also, on the opening night, many of the audience left before the final curtain, which came down at 11:35.

While many good things were said about the play, the complaints about its length from the press, coming after the disappointment of *Back to Methuselah,* the failure of which we felt was largely due to its overlength, caused us to cable to Shaw the next day for permission to cut the play. Alas, we had bitten granite. My own personal cable, equally unsuccessful, was as follows:

> One critic comparing you with Shakespeare says that Joan cannot be successfully given until after your death because it can then be cut. Splendid opportunity to prove again that you are greater than Shakespeare by cabling the Guild to use its discretion in making some omissions of unessentials. Guild has done splendid work. Sure you would agree if you were here.

We even persuaded Winifred Lenihan to cable in her own name, asking him to shorten the play. G. B. S. replied to her:

> The Guild is sending me telegrams in your name. Pay no attention to them.
> SHAW.

Ben Jonson wrote of Shakespeare that he was one of the most long-winded of men. I venture to say the same of Shaw, and that many of his plays will never be seen at their best until after the copyrights have expired. In later years, I felt a relaxing of the relentless rule. On one occasion, Shaw said

George Bernard Shaw in the latter part of his long life.

The Irish playwright as he appeared during one of Lawrence and Armina Langner's visits to his home, Ayot St. Lawrence, in 1948. He is seated in the doorway of his workshop.

George Bernard Shaw with Maurice Colbourne, who produced the former's *Geneva* first in Canada, then, after the Guild turned it down, in New York, with Gilbert Miller as co-producer. It was not successful.

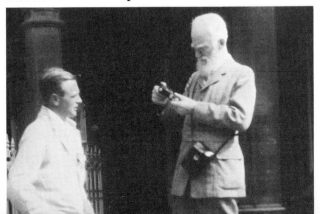

to me, "If only you would not bother me with asking for permission—!"

This reminds me of a remark once made to me by Mrs. Shaw. "Of course, Mr. Shaw is a strict vegetarian, but I've noticed that when he is traveling, he doesn't inquire too closely into the origins of the soup!"

Despite the length of *Saint Joan,* the large theatre-going public came to see it. A few weeks later I was writing G. B. S. as follows:

It is extremely annoying to have to admit that you are right. People are coming in droves to see *Saint Joan,* and it is a great success. I have complete confidence in your business judgment. I still hold my own opinions about the length of the play.

G. B. S. also wrote me further on the subject of publicity for *Saint Joan.*

The great press feature of the production was the notice by Pirandello, which you never even mentioned. *The N.Y. Times* has sent it to me specially with an invitation to comment. Perhaps I will; in the meantime let Terry sit tight on that article that I sent her when you had cabled a ghastly failure. She had better send it back to me.

By the way, you must stop your people from giving away my private business letters to the press. It is impossible to correspond on such terms. Nothing requires greater tact and knowledge of what is allowable than giving to the press matter not meant for it; and the silly young folk who become press agents because they are congenital unemployables are the last in the world to be trusted with such delicate business. You must give a flat instruction that nothing that I write, past or present, is to be given to the press without my express permission.

Terry's latest is a request for a new play to open the new theatre next January. She should have saved up *Joan* for it. I have no more *Joans* in me. Are you going to put in a revolving stage? It would have come in very handy for *Joan.*

He also gave me his views on the photographs we sent him:

The pictures have arrived. I had a long letter from Simonson, the Reformed Smoker (or *has* he reformed?), about it. On the whole there is nothing to complain of, which is a pity, as I complain so well. However, lots of things are wrong; so here goes.

In Act I the steward should be much older than Baudricourt; and both Baudricourt and Poulengy should be in half armor and be obviously soldiers and not merchants. This is important, as it strikes the note of France in war time. As it is, Poulengy's coat should not be belted. Baudricourt should be smart, a *beau sabreur.* The steward should not be a zany, but a respectable elderly man whom nobody nowadays would dream of assaulting. Otherwise B's handling of him becomes mere knockabout farce.

In the second act Joan's hair should be bobbed; and she should be dressed as a soldier, quite definitely masculine in contrast to her girlish appearance in the first act. And at the end of the act she should be in front of all the rest, in command of the stage in the good old-fashioned way from the point of view of the audience, and not beautifully composed in the middle of the picture with all the other people turning their backs to the spectators. Why don't you carry out my directions and get my effects instead of working for pictorial effects. As to the Dauphin I believe his wig is wrong. His portrait shows that his hair was completely concealed by the fashion of the time, giving him a curiously starved and bald appearance that would be very effective on the stage. The Bishop looks about right for the Inquisitor and the Inquisitor for the Bishop. My effect of a very mild and silvery Inquisitor and a rather stern Bishop has been missed as far as the makeup is concerned. The altar and candles in the middle of the cathedral scene are feebly stagy, and do not give the effect of a corner of a gigantic cathedral as my notion of one big pillar would. And it leads to that upstage effect, with a very feminine operatic-looking Joan in the centre, which I wanted to avoid. The drag towards the conventional is very evident, and is the last word in operatic artificiality (an angry woman tears a thing downward and throws it to the floor); but still, it is all very pretty in the American way, and might have been worse. I am going to see Charles Ricketts' plans and sketches for the London production this afternoon; and it will be interesting to see what he makes of them.

Meanwhile, the demand for seats for *Saint Joan* had increased to such an extent that we had to move to another, larger theatre, of which fact I informed G. B. S.; and we requested him to write us some articles and letters that we could use to publicize the play at its new home. I also sent him a copy of a skit I had written on *Joan*.

My last letter from G. B. S. on the subject of *Saint Joan* was as follows:

What an unreasonable chap you are, wanting your letters answered! I never answer letters: if I did I should have no time for anything else. The skit on *Joan* tempts me to write it up for London. The Play has repeated its American success here: it is going like mad; and everyone, to my disgust, assures me it is the best play I have ever written. Sybil Thorndike's acting and Charles Ricketts' stage pictures and costumes have carried everything before them. I am convinced that our production knocks the American one into a cocked hat. Why don't you come over and see it?

I had a letter (among many others) about your production from Rebecca West, in which she makes the astonishing remark that I ought to amplify the Inquisition speech, and goes on to complain that though it is "quite beautifully delivered," people don't get the meaning of it. As it lasts seven or eight minutes and is one of the successes of the production here, I am surprised. Is there anything wrong with it? The press notices here were just like the American ones: play too long; cut out the epilogue; magnificent play only needing the blue pencil to be a success, etc., etc.

Cardinal Hayes's medal was a Godsend, as a press correspondent named Thomas had just written to the French papers to say that I had "bafouee" Joan. The medal brained him and left him for dead.

I received Terry's demand for articles and so forth with the composure of a man swimming the Niagara rapids and being asked casually for a light. Terry thinks I have nothing else to do but job about as her press agent, and throw in a play occasionally. She should thank God for having done so well.

During my annual trips to Europe to visit my London office, I always called on the Shaws. It was my desire that the Guild should cement its relationship with him, and I tried in vain to have this set forth in writing. Notwithstanding the fact that the Theatre Guild produced more plays by Shaw than any other management, the only contract we had with him, other than the original *Heartbreak House* document, was the following written on a half sheet of notepaper:

June 14, 1922

My dear Langner,

Yes, your letter of the 12th correctly summarized our understanding except that though I have stood out for a minimum payment of $2500 win lose or draw. I have never asked for an advance, or been in a hurry for a contract. Of course I have no objection to either; but I wish to affirm that it is the Guild and not the Author that gets these attacks of nerves. . . . Meanwhile I am not to deal with the plays in New York without giving the Guild a look in unless I yield to an overwhelming impulse to treat them shabbily and lose my reputation for being the most reasonable man now living.

To this should be added the following legend on the back of a picture postcard from Madeira in 1923:

Now the Actors Theatre, which has done pretty well with *Candida,* wants to reap the harvest you have sown; but I am telling them and all other applicants that you have an option on all my plays, and that they can have only your leavings, if any.

Shaw was always an excellent businessman. His business advice to Ervine, and undoubtedly to all other authors, was stated tersely: "Build up your copyrights." I have retailed this advice to many an author flushed with success in Hollywood, when he had either sold his stories outright, or worked for a salary; had he done the same amount of work and held on to his copyrights, in time these would have worked for him, as they did for Shaw.

When I was in London in the summer of 1922, Shaw told me of the unhappy plight of his Austrian translator, Trebitsch, now ruined by the war, who had written a drama called *Jitta's Atonement.* "But how could you translate it when you don't know German?" I asked. "I have a smattering," he replied. "Besides," he added, with a twinkle, "translating isn't just a matter of knowing the language. The original play was a tragedy —which was all right for Austria—but it would never go that way in England and America, so I turned it into a comedy!" Shaw offered this play to the Guild, and while it was being considered, Bertha Kalich approached us for the American rights. We acquiesced and Shaw wrote me:

The Guild has cabled to me to give *Jitta* to Madame Kalich, probably blessing her for having extricated it from a difficult situation. But I am not at all happy about it. She seems the right woman for it; and she is very keen on it; but from what she has said to me I suspect that if the production is left in her hands she will suppress the comedy side of my version, and revert to the unrelieved gloom of the original; and I don't think this will succeed in America, because it means that the last two acts will merely wallow gloomily in the memories of the first.

I saw your press communication about the play; but I do not want it suggested that it is 95% Shaw and 5% Trebitsch. Novelty is always valuable; and novelty is the one quality that I have lost hopelessly with the affirmation of my reputation. The line to take is to boom Trebitsch in New York (steps are being taken to that end on this side), and to suggest that as what has been lacking in my plays is HEART, the combination of the emotional Trebitsch with the intellectual Shaw is ideal, and will make the most dramatic event of the season. . . .

Alas, *Jitta's Atonement,* which the Theatre Guild rejected, didn't succeed even as a comedy, but the play stands as evidence of the kindness and loyalty of Shaw to his friends when in trouble, financial and otherwise. The famous French actor Gemier once told me that Shaw had been so atrociously translated into French by his authorized translators, that his plays were seldom given in France, but that his loyalty to these translators was so great that it was impossible to have better versions made by other translators.

In the summer of 1927, I dropped a line to G. B. S. telling him we would be visiting my sister Gladys at Milan. He thereupon invited us to visit him and Mrs. Shaw at Stresa on Lake Maggiore.

About the middle of August we arrived at Stresa and put up at Shaw's hotel, the Regina Palace, an ornate buff-colored barracks-like structure overlooking the lake. G. B. S. had reserved our room for us, and greeted us on our arrival.

"You must stay here for a few days," he said, and added, "but Americans are not very welcome here, on account of the Sacco-Vanzetti case."

After settling comfortably in our room for the night, we were awakened at what seemed to be an unearthly hour by a loud knocking at our door.

"Come along, wake up!" cried Shaw from outside. "It's seven o'clock, and if you want to come swimming with me, you'll have to hurry up! See you at breakfast!"

"Do you want to get up this early?" I remarked drowsily to Armina.

"Of course," she cried, leaping from her bed like a gazelle. "How often will you have an opportunity of swimming with G. B. S.?"

I was stumped. First of all, I don't swim very well—about fifty strokes, and I am winded. Secondly, it was blowing quite hard the night before, and I was sure the lake would be full of waves, which have an irritating habit of getting into my eyes, ears, and mouth.

"Up you get," she cried. "You can't keep Shaw waiting for you!"

So I got up, protesting mildly, and down we went for breakfast. G. B. S. was waiting for us.

It was his custom each morning to cross the lake in a motorboat, then moor his boat off the estate of Albert Coates, the conductor, swim for the shore, and end up with a sunbath on a grassy meadow which sloped down to the beach. We boarded the motorboat dressed in our bathing suits, crossed over toward the other side of the lake, and at what seemed to me to be an enormous distance from the shore, G. B. S. dived in off the side of the boat. As his head and shoulders emerged from the lake and he shook the water out of his white hair and beard, the sun caught his pink cheeks and blue eyes, and he looked for all the world like Father Neptune emerging from the waves.

"Come on in, it's fine!" he shouted.

Armina, like most California-bred girls, was somewhat of a mermaid, and in she dived. I cautiously lowered myself down the side of the boat, looking nervously at the shore which seemed miles away. "I suppose the motorboat will keep moving slowly behind us," I thought, throwing discretion to the winds and timidly striking out in the direction of Father Neptune and the mermaid. I kept going for a while, as the waves waved wildly, and the other swimmers swam rapidly ahead of me toward the shore. I looked back to reassure myself that the motorboat was following me. It was not. The Italian boatman had stopped his engine and was settling down to a comfortable siesta. I was torn between the choice of drowning or calling for help. I called for help. The motorboat started up, G. B. S. and Armina swam back, and between the three of them I was heaved out of the water and ignominiously ferried to the shore. Some years later, when recounting this incident, G. B. S. remarked that it was the greatest compliment ever paid him.

"Lawrence Langner," he said, with a twinkle in his eye, "followed me to such an extent that when I jumped into Lake Maggiore, he jumped in after me without being able to swim a stroke, evidently thinking that my mere presence would save him from drowning."

Our next Shaw play, *The Simpleton of the Unexpected Isles,* was produced in the spring of 1935. Like *Too True to Be Good,* it was a conversation piece, only the conversations were longer and longer. Notwithstanding an excellent cast which included Alla Nazimova, Romney Brent, Lawrence Grossmith, McKay Morris, Rex O'Malley, and Viola Roache, the play was again received with indifference on the part of the critics, and registered a further financial loss for the Guild. In spite of this, I believe that it contains some of Shaw's most inspired writing, and at some future time a public will be found for this magnificent allegory.

In August of 1938, I received from G. B. S. a privately printed copy of his latest play, *Geneva.* By this time the possibility of a war with Germany was on everyone's mind, and the Theatre Guild had been, wherever possible producing plays which would arouse the nation to the dangers to democracy everywhere, should Hitler's dream of world domination by the German "superman" come to be generally accepted. On reading the copy of *Geneva,* I was furious with the way Shaw had dismissed Hitler's heartless treatment of the Jews—a treatment which was later to culminate in the killing of over four million of them in the concentration camps of Buchenwald and Oświecim. I delivered a frontal assault on G. B. S. by letter on August 26, 1938, which, believe it or not, caused him actually to revise the third act of the play, and to change the character of the Jew. "To please you, Lawrence," he replied, "I have written up the part a bit." Shaw also wrote me, "You may now put the copy I sent you in the fire as useless, or, better still, sell it as a curiosity!"

We did not produce *Geneva* even in its revised form, for it seemed to us to be merely another conversation piece, and we felt that we could not risk the financial sacrifices involved. Later on Terry and I went to Canada to see

Geneva as produced by Maurice Colbourne, but it did not interest us sufficiently to bring it to New York. However, Colbourne and Gilbert Miller took the chance, and the play opened in New York on January 30, 1940, and met with the failure which we had anticipated.

Later on, Shaw sent us his play, *The Millionairess,* which the Guild also decided not to produce at that time, though it did in 1952. As I liked the play, I put it on at the Westport Country Playhouse, in the summer of 1938, with Jessie Royce Landis in the title role of Epithania Fitzfassenden. The play was delightful and was extremely well received by the audiences. I should add that in addition to producing *The Millionairess* at Westport, we also produced *Fanny's First Play, Captain Brassbound's Conversion,* and *You Never Can Tell.*

In 1938, Armina and I wrote a play called *Suzanna and the Elders* which was partly suggested by the Oneida community, a utopian colony settled in upstate New York. We dedicated it to Mr. and Mrs. Shaw, and were deeply touched by a sentence written by G. B. S. at the end of a postcard acknowledging our dedication:

We are dreadfully old, and forget everything; but we have not forgotten you.

Mrs. Shaw's health began to fail in the latter part of the 1930's. The last time we saw her was on our visit to England for the London production of *The Pursuit of Happiness.* We tried to take G. B. S. with us to see a matinee, but he pleaded that he had read the play, which he found rather shocking, and that he now avoided the theatre as the plague. We learned through the newspapers of Mrs. Shaw's death in 1943. Armina and I wrote G. B. S. letters of sympathy, which he did not answer. Instead he sent us a beautiful photograph of Mrs. Shaw, as though words were meaningless on such an occasion.

Some years later, the story of Mrs. Shaw's funeral service was recounted to Armina and me by someone who heard it from one of the two persons who attended. Accompanied by Lady Astor and Shaw's faithful secretary, Miss Patch, they drove to the service. Shaw was silent and preoccupied. Then some of Mrs. Shaw's favorite music was played on the organ. After the resounding tones of Handel's *Largo* rang out, Shaw began to sing as though inspired, his eyes shone and his voice sounded young and clear, his spirit soared as though he was singing to his beloved Charlotte, as though he felt that her presence was near him and she did not wish him to grieve for her. After this, purged of his grief, Shaw became himself again, and on making some passing quip on his way home, Lady Astor is said to have remarked, "You really *are* a wicked old man!" When this story was told me, I remembered again Shaw's telling me that Saint Joan herself had guided his hand as he wrote his play about her. Behind the philosopher and the poet stood the mystic. Perhaps he felt that Charlotte Shaw was not really dead—but had merely passed over into another dimension of space in which they would meet again.

During the month of January, 1947, when Theresa Helburn and I were in London for the production of *Jane,* a play by S. N. Behrman based on a story by Maugham which we were unable to cast in America, we decided to call on G. B. S. and discuss our general arrangements with him. I called on Miss Patch who made the appointment with G. B. S. and gave us printed instructions on how to reach Ayot St. Lawrence.

The following day Terry and I hired a limousine and drove out to visit G. B. S. As we settled down in our car and drove through the winding roads which took us out of the London suburbs until we reached the Great North Road, we studied the printed drections which Shaw himself had written, showing us how to reach his country home. Only a playwright could have written such directions, and only a stage manager could have followed them.

Driving through the snow we read, "The lane twists about and rises and dips and ·rises again. At the top of the second rise, at a signpost marked 'to Welwyn,' bear left into the village of Ayot St. Lawrence. Drive through it past the ruined church; and at the end, where the road divides, Bernard Shaw's gate is facing you in the angle." Our chauffeur was no stage manager, and it is not surprising that we got lost several times in the snow. We finally arrived at the ruins of the church and descended from our car at Bernard Shaw's gate, fully expecting to meet the ruins not only of a church but also of a playwright.

We walked through the snow to the porch of Shaw's red-brick house, and the door was opened by a bored-looking housekeeper who has doubtless let in many boring callers during the past twenty years. She showed us into a comfortable little sitting room with four large chairs drawn up in front of a glowing coal fire. Around the room there was a good deal of bric-a-brac, a model of a small breakfront desk, and a Chinese scroll on the wall. Theresa and I sat in front of the fire, and thawed out until G. B. S. appeared and greeted us. He was no longer the tall, handsome, white-bearded figure I had once known, but resembled a Chinese philosopher or sage carved out of yellowing ivory, for his hair was streaked with yellow and his beard was shorter and irregular, as though he had bitten it off somewhat around the edges. I thought of Jaques' speech on the seven ages of Man in Shakespeare's *As You Like It.* At sixty-five Shaw had resembled "the justice . . . with eyes severe and beard of formal cut, full of wise saws and modern instances." As a vegetarian, however, he was lacking "the fat round belly with good capon lined." A lining of good vegetables, no matter how filling, can never produce the effect of a lining of good capon.

Shaw at the age of ninety was still in the sixth age of Man, wearing gray plus fours in which he looked indeed "the lean and slipper'd pantaloon," and he walked, acted as though like a man in his early seventies.

"What are you doing these days?" asked Terry. "I am being quite busy," said G. B. S. "First of all I am writing a new play for the Malvern Festival. There will be some plot and a good deal of conversation. I don't get so many new ideas now. After I had finished writing the play, I found that several of the things I had written had already appeared in some of my other plays. You know," he said, as though he was quite surprised at the fact, "it's rather hard to get new ideas at ninety. I rewrote the play and took out everything I had said before and now it's in fine shape." I asked if we might do it in New York after the Malvern production. "Certainly," he replied, "if you want to! It's called *The Unfinished Comedy.*" (Later the play was retitled *Buoyant Billions.*)

I asked G. B. S. what he thought of the condition of the theatre in England under the socialism which he had advocated. "Dear me," he said. "We haven't Socialism in this country— merely Trades Unionism. Most of the Trades Unionists don't know what Socialism is. On the other hand it's a good deal better than what you have in the States. The average American has the mentality of the village blacksmith. He knows what is going on in his own community, but hardly anything about the rest of the world. In my opinion Henry Wallace is the only man in the United States who really understands world affairs." He hoped Wallace would run for President on the Democratic ticket, even if he couldn't be elected. He thought it would be good to have world issues debated on Wallace's level during the next Presidential campaign. I suggested that if the British were ever able to vote for an American President, Wallace might have a chance, but I doubted it otherwise.

Talking of world issues, Shaw didn't think it mattered very much whether every nation shared the secret of the atomic bomb. "One thing ought to be self-evident to everybody," he said. "None of the peoples throughout the world want to destroy themselves. Indeed," he said, "from one point of view it's too bad the Japanese didn't appeal to the conscience of the world after the atom bombs were used at Hiroshima and Nagasaki. I think the conscience of the world would have stopped the United States from using any more of these bombs, just as the conscience of the world stopped the use of poison gas." I told G. B. S. I knew poison gas had been stopped not because of the conscience of the world, but because everybody had plenty of it. However, he stood his ground, as usual.

While we were having tea, he inquired about the state of the theatre in America. We told him our problems, and how the mounting costs were making it increasingly difficult to take chances in the theatre by way of experimental or noncommercial productions. "I see," he said with a smile. "You are caught between the cruel landlord and the relentless playwright." As we had hoped to persuade G. B. S. that his royalties, the highest in the world, ought to be reduced somewhat, I winced at the way he pronounced the word "relentless." "The theatre is not merely up against the landlord and the relentless author, but rising salaries as well," said Terry. "I agree with you," said G. B. S., and for a moment I thought, "Aha! Being a capitalist millionaire has taught him something." "The actors are overpaid," he said, "and it's entirely unnecessary. They would all be willing to work for less." And he instanced how Miss Gertrude Kingston told him that she had to ask a West End manager for £40 a week, in order that she might get a good dressing room, for they had a way of putting the inexpensive actors on the upper floors. However, she was willing to work for a third of that amount with Vendrenne and Barker because she was on a yearly

contract and could count on work all year round. "Until you get the theatre on that basis, you'll have to overpay," he added. "As to myself, I am now a classic. Of course I have to have my royalties, but if the royalty is only ninepence, why, I touch my hat and say 'Thank you.'" "How can anyone put on one of your plays and pay only nine-pence royalty?" I asked. "Oh, some village amateur dramatic group," he replied. "They do the classics."

We expounded the theory that since it costs at least fifteen thousand dollars a week to operate one of Shaw's plays, his royalty of 15 percent was too high. "I'll make you a proposition," said G. B. S. "I'll give you my plays royalty free up to fifteen thousand dollars." Our faces lit up happily, but only momentarily. "Any receipts over that, I'll take half—and of course," he added, "you'll have to play in a very large theatre." A rough calculation showed that G. B. S. would gain considerably more on this basis than before, so we said, "No, thank you. We'd rather pay the 15 percent." As a capitalist millionaire G. B. S. hadn't changed so very much, I thought.

We talked happily of many more things until it was time to leave. "We'll be back here soon with *Oklahoma!*," said Terry cheerfully, as we put on our coats in the hall, "and you'll have to come to see it." "No," said G. B. S. rather sadly, "I'm afraid I won't. I've lost all interest in the theatre, and I'm not much interested in anything else either."

He insisted on coming out of the front door to see us off. The snow was all around us as he stood outside the door, the light falling on his bare head and hair, giving him a translucent quality, almost saintly, like a halo.

On our way back Theresa said that she thought he must lead a lonely life so far out in the country. I said I didn't think so—that I felt the key to his character was to be found in the Preface to *Man and Superman,* in which he wrote, "There are no passions like the passions of the mind." I thought that G. B. S. had indulged this passion all his life, and that as he grew older he had more chance to indulge it, and that with it he would never be lonely.

In July of 1947, I wrote G. B. S. suggesting that we produce *You Never Can Tell, The Devil's Disciple,* and *Arms and the Man.* G. B. S. replied on a postcard:

Judith in the *D's D* is weakly sentimental: Katharine Hepburn is too strong for her.

Dick is not a raffish profligate: he is a tragic figure in black, like *Hamlet,* or Buckingham in *Henry VIII.*

I must let Alfred Fischer go where he chooses, as he did very well for me in Germany; but you should be able to give him as good terms as any other management, or better; and I should prefer yours. Hardwicke would of course be perfect as the waiter. It would be wise to wait for him.   G. B. S.

We informed G. B. S. that if and when we produced *You Never Can Tell,* we would take in Mr. Fischer as an associate producer, and an arrangement was made with Mr. Fischer. We finally decided not to wait for Cedric Hardwicke, but to produce the play with Leo G. Carroll in the part of the waiter. We made contracts to bring several players over from England and proceeded to put the play into rehearsal under the direction of Peter Ashmore who came over from London. After most of the actors' contracts were signed, a theatre engaged, and the entire project was under way, we received a cablegram from G. B. S. on November 14, 1947, reading as follows:

Taxation obliges me to defer further revivals. G. B. S.

We naturally assumed that in stating that further revivals were to be deferred, G. B. S. did not include *You Never Can Tell,* which was already under way, and which he had promised to us, and we therefore proceeded with this production, apparently to G. B. S.'s satisfaction. However, on January 10, 1948, when we were just about to go into rehearsal, we received a new cablegram from G. B. S. reading as follows:

Produce nothing of mine until presidential election is over. SHAW.

Hindsight compels me to admit that it was too bad we did not cancel all the contracts, and follow G. B. S.'s instructions. It would have saved us a great deal of money and trouble. However, since we had already entered into the production contracts on *You Never Can Tell* with G. B. S.'s blessing, we cabled him that his request had come too late for us to stop the production. Moreover, Peter Ashmore, who had directed the play in London, was already at work.

Unfortunately, while *You Never Can Tell* was liked in Boston and Philadelphia by our audiences and the out-of-town critics, the drama critics

of New York took it to pieces, notwithstanding the fact that, in my opinion, it was given an excellent production and was very much liked by our public; in fact, to test this out, we took a vote of the fifteen-thousand-odd subscribing New York members of the Theatre Guild, and well over two-thirds were delighted with the play. However, running expenses were very high, the summer was coming on, and we felt it expedient to close after a few weeks' run.

During the summer of 1950, Armina and I were in London for the opening of Rodgers and Hammerstein's *Carousel,* and we asked G. B. S. if we might visit him. The answer came back on the usual postcard, telling us to come, but that he had been ill with lumbago. This was destined to be our last visit.

We arrived at Ayot St. Lawrence in the late afternoon, and soon after, G. B. S. came into the room, looking frail and bent over, and walking with the aid of a stick. "Don't talk such nonsense," he replied to my remark that I thought he looked well. "I am decaying and disintegrating. I am not the man who wrote those plays." We sat and talked to him for a while, and he seemed gentler and more contemplative than ever before. In the course of our conversation he remarked, "Lawrence, I have told you several times now, you must regard me as being officially dead. I have made all arrangements so that my business affairs will proceed just as though I *were* dead." "But, G. B. S.," I replied, "whenever we want to do a play of yours, we still ask your permission, even though the Guild and the Westport Country Playhouse have produced over twenty of your plays." He answered in tones which sounded rather virile for one officially dead. "What, *only* twenty?" "Yes," I replied, "that's more than any other management has ever produced." By this time G. B. S. was coming to life rapidly. "I've written fifty," he said with a smile. "Why don't you do the other thirty?"

We then asked G. B. S.'s permission to produce *The Millionairess* with Katharine Hepburn, in accordance with his suggestion made some years earlier. "Is she a good athlete?" asked Shaw. "Indeed she is," said Armina. "She plays tennis every day, and takes long walks." And I added, hoping to clinch the matter, "She's as strong as a horse!" "Then you'll have to watch out," said Shaw, "for she'll have to play a scene where she applies jujitsu to her leading man, and she'll kill him if she isn't careful!" He then threw his head back and laughed heartily. This was the last time I heard him laugh.

He explained that he would never permit his plays to be done on television or in cut versions on radio, and when Armina remarked that cut versions of Shakespeare had been done successfully on radio, his eyes twinkled as he remarked, "My dear girl, it's bad enough to do that to Shakespeare, but it's sacrilege to cut Shaw!" I told him that I had brought a movie camera along to take a picture in place of the one which Pascal had muffed. "Come outside," he said. "If it's a movie camera, it calls for a director. Now you, Armina, will take a picture of the door to stimulate the interest of the audience. Then, after a moment of suspense, the door will open and I will come out. Then I will sit in my chair, Lawrence will come around the corner, and I will rise and greet him cordially." G. B. S. acted the picture as planned, but when it came time for him to rise from his chair and greet me, the ninety-four-year-old actor was somewhat less than sprightly. I shall always cherish this picture, and the one that follows it. "I think I'd better not see you off," he remarked, and I remembered his old custom of walking down the driveway to wave us good-bye. My last picture of him standing by the roadside, endeavoring to draw his bent-over body into the erect position in which he had always held himself, while he smiled and waved to us, brought tears to my eyes. There will never be another of his stature in our time.

During the past thirty years, the Theatre Guild has presented more of Shaw's plays than any other management, while the Westport Country Playhouse has presented seven. On balance, our relationship earned for G. B. S. somewhere in the neighborhood of $350,000 and has cost the Theatre Guild about the same amount. But had it cost the Guild ten times that amount, it would have been more than worth it to us. Our presentation of his plays to American audiences gained us a following which benefited all the other writers whose plays we produced during this period. But more than that, we counted his plays among the most precious contributions to the modern theatre, and in presenting them, we fulfilled one of our best reasons for existing.

I felt singularly ungrieved at G. B. S.'s passing, because I knew he wanted to die. I knew he felt that he had outlived his own brain and body, when he remarked to me, "Lawrence, I am not the man who wrote those plays," and he did not want to outlive that man. That man was a leader of our generation all over the world—in the theatre and out of it—and that man knew his days were over. The theatre has been very fortunate in the fact that some of the great geniuses of the world have written for it. One of these was Shakespeare, another was Shaw. The fact that Shaw was a great reformer, philosopher, thinker, and humorist—the fact that he used the theatre as his medium of expression—has made the theatre a greater place for his being in it, and it will be a lesser place for his passing.

After we learned of Shaw's death, I suggested that the Theatre Guild sponsor a memorial service dedicated to his memory. This took place on November 19, 1950, at the old Guild Theatre. The speakers made the occasion one of high celebration that the theatre had been blessed with so distinguished a genius, intermingled with grief at his passing. But the best part of the service was Shaw's own words, for at the conclusion Peggy Wood, Burgess Meredith, and Walter Abel played the last scene from *Candida;* John Gielgud read the "Statement of Faith" of Dubedat from *The Doctor's Dilemma,* and finally Katharine Cornell, with a sweep of emotion which carried the audience along with her, read the great speech of Saint Joan and ended the memorial with the ringing words, so applicable to Shaw himself:

"O God that madest this beautiful earth, when will it be ready to receive Thy saints? How long, O Lord, how long?"

IV

1926-1929

By 1926, the Guild had made a couple of tentative moves in the direction of putting its shows on tour, following their opening in New York, and the organization of the Guild Acting Company was to help implement the idea significantly. But the first concrete step toward a "road" plan was suggested during the winter of 1926 when Samuel Insull, a public-utilities tycoon from Chicago, visited Warren Munsell, the Guild's manager. Mrs. Insull, he explained, was an actress, working at the time with a Chicago company, and this accounted for his interest in the stage. If the Guild Acting Company would come to Chicago the following season he said he would underwrite the venture, which would be on a subscription basis, similar to that used successfully in New York. The first four of six plays would be produced by the Guild, the remaining two by the Chicago company.

It was apparent that Mrs. Insull was eager to act in a Guild company, which she eventually did, playing a role in *Caprice* during the 1928–1929 season. Largely through her enthusiasm and her husband's agreeable help, the Guild began a Chicago season in autumn of 1927 with the Lunts in *Arms and the Man* and *The Guardsman*. Following the opening of the second play at the Studebaker Theatre there, Philip Moeller and Lawrence Langner walked along Michigan Avenue and talked about the possibility of bringing Guild plays to all parts of the United States, and at that time began the planning which eventually brought it about. That same season an acting company was sent on tour, under the flag of the Judson Concert Bureau, with Florence Eldridge, George Gaul, and Fredric March as principal players. They carried adaptable scenery, which could be set up in theatres, schools, or gymnasiums, and presented a repertory which included *Arms and the Man, Mr. Pim Passes By, The Silver Cord,* and *The Guardsman.* Though they performed in 132 communities that season, the venture was not a happy one. One-night stands gave the company no time to rest, and the accommodations frequently were terrible. The experience strengthened the Guild's decision to handle its own tours, rather than letting them be booked by any of the established concert-lecture managements.

It was around this same time that the Guild began to publicize its own activities among its 25,000 subscribers with the new *Theatre Guild Quarterly,* shortly after made into a monthly called *The Theatre Guild Magazine.* It reached 50,000 circulation in two years, and continued to flourish until 1932, when it was taken over by John Hanrahan, who had been on the staff of *The New Yorker;* at the time it was renamed *Stage Magazine.* It survived seven more years, finally succumbing in 1939.

The mid-twenties also saw the launching of a School of the Theatre, which Theresa Helburn and Lawrence Langner supported over the doubts of other board members. Winifred Lenihan, an actress with more talent than patience, headed it for a while but finally quit after a tenure which must have been as hard on the pupils as it was on her. Some of them did pretty well in the arts either because of or in spite of this experience—Lucia Chase (who later guided the Ballet Theatre), Cheryl Crawford, Arlene Francis, and Linda Watkins.

Franz Werfel's *Juarez and Maximilian* raised the curtain on the 1926–1927 season. In the cast were Harold Clurman, Edward G. Robinson, Morris Carnovsky, Alfred Lunt, Cheryl Crawford, and Sanford Meisner. Regardless of this luster, it was the only one of fifteen consecutive plays produced by the Guild's Acting Company which was not financially successful.

So the Guild turned—again—to Shaw, this time to inaugurate their alternating repertory system, which achieved a compromise between repertory in the traditional sense (several plays being done by a company in the same season or even successive seasons) and the Guild's own system of long runs. A play would be produced for a week, then the same actors would be used in a second play for a second week, then back to the first play, and so on. Langner listed the advantages as these:

The actors played a different part each week, so they did not become stale.

The system lengthened the run of a weak play, since the box office was open for two weeks to sell seats for one playing week.

Good actors were willing to do smaller parts for one week, if they appeared in better ones the next week.

Labor costs were lower than those of ordinary repertory.

The best actors were not tied down to a single play, but were used in two or more.

When the plays were sent on tour under this system, rail fares were cheaper as each company played two or three plays, and stayed longer in each city.

The Acting Company formed for this consisted of Helen Westley, Alfred Lunt, Lynn Fontanne, Dudley Digges, Henry Travers, and Ernest Cossart; among others added later were Clare Eames, Margalo Gillmore, George Gaul, Glenn Anders, Earle Larimore, Tom Powers, Edward G. Robinson, Claude Rains, Edgar Stehli, Erskine Sanford, and Philip Loeb.

To expedite further the alternating repertory Langner suggested sets built of standard flats in neutral colors, so that they could be used in more than one play. Simonson and other designers weren't happy about this, but the unit set idea did prove practical.

The first play to implement the system was Shaw's *Pygmalion,* with Lynn Fontanne modeling her Eliza Doolittle on Hogarth's "Shrimp Girl,"

Juarez and Maximilian—Alfred Lunt portrayed the ruler of Mexico with Clare Eames as the Empress Charlotte. *Vandamm photograph.*

Juarez and Maximilian—Dudley Digges as the Archbishop Labastida and Edward G. Robinson as Porfirio Diaz. *Vandamm photograph.*

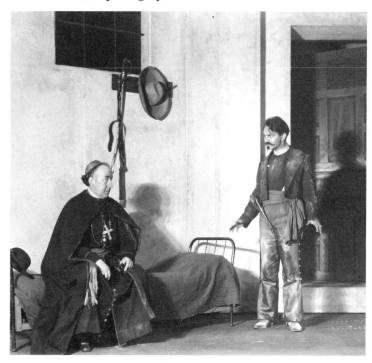

Juarez and Maximilian—Maximilian (Alfred Lunt) surrenders to the Juaristas. *Vandamm photograph.*

which hangs in the National Gallery in London. It was a great success, presaging the absolute triumph of Lerner and Loewe's *My Fair Lady,* based on this same play in later years. Still, Brooks Atkinson felt the play had lost some of its luster in the thirteen years since it was written. Mrs. Pat Campbell had played Eliza in the original New York production before the war, as she had done the role in England in 1914. Its world premiere had been staged in Vienna a year earlier. Highly pleasing to Guild audiences, besides Miss Fontanne, were Reginald Mason as Henry Higgins and Henry Travers as Eliza's dustman-father, Alfred Doolittle. Jo Mielziner designed the settings; before this he had done settings for *The Guardsman.*

Ned McCobb's Daughter, by Sidney Howard, alternated in repertory with *Pygmalion,* also earning its keep with 129 performances starting with the November 29, 1926, opening. It is a well-crafted play, with sharply delineated characters, drawing its spice from the spirit—good and bad—of New England farm folk.

Howard was also the author of *The Silver Cord,* which followed *Ned McCobb's Daughter* and opened December 20 at the John Golden Theatre. Alexander Woollcott wrote in the *New York World:* ". . . for Mr. Howard is the Guild's ringing answer to the restive charge that it is not interested in the American playwright. The Guild is passionately interested in the American playwright, the playwright being Mr. Howard." The earlier staging of Howard's *They Knew What They Wanted* contributed, of course, to the critic's conclusion. Reviewing the new Howard play in the *Telegram,* Frank Vreeland referred to it as *She Knew What She Wanted* and the head on Gilbert W. Gabriel's review in *The Sun* read: *"They Knew What Mother Wanted."*

The title refers to the thread—or apron string—with which a mother tries to bind her two sons, "secluding them," continued Vreeland, "from the rest of the world, especially other womenkind, and segregating them in an artificial little paradise while her mother-love, an iridescent but forbidding dragon, mounts guard at the gates with ferocious tenderness." Ruthlessly probing, the play earned critical approval, including at least one opinion that it was more deserving of the Pulitzer Prize than *They Knew What They Wanted.* Langner, who considered this drama the playwright's masterpiece, felt it was at least partly autobiographical. Laura Hope Crews's performance as the

Pygmalion—Henry Travers as Alfred Doolittle. *Vandamm photograph.*

Pygmalion—Lynn Fontanne as Eliza Doolittle. *Vandamm photograph.*

Pygmalion—the second meeting between Eliza Doolittle (Lynn Fontanne) and Dr. Henry Higgins (Reginald Mason). *Vandamm photograph.*

Ned McCobb's Daughter—Alfred Lunt as George Callahan knocks down his wife, Carrie (Clare Eames), who also is the title character. *Vandamm photograph.*

Ned McCobb's Daughter—Alfred Lunt on top, Earle Larimore down, with Margalo Gillmore, Philip Leigh, and Clare Eames watching. *Vandamm photograph.*

Clare Eames, who appeared as *Ned McCobb's Daughter,* with her own daughter.

The Silver Cord—Earle Larimore, Elisabeth Risdon, Margalo Gillmore, Eliot Cabot, and Laura Hope Crews. *Vandamm photograph.*

mother was singled out for special commendation, as was the direction and pacing by John Cromwell, described by one observer as honest, pliable, and galvanic.

One incident illustrates the almost psychotic protectiveness of the mother toward her sons. Hester, the despairing fiancée of one of the young men, has run outside to drown herself in the lake, and the two brothers rush out to rescue her. "Boys, boys, come back for your overcoats!" the mother shouts from the window. "You'll catch cold in this weather!" This might border on exaggeration, and not all of the play is this explicit; some is quite subtle. But Howard's exaggeration is grimly purposeful, as in this instance, and it makes a ring-ding of a second-act curtain.

Jacques Copeau, who collaborated the dramatic adaptation of Dostoevski's novel *The Brothers Karamazov* with Jean Croué, was brought from Paris to direct the Guild's production, which was the first done in English in the United States; there had been two Russian productions, one by the visiting Moscow Art Theatre. Copeau's handling of the brooding drama made this one more in the Guild's mounting list of successive

The Brothers Karamazov—in the usual order, George Gaul, Alfred Lunt, Morris Carnovsky, and Edward G. Robinson. *Vandamm photograph.*

hits, and ignited all sorts of discussion about how a Dostoevski masterpiece should be staged. As adapted by the Moscow Art, the play seemed to center on Ivan, the cruelly intellectual son of Feodor Pavlovitch. Copeau presented the romantic wastrel Dmitri as the core of all the turmoil—perhaps the natural emphasis for a Frenchman to give the story. Kelcey Allen, critic of *Women's Wear Daily,* summed up the prevailing opinion with:

> The Copeau version is a most creditable achievement, for it has caught the somber spirit, the sinister and menacing sense of impending tragedy of Dostoevski's work, and from the rambling, disjointed verboseness of the novel there issues forth a stirring drama of poignance and depth which, in its cumulative force of imminent doom, is overpowering.

At the time, a searching, perceptive evaluation of Copeau and his work was written for the *New York Post* by the young Harold Clurman. This was one of several sometimes subtle indications that the work of the director (also the co-author in this particular case) was starting to be noticed, and commented upon critically. Audiences too began to note the function of the director, apart from the acting and physical mounting, when they appraised their own favorable or unfavorable response to a Guild production. It was being proved that good provocative theatre makes better audiences—and critics.

> The major portion of the drama of Pirandello consists in a kind of metaphysical masochism. The Italian lays hold of a philosophical paradox, and derives an intense orgastic pleasure from belaboring himself with it. Where Shaw takes the same paradox and uses it sadistically upon his audience, his Latin contemporary bares his own flesh to it. In his ability to laugh at his self-imposed torture lies the latter's genius.
>
> The technique of the outstanding Pirandello drama is that of a philosophical detective play, with Truth as the mysterious and evasive culprit and all the characters of the play as sleuths. *Right You Are If You Think You Are,* excellently produced by the Theatre Guild, is typical of the leading elements in the Pirandello canon. As a tour de force in mystification, it must rank as a noteworthy achievement.

The Brothers Karamazov—they didn't get along. That's Alfred Lunt kicking Edward G. Robinson, while brothers George Gaul and Morris Carnovsky react each in his own way. The gentleman with the walking stick is Dudley Digges. *Vandamm photograph.*

Jacques Copeau adapted Dostoevski's *The Brothers Karamazov* for the stage and directed the Theatre Guild production.

Right You Are If You Think You Are—Edward G. Robinson, Armina Marshall, and Beryl Mercer in Pirandello's dramatic enigma. *Vandamm photograph.*

Right You Are If You Think You Are—this Jo Mielziner set cost $500. The year was 1927. *Vandamm photograph.*

Thus did George Jean Nathan welcome the Guild's matinee presentation of the Pirandello play which had come upon the New York theatre scene in mid-February of 1927. It was not an American premiere; that had taken place with a student production at Cornell University, with Franchot Tone as one of the young players. Nor was it New York's first exposure to the Italian writer; his *Enrico IV,* under the title of *The Living Mask,* had been done three years earlier. But, as remarkably good Pirandello, intelligently staged by Philip Moeller, it drew attention to one of the most fascinating dramatists of the early twentieth century.

The play, certainly well-known by now, begins with a mystery: why does the new secretary to the town Precept live with his wife on the top floor of an apartment, in which his mother-in-law lives on the ground floor, and never permit his wife and mother-in-law to get together? The two women communicate only by shouting or exchanging notes in baskets raised and lowered. Eventually each of the principals offers an explanation, and each is different from the next. Which is right? The one you wish to believe is right. Pirandello makes his point.

S. N. Behrman was one of the many playwrights discovered by the Guild, which eventually produced eleven of his generally well-worded comedies and dramas. His *The Second Man* had in fact been turned down by the company's playreader, Courtenay Lemon, but a friend of Behrman's urged Langner to look at it. He liked the lightweight but rather deft piece, as did Theresa Helburn and Philip Moeller, so they prepared what turned out to be a successful production featuring the Lunts, Earle Larimore, and Margalo Gillmore. This too clicked with Guild audiences to conclude a genuinely triumphant season, and to set the stage for an equally good one to come.

A retrospective appraisal such as this is bound to stir flickers of emotion which could not have been anticipated at the time these plays were being produced. For example, mention *Porgy,* the Dorothy and Du Bose Heyward drama about the crippled Negro of Catfish Row in Charleston, South Carolina, and suddenly we are enveloped in the music of Gershwin's *Porgy and Bess,* the folk opera based on this play which was not to appear on the theatre scene until the following decade.

Well before the music was added and the script was rewritten as a libretto, this story cap-

Samuel Nathaniel Behrman began a long and productive association with the Guild with *The Second Man* in 1927. They were allied on eleven of his plays. *Vandamm photograph.*

The Second Man—Alfred Lunt and Margalo Gillmore. *Vandamm photograph.*

The Second Man—Lynn Fontanne had to wear a white wig in order to appear thirty-five. With her, Alfred Lunt.

Porgy—Evelyn Ellis as Bess, Jack Carter as Crown. *Vandamm photograph.*

Porgy—Frank Wilson in the title role. *Vandamm photograph.*

Porgy—Percy Verwayne as Sportin' Life. *Vandamm photograph.*

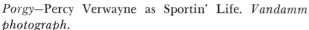

tured the imagination and heart of almost everyone who encountered it. Opening October 10, 1927, to begin the Guild's tenth season, *Porgy* ran for 217 performances, plus 137 more in a revival the following year. This play, the first work of stature about American Negro life, was purchased by the Guild, but no one was eager to direct it. Rouben Mamoulian, a young acting teacher from Rochester, New York, Moscow, and Tiflis, had been engaged to work in the newly formed Guild School. He successfully undertook the job, and his remarkable handiwork made a name for the play, as well as for himself. Frank Wilson was Porgy, with Jack Carter as the murderous Crown, and Evelyn Ellis, identified then not as "Bess" but as "Crown's Bess" in the program.

Using a Negro cast in *Porgy* was almost a Broadway innovation; at the time it was more the practice to use white actors made up as Negroes, except in comedy and housemaids' parts. The Guild turned to Shaw's *The Doctor's Dilemma* to put its regular company back to work in its next play, which opened on November 21. Morris

Porgy—a scene on Catfish Row. *Vandamm photograph.*

Carnovsky, Dudley Digges, Helen Westley, Alfred Lunt, Lynn Fontanne, Earle Larimore, and Ernest Cossart performed this saber-cut at the English (and, by implication, American or any other) medical profession, which, interestingly enough, doctors seemed to especially enjoy. It has several plot threads, but the principal one concerns a physician who must decide which of two patients he should save. His love for the mistress of one patient complicates the decision.

Nothing in the Guild's tenth season—which was a very good one in terms of theatre art and income—was as important or pivotal as the beginning of its association with Eugene O'Neill. For some time, the occasional criticism leveled against the Guild included the charge that despite their well-publicized resolve to produce works of promising American writers, they had never done an O'Neill play, though he had been around, as a functioning playwright, ever since the formative seasons of the Provincetown Players a decade before.

The truth was that Lawrence Langner had

Rouben Mamoulian, who had been brought from Rochester, New York, to teach in the Guild school, volunteered to direct *Porgy*. It was the first of many directorial achievements, including *Oklahoma! Vandamm photograph.*

The Doctor's Dilemma—Shaw's play united the Lunts once again. With them is Baliol Holloway.

been after O'Neill from the very beginning, but without much luck. The two of them had met and immediately hit it off the summer of 1917, when O'Neill was living in an abandoned Coast Guard station, redecorated, according to rumor, by Robert Edmond Jones. Langner had gotten the Washington Square Players to produce O'Neill's *In the Zone,* and wanted him to let the Guild undertake his plays from the opening season of the latter group. Unfortunately, five of his plays were turned down in succession by the Guild's directors, which certainly strained relations. Langner and Maurice Wertheim tried unsuccessfully to correct the situation.

In early 1927 Langner went to Bermuda to recover from a severe cold, knowing that O'Neill was staying there. The visit turned out to be both cordial and productive. The writer agreed to give the Guild *Marco Millions,* which it opened on January 9, 1928, and far more important, the world premiere of *Strange Interlude,* which three weeks later began an unbroken run of 426 performances.

Marco Millions is not the best of O'Neill, a fact recognized by a few critics who covered its opening; nevertheless the playwright was credited with "sardonic satire and mordant irony" rising from the "sheer poetry" of his play. Richard

Marco Millions—a departure from most of O'Neill's plays was this one with its exotic Eastern characters and settings; the latter by Lee Simonson, who also designed the costumes. *Vandamm photograph.*

Watts, Jr., writing then for the *New York Herald Tribune,* wondered about O'Neill's seeming hatred for the hapless Marco Polo, finding it as total a denunciation as any since Shakespeare pilloried Richard III. Guild director Rouben Mamoulian and designer Lee Simonson flooded the stage with oriental opulence. The play earned unstinted praise from *The New York Times*'s usually restrained Brooks Atkinson, with just about everyone admitting that it was a gorgeous spectacle. Alfred Lunt made a resourceful Marco Polo and Margalo Gillmore stirred Alexander Woollcott to verbal ecstasies in her portrayal of the Princess of Cathay. She didn't do as much for Leonard Hall of the *Telegram,* who found her "pretty much the brightest girl in the class reciting on Friday afternoon." It was generally recognized that the play is considerably more than a pageant; O'Neill's representation of the ancient explorer as a Venetian Babbitt made its sharp point.

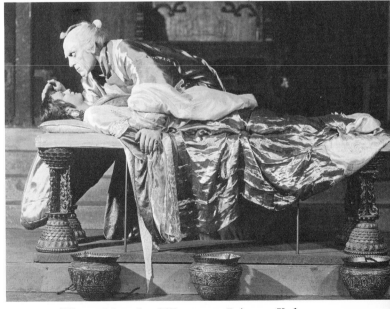

Marco Millions—Margalo Gillmore as Princess Kukachin, Baliol Holloway as Kublai Khan. *Vandamm photograph.*

At 5:30 P.M. on Saturday, January 30, 1928, the curtain at the John Golden rose on a play which was to win a Pulitzer Prize, earn lasting honor as an American classic, and significantly if subtly alter the course of the drama in the twentieth century. O'Neill's *Strange Interlude* was unusual in a number of ways, the first to draw comment being its length; in nine acts, it played for six hours, with a dinner break in mid-evening. Because it was unusually candid for the times, and even mentioned such dark matters as abortion, its effect on the public morality was a matter of concern in a few places, such as New York and Boston. "Banned in Boston" was good for the box office, of course, and even though Boston officials offered to adopt a more liberal attitude if the Guild would make a little donation of $10,000, the company decided instead to stage it in nearby Quincy, Massachusetts, where it was even more successful than it might have been in the larger city. Fleets of buses brought people from Boston, so nothing was lost. In fact, one Quincy restaurateur who happened to be on the verge of bankruptcy did so well with the *Strange Interlude* intermission business that he was able to start a national chain of restaurants bearing his name—Howard Johnson.

But what really stirred those who came to see O'Neill's play was its uncanny penetration of people's minds. The device was simple enough; he merely had the characters speak their thoughts, in asides to the audience, before they said whatever they had to say to the other characters in the scene. Nevertheless, it was disturbing, not solely because of what was said—or, more precisely, thought—but because the man or woman watching the play

Strange Interlude—this was the second O'Neill drama to open in January of 1928. Above, Glenn Anders, Lynn Fontanne, Tom Powers, and Earle Larimore.

Strange Interlude—Lynn Fontanne and Helen Westley. *Vandamm photograph.*

realized that thought had ceased to be private. If they had read some of the early psychoanalysts they would have known that the invasion of the mind had started long before, and that our secret selves were bound to become progressively less secret. But introspection as a public entertainment seemed, somehow, improper, or even indecent. Nakedness was wrong, in the prevailing thinking, and this was a kind of mental nakedness.

The fact that the play centered on a woman, and revealed some very intimate aspects of her mind, made it even more distressing—or intriguing; even those who overtly or covertly disapproved of the play were fascinated by what went on in the mind of Nina. Portrayed by Lynn Fontanne in a role which most actresses of the time would have hesitated to try, Nina refuses to give herself to her beloved Gordon before he leaves to go to war, and suffers agonies of self-recrimination for not having done so, when she learns he'll never return. She tries to assuage her guilt by giving herself to any veteran, eventually marrying Gordon's admirer, the colorless Sam,

who makes her pregnant. But Sam's mother tells her there is insanity in the family, so Nina aborts the child and has her dear friend Dr. Darrell plant a replacement. It is the relationship of all these, including the son in years to come, that brings the intense and relentless drama to its conclusion.

With the enormous success of *Strange Interlude,* the Guild system of alternating repertory had to be put aside temporarily, and only one more play opened that season. It was Stefan Zweig's adaptation of Ben Jonson's *Volpone,* which was presented at the Guild Theatre in April. It was received cordially, and drew further comment lauding the ensemble playing of the Guild troupe. Dudley Digges appeared as the fox (Volpone), with Alfred Lunt as Mosca, the gadfly.

Friedrich Holl, who had produced *Faust* in Germany, was brought to New York to direct the Guild's production, which opened its eleventh season on October 8, 1928. Goethe's dark and massive masterpiece proved feeble entertainment, as Percy Hammond of the *Tribune* appraised it, and audiences tended to find the experience grim.

Things picked up whenever they went on—or, in a sense, back—to Shaw, replacing Faust with the Irish playwright's *Major Barbara* a few weeks later. Following a London opening late in 1905, the year in which it was written, the satire made its way to this country in 1915. When the Guild opened it thirteen years after that, the play hadn't aged in the least—something which still can be said of it, even if some of our attitudes about capitalism and poverty have since altered. Winifred Lenihan, who had been Saint Joan a few seasons earlier, became Barbara Undershaft—social worker, Salvation Army major, and rebellious daughter of a millionaire munitions magnate.

The title, *Wings over Europe,* sounds like one of the many war-aviation movies which flooded the screen in the decade or two after World War I (and again after World War II, for that matter, though with different wings). Actually it was an uncannily prophetic drama about a young scientist who develops an atomic bomb and believes it can be employed to implement a plan for lasting and universal peace. While the scientist is almost fantastically and unbelievably idealistic, the political leaders don't sound that different from some of those who were to wrestle with this very real problem only a few years later.

Among the critics, few were so brash as to

Volpone—the battered Volpone (Dudley Digges) is on the floor, with Helen Westley beside him. Standing facing them are Ernest Cossart as Corvino and Margalo Gillmore as Colomba, with the wily Mosca (Alfred Lunt) at far right.

Faust—Graham and Tristan Rawson adapted the Goethe drama, in which George Gaul played the title character and Rita Vale personified Lilith. *Vandamm photograph.*

Major Barbara—Percy Waram as Bill Walker. *Vandamm photograph.*

Major Barbara—Dudley Digges as Andrew Undershaft. *Vandamm photograph.*

Major Barbara—Frieda Inescort as Shaw's heroine in the touring company. Winifred Lenihan did the role in New York. *Vandamm photograph.*

Major Barbara—Elliot Cabot and Winifred Lenihan. *Vandamm photograph.*

Wings over Europe—Alexander Kirkland (back to camera) is the young scientist offering his discovery of nuclear power to the British Cabinet in this prophetic drama. *Vandamm photograph.*

Wings over Europe—Ernest Lawford. *Vandamm photograph.*

say the whole thing was farfetched; even in 1928 things were happening so fast that you were careful about pooh-poohing anything that smacked of the future. But nobody was quite as alarmed as subsequent history would have warranted. The play is theatrically effective in some of its scenes, abstract in others, but quite possibly worth looking at again today, in the light of what has happened since it was written by Robert Nichols and Maurice Browne. The Guild production proved popular, but with its all-male cast, it did not fit into the alternating repertory plan and was soon replaced.

Philip Moeller branched out in *Caprice*, which enchanted audiences here and in London, as well as on the road, starting with its Boston opening on December 17, 1928, and its New Year's

Caprice—London as well as New York enjoyed this sophisticated comedy which employed the talents of Douglass Montgomery, Lynn Fontanne, Alfred Lunt, and Lily Cahill. *Vandamm photograph.*

Eve debut in New York. Along with directing it, he prepared the English adaptation of G. Sil-Vara's comedy, *Mit Der Liebe Spielen,* and even wrote words and music of a waltz, "Ilsa," used during the production. Actually, Sil-Vara probably could have translated his own play; the Viennese playwright, novelist, essayist, translator, and journalist had lived in London for ten years and spoke English flawlessly. The comedy contrasts love which is a devotion and love which is a game in the present and past of a Viennese attorney, with Alfred Lunt in that role. Lynn Fontanne was his contemporary diversion, and Lily Cahill the woman out of his past, who returns bringing the sixteen-year-old son born of their dalliance. This kind of champagne effervescence did a great deal to advance the already impressive popularity of the Lunts, particularly after the Guild moved it to the St. James's Theatre in London.

Eugene O'Neill had planned *Dynamo* as "the first of a trilogy, written on the general subject, more or less symbolically treated, of the death of the old God and the spiritual uneasiness and degeneration into which the sterile failure of Science and Materialism to give birth to a new God that can satisfy our primitive religious crawlings has thrown us," as he had written to Langner in the fall of 1928. Possibly because it was not a striking success in the subsequent Guild production, closing after fifty performances, or because O'Neill decided not to pursue this particular line of dramatic thought further, he never completed the intended trilogy.

In the story, the serious, overwrought son of a puritanical minister falls in love with the daughter of the man who runs the nearby power plant. Resenting his father's dour attitudes, the boy runs away, returns months later eventually to consummate his love with the girl, after he has taken a job in the power plant. He has decided that God is dead and that Electricity has replaced Him, but this still doesn't quiet his overpowering sense of guilt. He finally commits suicide by embracing the dynamo which, apparently, is not properly grounded. Glenn Anders portrayed the young man, with Claudette Colbert as the girl. Right after the play closed, Miss Colbert went to Hollywood—and stayed. According to Robert Littell of the *New York Post:*

> *Dynamo* is, on the whole, not a good play at all, but, except for its first act, an insistent, pretentious and solemn fumbling after large, vague truths, presented by the Guild rather better than it deserves. . . . It wallows a good deal among ideas and symbolism, about none of which Mr. O'Neill seems to have done any hard, clear thinking.

Dudley Digges, long the Guild's busiest actor as well as one of its best, turned director

Dynamo—Glenn Anders was the tragic hero-victim of O'Neill's drama, shown here with Helen Westley and George Gaul as his parents. *Vandamm photograph.*

Dynamo—a climactic scene, with Glenn Anders clinging to Claudette Colbert.

for *Man's Estate,* by Beatrice Blackmar and Bruce Gould, along with acting one of the principal roles. It opened April 1, 1929, at the Biltmore. "Unhappily ordinary, untidy and unhinged," in the opinion of the New York *American*'s Gilbert Gabriel, the bitter comedy deals with a young idealist trapped by his own Babbitt background. He wants to design fine buildings but an enforced marriage to the girl he has gotten pregnant finally traps him in the hardware store in a midwestern town. Then and to a certain extent now, it was

standard practice in the theatre to present the American Midwest as somewhere to escape from, as well as the nurturing soil for all sorts of repressive and reactionary attitudes.

The eleventh season came to its conclusion with Francis Langer's *The Camel Through the Needle's Eye,* which presented a somewhat different aspect of premarital sex. In that case, a rich young man becomes involved with a little blonde flower of sin who, it turns out, has a backbone of steel. Not until he tells off his stuffy father

Man's Estate—Earle Larimore and Margalo Gillmore, tenderly involved. *Vandamm photograph.*

Man's Estate—Earle Larimore and Margalo Gillmore getting married. *Vandamm photograph.*

The Camel Through the Needle's Eye —Lee Simonson's second-act set. *Vandamm phótograph.*

does she agree to marry him, after which they are, assumedly, happy despite his burden of wealth. The production was most brightened by Helen Westley's work as an old harridan of the cellars, who sends her gouty male companion out on the streets to throw epileptic fits and lead home the charitably inclined. Here they are overwhelmed by the scent of cabbage, which she has cooked to reinforce the aura of poverty, and subsequently milked of their donations.

Essential to any accounting and appraisal of the Theatre Guild is a consideration of its play-readers. They did not make any final decisions; this was the prerogative of the ruling sextet—Helburn, Langner, Westley, Moeller, Simonson, and Wertheim. But from the beginning they were, in most instances, the first to read any play offered for possible productions except, as occasionally happened, when someone who knew one of the directors would give a script directly to him. After the first few years, as the Guild grew not only in the size of its operation but in prestige, plays were increasingly being submitted, which meant that, busy as the directors were with the myriad details of production and of running the organization, somebody had to read them first. A play-reader carried—and carries—a heavy responsibility. He can turn down a script which, accepted by another producer, might become a hit. Almost anybody who has functioned in the theatre in a decision-making capacity for any length of time carries the scars of a few such unhappy experiences. But if he's good at the job, he can tell fairly quickly which scripts are good, which might possibly work, and which are not worth considering. He should be able to spot talent in a playwright even if the play submitted is unsuitable. And when a script is interesting though faulty, he must be able to say just what alterations, additions, or deletions are needed to make it possible and, hopefully, profitable.

Of all the Guild's play-readers, the most distinguished and able was John Gassner, who came into the organization in 1929, originally to examine only American and British plays, but within a short time he was reading all the foreign possibilities as well. Gassner had been graduated from Columbia University in 1924 and earned his master's degree there the following year. By 1928 he was teaching at Hunter College in New York and shortly after at Brooklyn College as well.

Already he was starting to show the versatility which was to persist throughout his professional life, carrying his horizons beyond theatre. For example, he was literary adviser to the Lehman brothers, who were bankers, and helped to write books on economics, such as *America Looks Abroad* and *The Standards We Raise*.

To understand Gassner's contribution to the Guild and, in fact, to theatre scholarship in this country, it is necessary first to look at the American theatre and the happy coincidence that introduced him and a few other singularly talented men and women (such as the Guild's organizers and directors) into it at the start of its first significant era. Prior to World War I, no one but an out-and-out chauvinist could pinpoint an American dramatic heritage of any real consequence. Plays had been staged in this country for more than a century, and quite a number had been written here. Yet any review of the nineteenth century in the United States is almost bound to focus more on actors and actresses than on plays and playwrights, except in terms of classics and a few contemporary European dramas. It wasn't that we lacked a theatre; at the turn of the twentieth century there was a playhouse in almost every American city and town of 800 or more population, but it was far more entertainment-oriented than idea-oriented, and it was American more in locale than in any developed artistic tradition.

Suddenly that changed. O'Neill, the Guild, the Provincetown Players, and the Washington Square Players all came on the scene within about four years—between 1916 and 1920. So it follows that anyone whose theatre involvement started then, or not long after those dates, would be blessed by an opportunity which simply had not existed before in this country, at least not in those proportions. The Guild, along with presenting the works of O'Neill (though they were neither the first nor the last to do so), helped to develop an American dramatic literature which had not existed before.

Almost as suddenly as all this happened, it became evident that we needed a new kind of theatre scholarship and criticism, directed not so much toward retrospective evaluation of old plays as toward timely analysis of the new. This meant that the cloistered study would not meet the need. If one were to understand this new life of the theatre, he had to be a part of it, to participate in the staging of the plays, or to be there when they opened; to know the playwrights and directors, to observe the way audiences responded, and to try, in the living situation, to discern the difference between theatricality and drama. In a sense, the critic had to be the scholar and the scholar had to be the critic. It was vital to bring to this new experience the learning of the past and an instinct for wisely evaluating the theatre of the present. The accident of being there, and being involved, was a singularly blessed one for men such as John Gassner, Harold Clurman, and a number of others who were young when this theatre era was still so vulnerably young, and who were able to grow not just on its perimeter, but deeply within it.

Gassner's work—before, during, and after his Guild involvement—always enabled him to maintain a close physical as well as intellectual association with the theatre in New York, which was and continues to be the most creative area of theatre in America, encouraging as the growth of regional theatre might be today. He was almost continually seeing plays—literally thousands of them over forty-plus years. When he wasn't seeing them, he was reading them, during fifteen years with the Guild, and writing the concise, explicit, and incredibly perceptive private critical analyses which guided the Guild directorship in most of its decisions. During the Guild years, he also was writing publicly published criticism. This exposure and activity, coupled with his steadily mounting authority in the total history and analysis of the world's drama, provided a double-barreled scholarship which few others, no matter how learned or dedicated, were in a position to match. Even if John Gassner had not been a remarkable man—and he was—he could not have helped being a richly experienced one.

He left the Guild in 1944, to become head of the play department for Columbia Pictures, a position he held for the next three years. He took a year off, in 1947 and 1948, for writing, travel abroad, and concentrated theatre-going. From 1948 to 1956 he taught at Queens College, and in the latter year he was named Sterling Professor of Playwriting and Dramatic Literature at Yale University, a position he filled no less than brilliantly until his death in the spring of 1967.

Gassner's play evaluations for the Guild were written in longhand, then carefully typed—usually by his wife and quiet collaborator, Mollie—single-spaced on white, yellow, or pink sheets of paper, in ascending order of their value as production possibilities. Collected in the Theatre Guild archives in the Beinecke Rare Book Library at Yale University, they are a rare resource for information about almost every play that was written during those fifteen developmental years in the theatre. While they have not been published, a great deal of Gassner's writing was. He produced about sixty books, mostly dealing with the drama, here and abroad, historical and contemporary. He was the foremost theatre scholar this country has ever produced.

Anita Block was one of the early play-readers, as was Cynthia Lathrop, who also edited the Guild's programs. Prior to the Gassner period the job was done for some years by Courtenay Lemon, a learned gentleman who was married to Djuna Barnes, a budding playwright and one of the most beautiful girls in Greenwich Village at the time.

Among others who looked over new scripts for the Guild were Kenneth Rowe, who wrote very professorial, essay-type reports; William Herman, whose comments were more concise; Phyllis Anderson, and Bea Lawrence.

V

Eugene O'Neill

by Lawrence Langner

THE IMPACT OF Eugene O'Neill on the American theatre was, in the first instance, one of romanticism rather than tragedy. His early one-act plays, with their rugged portrayals of sailors before the mast, brought a breath of fresh sea air into the theatre which culminated in the *Moon of the Caribbees, The Emperor Jones,* and *Anna Christie.* Side by side with those were the more tragic one-act plays such as *Before Breakfast* and *Ile.* But it was only with the production of *Beyond the Horizon* that O'Neill's tragic gifts were felt with full force and effect, and from there on, the critics who wrote for the theatre and the people who worked in it realized that here was a man of genius capable of writing tragedy in its highest form. His great plays crashed into the American theatre like giants crashing through an undergrowth of lesser plays. Before him were the tepid realistic plays written in pale imitation of Ibsen, such as Eugene Walter's *The Easiest Way* and James A. Herne's *Margaret Fleming.*

From *Strange Interlude* on, O'Neill showed a unique ability to pile dramatic situation on dramatic situation, to build from one climax to a greater climax, and to stir the emotions of an audience in mounting suspense until the tension became almost unbearable. These qualities of his writing became evident in his middle period, and marked him as the greatest dramatist of his day, comparable only to the greatest masters of ancient and modern times.

In the beginning of his writing career O'Neill was blessed with a sympathetic group of theatre workers in the Provincetown Players, led by George Cram (Jig) Cook and James Light, both of whom contributed greatly to his birth as a dram-

Eugene O'Neill, photographed by Carl Van Vechten at Sea Island, Georgia, 1936.

atist. Jig Cook came first and James Light later, as Gene demanded the theatrical competence of Light as well as the mystical enthusiasms of Cook. But it was the "uptown" managers, such as John Williams, George Tyler, and Arthur Hopkins, who first brought about a marriage between O'Neill and the professional theatre, and peopled his plays with the best actors the theatre could afford. Yet even when he was in swaddling clothes in Greenwich Village, O'Neill was fortunate in the casting of his plays. Charles S. Gilpin in *The Emperor Jones,* Mary Blair and Louis Wolheim in *The Hairy Ape,* Mary Pyne in *Before Breakfast,* all gave unforgettable performances which carried O'Neill's fame from the Village to Broadway.

At the time when I first worked on the production of an O'Neill play (other than *In the Zone* produced by the Washington Square Players about 1917), his reputation was already securely established by the successful productions of *Beyond the Horizon, The Emperor Jones, Anna Christie, The Great God Brown,* and so forth. We of the Theatre Guild were no pioneers in producing O'Neill. Far from it. But during his early period we were engaged in attaining professional competence and a theatrical following which served O'Neill in good stead by the time he was writing his later masterpieces. Nine of his plays were produced by the Theatre Guild in succession, as he wrote them, and during the latter part of his lifetime he regarded the Guild as his theatrical home until the time arrived when he could no longer, for reasons of health, be present during rehearsals, and therefore held up the production of his later plays. I am not unhappy that he did not witness some of these later productions done by others. He would have vomited with disgust at some of them. Others he would have cheered. As it was, the producers were deprived of his help in translating his plays from the printed page to the stage, so that they lacked the pruning and revisions which were always part and parcel of his final contribution to his writings. Neither directors, actors, nor managements can therefore be blamed if some of these later plays in production did not add the luster to his fame which was actually merited.

I first met Eugene O'Neill at Provincetown in the summer of 1917. He lived on the edge of the ocean in an abandoned coast guard station, which was formerly the home of the famous Mabel Dodge, and to reach his home it was necessary to trudge for about three miles across the sand dunes. Rumor had it that Robert Edmond Jones had decorated the house in the gay blue-and-white color scheme which it then wore, and the large room which formerly contained the coast guard lifeboat was now the living room.

On the beach just below the house was the wreck of a large schooner, and O'Neill, costumed in a bathing suit, took me onto the beach where, somewhat superfluously, I emptied the sand out of my shoes. The resounding surf, the background of the wrecked sailing ship, and the lithe, muscular body of O'Neill, his dark Irish eyes set deep in his suntanned face, made an appropriate O'Neill setting for my first meeting with our foremost playwright, with whose destiny my own was later linked for so many years. We talked over the production of *In the Zone* by the Washington Square Players, after which he invited me to join him in a swim. This I refused, being no swimmer in a high surf (or even in a low one), whereupon O'Neill plunged in and displayed his prowess with a swift overarm stroke of which he was very proud. Like Bernard Shaw's, O'Neill's favorite sport was swimming; indeed it was the only form of athletics in which he indulged during the time I knew him. My last view of him, as I bade him farewell at this first meeting, was his silhouette at the side of the house, the ocean behind him and the wind blowing his hair awry. It was also my last view of the old coast guard station, for the restless Atlantic swallowed it up a few years later and not a trace now remains but the endless ocean and the lonely dunes.

"What do you think is the finest thing I could do to help the American theatre?" my friend Maurice Wertheim asked me with enthusiasm one day as we walked down Sixth Avenue toward the Garrick Theatre. "Subsidize Eugene O'Neill so that he can write plays for the next two years without any financial worries," I said. "All right," said Maurice, "go ahead and sound him out." I passed on the suggestion through a friend and this resulted in my receiving the following from Gene dated January 10, 1921:

Indeed I'll be glad enough to talk it all over with you when I get to town again—the first part of February probably. I'll confess your proposition has me puzzled. Granted its generous interest, it yet seems to me inconsistent. I am in no dire straits for money, as you must know. Even if I were, my poverty-stricken years of the past are proof enough that there is no danger of my street-walking along Broadway. I simply ain't that kind of a girl.

But, after all, all that part of it is immaterial. I know what you were driving at and, as I have said, I appreciate the interest. However, the whole thing, to my mind, boils down to this: Either you have faith in my plays, or you haven't. If you have, you produce them. If not, not. And you have turned down three of mine already. In rejections of my work you have a clear lead over any other management. These facts, you must acknowledge, are a bit inexorable. Your committee's judgment is not in question here. Perhaps they were right, perhaps wrong. A jury of our peers might well disagree forever on that point. And certainly they—the committee—were entitled to their verdict made in good faith. The thing is, how do you expect me to reconcile your adverse judgments with your alleged appreciation? It is all very well to talk of my future work, but if everyone had done that I would have no past nor present to build a future upon. The only help I need or would accept from anyone is a hearing—a fair hearing as in *Jones* or *Anna Christie*. And my obligation, both as a man and as a playwright, lies toward those who have helped me to that hearing and thereby proved their faith in me in the one way it can be proved.

So there you have my side of it; and it seems to me there is little else that can be said.

All this without any trace of hard feeling on my part, I know I don't have to tell you that. It is merely a question of unprejudiced disagreement, but I am afraid the evidence indicated that your committee and I are doomed forever to disagree.

In the spring of 1927 I suffered from a severe cold and was advised by my doctor to take a couple of weeks off to recuperate. By this time the producing firm with which O'Neill had associated himself had dissolved, and O'Neill spent most of his time in Bermuda. I had a hunch that a visit to Bermuda might not only restore me to health but also enable me to restore the personal relation which had formerly existed between O'Neill and myself, and which had very naturally become cloudy for the reasons I have explained above. My hunch turned out to be correct.

O'Neill welcomed me warmly, and we had some talks about the possibility of the Guild producing *Marco Millions*. From that he went on to discuss the future of the American theatre, and what he hoped to contribute toward it. Walking up and down the sandy beach near his white-roofed coral house, which had been built by a seventeenth-century privateer and stood at the edge of the sea, Gene explained that he was experimenting with ways and means to break down "realism" in the theatre, and had just finished a play in which the characters not only talked to one another but also spoke their thoughts in a form of aside which he thought the audience would accept. The idea fascinated me and I asked him if I might read the play, which he informed me was called *Strange Interlude*. He also told me that it would take six hours to play it. In view of our experience with Shaw's *Back to Methuselah*, this did not daunt me.

A few days later I was invited to O'Neill's home for a swim and dinner afterward, and I spent the evening with him discussing the theme of the play. He told me that he had already promised it to a well-known American actress who was his first choice, but that if I liked the play and she did not, I might have it for the Guild. Meanwhile, I could read it and let him know what I thought of it. He then handed me the first six acts of the manuscript, which I still possess. It was half again as thick as any ordinary play, for not only was it a double-length play, but so long that nearly forty pages were subsequently cut out of it. Clutching the precious manuscript to my bosom I returned in the horse cab which had been ordered for me (there were no automobiles in Bermuda at the time), and drove along the shore road in a gale which at times seemed so strong that I feared horse cab, *Strange Interlude,* and I would be blown together into the sea.

I went to bed intending to read at least part of the play before I fell asleep; the storm outside grew more and more violent as the play grew more and more exciting. The tropical thunder and lightning, and the fierce howling of the gale which began to assume hurricane proportions failed to interrupt me. All night long I read and read, and at four o'clock in the morning, my eyes strained and throbbing, I finished the sixth act. Before I went to sleep I examined my feelings about the play as far as I had read. I judged it one of the greatest plays of all time.

The storm died down during the night, and the next morning was bright and clear; as soon as I was awake I telephoned Gene and told him how enthusiastic I was about the play. He invited me over to his home again. This time he definitely promised me that if the actress to whom he had offered the play did not care to do it (and he thought there were certain reasons why she might not), the Theatre Guild could have it. Then he gave me a breathtaking exhibition of his over-arm stroke, which I photographed with my Cine-Kodak.

After my return to New York, I wrote Gene telling him I had stirred up some interest in *Marco Millions* and asked him to send us a copy of *Strange Interlude*. On the arrival of the manuscript, I circulated it among my fellow directors. To my horror, they did not all share my enthusiasm. One of them even went so far as to say that if all the asides were taken out, the play would be greatly improved. I wanted to choke him, but restrained myself.

At the next board meeting I pressed the matter with enthusiasm, having also heard from O'Neill that the play was now released for us if we wanted it. Many and varied were the objections to the play at the board meeting, and I became frantic. To quiet me down they offered to bring O'Neill to New York to discuss the play, and in the meantime bought his play *Marco Millions*. These tactics did not suit me at all. Aided by Theresa Helburn and Maurice Wertheim, I conducted a frenzied campaign to secure the production of *Strange Interlude*. On April 21, I wrote the board a stinging letter:

In *Strange Interlude* we have probably the bravest and most far-reaching dramatic experiment which has been seen in the theatre since the days of Ibsen. O'Neill's genius was never more clearly shown than in this play. . . . This play contains in it more deep knowledge of the dark corners of the human mind than anything that has ever been written before. It proclaims O'Neill the great dramatic genius of the age. As an important experiment, it knocks *Back to Methuselah* into a cocked hat. . . .

None of O'Neill's plays is as perfectly written as this play; if the Guild did it, none would be better produced. If we fail to do this great experiment, if we lack the courage and the vision, then we should forever hang our heads in shame, for we will have lost one of the greatest opportunities in our history. Indeed, the theatre being what it is today, it almost devolves upon the Guild to produce this play, as the only surviving art theatre in America, for the demise of the other art theatres, such as the Neighborhood Playhouse, places upon us the solemn responsibility of being the first to recognize the work of genius and to dare to experiment, even if it be accompanied by financial loss, if that experiment be in the direction of greatness. One thing we can never lose by such a course—our prestige and our self-respect.

My letter had its effect. The Guild Board decided that the play would be produced if Gene were willing to cut it sufficiently, but that *Marco Millions* should be presented first. I wrote Gene on the subject of cutting the play, to which he replied:

You should have enough confidence in my ability to trim this play down to be able to predict for yourselves what the final product will be. After all, you are not dealing with any novice in the theatre, and anyone who has ever worked with me—Bobby [Robert Edmond Jones], Kenneth [Kenneth Magowan], Arthur [Hopkins], etc.—will testify that I don't have to be urged but am always on the lookout for helpful cuts right up to the last week of rehearsals. And the legend that I don't attend rehearsals is all rot. I didn't in the old Provincetown Players days because I was never in New York and when I was I was never "on the wagon." But of late years it has been different. Except in cases where I saw that my play was being given no chance and it didn't matter whether I was there or not, I have been very much on the job. *Beyond the Horizon, Anna Christie, Hairy Ape, All God's Chillun, Glencairn* cycle, *Desire Under the Elms,* and *G. G. Brown,* are examples of when I was. And I should most decidedly be there from the first day to last if I were doing stuff with you people because I would be genuinely interested.

It seems difficult to realize, now that *Strange Interlude* is regarded as an American classic, that we had great difficulty in securing an actress to play the role of Nina, but at that time the Freudian implications of the play were, generally speaking, unknown in the theatre, and Nina was generally regarded as an unsympathetic role. We were fortunate in finding in Lynn Fontanne an actress who was courageous enough to essay the role. Fearing that Lynn might not like the part, Theresa Helburn and I made a special trip to Baltimore where she was playing at the time, and on the train we went over each and every argument we might be called upon to use. We were invited to supper with Alfred and Lynn after the performance and arrived at the Lunts' apartment at the Belvedere Hotel so charged with our arguments that we were almost ready to pop. We were somewhat chagrined to hear Lynn tell us that she had decided, without any question, to play the part, for we were so intent on convincing her that we were almost disappointed to learn that she had already convinced herself without our help.

With an excellent cast which included Earle Larimore, Glenn Anders, and Tom Powers, the play went into rehearsal and opened at the John Golden Theatre on January 23, 1928. The rehearsals were marked by considerable argument, for time after time Gene insisted on cutting out comedy lines or "laughs" when, in his opinion, they interfered with the emotional build of a scene. Philip Moeller, who directed the play so brilliantly, adored the comedy, and every time Gene solemnly cut out an amusing line, Phil would plead vociferously for its return. "I hope he doesn't realize that line is funny," Phil once remarked to me, "for if he does, out it'll go." Every now and again Gene would retire to the lounge with me, and give vent to his feeling about some of the acting in language he certainly did not learn in school at Stamford. He was never too pleased with his actors in rehearsal, and once he told me that he adopted the technique of asides which showed what the characters were thinking in *Strange Interlude* because the majority of actors were incompetent to do so. This, however, can be taken with a grain of salt, like some of Shaw's remarks on the same subject. No author ever succeeds in getting a complete realization of the part he has created, and he blames the actor because the actor is unable to achieve the impossible. On the other hand, I have seen many creative actors add dimensions to a part which the author never dreamed of.

The night *Strange Interlude* was presented to a waiting world I ran out to a neighboring drugstore during each intermission and phoned a blow-by-blow account to Gene who was waiting in his hotel to hear how the play was received. The next day the dramatic critics outdid themselves in praising this play which, although it ran for nearly five hours, did not seem a minute too long.

Instead of our patrons objecting to going out for dinner during the long intermission after Act 5, they seemed, on the contrary, to enjoy it. Going to the John Golden Theatre became a sort of adventure which not only enriched the Guild and the author, but also all the restaurants in the neighborhood. One of these prepared a sandwich in half-a-dozen layers and called it the "Strange Interlude Sandwich"!

The asides in the play were the cause of much comment. "One reason *Strange Interlude* is such a success," a wag was heard to say, "is that many of the audience learn for the first time the surprising fact that people actually think." I was personally amazed at the success of the play, for while I knew it to be a great play, I did not dream it would command the popular success which it was to achieve. Indeed, it earned nearly three hun-

dred thousand dollars for O'Neill and a little more for the Guild, all of which we lost later.

As *Strange Interlude* settled down for a steady run in New York, we decided to send out road companies of the play, and we found that the rest of the United States was just as excited about *Strange Interlude* as was New York. Pauline Lord and Judith Anderson in turn played the role of Nina on the road, while later on Mary Ellis and Basil Sydney took a company of the play to London where, however, it achieved only a moderate success.

I treasure as a memento of the production of *Strange Interlude* the MSS copies of the play in the form in which it went into rehearsal. On the copy which contained Acts 1 to 5, O'Neill wrote:

To Lawrence

Who saw the promise in this child
when it was only six acts old.

Gene

On the copy which contained Acts 6 to 9 he wrote:

To Lawrence

With deep gratitude for his appreciation of this play and his help in putting it over on the grand Committee.

Gene

In September, 1928, I received a letter from Gene sending me a copy of his new play *Dynamo*, from which I quote:

. . . I've finished *Dynamo* and feel it's the real stuff. You will judge when you read it . . .

One thing I want to make plain about *Dynamo* (perhaps on the program) is that it's the first of a trilogy written on the general subject, more or less symbolically treated, of the death of the old God and the spiritual uneasiness and degeneration into which the sterile failure of Science and Materialism to give birth to a new God that can satisfy our primitive religious cravings, has thrown us . . .

We produced *Dynamo* at the Martin Beck Theatre with an excellent cast, Philip Moeller directed the play, but it was diffused in effect, and the meaning was difficult for the audience to understand. We greatly missed Gene at rehearsals for clarification and cutting, and had to do the best we could.

Dynamo, although it excited considerable

interest, was not popular, and we were reluctantly forced to close the play after fifty performances. *Dynamo,* with its intuitive foreknowledge of what was to be discovered later as to the universal nature of energy, was produced in 1929, the same year that we presented *Wings over Europe,* an extraordinary play that foretold the discovery and probable results of the atom bomb fifteen years before the bomb was actually exploded at Hiroshima. We asked Gene to come to New York to help us stage the play but he decided not to do so, a decision he regretted later. After the failure of *Dynamo,* Gene never stayed away from the initial production of any of his plays.

During the 1930's the Theatre Guild produced three of O'Neill's plays, *Mourning Becomes Electra, Ah, Wilderness!,* and *Days Without End.* I worked on all these plays, and acted, when he was not in town, as liaison between him and the Guild. I received a letter from Gene in the summer of 1929 in which he stated:

I haven't got a hell of a lot of work done in the past two months, as you can imagine, what with moving, settling down, plagiarism suits, and getting married, but from now on I'll be hard at it. I'm attempting something big and new—the most ambitious stuff I've ever tackled, but it sure looks good.

The "something big and new" was *Mourning Becomes Electra,* while the plagiarism suit was that brought by a writer named Gladys Adelina Lewys.

Later on he wrote:

As for work, I am at it in my tourelle every day from nine or quarter to, until lunch time at one-thirty and I am getting a lot done and hope to have the first draft of the whole opus finished by the middle of February, if my present gait keeps up. I worked on the preliminary doping out all last summer and then got off to a couple of bum starts that ate up time. Also there were interruptions like having to go to Paris for three weeks, every day of which I was in the dentist's chair. But now I am off on the right foot and well into it. It involves a lot of hard labor—more than there was in *Interlude*—but I think it will be worth it. No, I am not going to tell you what it's all about. Suffice it that it's the most ambitious thing I have undertaken. This doesn't mean that there is any elaborate new experiment in technique involved, or that I am trying to evolve a new language like Joyce. There isn't that about it.

And I'm not coyly withholding the secret for any other reason except that, remembering my blundering about *Dynamo,* I simply have a reaction against saying a word about this in advance. I would rather wait until it is all done as well as I can do it and then let it do the talking for itself. Also I want to let it become exactly what it wants to be and not be forcing it into my preconceptions. It might very well turn out to be nothing like what I would describe it as at this stage of creation.

His next letter, dated February 19, 1930, again referred to *Mourning Becomes Electra.* He was pleased with the progress he was making on it. He was not certain when it would be in shape to be shown to the Guild, as he intended "to write the whole thing from cover to cover three times in longhand in order to get all there is out of it." He added that he was going to follow this procedure henceforth with all his plays.

The manuscript of the new play, *Mourning Becomes Electra,* which was actually three plays in one, arrived in New York just about the time we received the decision that Gene had won the *Strange Interlude* plagiarism suit. After reading it, I wrote him:

. . . I could not put it down, once I started reading, and had to go on and read the three plays, one after the other. The effect was to knock me silly for the rest of the day.

Mourning Becomes Electra is thought by many discerning critics to be O'Neill's greatest play. It progresses from ever-increasing climax to climax with a crescendo effect which leaves one staggering at the end. The fact that the play ran for five hours was all in its favor, for to see it was such an experience that for days after playgoers could talk of nothing else, and consequently sent all their friends to the theatre to see it, too. *Mourning Becomes Electra* was not only one of our greatest artistic successes; it was also a financial success, and carried us through one of our most difficult seasons.

Seven weeks were given to rehearsals, and at the end of this both Philip Moeller who directed the play and O'Neill who stood by for all rehearsals were in a state of exhaustion. On opening night the audience sat enthralled by the magnificent play, acting, and settings. With the acting of Alice Brady, Alla Nazimova, and Earle Larimore, the magnificent direction by Moeller, the inspired support of the cast, and the stark Grecian columns and Victorian interiors of Robert Edmond Jones, *Mourn-*

ing Becomes Electra was a high watermark in the American theatre.

The day after the opening the New York drama critics saluted its advent with an accolade of praise which has never been surpassed or even equaled. If any of my readers are so ill-advised as to wish to become drama critics, they will gain a liberal education in how to write readable reviews under conditions of great mental excitement, by consulting, in the libraries, the New York daily papers for October 27, 1931.

In the spring of 1933, Gene was writing a new play, *Days Without End,* which would show that love could last beyond life. In writing it, it seemed as though he had gone back to his early religious feelings and was affirming his belief in the afterlife. The regularity of home life at Casa Genotta made for ideal working conditions, and just as Le Plessis had produced a background for the enormous task of *Mourning Becomes Electra,* so, here on Sea Island looking out over the ocean, Gene brooded over other plays to be written in the future. A few weeks after our return I received Gene's letter of May 15 from which I quote. The play, first called *An End of Days,* became later *Days Without End.*

> For heaven's sake, don't count on this opus for next fall—or even next season. When I read it, I may feel so sick of it I won't want to touch it again for six months or so—or I may be too enthused about the one I'm outlining now to work on the other again for a while. Or— But there are so many "ors." The best thing for you all to do is go ahead with your plans without considering it even as a possibility—but with assurance (I *can* speak surely here)—that if there is no play from me next season there will *surely* be *two* (perhaps three) for the following season. If you go ahead on this basis, then if I get *An End of Days* right in time for next season and you *can* cast it and make room for it—well, all the better! But I would not be playing fair with the Guild or myself if I did not make the extreme uncertainty about the next session absolutely clear. Sabe?

Gene's next letter was unexpectedly more optimistic. The play was finished and he thought it "a damned interesting piece of work." He also made reference to "another play." This was *Ah, Wilderness!* While he was struggling with *Days Without End* and under the usual strain which his writing imposed on him, he awoke one morning supremely happy, having dreamed an entire play which reminded him of his own childhood. He rushed to his study, poured out the play on paper, and finished it in less than four weeks. "It was," he told me, "like a holiday from the other play."

Gene and Carlotta arrived in New York in due course, and we received the manuscript of *Ah, Wilderness!* which we all read and liked. There were some differences of opinion about *Days Without End,* however, and Gene sensed the controversial nature of the play and was greatly worried as to which of these plays should be produced first. On August 7, 1933, he wrote me from Faust, New York, putting his anxieties into words:

> *Days Without End* is nothing if not controversial, especially in its Catholic aspect. It is sure, fail or succeed, to arouse much bitter argument. It will be well hated by the prejudiced who won't see the psychological study end of it but only the general aspect. And, technically too, there will be much argument pro and con. Now I feel strongly that such a post-production atmosphere, if *Days Without End* were done first, would be fatal for *Ah, Wilderness!*
>
> Give all this careful thought, all of you, and I know you'll agree.

A day later he was still confused and wrote me again:

> There is a lot to be said on both sides, and I've been saying it all to myself until I'm quite gaga and confused and my opinion is worthless. All I know is that any play of mine that immediately follows *Electra* is in a bad spot— no matter how good it is; and I'm so close to both these two plays that I really don't know just how good or bad either of them is. This is particularly true in the case of *Ah, Wilderness!* which is so out of my previous line. Has it got something finer to it than its obvious surface value—a depth of mood and atmosphere, so to speak, that would distinguish it from another play of the same genre, the usual type? I felt it had when I wrote it. (Nathan, for example, says most emphatically yes.) But now, frankly, I'll be damned if I can trust myself to judge. I simply don't know. It's up to you Guilders to decide. Has it charm and humor and tender reminiscence enough to disarm the people who will feel that dramatically it is a terrible let-down after *Electra?*

On August 14 I wrote him that, for a variety of reasons, we preferred to produce the comedy first. During the rehearsals of *Ah, Wilderness!* Gene attended the theatre regularly and made considerable cuts. Indeed he was usually extremely cooperative in regard to cutting, and once he was in a cutting mood, he cut faster than the director asked in rehearsals. He was not at all happy, however, when the play took to the road, and he had to spend a week in Pittsburgh. I had the greatest difficulty in getting him to come to the theatre at all after the dress rehearsal, and even then he would come in only for certain scenes. I asked him why he had this phobia against attending performances of his own plays, and he told me that it did not relate to his own plays, but to being present in a crowded theatre, which made it very difficult for him to sit still and watch the play. On other occasions, I have been with him in crowded arenas such as Madison Square Garden where he would spend hours watching the six-day bicycle race and more recently at prizefights in Madison Square Garden, where he did not appear to have the slightest discomfort in mixing with crowds of thousands in a large arena.

Ah, Wilderness! opened at the Guild Theatre October 2, 1933, and was received with delight on the part of the critics and audiences. All Gene's fears about the reception proved to be unfounded, for the play's quality of nostalgic sentiment made it overnight a piece of Americana as indigenous to our soil as a folk song. And with the passage of time, this play has proved the most endearing, if not the most enduring of his works. The story of the boy, who was Gene, his adolescent adventures, and the tender understanding of his father and mother make a picture of the decencies of American family life which no play has surpassed in the theatre. It continued to run for a whole season with George M. Cohan at his best, until Cohan's bad habit of elaborating the comedy made the play seem unnecessarily long. Later it was played on the Coast by Will Rogers, and by Walter Huston in the motion picture. Gene felt that we used the wrong emphasis in employing these outstanding actors for the father, for he regarded the boy as the leading character.

After the successful opening of *Ah, Wilderness!* we went to work on *Days Without End.* Gene seemed to be especially timorous about this play, mostly I believe, because it represented a very deep change in some of his views of life and also because it might be possibly interpreted as a return to his early Catholic faith. His struggle over this was

shown not only in the difficulty he had in writing the play, but the first version had a Protestant minister, which he later changed to a Catholic priest. This was the right thing to do, for surely this play sprang out of a deeply rooted sectarian revolt. Gene's letter to me on October 29, 1933, shows some of his doubts in the situation:

> I'm especially anxious to have your sympathetic backing on this particular play, not only because it's a tough one to get over and is bound to arouse a lot of antagonism, but because I want to lean over backwards in being fair to it and getting the best breaks. For, after all, this play, like *Ah Wilderness!* but in a much deeper sense, is the paying of an old debt on my part—a gesture toward more comprehensive, unembittered understanding and inner freedom—the breaking away from an old formula that I had enslaved myself with, and the appreciation that there is their own truth in other formulas, too, and that any life-giving formula is as fit a subject for drama as any other.

Days Without End opened in New York on January 8, 1934, at Henry Miller's Theatre and was as badly received by the critics as *Ah, Wilderness!* had been well received a few months earlier. I fear that these gentlemen were afraid that O'Neill was going back to his early faith, and attacked him from that point of view as much as for the play itself. This, of course, was not correct, and had they been able to take a more objective view of the play, it would have fared much better, as indeed it did in such countries as Sweden, Italy, and Germany. Gene was bitterly disappointed with the reception of the play, and returned soon after to Sea Island. Before leaving, he confided to me that he had plans for executing a major work in the theatre which would take years of his time to write, and I left him with the feeling that although he was discouraged, he would nevertheless soon forget what had happened to *Days Without End* in the excitement and interest in this new major work. When the book of *Days Without End* was finally published Gene sent me an autographed special edition of uncorrected proofs on the title page of which, in his neatest of neat handwriting, appeared the following inscription:

DEAR LAWRENCE:

Again, thanks for your fine cooperation in helping this opus to a fine production! Whatever its fate in the Amusement Racket which

New York vaingloriously calls The Theatre, it will have been heard by a few of them it was written for, thanks to the Guild, and will live for them. So what the hell!

GENE

January 27, 1934.

In the spring of 1935, Russel Crouse, our press agent at the time, since distinguished for his brilliant co-dramatization of *Life with Father* and other plays, went down to visit Gene, and brought back the news of the new cycle of plays on which Gene was working. In March Armina and I spent some days at Nassau, and on our way back we paid a visit to the O'Neills. I found Gene deeply engrossed in his new cycle. I called it his six-day bicycle race, for which he was stripped for action like a pugilist. His habits were most regular, and everything ran like clockwork.

The first morning I was there, Gene, after doing his morning's work, came out and sat on the beach where I was taking a sunbath, and as we both looked out over the ocean, the waves breaking at our feet a few yards away, he told me about his plan for his new plays. They would take literally years to write. We were not to expect to receive the first of them until the last was completed because he would be making changes in them until the very last one was done. Each play would be complete in itself, yet each of the plays would be part of a whole, which he called *A Touch of the Poet*. The plays would deal with several generations of a family, an admixture of old Puritan New England stock and Irish-American blood, and it was the Irish in the admixture which gave the cycle its title, for the touch of Irish blood gave the touch of the poet. Characters were to be in their youth in one play while they would be parents or grandparents in later plays in which the main stories were based on the lives of their children and children's children. Galsworthy's *The Forsyte Saga* seemed like child's play in comparison, as Gene traced the effect of the grandparents on the children and their grandchildren, reminding me of the biblical prophecies as to the sins of the parents being visited upon their children unto the third and fourth generations. I marveled at the scope of the work he was attempting, and wondered whether, in the hot damp climate of Sea Island, he would have the strength to last out the ordeal he had set for himself. Gene continued with his work, however, and reported the progress he was making in a letter to me of August 12, 1936.

I hope you yourself don't believe the Cycle is "an American life" in any usual sense of the word, or you're going to be disappointed. I mean, I'm not giving a damn whether the dramatic event of each play has any significance in the growth of the country or not, as long as it is significant in the spiritual and psychological history of the American family in the plays. The Cycle is primarily just that, the history of a family. What larger significance I can give my people as extraordinary examples and symbols in the drama of American possessiveness and materialism is something else again. But I don't want anyone to get the idea that this Cycle is much concerned with what is usually understood by American history, for it isn't. As for economic history—which so many seem to mistake for the *only* history just now—I am not much interested in economic determinism, but only in the self-determinism of which the economic is one phase, and by no means the most revealing—at least, not to me.

He added:

Try a Cycle sometime, I advise you—that is, I would advise you to, if I hated you! A lady bearing quintuplets is having a debonair, carefree time of it by comparison.

A hell of a hot oppressive summer here. Carlotta and I are neck and neck toward the Olympic and World's sweating record! We just continually drop and drip.

The dropping and dripping ultimately became too much for Gene, and with considerable reluctance, they left Sea Island in the hopes of finding a better climate in the Pacific Northwest. It was during this period that Gene won the Nobel Prize for literature, which of course pleased all of us greatly. Later, at my request, he showed me, with almost childlike pleasure, the black box which he opened to display the large gold medallion symbolizing the greatest honor awarded to an American playwright. There was not the slightest suggestion either of undue pride or modesty on his part. He took it in his stride.

Finally they moved on south into California, where Carlotta O'Neill designed and built the modest but extremely handsome home known as Tao House, facing Mount Diablo in Contra Costa County, about an hour out from San Francisco. Here, for the first time in years, Gene was able to enjoy bearable weather the year round. And here he settled down to write on his cycle.

During the latter part of the thirties, I had

little news from O'Neill, who was busily engaged in writing the monumental cycle of nine plays he had projected for himself. In our conversations and his press releases, he had stated that he did not want any of these plays to be produced until all were completed, partly because he wished to finish them as a complete work of art before any individual play was presented. In the early part of 1940 I wrote him suggesting that we make a start with the cycle the following season, to which Gene replied under date of March 10.

You can't begin producing the cycle until the first plays are ready, even if I wanted any of it done before it's all completed, which I don't. So I tell you again, forget it. Go on as if you had never heard of it. I've made myself put it aside for the past seven months. Had gone terribly stale, as I told you when we talked over the phone, and did not start the fifth play beyond getting it all ready to start. Since then I have been working on other things. But forget that, too, until further notice, because it does not mean I will have anything for you to consider in making your plans for next year.

Later on, a mention in the newspapers about a new O'Neill play called *The Iceman Cometh* aroused our curiosity; the situation was explained fully by Gene in his letter of July 17, 1940:

One reason I haven't sent you or Terry a script is that there are only two in existence. I have one and I sent the other to Bennett Cerf to lock in the Random House safe for safekeeping—but not for publication. Don't blame Bennett for not telling you or Terry. I made him promise to keep it dark from everyone, bar none. Frankly, I did not want you to see it yet—in New York. I was afraid you would want to produce it right away and I don't want the strain of any production now. There are other good reasons against it, too. On the other hand, if you or Terry happened out this way, as you thought you might, then I could give you the script to read with the proviso that production was out for the present, and do all my explaining why at the same time. But the idea of trying to do all this in letters simply had me stopped. Hence the secrecy. To tell the truth, like anyone else with any imagination, I have been absolutely sunk by this damned world debacle. The Cycle is on the shelf, and God knows if I can ever take it up again because

I cannot foresee any future in this country or anywhere else to which it could spiritually belong.

Well, to hell with that. I'm writing this to explain my past few months' secrecy re the completion of *The Iceman Cometh,* and to say if you and Armina, Terry and Oliver, want to read this opus you can get the script from Bennett. I'm writing to release him from his pledge of secrecy as far as you and Terry are concerned. But give it back to Cerf to lock up in the safe afterwards, and *please don't* let anyone else see it. Remember only two scripts exist and it's no time to let too many people, even in the Guild, really know about it yet. And forget about any production.

I'm working again on something—not the Cycle—after a lapse of several months spent with an ear glued to the radio for war news. You can't keep a hop head off his dope for long!

Terry and I both read the new play, and felt it to be one of Gene's major works. Gene replied to my comments in a letter dated August 11, 1940:

Many thanks for your letter regarding *The Iceman Cometh.* I'm damned pleased you liked it so well. Personally, I love it! And I'm sure my affection is not wholly inspired by nostalgia for the dear dead days "on the bottom of the sea," either! I have a confident hunch that this play, as drama, is one of the best things I've ever done. In some ways, perhaps *the* best. What I mean is, there are moments in it that suddenly strip the secret soul of a man stark naked, not in cruelty or moral superiority, but with an understanding compassion which sees him as a victim of the ironies of life and of himself. Those moments are for me the depth of tragedy, with nothing more that can possibly be said.

Gene could not get the war out of his mind. Early in 1941 he wrote me:

Yes, you're right, the world chaos is always on one's mind no matter what one does, and the nearer spring comes with its invasion of England threat, the greater the tension will grow. I doubt if I will be able to find any escape in writing, although I shall try. When there is too much tension, something in you goes on strike. Of course, I've done little since I've been sick except fiddle around with a few notes.

Regarding *The Iceman Cometh,* it is no time for that. And no time for me, believe me, to bet my health against the strain of producing it.

In the early summer of 1944, Armina and I visited the O'Neills when they were living at the Huntington Hotel, San Francisco. Gene was hard at work making final revisions on some new plays. We discussed what plays were in shape for production and were being typed in final draft in San Francisco. Gene recited the titles of the plays which he had written. First of all came *The Iceman Cometh,* which he was willing to allow us to produce a little while after the war was over. He felt the timing for the play's opening was very important, and that if it were to be produced immediately after the war was over, the pessimism of the play would run counter to public optimism, and would result in a bad reception by the audience. He thought a year or so after the peace, there would be considerable disillusionment, and that the public would then be more inclined to listen to what he had to say in this play.

Just as Armina and I were about to leave Gene's apartment, he handed me, with one of his shy smiles, two manuscripts, one of which was his new play *A Moon for the Misbegotten* while the other was a long one-act play entitled *Hughie.* "I would like you to read these while you are here in San Francisco," he said, "and tell me what you think of them."

On returning to our hotel that evening, we read both the new O'Neill plays. I was particularly delighted with *A Moon for the Misbegotten,* which I regard as one of the greatest plays O'Neill has ever written, and one of the few truly great tragedies written in our times. The play has, in its final act, and at the end of the second act, the spiritual uplift which is the characteristic quality of all great tragedy, and along with it is such a profound knowledge of the good and evil in humanity as to raise it head and shoulders above *Anna Christie,* which it resembles to some extent in its father-daughter and lover relationship. Indeed, the maturity which Gene had reached as a dramatist can well be measured by contrasting these two magnificent plays; the first, *Anna Christie* with its partly happy ending (and I am not averse to happy endings), and *A Moon for the Misbegotten* with its ruthless, tragic finality.

After a second reading of the play I began to realize some of the troubles which awaited us

in casting it, for the leading woman was to be a veritable giantess—indeed, exactly the kind of woman who, when she comes to see you and asks you to advise her whether she should attempt a career in the theatre, you look embarrassed and reply, "Well, I'm afraid you're rather a big girl; how are we to find a man tall enough to play opposite you?" Yet, here in this play O'Neill wrote the tragedy of an oversized woman, making it an oversized job for any producer to find the right actress for the part. In addition to the physical requirements of the actress, she must be tremendously experienced in the theatre and must have exactly the kind of emotional acting experience that it would be difficult for a girl of her stature to obtain. I made a mental note of all the very big girls I knew—emphasizing the Irish quality which was needed—and the following day I went around to see Gene again. I told him I had read both of the plays and gave him my opinion of them. The one-act play entitled *Hughie,* which was in the form of a long monologue by the rooming clerk of a cheap hotel, struck me as a magnificent task for any character actor. Gene told me that he had another one-act play which, together with this play, might make a full evening in the theatre, but he did not give me this other play as it needed some further revisions. There were to be five other one-act plays in monologue form, and the series was to be called *By Way of Obit.*

After I had described my feelings about *A Moon for the Misbegotten* to Gene, he said, "Well, if you like it so much, Lawrence, you can have it." Naturally, I was overjoyed, and told him we would produce it any time he wanted, and that as I was going to Hollywood I would immediately get in touch with Barry Fitzgerald, as we thought he would be ideal for the father. After some discussion, it was decided that it would be better to produce this play before *The Iceman Cometh,* and we decided to go ahead immediately with the casting. During our interview that day Gene remarked, "As you like *A Moon for the Misbegotten* so much, you can ready my other play, *A Touch of the Poet,* and we'll talk about the casting of that play as well." He then gave me the manuscript of this new play, which had just been finally typed, and after I read it I realized that it, too, was one of Gene's greatest plays. *A Touch of the Poet* also carried with it some extremely difficult casting problems, and we discussed these in considerable detail before we left

San Francisco. It was decided, however, that *A Touch of the Poet* should be the last of the three plays to be produced, and that the long one-act play, *Hughie,* should await the completion of the other one-act play before production.

In the fall of 1945, Gene and Carlotta O'Neill felt it was imperative for them to come East. It was decided that we would cast *The Iceman Cometh* and that this play should be the first of the O'Neill plays presented by the Guild at the opening of the following season. The winter was spent in casting the play, and Armina Marshall acted as associate producer and worked unceasingly with Gene, Eddie Dowling, Theresa Helburn, and me in securing the very finest cast we could possibly obtain for the play. After a few weeks in New York, Gene's health improved, and especially after he began work on *The Iceman Cometh.* He enjoyed his visits to the Guild offices each afternoon, and he began to put his manuscript into final shape. We all felt the fact that he was at work again in the theatre was doing wonders in bringing him back to health. One afternoon in May, 1946, we assembled in the large rehearsal room of the Theatre Guild building and read *The Iceman Cometh* aloud. This was valuable not only for purposes of cutting, but it also gave us an opportunity to hear how the actors fitted the parts, and the parts the actors, how their voices sounded in the roles, and how their personalities seemed to fit in with the words which they uttered.

During the month of September, 1946, *The Iceman Cometh* went into rehearsal, and Gene attended each morning and worked hand in glove with Dowling in the direction of the play. Every move of every actor had been clearly thought out in Gene's mind, and he was of enormous help in the staging of the play. He did a great deal of cutting prior to going into rehearsal, but not, in my opinion, as much as was needed, and there were some exchanges between Gene and myself on the subject of reducing the length of the play. On one occasion I told Gene that at my request my assistant, Paul Crabtree, who played the part of Dan Parritt, had counted the number of times a certain point was repeated, and this, in actual fact, was eighteen times. Gene looked at me and replied in a particularly quiet voice, "I *intended* it to be repeated eighteen times!"

Gene was not willing to have the play open in an out-of-town city, as was our usual custom, but insisted on following his own practice of having the play open "cold" in New York. This called for considerably more time for rehearsal, but this was arranged for, and on October 9, 1946, the play opened at the Martin Beck Theatre, making a tremendous impression upon its audience. Owing to the length of the play, we began at 5:30 in the afternoon for the opening, took an hour and a half for dinner, and the play concluded at 11:30 P.M. Later on we started the play at 7:30 P.M. and ran straight through the evening, but while this pleased Gene, it did not please me, for in my opinion it put too severe a strain on the audiences.

During the opening-night dinner intermission, unfortunately for us all, James Barton, the actor playing the part of Hickey, was forced to entertain a crowd of friends, including Babe Ruth and his family, in his dressing room, instead of resting, so that by the time he came to make the famous speech which lasted nearly twenty minutes in the fifth act, he had little or no voice left with which to deliver it. As a result, the last act, which should have been the strongest of all, fell apart in the center. Notwithstanding this fact, the audience was deeply moved, and there was a great ovation at the end of the play, while the critics, for the most part, gave the play the greatest acclaim.

At the opening performance, I telephoned Gene during the dinner intermission, telling him I felt the play was going well, and he suggested we all come up and see him after the play was over. When we arrived at the apartment I proceeded to recount the details of the opening night. I could not help remarking to Gene that, in my opinion, *The Iceman Cometh* like *Saint Joan* would never be properly presented until after the expiration of the copyright, when it might be possible to cut it. Gene smiled at me in his usual disarming way and said it would have to wait for just that. Later on I asked Gene if he would mark my copy of the play with the places where he would agree to cut and where he would not. It was astonishing to see how boldly he wrote the word "No" in blue pencil against most of my proposed cuts and how tremulously he wrote his infrequent "Yes." Then he wrote on the front page of the manuscript: "To Lawrence Langner, The hell with your cuts! Eugene O'Neill."

I recount these details to show that Gene has never at any time truckled to the box office. If, in his opinion, the play could not be cut without mutilating it, it mattered very little to him that its length affected the attendance at the theatre, for he wrote his plays for those who could take them and not for what he called the "entertainment racket." As it was, *The Iceman Cometh* had a considerable run, and one which I think would have been much longer had not James Barton developed a case of laryngitis, so that it became increasingly difficult to hear him during the latter part of the play.

The following fall, having searched incessantly for an Irish giantess to play the part in *A Moon for the Misbegotten*, we ultimately collected a cast together including Mary Welsh, a tall, handsome, strapping girl of Irish extraction, and an excellent actress. She did not weigh nearly enough, however, and she had to fatten up for the proceedings, finally raising her weight to about 170 pounds so as to fill the bill in this regard. James Dunn was cast in the part of Tyrone and James M. Kerrigan in the part of Phil Hogan. The play was placed in rehearsal in February, 1947, and was directed by Arthur Shields, brother of Barry Fitzgerald. Gene at this time seemed to be dominated by a belief that in order to bring this play to successful fruition, it was necessary that everyone connected with it should be Irish or Irish-American.

During the first rehearsal, the actors sat around a table and began to read the play. Dunn read a few speeches and remarked, "I wish I had been taught to read in school." When we reached the third act, with its tragic situation, Dunn began to cry. "I'm sorry," he said. "This is just too much for me." "Take a rest," said Arthur Shields, the director, in his rich Irish voice. "No," replied Dunn. "I'll go right ahead." He continued to read, but was so overcome by tears that he could not continue. We all decided to take a rest. After a while Mary Welsh began to cry and had to stop reading, by which time everybody sitting around the table had tears in their eyes. Said Dunn, "We're *all* crying now. I guess it will be the management's time to cry later." How right he was.

After the play had been read aloud, Gene expressed considerable misgivings. Since all our contracts were signed and the scenery was already built, we suggested that the play be tried out in some of the Midwestern cities. This plan was agreed to with some reluctance by Gene.

On February 20, 1947, *A Moon for the Misbegotten* opened in Columbus, Ohio, and the town was in a state of great excitement. The play was received with mixed feelings on the part of the audience, being slightly overlong, a fault which Gene remedied later on. At the end of the second act I noticed that a group of people rose from their seats and left the theatre. I wondered whether they had been upset by some of the language in the play, and I asked the doorman whether they left on this account. "No," he replied. "They just said they were Irish." As was so often the case with Gene's plays, whenever he depicted Irishmen on the stage who were not models of sobriety, there was always a great outcry against him on the part of the Irish that he had libeled their race.

The play toured several cities and when it reached Detroit, I received a telephone call from Armina, who was acting as associate producer, telling me that the police had threatened to close the play unless some of the alleged profanity was removed. Terry Helburn was present at the Detroit opening and between the two of them, they withstood the threats of arrest. Armina's own account of the Detroit incident is as follows:

The morning after we opened, I wakened and ordered coffee, and the waiter brought in the morning paper at the same time. When I opened it, across the front page was the startling headline, "O'Neill Play Closed For Obscenity." Later, Terry and I went to the Cass Theatre office to meet the police officer who acted as censor. One of the objections he made was that the word "mother" was used in the same sentence with the word "prostitute." He mentioned other words which, he said, should not be used on the stage. He continued, "Now mind you, the actor can go ahead and say the sentence right up to the obscene word, and then he can make a gesture. But he cannot use the word." I said, "You've allowed the *Maid of the Ozarks* to play here in Detroit, and yet you will not allow a play written by Eugene O'Neill, the greatest playwright in America, who won the Nobel Prize?" He said, "Lady, I don't care what kind of prize he's won, he can't put on a dirty show in *my* town." I answered, "This is not a dirty show. This is a great play— which *Maid of the Ozarks* is not." "Lady," he replied, "when the *Maid of the Ozarks* came here, it was a very different play. I helped rewrite *that* play, and we finally let it stay here." To this I replied, "Well, I'm afraid you'd have your problems cut out for you to rewrite a play by Mr. O'Neill." This upset him considerably, for he burst out with "Listen, lady, I don't have to sit here and take that from a woman." Then Jimmy Dunn came in, and pacified him. He agreed to talk it over with Jimmy, but he said he wouldn't have women around, so Jimmy went with him and they actually deleted about eight words. By this time the reporters were there. The police officer realized he had made a laughing stock of himself, and to show that everything was all right, and that we were all happy about the affair, he wanted his picture taken with Terry and me, to which I said, "Over my dead body," and we didn't!

A Moon for the Misbegotten closed in St. Louis, and it was decided to reopen it later with a new cast. However, because of his illness, Gene asked us to defer this until he was feeling better, and he also asked us to postpone the production of *A Touch of the Poet* for the same reason. This we agreed to, notwithstanding the fact that two of the best directors in the country were eager to direct the plays.

The state of Gene's health, due to Parkinson's disease, unfortunately grew worse, and ap-parently made him unwilling to risk the production of his unproduced plays, which were the only truly great plays which had passed through my hands since the war.

I often visited him at his home in Marblehead, perched on bleak rocks and overlooking the ocean, and I would ask him not to postpone further our production of these plays, if not for his own sake, for the sake of the American theatre, which stood so badly in need of his greatness. However, when I last raised the subject, we were sitting together in his study, and I asked if we might produce *A Touch of the Poet* with Elia Kazan of whom he had approved directing it. "I don't be-lieve I could live through a production of a new play right now," he replied, and to my protesta-tions that we would do everything possible to make things easy for him, he answered, "No, that's my last word on the subject." He never recovered his health. Later on, we received a letter from Mrs. O'Neill's lawyers asking us to relinquish our contracts on these plays. This we agreed to. After O'Neill's death, both *A Touch of the Poet* and *A Moon for the Misbegotten* were produced on Broadway.

VI

1929-1939

THE GERMAN novelist and dramatist Leonhard Frank adapted his own story into the script of *Karl and Anna* with which the Guild resumed its operations in the fall of 1929. Whatever its appeal in its original form, this poignant love story proved just too cumbersome on stage and was generally counted a disaster. Karl and Richard are two German soldiers in a Russian prison camp. As Richard talks glowingly about his wife, Anna, Karl cannot help falling in love with this girl he has never known. When he escapes, not knowing if Richard has been killed or not, Karl goes to Berlin, posing as Richard. Anna, lonely, introduces him to her neighbors as her husband and love develops between the two. Inevitably, the real Richard finally comes home, but by this time Anna is irrevocably committed to Karl.

Second of three successive failures in that twelfth season was Romain Rolland's *The Game of Love and Death,* which takes place at the climax of the French Revolution and was one of a series—a polytych, as Rolland put it—devoted to that upheaval in the history of France. Alice Brady scored a personal success in this, as she had in *Karl and Anna,* which helped but did not save the production. The fact that Rolland dealt with the play's several crises not so much as action but as a philosophic statement of the conflict brought about by the Revolution probably accounted for its lethargic reception by audiences. The prevalent feeling was that while Rolland had written well in *The Game of Love and Death,* he had not written well for the stage. Also, the play might have worked better if audiences had seen it in context with the more heroic plays of the series, *The Fourteenth of July* and *The Triumph of Reason,* which precede and follow it.

S. N. Behrman's *Meteor,* which came next, also failed to start a stampede toward the box office, even with the Lunts in the leading roles. Alfred played the young man blessed or cursed with the ability to see the future, and with a ruthless ambition. The time comes when his friends begin to think him insane, though—and this seems to be Behrman's point—it is his very sanity, his tragically clear perception, that prompts him to behave as he does. Originally written in four acts, it was cut to three for the New York opening, and suffered in the transformation. Langner has pointed out that Behrman's characters were always fascinating and his dialogue scintillating, but that the playwright frequently had a bad time with dramatic structure. Apparently that was part of the trouble with *Meteor.*

Karl and Anna—Otto Kruger, Alice Brady, and Frank Conroy in the German drama of two men in love with the same woman. *Vandamm photograph.*

The Game of Love and Death—Otto Kruger and Alice Brady were paired again in this drama of the French Revolution. *Pinchot photograph.*

The Game of Love and Death—Alice Brady. *Pinchot photograph.*

Meteor—"There's bad news tonight," judging by this moment involving Alfred Lunt, Lynn Fontanne, and Douglass Montgomery. *Vandamm photograph.*

The Apple Cart, Shaw's self-styled political extravaganza in two acts and an interlude, is set in the future—the 1960's—when King Magnus is ruler of Great Britain, and the United States is seeking readmission to the British Empire. Dr. Joseph T. Shipley has described it in part as "two dramatized political discussions separated by a frolic of the monarch and his 'platonic concubine,' which ends in a wrestling match because she wants him to stay and he wants to get home in time for dinner with his wife." The play gives the impression that democracy simply hasn't worked (perhaps that's the apple cart that is upset). Dresden, Germany, banned it as reactionary. The Guild's production opened in New York on February 24, 1930, following a week's run in Baltimore, with Tom Powers as the king and Claude Rains as his prime minister, Proteus. In the play's denouement, the king threatens to resign his throne and run for parliament. Rather than face him as a political opponent, his adversaries back down, on the conclusion that the monarchy is less an evil than anything which might replace it.

Another imported play that season was

The Apple Cart—Claude Rains as the prime minister, Tom Powers as the king, and Eva Leonard-Boyne as the postmistress in Shaw's political extravaganza. *Vandamm photograph.*

The Apple Cart—Tom Powers plots with Violet Kemble-Cooper. *Vandamm photograph.*

Rouben Mamoulian's acting version of Turgenev's *A Month in the Country,* a production made memorable by the magnificent performance of Alla Nazimova. The Guild's revival of this pioneer naturalistic play resulted in new productions of it all over Europe. It was an American premiere of the play; in fact, his *The Lady from the Provinces,* done as a curtain-raiser for *The Brothers Karamazov* by the visiting Moscow Art Theatre, had been the first Turgenev ever staged here. Stanislavsky, writing in *My Life in Art,* says that he chose to do this play because of its complex psychology built on the most delicate curves of the love experience.

Langner, in *The Magic Curtain,* recalls that Nazimova had a disconcerting way of playing a part differently from night to night, and this applied to her Natalia, the bored wife who falls in love with her son's tutor and competes for him with her seventeen-year-old ward, Viera.

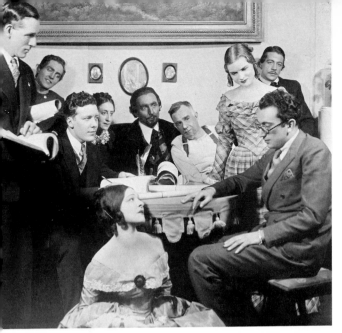

A Month in the Country—Nazimova (foreground), director-adapter Rouben Mamoulian (wearing glasses), and others of the cast at a read-through of the Turgenev classic. *Vandamm photograph.*

A Month in the Country—Henry Travers. *Vandamm photograph.*

A Month in the Country—Earle Larimore. *Vandamm photograph.*

A Month in the Country—sketch of Franchot Tone, by Baldridge.

She sometimes played Natalia as a charming and delightful woman; at other times, she would play her as a sulky and lovable creature, while another time she would make her positively mean and disagreeable; and what was more extraordinary, whichever characterization she happened to choose on the particular night she was playing it, this characterization was completely consistent from the beginning to the end of the play.

Incidentally, the role of a maid in this was played by Katharine Hepburn.

The problems of disillusion among the lost generation of World War I were examined in Philip Barry's *Hotel Universe*, which was an April offering at the Martin Beck Theatre in New York. Set in the south of France, it presents several young people tortured by individual and collective doubts, though their conversation is, on the surface at least, more flippant than ponderous. An old man, a physicist, comes among them to help them relive their pasts, come to terms with the present, and equip themselves psychologically for the future. Freudian, of course, and familiar in terms of some of the forthcoming plays which also were to thrust several assorted and emotionally assaulted people into one place (a hotel, often enough), it was at the time sufficiently unique to sustain interest, even if it left bewildered a few viewers, such as Percy Hammond of the *Herald Tribune*. At the end of his review he paid a kind of backhand compliment to the producers:

> Most of the "scenes" in the play seemed more important as exhibitions of acting and direction than of Drama, and they were all victories for Mr. Moeller, who as a director can pull more live rabbits out of a flower pot or a bowl of fish than any of his, if any, fellow prestidigitators. I could understand Mr. Moeller and the good actors of *Hotel Universe* last night even if Mr. Barry, the author, was a sophomoric puzzle. One of the few menaces of the Theatre Guild's attitude to Art in the Drama is that it has the skill, the power and the prestige to make little plays seem big.

The season also included a studio production of *Red Rust,* by V. Kirchon and A. Ouspensky, and a third edition of the surefire *The Garrick Gaieties*. The studio was a company of young players who did experimental plays. *Red Rust* had been first produced in Moscow in 1927

Philip Barry, whose *Hotel Universe* was the first of five of his plays and one adaptation done by the Theatre Guild. *Vandamm photograph.*

Hotel Universe—Morris Carnovsky and Ruth Gordon. *Vandamm photograph.*

Hotel Universe—Glenn Anders and Katherine Alexander. *Vandamm photograph.*

Hotel Universe—Glenn Anders, Katherine Alexander, Franchot Tone, and Earle Larimore. *Vandamm photograph.*

Red Rust—this Russian ideological play was prepared by the Theatre Guild Studio, a group of young performers who did experimental drama. *Vandamm photograph.*

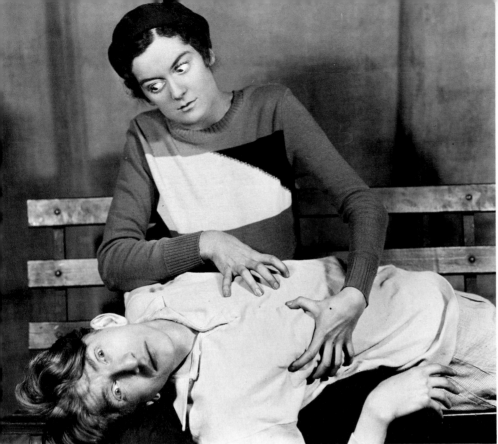

The Garrick Gaieties—another Studio production of the 1929–1930 season was a third edition of the Theatre Guild little revue. Above, Rosalind Russell and Sterling Holloway.

The Garrick Gaieties—introducing Imogene Coca. *Vandamm photograph.*

at the Trades Union Theatre, and presents a panorama of Russia at that time; naturally its content was heavy with political ideology.

Though no one in the Guild could have suspected it at the time, the season of 1930–1931 contained the beginnings of a project which, a dozen years later, would reshape the course of the American musical theatre and, not incidentally, make them more money than any show in the Theatre Guild's history. They were to have opened in the fall of 1930 with *Green Grow the Lilacs,* by thirty-one-year-old Lynn Riggs, but Arthur Hopkins was staging another Riggs play, *Borned in Texas,* at the same time, and the playwright didn't think he could attend rehearsals for both. So the Guild delayed its production, subsequently presenting it as the fourth attraction of the series. Nothing ever was heard again from *Borned in Texas,* which apparently had its time on the stage and went its way, but *Green Grow the Lilacs* was to re-emerge during World War II as *Oklahoma!*

As a substitute, they began their season with *Roar China,* by S. M. Tretyakov, a clamorous, wildly propagandistic pageant which apparently had started life as an actual event witnessed by the playwright, who then wrote it up as a poem and eventually as a drama. A big hit in post-revolu-

tionary Russia, it wasn't as successful in wooing Americans either into the communist philosophy or the conviction that it was dramatically worthwhile. But it was a spectacular eyeful, with its no-curtain set and the terrifying copy of a Russian tank, not to mention a British warship, on stage.

In the play, a cowardly, bullying American in China falls overboard and is drowned during an argument with two natives. So the captain of the British warship decides two members of the Chinese boatman's guild must be hanged—any two.

Roar China—spectacular but dramatically deficient was this noisy example of communist propaganda, even if it was based on truth. *Vandamm photograph.*

When the execution is about to take place, the townspeople revolt, the ship fires its guns, and all hell breaks loose. It was dramatic enough to inspire even so thoughtful a critic as John Mason Brown to call it a major triumph of the Guild's career and "one of the most visually exciting productions that our theatre has ever seen," also qualifying the play itself as "ridiculously overdrawn."

Robert Littell of the *World* noted:

It is for such things as *Roar China* that the Theatre Guild was born on a Broadway which, but for the Guild, would never have known how Soviet Russia felt about China in 1926 and would never have seen that feverish, deluded hope translated into a gigantic, sprawling, spectacular melodrama, that makes your heart bleed quite a lot for the poor coolie as he writhes under the heel of the white oppressor.

Roar China proved as difficult backstage as it was onstage. There had been a growing competition among the Guild's directors, which came to a head when this production was being planned. One faction wanted it directed by Herbert Biberman, who recently had spent several months in Soviet Russia and who, as Langner recalled in his autobiography, "seldom talked any quieter than

in a loud shout." The opposition on the board wanted young Rouben Mamoulian, who had the successes of *Marco Millions* and *Porgy* to his credit, and whose heritage was Russian and Armenian. Philip Moeller also coveted the assignment. Biberman finally got it, and Mamoulian left to become a tremendous success in Hollywood, to the Guild's loss. At the time, one of the forty-five Chinese who had been cast in the play had a habit of commenting, "It looks black from where I sit," and the Guild board found themselves adopting the expression.

One week after launching *Roar China* at the Martin Beck, the Guild opened Maxwell Anderson's *Elizabeth the Queen* at the Guild Theatre, on November 3, 1930, to become one of its notable successes. As might be expected, Alfred Lunt was Essex, with his wife, Lynn Fontanne, in the title role. Because Anderson's play originally was named *Elizabeth and Essex*, the impression persisted that he had based it on Lytton Strachey's then-popular biography of that title. This was not the case, but to be on the safe side, he renamed it.

At the time, the subject of England's virgin queen was popular in several areas. In England, Clemence Dane had written a new play about the royal lady, as had H. R. Lenormand in France. That same season Reinhardt had a play about

Elizabeth the Queen—the Lunts portrayed Essex and England's monarch in Maxwell Anderson's historical drama.

Elizabeth in production in Germany. Lee Simonson's fine sets and costumes and Philip Moeller's discerning direction helped win the prevailingly favorable comment, in which the drama itself was both praised and picked at. John Mason Brown, Percy Hammond, and Robert Littell were each so impressed with Miss Fontanne's evocation of Elizabeth that they felt it was the strength of the evening. Among other critics, Brooks Atkinson and Charles Darnton were more impressed with the play itself, particularly the beauty of Anderson's writing. At the pre-Broadway opening in Philadelphia, audiences were expecting more of the Guild's "tricks," by which was meant the updating in language and costume of historical situations, as had been done in several previous productions. Instead, they were surprised by—in the words of a Quaker City reviewer—". . . a straightforward, unequivocally romantic drama set in the purely classical mold and never for a minute dependent on interpolations of the modern vernacular or tongue-in-cheek diversions." Anderson, in fact, did not resort to Elizabethan speech, which he might have, to make it much more authentic, but he did write the English language quite beautifully, and it was as beautifully spoken by the Lunts, Percy Waram as Raleigh, and the rest

of the fine cast. The play centers on the love of Elizabeth and Essex, and on their respective love of power. Elizabeth finally promises to share her throne with the ambitious Essex if he will drop his plan to capture London and the palace. After he dismisses his guard, she has him arrested and imprisoned in the Tower of London. There is a touching scene in which the stubbornness of each forces her to condemn him to death, and him to accept that fate rather than a subservient position as her consort.

A title change also was destined for the Guild's third play, which was *In the Meantime* on tryout tour but *Midnight* when it came to New York, with Glenn Anders, Linda Watkins, and Frederick Perry in leading roles. Described as a "melodrama of ideas," it purported to show the "unceasing conflict between law and justice and how our national ideals may be buffeted about by the winds of politics." Playwrights Claire and Paul Sifton wrote about a woman about to be executed for murder, and how her fate is affected by the foreman of the jury and, indirectly but irrevocably, by the members of his family. It was the Guild's first American melodrama and managed to become both a critical and a popular failure.

"But is it art?" asked the Boston *Advertiser*

Midnight—Linda Watkins and Frederick Perry in a melodrama which disappointed critics and paying customers. *Vandamm photograph.*

Green Grow the Lilacs—strongly resembling the characters of *Oklahoma!*, which was to be adapted from it a dozen years later, are these people of Lynn Riggs's play. In the opening scene, Franchot Tone as Curly and Helen Westley as Aunt Ella. *Vandamm photograph.*

Green Grow the Lilacs—June Walker as Laurey. *Vandamm photograph.*

Green Grow the Lilacs—June Walker, Helen Westley, and Franchot Tone. *Vandamm photograph.*

following the December 13 opening in New England of Lynn Riggs's *Green Grow the Lilacs,* prior to its New York premiere on January 26. "Any playwright that offends good taste or unduly sacrifices Illusion to Reality has not wrought a good drama," concluded critic Leo Gaffney in stentorian, Old Testament tones. He was most incensed by Riggs's presentation of a villain—Jeeter (called Jud in *Oklahoma!*), who lives in the smokehouse where he keeps pictures of naked women—who has a "filthy mind."

The truth—which we can discern better from today's vantage point—was that Riggs had written a psychological play, probing deeper into the nature of personality than did most of the contemporary stage fare. This frequently is overlooked by critics and lay theatregoers who have dismissed *Oklahoma!*, musical son of *Green Grow the Lilacs,* as mere song-and-dance entertainment. It too has this quality of conflict between the sick mind of Jud and the more normal attitudes of the young lovers, Laurey and Curly. And its realism, far from being considered a fault, has become an asset, just as the theatre itself was moving from illusion toward reality—a movement under way in Ibsen's time in the late nineteenth century.

Should anyone need to be reminded of the

Green Grow the Lilacs—the Guild rounded up some real cowboys for the chorus, including Jackie Miller (left) and Slim Cavanaugh (tall man in back). *Vandamm photograph.*

Green Grow the Lilacs—Clare Woodbury later replaced Helen Westley as Aunt Ella. *Vandamm photograph.*

Green Grow the Lilacs—Richard Hale as Jeeter Fry (the name was changed to Jud Fry for *Oklahoma!*) and Franchot Tone as the original Curly. *Vandamm photograph.*

plot, the breezy, amiable, and personable Curly (Franchot Tone), a cowhand, loves Laurey (June Walker), but teases her to the point that she agrees to go out with Jeeter. But Curly takes Laurey away from Jeeter and marries her. At the shivaree —the celebration following the young couple's wedding—Jeeter first tries to set fire to the haystack on which they're being bounced by their friends, then attacks Curly with a knife. But Jeeter falls on his own blade and dies. The Guild production was augmented by cowboy laments and border ballads (the title itself is from such a song), and audiences were exhilarated by the cowboy flavor, previously an almost exclusive property of the movies. It got a good press and enjoyed a successful run. Richard Dana Skinner in *The Commonweal* wrote: "Mr. Riggs's play is the only logical candidate up to now for this season's Pulitzer Prize" (which was awarded to Susan Glaspell for *Alison's House*). Walter Winchell hated the play but admitted that ". . . the performance of Franchot Tone gives the show its pace and what little excitement it contains."

There is a strange and quite unintentional link between Austrian playwright Hans Chlumberg's *Miracle at Verdun,* which had its American premiere March 16, 1931, at the Martin Beck, and Shaw's *Saint Joan.* In the epilogue of the latter, Joan is elevated to sainthood by the same Roman Catholic Church which had burned her almost five centuries before. At this news, she decides it is time to return to life among the living, but her friends and former enemies convince her that to do so would only mess things up. Whereupon she closes this shining drama with the words: "When will Earth be ready to receive Thy saints? How long, O Lord, how long?"

In *Miracle at Verdun*, the French and German dead of World War I, buried in a common, mass grave, begin to rise. They take their crosses on their shoulders, gravely salute one another, and start their long trek toward home. But word of their resurrection, preceding them, greatly disturbs the French minister, in bed with his mistress; the German head of state, the English counterpart; also wives who have remarried, and men who had taken the jobs of the war dead. They finally are told they are not wanted—the world no longer has a place for them—and they are ordered back to their grave at Verdun, to which they return in the sardonic conclusion of this symbolic and bitter parable.

It was a pioneer experiment in mixed media, with motion-picture projections and amplified sound used during the progress of the stage drama, and the expense of staging *Miracle at Verdun* almost crippled the Guild financially. "More muddle than miracle," commented Brooks Atkinson about both the play and director Herbert Biberman's attempts at solving its staging problem. Reading the mostly negative critical comment at the time—directed more against the staging than the play itself—leads one to wonder if it might be tried again by some enterprising

Miracle at Verdun—the French and German dead of World War I rise from their common grave, lift up their crosses and start the march home to a world that doesn't want them back. *Vandamm photograph.*

group today, in the hope of better and more clearly realizing the drama's message. The fact that we have been through more wars, and have buried infinitely more dead, would not necessarily invalidate it. However, rewriting probably would be indicated. Gilbert Seldes and others remarked enthusiastically about the power of the opening scene, in which action on stage and projections of filmed battle scenes on the arms of a great cross had the effect of instantly quieting the first-night chatter.

Getting Married, which probably can be described as lesser Shaw, wound up the theatre year to something less than cheers. However it was at least indulged, as by Atkinson who appraised it in these words:

> Riding on Mr. Shaw's intellectual merry-go-rounds is always a pleasant sensation. Before you are thoroughly acquainted with the chief situation of *Getting Married,* the sensation is as giddy as ever. Given a green-grocer who is the village sage, a bishop who thinks reasonably in spite of his vestments, a divorced lady who wants both her husband and her lover, and a pair of young people who rebel against the marriage laws when the wedding guests already are assembled at the church, and you have the materials for at least a sprightly entertainment. . . . Eventually Mr. Shaw works up to the rowdy scuffle with which he translates ideas into horseplay and creates the illusion of drama.

Dorothy Gish portrayed the covetous wife, with Henry Travers as the grocer, Ernest Cossart as the general, and Reginald Mason as the bishop.

The fourteenth season got an early start, though not a very encouraging one, on September 21, 1931, with the opening of *He,* by Alfred Savoir (1883–1934). Considered a French playwright, though born in Poland with the name of Posymanski, Savoir had achieved a modest success in the United States with *Bluebeard's Eighth Wife,* in 1921, and *The Lion Tamer,* five years later. He had a talent for comedy, as in the first of these, and a skill at devising meaningful symbols, as in the second.

Neither of these abilities manifested itself in *He.* Originally the title character was to have been played by Paul Muni, who withdrew prior to the out-of-town opening and was replaced by young Tom Powers, with Claude Rains as an elevator man who figures prominently in the plot. A meeting of the International Society of Free Thought is convened at a hotel in the Swiss Alps. This seems to have been the original "God is dead" gathering, except for He, a rather Breezy young man who claims he is God. The others scoff at first, then turn to him for assurance when a blizzard cuts them off from the rest of the world and creeping ice threatens to push the hotel off the mountain. Eventually it is revealed that He is an escapee from a mental hospital. Chester Erskin, who prepared the adaptation in English, also directed, and he was soundly lambasted by critics and audiences. The play was deemed sluggish, flat, and uninteresting. Even one of the relatively kind reviews mentioned that the Guild was "fortunate in the possession of so understanding and patient an audience of subscribers."

O'Neill's *Mourning Becomes Electra,* which opened the night of October 26 in New York, was directed by Philip Moeller, designed by Robert Edmond Jones, and acted by a superb cast headed by Alla Nazimova, Alice Brady, and Earle Larimore. Not only did it qualify for unprecedented superlatives from audiences and reviewers (in *The*

Getting Married—Henry Travers and Margaret Wycherly as two of Shaw's spirited people. *Vandamm photograph.*

He—Claude Rains portrayed an elevator operator at a Swiss resort. The title role was played by Tom Powers.

He—Edith Meiser. *Goldberg photograph.*

113

Mourning Becomes Electra—Alice Brady and Alla Nazimova pose before Robert Edmond Jones's stately setting of the Ezra Mannon mansion. This is one of the best-known and most reproduced theatre photographs ever taken by Vandamm.

Mourning Becomes Electra—Alice Brady as Lavinia, Lee Baker as Brigadier General Mannon, and Alla Nazimova as Christine. *Vandamm photograph.*

Nation, Joseph Wood Krutch wrote: "It may turn out to be the only permanent contribution yet made by the twentieth century to dramatic literature"), but it inspired some of the most penetrating dramatic criticism to appear in the American press. As any critic knows, it is easier to pinpoint the faults of a bad play than the majesty of a great one. Here was a drama so compact, despite its five-hour length, so rich in ascending climaxes, so profound in its meanings, and so overwhelming in its dramatic power that critics surpassed themselves in what must have been an awesome problem of literate appreciation. Certainly one of the finest reviews to be written under the pressure of a deadline (which is the circumstance under which some of the most cogent critical writing has been done) was that by Brooks Atkinson who, speaking of "the formidable earnestness of Mr. O'Neill's cheerless dramatic style," goes on to say:

Mourning Becomes Electra—Alla Nazimova (Christine) with Earle Larimore (Orin). *Van-damm photograph.*

Mourning Becomes Electra—Judith Anderson and Walter Abel appeared in the O'Neill tragedy on tour.

Robert Edmond Jones (1887–1954) was one of the most creative designers in the history of the American stage. He did a dozen O'Neill plays, including *Mourning Becomes Electra.*

Using a Greek legend as his model, Eugene O'Neill has reared up a universal tragedy of tremendous stature—deep, dark, solid, uncompromising and grim. It is heroically thought out and magnificently wrought in style and structure, and it is played by Alice Brady and Mme. Nazimova with consummate artistry and passion. Mr. O'Neill has written overwhelming dramas in the past. In *Strange Interlude* he wrote one almost as long as this trilogy. But he has never before fulfilled himself so completely; he has never commanded his theme in all its variety and adumbrations with such superb strength, coolness and coherence. To this department, which ordinarily reserves its praise for the dead, *Mourning Becomes Electra* is Mr. O'Neill's masterpiece.

The following Sunday, Atkinson made another cogent point about the play:

> Although most of us have been brought up to bow and genuflect before the majesty of Greek tragedy, it has remained for Mr. O'Neill to show us why. His modern psychological play, *Mourning Becomes Electra,* brings the cold splendors of Greek tragedy off the sky-blue limb of Olympus down to the dusty forum of contemporary life.

O'Neill patterned his trilogy after the Oresteia of Aeschylus, even to using names that suggested the Greek characters—Ezra Mannon for Agamemnon, and Orin for Orestes. In *Homecoming,* Christine Mannon is having an affair with her cousin while her husband is away, occupied with the Civil War. Their daughter, Lavinia, tells her father about it, but when he comes home, his wife poisons him. In *The Hunted,* Christine's son Orin shoots her lover and drives Christine into suicide. *The Haunted* shows Lavinia and Orin, sister and brother, returned from a long voyage but still burdened with the weight of their tragic family and disgust at their own incestuous feelings. At the end, Orin shoots himself, and Lavinia condemns herself to eternal incarceration in the Mannon manse.

In later years, negative opinion about the play appeared to counter the adulation it had earned at its opening. Joseph T. Shipley has pointed out that whereas the Aeschylus trilogy represents three stages of the spirit—the curse, the doom, and the deliverance—O'Neill fails to show any spiritual redemption: ". . . his trilogy but lengthens out the doom." The critic also believes Electra fails to achieve the psychological catharsis of classic tragedy, and that it pyramids the theme of incest beyond belief.

What O'Neill might have answered can only be speculated. It is likely that he did not intend an entirely literal adaptation of the Greek original, but a play more tangential. This was the procedure Archibald MacLeish used years later when he wrote *J.B.*, which seems to parallel the biblical Book of Job. He compared the project with building a little structure against, and supported by, a great wall. He was not rewriting Job,

but using it to support his parable. At any event, *Electra* on its own represents a kind and strength of dramatic power which had not been achieved by an American writer up until then, nor surpassed, often, if at all, since.

The brooding O'Neill masterpiece had to be followed by something lighter, and Robert E. Sherwood's *Reunion in Vienna* served very nicely, starting in mid-November. The Lunts played it, not just in New York but, as was their usual practice, on the road as well, later taking it to London. (How different from today, when even minor

Reunion in Vienna—Alfred Lunt was the Hapsburg Prince, reduced to driving a taxicab in Nice, who returns to Vienna to resume for one night the affair with his mistress (Lynn Fontanne) of ten years earlier. *Vandamm photograph.*

players balk at the rigors of the road.) One night in New York the humor was heightened unintentionally when Alfred Lunt, who was required to lift Helen Westley's skirt and spank her red bloomers, discovered at that moment that she had forgotten to put them on.

Lunt portrayed the Hapsburg prince, banished for a decade, who returns to his Vienna in the guise of a taxi driver, in order to resume, if he can, the affair with his former mistress (Miss Fontanne), now wed to a distinguished psychoanalyst. The resumed affair is prankish, romantic, and delightful, and the Lunts played it, in Gilbert W. Gabriel's words, "swiftly, dashingly, humorously and ornamentally." He also commended the "wholly expert and blissful direction by Worthington Miner."

Earlier in this same season, the Guild had sponsored, though not produced, *The House of Connelly,* by Paul Green, as the first production of the newly formed Group Theatre, and its reception was most encouraging. The Group Theatre had its origins three years before, in 1928,

Worthington Miner's directing assignments for the Theatre Guild included *Reunion in Vienna* and *Jane Eyre. Vandamm photograph.*

The House of Connelly—the Theatre Guild sponsored the Group Theatre in the latter's production of this Paul Green drama, during the 1931–1932 season. The players are Margaret Barker and Franchot Tone. *Vandamm photograph.*

Reunion in Vienna—Alfred Lunt with Helen Westley, whose role as the grande dame of a celebrated hotel was modeled after the famous Madame Sacher of Vienna.

when two former Guild directors, Harold Clurman and Lee Strasberg, decided to organize a group to do experimental plays. Later they were joined by a third director, Cheryl Crawford, who had been a casting director for the Guild. The Group Theatre was to exert a significant influence on the course of the American stage during the years in which it was functioning, and many presently famous names, in addition to the three above, were to come out of it.

Imported from Ireland for a February 29, 1932, opening was Denis Johnston's *The Moon in the Yellow River,* an episodic and dramatically untidy exercise that pleased very few of its viewers. The title is from *Epitaph Li Po,* by Ezra Pound: "And Li Po also died drunk. He tried to embrace a moon in the Yellow River." It was followed by Shaw's *Too True to Be Good,* in which the Irish satirist took off once more on the state of the world, the attitude of modern young women, the state of medicine, the aptitude of British army officers for their jobs, the benefits of fresh air and exercise, and the state of the world following the World War. Shaw made no bones about the nature of his plays, labeling this one "A collection of stage sermons by a Fellow of the Royal Society of Literature." Good players added to its interest —Hope Williams, Beatrice Lillie, Leo G. Carroll,

The Moon in the Yellow River—William Harrigan, Henry Hull, and Gertrude Flynn. *Vandamm photograph.*

The Moon in the Yellow River—a fearsome moment in the second act. *Vandamm photograph.*

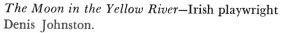

The Moon in the Yellow River—Irish playwright Denis Johnston.

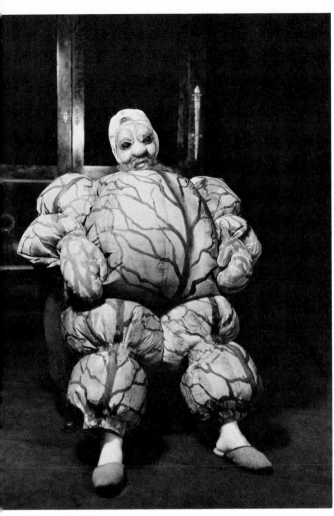

Too True to Be Good—inside Jonel Jorgulesco's costume is Julius Evans as The Monster. *Vandamm photograph.*

Claude Rains, Hugh Sinclair, Ernest Cossart, Julius Evans, Minna Phillips, and Alex Clark, Jr. Despite this, the combination of so much dialogue and so little action made the play less than thrilling to sit through, which has been the case with its occasional revivals.

Until 1932, touring theatre in America was in what the Irish playwright O'Casey might have described as "a state of chassis." The Shubert management, on the one hand, and Klaw and Erlanger, on the other, were competing desperately and destructively. When one booked a strong play or star into a city, the other would bring in an equally attractive personality, with the result that neither made as much money as they could have by some sort of an alternating plan. This hurt the Guild, which up to that point was booking out-of-town performances through Klaw and Erlanger.

Soon after Franklin D. Roosevelt took office and the National Recovery Act was put into effect, Langner became acquainted with Marcus Heiman, Erlanger's wealthy partner, who was doing what he could to save theatres which threatened to succumb to the economic pressures of the Depression. Langner introduced him to Earle Bailie, one of the Shuberts' bankers, suggesting the two discuss a cooperation which would permit a theatre season in the large cities that would spread its offerings over a half year or more. Eventually Heiman and Lee Shubert worked out the plan for the United Booking Office, which provided a much more sensible distribution of plays, regardless of who owned the theatres involved. At the same time, the Theatre Guild subscription and the Shubert subscription were merged into the American Theatre Society, of which, Langner became president. Prior to this, the Guild had toured only its own plays, but after ATS was formed other

Too True to Be Good—Ernest Cossart greets Beatrice Lillie, who is attended by Hope Williams and a skeptical Leo G. Carroll. *Vandamm photograph.*

Too True to Be Good—adorning Jonel Jorgulesco's set are Ernest Cossart, Minna Phillips, Claude Rains, Hope Williams, Leo G. Carroll, Hugh Sinclair, Beatrice Lillie, and Frank Shannon. *Vandamm photograph.*

managers joined, so that the selection of stage offerings in each city was far more extensive.

Under the name of the Theatre Guild–American Theatre Society, a subscription program was installed in Chicago, Boston, and Washington, along with New York which had had Guild subscription from the beginning. Eventually it grew to include twenty cities and reached as far as San Francisco with a total subscription by 1946 of about 150,000 members. Today the TG-ATS tours play each season to Boston, Chicago, Cincinnati, Cleveland, Columbus, Denver, Kansas City, Los Angeles, Louisville, Philadelphia, Pittsburgh, St. Louis, San Francisco, Toronto, Washington, and Wilmington, Delaware.

Pearl Buck's novel of China, *The Good Earth,* had won a Pulitzer Prize and had gone into its twenty-third printing when the Guild decided to start its fifteenth season with the dramatic adaptation by the father-and-son team of Owen and Donald Davis. It was not a good choice, being composed of ten episodes from a book which was not in the least episodic, and it never had the movement or persuasion of a play. George Jean Nathan wrote that ". . . trying to adapt *The Good Earth* to the stage form is something like trying to adapt the *Earl Carroll Vanities* to the novel form. It doesn't fit itself into the proscenium arch." Another problem was that on opening night, Nazimova, playing the slave O-Lan, was

The Good Earth—Alla Nazimova. *Vandamm photograph.*

The Good Earth—Claude Rains and Henry Travers. *Vandamm photograph.*

The Good Earth—Sydney Greenstreet. *Vandamm photograph.*

121

The Good Earth—key roles were played by Claude Rains (left), Henry Travers (on the bed), and Alla Nazimova (carrying chest). *Vandamm photograph.*

nervous and slowed up her performance so as to add twenty minutes to the playing time of a production, which was anything but swift even without such hesitation. The effect of this was reflected in the newspaper notices the following morning, and the play never recovered.

Biography, by S. N. Behrman, was a favorite of the Guild's Lawrence Langner, who considered it one of the best comedies ever written in this country, and it began the group's association with the comedienne Ina Claire. "Ina ranks with the best actresses of this period," Langner later wrote, "her style reminding one of the expert comedy acting of the earlier Minnie Maddern Fiske and Marie Tempest. She was one of the

prettiest women I have ever known, with blonde hair, laughing Irish eyes, piquant features, a beautiful figure, and a sense of humor that worked without ceasing, both on the stage and off. But beyond this, she had a deep emotional quality which, alas, she seldom permitted herself to display."

As a painter whose zest for life fails to find its way to her canvas, Miss Claire agrees to write her autobiography for a magazine, to the consternation of her several former lovers. One, now a candidate for the Senate, is influential enough to keep the story out of print, which provokes its intense young editor to quit his job. To enable the editor to keep his career and his convictions, the artist voluntarily destroys her manu-

Biography—this S. N. Behrman comedy began the Guild's happy association with Ina Claire; she portrayed a painter whose autobiography threatened the peace of mind of several former lovers. *Vandamm photograph.*

Biography—Alexander Clark, Ina Claire, and Arnold Korff. *Vandamm photograph.*

Ina Claire's mischievous charm endeared her to audiences and to the people with whom she worked. *De Mirjian photograph.*

script. The sophistication of the story, and the deftness of its dialogue, appealed to audiences; it ran for 267 performances following its December 12, 1932, opening. The following season Miss Claire did it with Laurence Olivier in London, and Ilka Chase toured in *Biography* in the United States.

Nothing so far had indicated that 1932–1933 would be much of a season for the Guild in terms of substantial drama, despite the wit and popularity of Behrman's play, and only one strong play was to follow that winter and spring while the nation was sinking into the deepest valley of the great Depression. That strong play was *American Dream,* by George O'Neil (not to be confused with *The American Dream* which Edward Albee was to write years later, or with anything of Eugene O'Neill's). It was a trilogy written to be played backwards. Director Philip Moeller decided to play it forward. The playwright, whose indicated talent was extinguished with his early death, probably was right. On a trip to New England, he had wondered what past generations of a family he was visiting would think about the contemporary world if they were to return to life. He started with the summer of 1933—actually a few months in the future, then depicted the family as of 1849, and finished with 1650. By reversing this order, the Guild defeated his purpose of using the present-future episode as the point of reference for any insights into the past generation. It was an unconventional play that detailed the deterioration of a line of sturdy pioneers, but not without bitterness, especially in the present-day scene. Most critics were dissatisfied with the play, though even more with the production. Still, there was enough recognition of George O'Neil's ability to make one wonder what else he might have produced if he had been granted twenty or thirty more years of life. Gilbert W. Gabriel concluded his review with an encouraging word for the playwright and the blunt statement: "I've seldom seen worse playing at any American first nightmare."

The redeeming effort for the first half of 1933 was Maxwell Anderson's *Both Your Houses,*

American Dream—a trilogy written to be played in reverse chronology featured Gale Sondergaard, Stanley Ridges, and Douglass Montgomery. *Vandamm photograph.*

American Dream—Gertrude Flynn and Douglass Montgomery in an episode set in 1650. *Vandamm photograph.*

Gale Sondergaard. *De Mirjian photograph.*

Both Your Houses—Walter C. Kelly, Shepperd Strudwick, and Mary Phillips. *Vandamm photograph.*

which won a Pulitzer Prize. Drawing its title from Mercutio's "A plague o' both your houses," in Shakespeare's *Romeo and Juliet,* it details the crushing of a young and politically innocent congressman (Shepperd Strudwick) by legislators from both major parties. As a member of the Appropriations Committee, he watches in dismay as a bill is loaded with "pork-barrel" projects. Unable to stop this waste of taxpayers' money, he adds more wasteful appropriations, assuming that the bill will become so ridiculous it will be defeated. But to his horror, the bill is voted through by both houses, and by a large majority. Anderson had researched congressional behavior thoroughly enough to come across with a realistic and upsettingly candid drama. Such things had indeed happened, and have happened since, if not always accompanied by a romance between the congressman and the committee chairman's daughter. Anderson's anger was transmitted to his audiences, which was just what he intended. A couple of critics did claim the play had come too late, and that Anderson was writing about the Herbert Hoover administration after the Franklin D. Roosevelt reign had just begun; they also claimed that there were more timely issues to write about, considering the state of the economy. While it was true that such pork-barreling might have been more characteristic before the Depression started,

Both Your Houses—Aleta Freel, Walter C. Kelly, and Mary Phillips. *Vandamm photograph.*

Morris Carnovsky, about the time he appeared in *Both Your Houses. Pinchot photograph.*

Maxwell Anderson appears in the Guild roster of plays six times. He wrote *Elizabeth the Queen, Both Your Houses, Mary of Scotland, Valley Forge, The Masque of Kings,* and *Candle in the Wind.*

enough of it continued to make Anderson's realistic satire durably pertinent.

Following its run of American plays, the Guild turned toward season's end to Italian playwright Luigi Chiarelli's *The Mask and the Face,* which had been produced in New York by Brock Pemberton in 1924, in an adaptation—much changed from the Italian original—by Chester B. Fernald. More faithful, and dramatically more sound was the version prepared by Somerset Maugham which the Guild used.

In the play, which is part comedy, part caricature of social custom, Count Paolo decides that his wife, Savina, has been unfaithful, but he likes her too well to do the expected thing, which is to kill her. So he sends her out of the country, then confesses that he has drowned her. At his trial, a man testifies to Savina's infidelity, at which the jury absolves her husband. Subsequently the count is so set upon by marriage-eager women that he decides to bring his wife back, and she arrives during the funeral of a woman found in the lake and believed to have been his wife. She has her inning with the man who had maligned her wifely virtue, after which she and her husband quietly slip away from the funeral.

Judith Anderson played the wife, with Stanley Ridges as the husband, and a young actor named Humphrey Bogart as the lawyer who claims to have been her lover. Shirley Booth also was in the cast, in a small role. Apparently the Guild's production wasn't the least bit Italian (Bogart especially was clobbered for his clumsiness), though Burns Mantle of the New York *Daily News* felt that it was "nothing much nicely done." Actually it's quite a clever and far from superficial satire which is admired and performed in many countries and languages.

In the wake of such dark O'Neill dramas as *Desire Under the Elms, Strange Interlude,* and *Mourning Becomes Electra,* the last two of which had been premiered by the Guild, audiences were surprised and delighted by his *Ah, Wilderness!* which began the Guild's sixteenth year in October of 1933. The truth is that O'Neill himself was surprised when this fictionalized episode from his boyhood, which he claimed came back to him one night in a dream, got written so quickly. He had it finished in four weeks, and he moved it ahead of *Days Without End,* which the Guild mounted three months later.

The Mask and the Face—the man with Judith Anderson looks like a young Humphrey Bogart. He is Humphrey Bogart. *Vandamm photograph.*

Somerset Maugham translated Luigi Chiarelli's *The Mask and the Face* for the Theatre Guild production. *Vandamm photograph.*

Ah, Wilderness!—Elisha Cook, Jr., as Richard. *Vandamm photograph.*

Ah, Wilderness!—George M. Cohan as Richard's father. *Pinchot photograph.*

Ah, Wilderness! is as pleasant and beguiling as so much else of O'Neill is foreboding or forbidding. Richard is the restless teen-age son of a wise and tolerant newspaper publisher in a Connecticut town. He wants to "live," a project abetted by Sid, his mother's drinking brother, and eventually goes off to sample the wine and women of dissolute New Haven. The toot doesn't last long nor is it particularly evil, and his sweetheart Muriel is eager enough to have him back when he comes home drunk and disillusioned that same night. The comedy dispensed its gently sentimental cheer for a full season, with George M. Cohan in one of his memorable roles as the lad's father. It was not entirely fortunate that Cohan kept embellishing his role until the performances were running far too long; however, few in the audience seemed seriously concerned. Later the part was acted by Will Rogers on the road and Walter Huston in films. In recent years, the play became a musical, *Take Me Along,* with Walter Pidgeon as the father, Robert Morse as the son, and Jackie Gleason as Uncle Sid.

An adaptation in rhyme of Molière's *The School for Husbands,* prepared by Arthur Guit-

Ah, Wilderness!—Gene Lockhart as Sid. *Vandamm photograph.*

Ah, Wilderness!—Marjorie Marquis as Essie.

The School for Husbands—Osgood Perkins and June Walker in the Guiterman-Langner adaptation of Molière's comedy. *Vandamm photograph.*

The School for Husbands—the dancing of Doris Humphrey and Charles Weidman was a bonus for Theatre Guild audiences. *Vandamm photograph.*

erman and Lawrence Langner, marked the Guild's first encounter with ballet. This was Langner's doing; he was fascinated by the dance. Besides the incidental ballet titled *The Dream of Sganarelle,* danced by Doris Humphrey and Charles Weidman, the production was embellished with French Bergerette songs sung by Osgood Perkins and June Walker. Luxuriously costumed and brightly played, the Molière piece was generally applauded in the press. Nevertheless it was not that strong at the box office, and left to tour the Guild subscription cities after a relatively brief stay at the Empire Theatre in New York.

    . . . It was rather magnificent, the success that Maxwell Anderson, Helen Hayes and the Theatre Guild jointly won at the Alvin Theatre last evening. It had a superlative quality, a certain lordly, professional dignity, the theatre does not often achieve. Five or six times a decade, perhaps. But not oftener. *Mary of Scotland* is so beautifully written, so nobly staged and spoken, it brings a definite majesty into the playhouse.

This was Burns Mantle's opening accolade in the *Daily News* following the November 27, 1933, opening at the Alvin. "This is the drama of heroes," wrote Brooks Atkinson, and John Mason Brown rated it the best historical drama to have been written by an American. Everyone cheered the way Anderson had brought forth the beauty of the English language, as he also had in *Elizabeth and Essex.*

    It was indeed an achievement, and one which was bound to recall the chronicle plays of Shakespeare, not necessarily to compare the two writers in terms of skill, but to note how successfully each had exploited the high drama of royal personages. Anderson set forth the resentment of the Puritan John Knox toward his Catholic queen, the intrigues that fettered her, the murders, the rebellion, the uneasy peace, her marriage to Darnley, and especially the ruthless scheming for undivided power by Elizabeth of England. With Helen Hayes as Mary, Philip Merivale as Bothwell, Helen Menken as Elizabeth, and the sustained and sustaining strength of Theresa Helburn's

Mary of Scotland—Helen Hayes as Mary, Helen Menken as Elizabeth. *Vandamm photograph.*

Mary of Scotland—Helen Hayes with Philip Merivale as Bothwell. *Vandamm photograph.*

direction, the drama was indeed, in Mantle's phrase, "rather magnificent." Robert Edmond Jones designed the sets and costumes, to add further luster to one of the landmark productions in the Guild's history. Fascinating as Anderson's regal and noble characters are, the play gains its deeper impact from the fact that they were concerned not just with themselves but with principles, with the destiny of a nation, and with bold ideas. There doesn't seem to be any historical record that Elizabeth visited Mary in prison, just before the latter's execution, but the scene is consonant with the nature of the two women and of their relationship. In any event, it is a climactic scene, brilliantly written, with Mary claiming that she has won through having loved, been a woman, and borne a child, while Elizabeth's life has been barren.

When Eugene O'Neill's *Days Without End* opened in January of 1934, many of the critics, along with a number of people who knew Gene, were inclined to interpret it as a return to the Catholic faith he had pretty much repudiated as a much younger man. The playwright anticipated, during the writing of this "modern miracle play," as he described it, that audiences might see it in that light, and he tried—unsuccessfully—to avoid giving such an impression. In his first version, called *An End of Days,* the clergyman in the story was a Protestant minister, but O'Neill eventually changed him to a Roman Catholic priest; the story simply worked better in a Catholic atmosphere.

Actually, and retrospectively, *Days Without End* might better be described as a romantic play, at least in its deeper objective and in its inspiration, than a religious one. Gene was married for the third time in his turbulent life, and his Carlotta, along with being a beautiful woman, seemed an ideal wife. All he needed to complete his life was a good working situation, which he did not find in their Park Avenue apartment in New York. Ilka Chase, a friend of both Gene and Carlotta, suggested Sea Island, Georgia. The couple went there in the spring of 1932 and built a home, called Casa Genotta, on the beach. Miss Chase, incidentally, was in the cast of this particular play when the Guild opened it at Henry Miller's Theatre less than two years later.

So it was in this relatively idyllic setting (apart from rattlesnakes, coral snakes, and summer dampness which corroded all the hardware on the house), that O'Neill wrote his somewhat mystical

Helen Menken at the time she was portraying Queen Elizabeth in *Mary of Scotland. Vandamm photograph.*

Days Without End—Eugene O'Neill wrote two roles to depict the evil (Stanley Ridges, in mask) and good (Earle Larimore) sides of one man's nature.

131

Days Without End—guided by a minister (Robert Loraine), the good John Loving (Earle Larimore) turns to prayer while his evil self (Stanley Ridges) plots his next move.

Days Without End—Earle Larimore and Selena Royle. *Miller photograph.*

Days Without End—the denouement before the cross.

drama. Lawrence Langner was convinced that it was "inspired by Carlotta and that in it Gene sought to express his hope for a love which transcended mortal life and could last forever." Both had previously found love not only unhappy but impermanent, and he was incurably romantic, as evidenced by his sea-roaming life and by many of his plays. It was, if such can be, a realistic romanticism; that is, he had come to know life bitterly enough to be entirely disillusioned, but deep down, any true romantic never gives up his quest. O'Neill was like that.

The fact remains that most people, not understanding the playwright as perceptively as Langner did, failed to pinpoint this motivation, and persisted in appraising *Days Without End* in essentially religious or moralistic terms. Oddly enough, in Europe, where it was received more favorably than here, it apparently was accepted more at O'Neill's own values. At least, its reception was not clouded by speculation about the author; England, Sweden, Germany, and Italy simply listened to the drama and made their own conclusions.

John Loving, the pivotal character, is presented in two aspects—and two roles: his better self is seeking enlightenment and an affirmation of the beauty of life, while the other sees life as hopeless, hates his devoted wife, and resents God for having made him an orphan. The device, incidentally, showed up thirty years later on the Broadway stage in Brian Friel's tender comedy, *Philadelphia, Here I Come,* in which a young man is portrayed by two actors, as his outer and inner selves. But the two John Lovings (played by Earle Larimore and Stanley Ridges) are irreconcilable; one finds love and security in his wife, while the other is too suspicious of even so good a love to accept it, and is deliberately unfaithful. The wife attempts suicide, which is hardly surprising under the circumstances, and is saved from death only when the good John prays before the cross and is redeemed in the sight of God.

The crux of most of the reviews was that despite any inspirational value or soaring spirituality, *Days Without End* was simply a bad play, and certainly below the level of workmanship expected from O'Neill. In fact, Gilbert Gabriel concluded his unfavorable notice in the *New York American* with a condemnation of the producers for staging it: ". . . But I was villainously certain by the churchly finale that the real miracle of this miracle play was this: that the Guild had summoned up the sheer masochistic generosity to do this *Days Without End* at all. Mea culpa." The Catholic press was much more enthusiastic, which is to be expected, although somewhere along the line someone made an artistic judgment; the play was not included on the Church's White List of recommended drama. Indicative of the reaction in the religious Establishment was this rave in *America,* a Catholic publication, by a Jesuit priest, Gerard B. Donnelly:

> I am still reeling from the shock of it. For I have seen a magnificently Catholic play—a play Catholic in its characters, its story, its mood and its moral. With a Catholic priest in it—the noblest priest in the history of the modern theatre. With Catholic prayers in it. With dialogue about the Faith, mortal sin, Confession and the Mercy of God. A play that defies all the Broadway traditions and dares to close with its hero kneeling in a Catholic church before a great carved crucifix.

"John Wexley writes with the coolness of a man who has been deeply stirred," observed

The New York Times critic Brooks Atkinson in his opening night review of *They Shall Not Die,* which bowed on February 21, 1934, at the Royale. Its subject, though not specifically identified as such, was the Scottsboro case, in which nine young Negroes were convicted of rape despite overwhelming evidence of their innocence, and sentenced to die. Ruth Gordon and Linda Watkins portrayed the two girls intimidated into making the rape charge, which Miss Gordon later repudiated in a powerful courtroom scene. Claude Rains was the defense attorney.

Abrasive drama today can be encountered on and off Broadway; these are the plays which intentionally upset the audience with the harshness of injustice, or even thrust guilt into the awareness of the unsuspecting theatregoer. There was less of it in the earlier years of this century, despite the heritage of a moralistic, intentionally disturbing theatre from Europe, but the social consciousness aspect of American drama really began to manifest itself in the 1930's. Wexley, instead of softening the bitter facts of the massive injustice down South, hardened them with touches that were theatrically effective even though they were entirely justifiable in terms of what actually had happened. As the play approaches its close,

the defense has proved beyond the shadow of a doubt that the nine Negro lads are innocent, and the judge has charged the jury with religious sincerity. Then Wexley is merciless enough to let the audience hear, offstage, the laughter of the twelve jurymen; obviously, guilt or innocence has nothing to do with the case.

They Shall Not Die earned critical approval and proved a success for the Guild. The predominantly white audiences were outraged at the inhumanity of the Scottsboro case, and at least began thinking that "free and equal" as defined in the Constitution might not do much good for the Negro population.

Jig Saw, a comedy which closed the season, was notable only as the vehicle which introduced Ernest Truex and Spring Byington to Guild audiences. It was by Dawn Powell, an Ohio girl who had written several romantic novels, some short stories, and three previous plays, one of which was made into a movie. After a brief run, *Jig Saw* apparently was dismantled; few people have heard of it since.

Earlier that spring the Guild had opened *Races,* by Ferdinand Bruckner, in Philadelphia where it ran for two weeks, but it never was brought by them to New York. Probably the first

They Shall Not Die—Ruth Gordon, Linda Watkins, Al Stopes, Ralph Theadore in John Wexley's drama about the Scottsboro case. *Vandamm photograph.*

They Shall Not Die—Ruth Gordon. *Vandamm photograph.*

Jig Saw—this comedy introduced Spring Byington and Ernest Truex to Theatre Guild audiences. *Vandamm photograph.*

Jig Saw—the dark-haired woman on the settee at left is Helen Westley, and Shepperd Strudwick is at the extreme right. In the center, Ernest Truex and Spring Byington. *Vandamm photograph.*

Jig Saw—Spring Byington and Cora Witherspoon. *Vandamm photograph.*

anti-Nazi play, it had been done in Zurich the preceding November, then in Vienna, Paris, and London. A Prague production was canceled because the actors were afraid, with good reason, that it could end their careers if not their lives. The play tells of a young medical student who for a time helps the Nazis in their persecution of the Jews, but finally helps his Jewish fiancée escape, knowing he will be punished for it. New York finally saw *Races* in 1935—it was not done by the Guild—and found it wordy and preachy. Perhaps if closer attention had been paid to what it had to say, the United States might have been better prepared to accept the reality of Nazism a few years later.

A Sleeping Clergyman proved hardly the play to awaken audiences to a new season—the Guild's seventeenth—in the fall of 1934, nor was it the kind of title to start a box-office stampede. James Bridie was the pseudonym of the author; he was really Dr. Osborne Henry Mavor, a Glasgow physician, who used the two names in an attempt to keep his two identities out of conflict. Ambitious in scope, it examined the strange course of heredity in one family from 1867 to the present. It begins with a young medical student dying of tuberculosis, not to mention indignation when his fiancée destroys his experiments. She is perhaps understandably piqued, in that she is with child by him. The daughter eventually born of this troubled union grows up to keep company with a blackmailing cad whom she murders and, after giving birth to the twins he had planted,

A Sleeping Clergyman—the young Ruth Gordon and Theodore Newton. *Vandamm photograph.*

A Sleeping Clergyman—Ruth Gordon a generation later in this play about heredity. With her is Ernest Thesiger. *Vandamm photograph.*

Valley Forge—hunger is the issue.

ran for fifty-eight performances. Joseph T. Shipley found it interesting as a twentieth-century view of the eighteenth century, presenting, as it did, General George Washington's discouragement during the bleak winter of 1778 in terms which make sense and invite contemporary parallels for a modern audience. His enemies at the time were not only the British, but the cold, the indecision and the bickering Congress, the colonists who were sick of the war and ready to make their own deals with the enemy, the businessmen whose profits were diminished by war, and the soldiers who wanted to go home or already had. But when

commits suicide. The twins begin badly enough, in the tradition of their parents and grandparents, but wind up as a secretary to the League of Nations and a physician who discovers a cure for the plague. In other words, heredity doesn't prove anything. The production apparently represented a high—or low—point in stage mumbling by Glenn Anders, who played the man in all three generations, and whose diction was described by one reviewer as "always extremely bad," adding: "He surpasses himself in this offering by swallowing six words out of ten and choking over the rest." This apparently inspired the usually clean-spoken Ruth Gordon, in the three women's roles, also to swallow her speeches.

Maxwell Anderson's *Valley Forge* opened at the Guild Theatre on December 10, 1934, and

Washington is in a mind to surrender to England's Lord Howe, it is the troops who reproach him, and help him form a fresh determination to persevere. The closing line bears repeating: "This liberty will look easy by and by when nobody dies to get it." Herbert Biberman and John Houseman directed *Valley Forge*, which starred Philip Merivale as Washington.

"The Sentimental Journey of an Exile" by Alfred Kerr, an article in *The New York Times* in August, 1933, inspired S. N. Behrman to write his then-timely comedy, *Rain from Heaven*, a Christmas offering by the Guild the following year. Like *Races* in Philadelphia the previous spring, it dealt with the rising tide of German hatred and atrocities against Jews, except that it takes place in the drawing room of a wealthy and

Valley Forge—Philip Merivale as General Washington. *Vandamm photograph.*

Rain from Heaven—John Halliday, Lily Cahill, and José Ruben.

Valley Forge—Margalo Gillmore as Mary Philipse and Philip Merivale as Washington. *Vandamm photograph.*

Rain from Heaven—Thurston Hall, John Halliday, and Jane Cowl.

attractive widow. Her guests include a refugee German music critic whose great-grandmother had been Jewish, and his former mistress, now married to an American who is organizing a Fascist youth group in England. In the light of what follows, some of its conclusions appear painfully innocent. For example, the partly Jewish critic finally returns to Germany to help fight Hitler, in noble contrast with a Russian emigré who tries to conceal his past. Maybe the Russian was smarter, as the other certainly would have been murdered by the Germans in time. But the play does succeed in putting forth several opposing attitudes—liberalism, nationalism, Nazism, bigotry—at a time when these were of more than academic interest. While Behrman could not see what the next decade would bring—World War II and the extermination of six million Jews by the Germans among other disasters—he recognized the moral and ideological climate.

If you remember *Escape Me Never,* it probably is because the play introduced Elisabeth Bergner to American audiences. Margaret Kennedy wrote it, and the Guild staged it in collaboration with Charles B. Cochran of London. Miss Bergner, born in Vienna, had achieved a glowing stardom abroad in roles ranging from Shaw's *Saint Joan* to Nina in O'Neill's *Strange Interlude.* Despite a good engagement in London, *Escape Me Never* seemed insubstantial to American critics, though there was general agreement that Miss Bergner's debut was a triumph. Miss Kennedy's play is a

Escape Me Never—Douglas Watson, Elisabeth Bergner, and Hugh Sinclair. *Vandamm photograph.*

Escape Me Never—Elisabeth Bergner, shown with Hugh Sinclair, was brought from Germany to star in Margaret Kennedy's poignant play. *Vandamm photograph.*

Escape Me Never—Eve Turner and Elisabeth Bergner. *Vandamm photograph.*

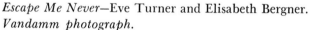

sequel to *The Constant Nymph* and, like that one, is based on a novel. Miss Bergner portrayed a stray teen-ager in Venice, with an illegitimate baby, who is picked up by one of the brothers of the Sanger Circus family and alternately loved and booted about thereafter.

Percy Hammond wrote:

Miss Bergner is an elfin actress versed in all the pixie magic of the stage. In the beginning scenes she plays a blond Topsy with a Jack Pearl accent and effective combination of mimetic gifts. She is addicted to scratching herself from head to heel and otherwise to be gamine and all that sort of thing, causing you to wonder why she is seductive to lovers of beauty and music. There is nothing in the reservoir of a keen mime's devices that does not come to her when she summons it. She haunts a ramshackle play hauntingly. In case your eyes wet easily they will be damp when her baby dies and her musical sweetheart kicks her out. Miss Bergner knows her way through the lanes and broad paths of *Escape Me Never*, which, I am reluctant to say, is a shallow bog. She enlivens if she does not illuminate a dull lesson in the theater.

The *New York Journal*'s John Anderson noted that "she plays with such disarming humility, with such tenderness and with, on rare occasions, such a sense of innocent mischief that she makes herself altogether captivating."

The Simpleton of the Unexpected Isles was the fifth play which G. B. Shaw entrusted to

138

The Simpleton of the Unexpected Isles—Lee Simon-son's setting. Vandamm photograph.

The Simpleton of the Unexpected Isles—Romney Brent and Nazimova. Vandamm photograph.

the Guild, and it enjoyed the services of Nazimova and Romney Brent. "Like *Too True to Be Good*," recalled producer Langner, "it was a conversation piece, only the conversations were longer and longer." The critics were unenthusiastic, and it proved a loser at the box office.

Financial matters were made worse by the "socially conscious" musical revue, *Parade,* which completed the Guild's seventeenth season, which represented a loss of about $111,000. Its sole assets were its introduction of comedian Jimmy Savo and the pattern it set for such later musical revues with timely ideological themes as *Pins and Needles* and *Call Me Mister.* At this time, Philip Moeller, Theresa Helburn, and Helen Westley were all in Hollywood, leaving only Langner and Lee Simonson to decide what to do next in New York.

Fortunately the season of 1935–1936 proved financially successful. Also the three errant directors returned from Hollywood, and the Guild outlook brightened accordingly. Five of the six productions earned a profit—*The Taming of the Shrew, Porgy and Bess, End of Summer, Idiot's Delight,* and *Call It a Day.* The only unpopular play was the season opener, *If This Be Treason,* by the Reverend John Haynes Holmes and Reginald Lawrence. The play, intended to show how Japan could be reasoned out of its course toward war, was contradicted by later events, such as their bombing of Pearl Harbor. Robert Garland in the *New York World-Telegram* observed: "It is impossible to approach *If This Be Treason* as just one more Broadway drama. In times such as these,

The Simpleton of the Unexpected Isles—Lawrence Grossmith. Vandamm photograph.

Parade—Jimmy Savo was the good-hearted little guy at odds with the Establishment in this pioneer "socially conscious" musical revue. *Vandamm photograph.*

Parade—Dorothy Fox and Charles Walters did several specialty numbers.

Parade—Vera Marshe and Earl Oxford. *Vandamm photograph.*

Parade—people laughed at Jimmy Savo—here tangling with the law—but the Theatre Guild lost $100,000 on the show.

If This Be Treason—McKay Morris played the President of the United States, with Armina Marshall as his wife. *Vandamm photograph.*

with civilization on the verge of suicide, it transcends the showshop."

When the Theatre Guild production of Shakespeare's *The Taming of the Shrew* opened in Pittsburgh, five months prior to its Broadway debut, Harold Cohen, writing for *Variety Weekly*, spotted it for the hit it was destined to become. This is not to say that the Shakespearean romp hadn't been a gladsome theatre piece during its preceding centuries, but in the hands of Alfred Lunt and Lynn Fontanne it became possibly better and certainly livelier than ever. Some time before, after finishing a tour of the Guild's *Reunion in Vienna*, they had left to go into an association with Noel Coward, opening with his *Design for Living*. A couple of years later Lawrence Langner and Helen Westley went to see them when they were appearing in Coward's *Point Valaine* and urged them to return to the Guild to do a Shakespearean production. *Shrew* intrigued them, and became the vehicle which not only brought them back to the fold but which started a new acting company that was to remain virtually intact for several highly profitable years. Alfred Lunt directed, eliciting the admiration in that capacity he had long enjoyed as an actor. *Variety* described it as "an informal harlequinade mixing farce and bur-

lesque and makes a legitimate lark of one of the theatre's heretofore sacred cows." Continuing:

Christopher Sly (Richard Whorf) sits throughout the play in a box down front, a sort of glorified stooge, guzzling ale and munching chicken legs while he voices his approval or disapproval of the performance. Three acrobats tumble on and off stage, a trio of alley-oopers satirizing a vaude tradition. Four dwarfs are present, all males, and they serve, among other things, as Katherine's bridesmaids; grotesque creatures in their bridal habiliments. A couple of actors supply the front and back legs of Petruchio's two horses and the shrew-tamer, most of the time, carries a long black snake-whip that he crackles with the ease and flourish of a Simon Legree.

Shrew abounds in surprises, not the least of which is that finish. It disclosed the now-happy couple aboard a winged chariot soaring through the clouds and stars to a heavenly destination and obviously eternal bliss.

The following February when the show was on tour, Ashton Stevens characterized it accurately as "low comedy with a high heart." Also in Chicago, Claudia Cassidy, then critic of the

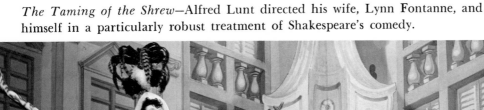

The Taming of the Shrew—Alfred Lunt directed his wife, Lynn Fontanne, and himself in a particularly robust treatment of Shakespeare's comedy.

The Taming of the Shrew—Sydney Greenstreet as Baptista.

The Taming of the Shrew—tamer Lunt and shrewish Fontanne. *Vandamm photograph.*

Journal of Commerce (before she went to the *Tribune*), disliked all the acting—including Miss Fontanne's Katherine—except that of Lunt, Sydney Greenstreet, Whorf, and William Clifford; then went on to wonder why Lunt hadn't directed the whole thing as the program stated he had.

Today, when even second-rate actors refuse to go out on the road because it is such a grueling existence, it is worth repeating that the Lunts regularly did, in this case taking *Shrew* all across the country and playing it to the hilt wherever they happened to be.

Rouben Mamoulian, who had staged *Porgy,* the Dorothy and Du Bose Heyward drama about Negro life on Catfish Row in Charleston, South Carolina, for the Guild in 1927, returned to help reshape it as an American Negro folk opera, *Porgy and Bess,* with music by George Gershwin, in the fall of 1935. It seems odd now that it ran for only 120 performances and did not even earn back its cost. Revived in New York in 1942, however, it enjoyed an engagement of 286 performances, and has been presented a number of times since. Part of the loss in 1935 was due to the cost of a forty-eight-piece orchestra, conducted by Alexander Smallens, in place of the usual musical comedy pit band of perhaps half that size. Nobody in the Guild complained, however; the larger orchestra was required, and it helped to make *Porgy and Bess* a landmark in the musical theatre. Tod Duncan as Porgy, Anne Brown as Bess, Warren Coleman as Crown, Ruby Elzy as Serena, and John W. Bubbles as Sportin' Life earned critical praise, as did the rest of the cast. Even with the Guild's tradition of fine settings, mostly by Lee Simonson, those designed for *Porgy and Bess* by Sergei Soudeikine were outstanding.

Not widely known is the fact that it was Warren P. Munsell, business manager of the Guild at the time, who conceived the idea of making *Porgy* into an opera, and talked George Gershwin and his brother Ira into doing it. When it opened, each New York paper covered it by both the music critic and the drama critic. Gilbert Gabriel quoted his own review of *Porgy* in 1927, in which he had written that the play would make an effective libretto for an opera.

If you were to ask what people really enjoyed in the theatre of the mid-1930's, the answer might well be Dodie Smith's English comedy, *Call It a Day,* though I hesitate to guess how it would fare in New York today. Gilbert Gabriel,

Porgy and Bess—Todd Duncan as Porgy, Anne Brown as Bess. *Vandamm photograph.*

Porgy and Bess—Anne Brown as Bess, Warren Coleman as Crown. *Talbot photograph.*

Porgy and Bess—Catfish Row, as evoked by designer Sergei Soudeikine. *Vandamm photograph.*

Porgy and Bess—composer George Gershwin. *Vandamm photograph.*

Porgy and Bess—lyricist Ira Gershwin. *Vandamm photograph.*

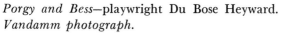
Porgy and Bess—playwright Du Bose Heyward. *Vandamm photograph.*

Call It a Day—Gladys Cooper and Philip Merivale. *Phyfe photograph.*

perhaps a bit more acerbic than most critics, though still favorable, viewed it as a fond scrutiny of that ancient English institution, the Nice Family. On a singularly felicitous early spring morning, the Hilton family awakens full of almost irresistible romantic impulses. Mr. Hilton (Philip Merivale) finds himself agreeing to meet an actress-client in her apartment at nine that evening to pursue some business. His proper wife (Gladys Cooper) feels very friendly toward a lonely rubber planter. The son is importuned by another young man, though this is understated ever so delicately, and some of the critics couldn't even bring themselves to mention it in their reviews. The elder daughter yearns for a portrait artist. The thirteen-year-old girl and the maid also have their romantic inclinations, the first rather diffuse but poetic, the second toward the butler next door. At nine that night all keep rendezvous, but are home and in their own beds by midnight. Nothing has happened. Arthur Pollock, writing in the *Brooklyn Eagle,* repeated that they had avoided tragedy. Admittedly, it would have been unfortunate if the boy had gone off with his male friend instead of being saved by the pure love of the girl next door. The other threatened alliances, while hazardous, hardly measure up to tragic proportions.

At any event, just about everybody loved the comedy, including the critic of *The New Yorker,* who went to see it twice. An exception was Brooks Atkinson of the *Times* who said of playwright Smith: "The commonplaces of theatre thinking keep her well inside the postprandial conventions when she is tracking down middle-aged philandering. Call it only an ordinary day in the final analysis." Nevertheless, the play enjoyed a good run, and the Guild replenished its treasury with the profits.

Atkinson preferred the more adult comedy of S. N. Behrman, and referred to *End of Summer,* the fifth Guild play of that season, as "a treasure-house of modern good-will," concluding his notice with "Many thanks for a civilized evening." In dialogue that was always intelligent and often brilliant, Behrman exposed the people gathered around a wealthy woman summering in Maine. The company includes a troubled and very modern daughter, her revolutionary boyfriend, another and cheerier revolutionist, a gloomy Russian, a scientist just fired for doing too well at his job, a psychoanalyst, and a grandmother. The principal theme was the ethics of a poor man marrying a rich girl, which was hardly a dramatic breakthrough, but there was nothing banal or hackneyed about Behrman's handling of it. There is

End of Summer—Ina Claire and Osgood Perkins.

Call It a Day—Philip Merivale, Jeanne Dante, John Buckmaster, and Gladys Cooper.

End of Summer—Minor Watson. *Vandamm photograph.*

considerably more to *End of Summer* than that, and skillfully fashioned roles enabled a fine cast to show to advantage. They included Ina Claire, Osgood Perkins, Mildred Natwick, Doris Dudley, Shepperd Strudwick, Kendell Clark, Minor Watson, Van Heflin, Herbert Yost, and Tom Powers. It would be hard to imagine more deft direction of such a play and company than that provided by Philip Moeller, who had worked with Behrman before and who knew how to keep a stageful of bright people always in focus. Despite Behrman's skill at writing dialogue and creating fascinating characters, his plays seldom went smoothly when they first went into rehearsal, and the construction of *End of Summer* improved markedly during its preparation. Miss Claire had a talent for spotting the diffused nature of a scene, and demanding that it be sharpened up. Langner relates how she would stand in the middle of the rehearsal room, look at the playwright, and say: "Sam, this play is about me, isn't it, so what do I do next?" Thus she kept the story intact with herself in the center of it, which was just what was needed.

A good season ended even better with Robert Sherwood's anti-war play, *Idiot's Delight,* which was to win him a Pulitzer Prize (the Guild's fourth; the others had been for *Both Your Houses,*

They Knew What They Wanted, and *Strange Interlude*). He gathered his characters at a winter sports inn in the Italian Alps, near the Swiss and Austrian borders. They include an old scientist seeking a cure for cancer, a young pacifist who believes the essential goodness of men will avert the next war (he was wrong), an international munitions manufacturer who knows it won't (he was right), the arms tycoon's mistress (Lynn Fontanne), a young English couple, and an American vaudeville entertainer (Alfred Lunt) who is shepherding a flock of six dancing blondes on a tour through Europe.

There could be no challenging Sherwood's high idealism. In the published version of his play he prefaces:

> I believe that the world is populated largely by decent people, and decent people don't want war. Nor do they make war. They fight and die, to be sure—but that is because they have been deluded by their exploiters, who are members of the indecent minority. . . . By refusing to imitate the Fascists in their policies of heavily fortified isolation, their hysterical self-worship and psychopathic hatred of others, we may achieve the enjoyment of peaceful life on earth, rather than degraded death in the cellar.

It was a fine idea, wittily articulated in *Idiot's Delight.* The fact that the world was plunged into war only shortly after did not invalidate Sherwood's fervor or his message.

One of the keenest observations about the play came from James Agate of the London *Times* when the play opened there in 1938: "It is very nearly a masterpiece of light theatre with a core of thought." The March 24, 1936, premiere in New York was greeted with exuberant reviews for the most part and started a run of 121 performances; a revival in August of that same year lasted 179 performances.

When *Idiot's Delight* was in rehearsal, producer Langner felt that the play was too light for the seriousness of its own implications. It was Miss Fontanne who suggested that Sherwood write the scene for her and the munitions manufacturer which more sharply defined the moral line of the drama. It was runner-up for the first New York Drama Critics Circle Award, which had gone to Maxwell Anderson's *Winterset.* The critics had organized that season, largely in protest against the Pulitzer Prize committee, which the

Idiot's Delight—Alfred Lunt and the dancing girls in a memorable scene from Robert Sherwood's Pulitzer Prize-winning play. *Vandamm photograph.*

Idiot's Delight—Alfred Lunt and Lynn Fontanne. *Vandamm photograph.*

previous year had selected *The Old Maid* as the year's finest play—a selection with which most of the reviewers had disagreed.

There is little reason to dwell on *And Stars Remain,* the nineteenth season opener, except to note that once again the use of an ingenious and inventive actor kept a bad play from becoming a total catastrophe. Written by twins—Julius and Philip Epstein—the play takes its title from a poem by Shelley and attempts to match S. N. Behrman at witty drawing-room dialogue, even to the point of using his familiar theme of liberal thought in a conservative atmosphere. Richard Watts, Jr., in the *Herald Tribune* pointed out that the play offered "neither the penetrating and tolerant insight of a Behrman nor the burning indignation of an Odets." Helen Gahagan (later to marry Melvyn Douglas and also to become a liberal representative from California in Congress) was the beauteous granddaughter of a crusty millionaire. Naturally, she falls in love with a liberal. What salvaged this tired plot was the performance of Clifton Webb as a young dilettante with vaguely liberal tendencies, who comments from a prone position on a couch through much of the play. It was only the second time Webb had been on the legitimate stage in other than a dancing-and-singing role. He had begun his career in his teens as a portrait painter, turned next to opera, then tried dancing which got him involved in theatre and, eventually, acting.

Philip Moeller, who directed many of the Theatre Guild productions, including *And Stars Remain.* He was one of the Guild's founders. *Vandamm photograph.*

And Stars Remain—Clifton Webb and Helen Gahagan. *Vandamm photograph.*

Equally lacking in durability was William McNally's *Prelude to Exile,* in which Wilfred Lawson played the German composer Richard Wagner and Eva Le Gallienne was Mathilde Wesendonck, wife of his benefactor, and in love with the young man who was then at work on *Tristan und Isolde.* Also involved with the composer were his wife, fighting a losing battle, and the very young Cosima Liszt von Bülow, who was destined to nail him—or he her—ere long. Prevalent critical opinion was that Wagner deserved a better play, and that the author had erred in making him seem such a dolt and such a shallow romantic.

The Guild's reputation was not helped by *But for the Grace of God,* by Leopold Atlas, which was the third try of the 1936–1937 season. Atlas had scored a modest success earlier with *Wednesday's Child,* and his new play evidenced a comparable sincerity and compassion. However, his theme—the evils of child labor in particular and poverty in general—was pretty much expounded in the first few minutes, and thereafter the play was not especially revealing. John Mason Brown's judgment of it as a decidedly unskillful melodrama reflected the general feeling.

Prelude to Exile—Eva Le Gallienne and Wilfred Lawson as the lovers Mathilde Wesendonck and Richard Wagner. *Vandamm photograph.*

Eva Le Gallienne at the time she was appearing in *Prelude to Exile. Pinchot photograph.*

But for the Grace of God—James McCallion (center) leads Paul White (left) and Robert Mayors in a robbery which nets them $8 and winds up in murder. *Vandamm photograph.*

But for the Grace of God—James Bell.

Jane Eyre, Helen Jerome's dramatization of the Brontë novel, was not the first play to be mounted by the Guild, then dropped during out-of-town tryouts. *The Lonely Heart* (1931), *The Pure in Heart* (1932), *Love Is Not So Simple* (1934), and *Five Kings* (1939), taken from the Shakespeare chronicle plays, were some of the others. But *Jane Eyre* was to bring Katharine Hepburn back to the stage, after a successful sojourn in Hollywood, so there was additional regret when it closed after engagements in Chicago, Cleveland, and Pittsburgh. She did work for the Guild again, and with spectacular success, in *The Philadelphia Story* a couple of years later.

Continuing a season of landmark indistinction, the indomitable producers turned to an old hand—Maxwell Anderson—for their next effort. *The Masque of Kings,* featuring Henry Hull, Margo, Dudley Digges, and Pauline Frederick, covered three key days in the troubled history of the royal Hapsburg family of Austria, and specifically the murder or suicide—or both—of the Crown Prince Rudolph and the young Baroness Mary Vetsera at the shooting lodge in Mayerling in 1889. As might be expected of Anderson, much of it was written with skill and compassionate insight; the fault was his tendency to overwrite—"to turn every action into a full-length speech," in Atkinson's opinion. Still, the play was conceded to be the Guild's best in a notably bad year and above the prevailing level of the commercial theatre. Incidentally, that season three Maxwell

149

Jane Eyre—two lovely portraits of Katharine Hepburn in an adaptation which the Theatre Guild produced on the road but which was abandoned before a scheduled New York opening. *Vandamm photograph.*

The Masque of Kings—Henry Hull as the Crown Prince Rudolph of Austria-Hungary; Margo as the Baroness Mary Vetsera.

Anderson plays were running in New York—*The Masque of Kings, Wingless Victory,* with Katharine Cornell, and *High Tor,* with Burgess Meredith.

From such serious, and indeed, tragic fare, the Guild returned to comedy of the frothiest sort to conclude the season. *Storm over Patsy* was adapted by James Bridie from a German play, *Storm in a Waterglass* by Bruno Frank and, according to the original playwright, given 6,500 performances in at least half-a-dozen languages. Bridie's version in Scotland and England had been called *Storm in a Teacup;* Roger Livesey, who appeared in it there, also performed in the American production and again was largely responsible for its appeal. Alexander Woollcott was instrumental in getting Livesey to New York, because originally Actors Equity had refused to permit the English actor to do the role here (the situation has not changed substantially today). But after Woollcott, having seen the play in London, wrote enthusiastically about Livesey to Frank Gillmore of Equity, the union reversed its stand. One

Storm over Patsy—Sara Allgood and the title character in the witness box.

owner (Sara Allgood) cannot pay the dog's long-overdue license fee. Subsequent events ruin the political career of the town provost, arouse the dog-loving electorate, and trigger two divorces and a love affair.

"It has become one of the quainter rituals of the Theatre Guild to open its season by rushing out onto its 52nd Street stage and falling flat upon its annually astonished face." *New York Journal-American* critic John Anderson might have been putting it more bluntly than necessary that October morning in 1937, but his point needed to be made; for years, and with very few exceptions, the Guild had begun its season badly. In this instance the choice was *To Quito and Back,* in which playwright Ben Hecht had written the role of an eminent novelist in what observers discerned to be either an autobiographical or wish-fulfillment fashion. The author leaves his wife to run off to Ecuador with a girl who, wrongly, expects him to get a divorce and marry her. They discuss

To Quito and Back—Sylvia Sidney holds Leslie Banks at point. *Vandamm photograph.*

condition, however, was that Livesey could not appear in any other American production for a year; the usual limitation was only six months.

Among critics, *Storm over Patsy* invited mild and indulgent approval up to the third act, which played better than the other two, and the company came in for some kind words such as these from the distinguished Stark Young of *The New Republic:*

Under Mr. Philip Moeller's direction the players are very delightfully together. They all seem to enjoy themselves and to be reaching after the laurels of character acting—no harm in that. You get the sense of nice people there behind the footlights, people too used to the amenities to be overanxious, and too pleasantly nurtured in this world to be hard-driven. The final result is not unlike certain situations in life; you are not bothered about the crux of events because you enjoy the company of the agents involved.

The crux of events is the threatened execution of a mongrel dog named Patsy because its

To Quito and Back—Walter N. Greaza appeared in Ben Hecht's semiautobiographical drama. *Talbot photograph.*

this and other matters at some length, after which he goes off and gets himself killed in the lost cause of General Zamiano's communist revolution. While most critics blamed Hecht for the play's ineptitude, one thought that Sylvia Sidney, as the girl, was "curiously out of it all," and others suspected Philip Moeller's direction was either confused or not sufficiently dynamic. Leslie Banks was cast as the novelist.

Adapting a famous novel for the stage always seems like such a good idea, but for a variety of sometimes obscure reasons, it seldom works. This was to be the case with Flaubert's *Madame Bovary* in the version which brought it to the Broadhurst Theatre early in the Guild's twentieth season. The French dramatization by Gaston Baty had been translated, adapted, and directed by Benn W. Levy as a vehicle for his wife, actress Constance Cummings, who had made about thirty motion pictures and scored a success with *Accent on Youth* on the New York stage in 1934–1935.

In a literal sense, at least, Levy's production detailed the sordid events in Emma's life, through sixteen explicit episodes. What it lacked was the Flaubert style, which alone sets that story apart from countless other accounts of ambitious young women, and without that style, there was insufficient reason for doing it. Better to read the book. At least, there was Miss Cummings' delineation of Emma, which won praise as a well-sustained tour de force and as the finest performance of her career. Lee Simonson's stunning costumes and sets were further compensations.

It was about time—if not long overdue—for the Guild to come up with a strong contender and they found it in *Amphitryon 38*, which was quality all down the line. Jean Giraudoux had written it, Sam Behrman had prepared the English adaptation, and the Lunts not only starred in it but conceived and supervised this production. It got rave reviews in San Francisco, where it opened, and in engagements across the country; in New York the press comment wasn't quite that glowing but was still enthusiastic. Bretaigne Windust directed the play. It also served to introduce the Lunt and Fontanne Acting Company, which developed a repertory.

Probably the oldest play the Guild had yet staged, it originated about 186 B.C. as *Amphitruo*, one of twenty extant comedies by the Roman playwright Titus Maccius Plautus (more recently, *A*

Madame Bovary—Constance Cummings as Emma Bovary. *Vandamm photograph.*

Madame Bovary—Constance Cummings and Eric Portman.

Madame Bovary—Ernest Cossart. *Vandamm photograph.*

Amphitryon 38—Alfred Lunt as Jupiter and Richard Whorf as Mercury plot a bit of mortal dalliance in the comedy adapted from a Roman diversion by Plautus. *Vandamm photograph.*

Amphitryon 38—Alfred Lunt as Jupiter in mortal guise and Lynn Fontanne as the earth lady he has come to seduce. *Vandamm photograph.*

Amphitryon 38—Sydney Greenstreet sounds the call. *Vandamm photograph.*

Amphitryon 38—Richard Whorf as Mercury. *Vandamm photograph.*

Funny Thing Happened on the Way to the Forum revived his name in the living theatre). Later the same story was retold by Rotrou in 1638, Molière in 1668, Dryden in 1690, and Von Kleist in 1807; Giraudoux estimated that there had been thirty-seven versions before his, which is why he named it *Amphitryon 38.*

While the hero Amphitryon is away at war, Jupiter makes the night extra long, so he can spend it in bed with the beautiful and staunchly faithful Alcumena (Alcmena), wife of Amphitryon, whose body the god assumes to pull off the deception. Giraudoux' piquant touch was to make their conversation about lovemaking rather than triumphs in battle. As Jupiter boasts of his exploits, Alcmena innocently puts him down by reminding him of other nights even more exciting and enjoyable. Not incidentally, Hercules was born of this union of god and mortal. George Jean Nathan estimated that the number of versions of the legend on stage was more like fifty or one hundred than thirty-eight; at any event, another was added in 1950 with the heavy-handed musical adaptation titled *Out of this World.*

Joseph Wood Krutch, writing in *The Nation,* paid a well-worded tribute to the stars and the playwright:

> Incidentally, also, it should be remarked that the whole business of parodying gently the daily life of the Greeks is managed with delicate moderation and that Mr. Lunt and Miss Fontanne have never been better suited than in these roles which exploit the most distinctive of their talents—that for the kind of acting which involves an almost imperceptible wink to the audience and which establishes what was called long ago the paradox of the comedian. Neither should one fail to remark that Richard Whorf as Mercury is almost as good in much the same way. But *Amphitryon 38* is more than a lark. Behind the wit and the mere spoofing alike lie the Frenchman's profound conviction that the charm of variety in love is a mystery at least as important and inexhaustible as any suggested by metaphysics or theology. If the gods themselves seek erotic adventures, that does not imply that the gods are trivial, but only that amorous curiosity is, after all, very nearly godlike.

The hypothetical next world war, which in reality was getting closer and closer, was the subject of Sidney Howard's *The Ghost of Yankee Doodle,* which arrived at the Guild Theatre in New York on November 22, 1937. A family of decent liberals, who lost a son and brother in World War I, try earnestly to keep out of the next one. But one member of the family must countenance the sale of munitions to Japan in order to keep his own business solvent, another must face the fact that pro and con war papers are selling better than the one he edits, and a daughter in love with a young intellectual is swept off her feet by a war hero. Performances by such as Ethel Barrymore and Dudley Digges were not enough to infuse a drifting and clouded drama with any semblance of life, despite the good sense of its message.

S. N. Behrman's *Wine of Choice* was ill-fated from its out-of-town beginnings. It had been a mistake to cast the English actor Leslie Banks, complete with his British accent, as a senator from New Mexico. A sarcastic newspaperman was enacted by Alexander Woollcott, and Miriam Hopkins was the girl. No one was happy with the play, and the day-to-day revisions of the script didn't help. Eventually Miss Hopkins quit in

The Ghost of Yankee Doodle—Ethel Barrymore consoles Dudley Digges. *Vandamm photograph.*

Wine of Choice—Leslie Banks, Claudia Morgan, and Alexander Woollcott. *Vandamm photograph.*

*Wine of Choice—*Leslie Banks. *Vandamm photograph.*

*Wine of Choice—*Alexander Woollcott. *Vandamm photograph.*

Pittsburgh, being replaced by Claudia Morgan, and director Philip Moeller gave up in Philadelphia, where Herman Shumlin agreed to do the job. The play made it into New York, but lasted only a few weeks. It was far from the best of Behrman.

Chekhov's *The Sea Gull,* in March of 1938, was the fourth production of this superb Russian drama in New York, this time with Lynn Fontanne, Uta Hagen, Margaret Webster, Alfred Lunt, and Richard Whorf, in a translation prepared by Stark Young. Langner had been involved with the Washington Square Players production in 1916. The Guild's production failed to stir great enthusiasm; one unenlightened reviewer (Sidney B. Whipple of the *New York World-Telegram*) blamed it on a "dull play." Others were aware either of a lack of the necessary ensemble playing, despite the individual brilliance throughout the cast, or the fact that the Lunts seemed to give only a surface reading. Quite probably no one, including director Robert Milton, approached it as Chekhov must be approached —with the awareness that the subtext, rather than the text, is the heart of the drama. In Chekhov

an audience must be alert not just to what is said, but what is strategically left unsaid; what is implied.

A political satire and spoof on the New Deal was *Washington Jitters,* by John Boruff and Walter Hart, which originally was prepared just for Guild subscribers but later was opened to the public. It was based on a novel by Dalton Trumbo, about a sign painter who, through a series of accidents, becomes the head of a government bureau. George Jean Nathan was quick to recognize the theme and plot as being the same as Gogol's *The Inspector General,* and to note that neither of the playwrights was a Gogol. Wolcott Gibbs of *The New Yorker* found it "as dismal and irritating a way to spend an evening as you can find this side of picking oakum."

Autumn of 1938 was a threshold of the future in more ways than most people suspected. Some of the forthcoming changes were obvious. Across the East River from Manhattan, the giant steel skeletons of the Trylon and the Perisphere were rising into the sky, soon to become the symbols of the New York World's Fair, opening

The Sea Gull—Uta Hagen as Nina, Richard Whorf as Constantine. *Vandamm photograph.*

The Sea Gull—Lynn Fontanne as Madame Trepleff, Alfred Lunt as the writer Boris Trigorin.

Washington Jitters—Fred Stewart portrayed a sign painter who accidentally becomes head of a government bureau in Washington. His companion in the boudoir just above is Helen Shields.

the following year. The *Playbill*, with the blithe inaccuracy which has been its hallmark up to the present, described the Fair site as being "not more than a stone's throw from Broadway," without specifying whom they might find to hurl a stone that far. But there were more profound changes afoot—changes which were to give the Guild an object lesson which apparently cannot be repeated too often. This was that the theatre is affected, often to an overpowering degree, by circumstances well outside the theatre. Consider the case of *Dame Nature*, which opened the twenty-first season.

The story is quite charming, even if it is not as unconventional as it was then. Leonie Perrot, a fifteen-year-old girl, operates a stationery store near a school. She becomes friendly with Paul, a pupil who is about her age and whose home situation is anything but happy; his mother keeps him in short pants to enhance her own aspect of youth, and both parents use him as an excuse for staying together even though they have ceased to care about their marriage. Eventually the teen-agers are intimate, and Leonie has a baby. Both take parenthood seriously, which forms an amusing and rather touching contrast with their actual innocence and very young attitudes. As might be guessed, the affair jolts Paul's parents, who do learn from it that they might be happier

by shifting their attention from themselves to the very young couple and their unexpected grandchild.

Written by André Birabeau and first staged with the title *L'Illustration* in Paris in 1938, *Dame Nature* was translated into English by Patricia Collinge and produced successfully in the summer of 1938 at Langner's Westport Country Playhouse. Both the French and English versions managed to retain the delicacy, both in humor and feeling, to keep the play amusing and touching without descending into the sentimentality which might have afflicted it in less fortunate circumstances. Worthington Miner directed the production, with settings by Norris Houghton, and the opening marked the Broadway debut of Montgomery Clift as the lad, with Jessie Royce Landis and Onslow Stevens as his parents, and Lois Hall as the girl.

Here, obviously, were all the ingredients for at least a moderate success. *Dame Nature* opened to mixed reviews, though with enough good comment to sustain an advertising campaign, and conceivably the play might have enjoyed a reasonable run. However, opening night was September 26, 1938. About the time the audience was gathering, news was breaking that Adolf Hitler had invaded Czechoslovakia. At intermissions and after the opening night performance, the audience could see the catastrophic news flashed on *The New York Times* building's electric sign at Times Square.

Langner felt that this accounted for the quick fold of what he admitted was, despite its great appeal at Westport, "our insubstantial comedy," and no one can say for sure what might have happened to it if war had not appeared on the horizon at that moment. Certainly the invasion of Czechoslovakia, and all that ensued, accounted for massive changes in our attitudes, and quite possibly the fate of *Dame Nature*—unimportant as that might have been either to the theatre or to history—signaled those changes. This does not mean that the move into World War II was instantly sobering, though it well might have been. Audiences during the next seven tumultuous years turned to comedy as an escape whenever they could, but it was not the same kind of comedy or escape which had sufficed before. Urgency entered into the theatre as it was entering into life. The gentle, discursive, or delicately symbolic play had a hard way to go against the reality which surrounded it. These were not alterations in public

Dame Nature—Montgomery Clift and Lois Hall portrayed two teen-agers who have a baby, and Morgan James is their friend. *Vandamm photograph.*

Dame Nature—Morgan James and Montgomery Clift entertain the latter's baby. *Vandamm photograph.*

Dame Nature—Onslow Stevens and Jessie Royce Landis are the parents who persist in thinking of their son (Clift) as a child, though he's already become a father. *Vandamm photograph.*

attitude which could be instantly and accurately card-indexed, with the result that for quite a while producers—including the Guild—had trouble finding the fare which was right for the times, at least by box-office standards. They did sense, almost immediately, that something quite deep was changing in the public tastes, but if they weren't sure what it was, neither was the public. One thing was obvious: a great deal of theatre which had proved serviceable enough as America was climbing out of the Depression suddenly seemed old hat. Actually, a decade was to pass before the massive alterations in our social, political, psychological, and esthetic attitudes were to manifest themselves in the American drama, as with Arthur Miller's *All My Sons* and *Death of a Salesman*, though even these were to be quickly superseded by more corrosively unsettling plays.

This effect of the world outside the theatre

on the theatre itself was noted the following February by New York *Daily News* critic Burns Mantle in his review of the Guild's treatment of Stefan Zweig's *Jeremiah:*

"That audience response is likely to be measured and subdued will be due to the temper of the times and to no fault of the Guild. Nor of Stefan Zweig, the author. The drama of lamentations has a hard row to hoe in a time of general lamentations."

Zweig had written his brooding drama in 1917, when the world was trapped in the stalemate of that grim war, though the Germany of that time was considerably different from Hitler's Germany. At least, a Leipzig firm published the play, with its anti-war message, while the Fatherland was at war; two decades later censorship would have permitted nothing so enlightened. The new acting version had been prepared by the eminent theatre

Jeremiah—Kent Smith as the prophet and Effie Shannon as his mother.

Jeremiah—Arthur Byron. *Vandamm photograph.*

scholar, John Gassner, who had recently joined the Guild as its dramaturge—play-reader and critic-in-residence—in collaboration with Worthington Miner, who directed. They used a translation into English by Eden and Cedal Paul, and Kent Smith played the title role. Zweig, who hated war, uses the prophet Jeremiah to give eloquence to his protest. Jeremiah opposes the mob seeking a war against Nebuchadnezzar and holds out later in the face of defeat against the siege that follows. The people defy and desert him, and he is tortured by King Zedekiah, whereupon the prophet curses God, only to return to his redeeming faith at the end of the drama.

Richard Watts, Jr., of the *New York Herald Tribune,* among other critics, noted that high purpose was not enough to sustain *Jeremiah,* summing it up as "a stuffy, long-winded and ostentatious drama." He also wrote:

It is, I am sure, a lofty and dignified narrative, filled with a valuable lesson for all of us and replete with significance for those who will hear. Unfortunately, I must remain among the groundlings. There is earnestness and a high idealism about *Jeremiah* and the Guild has cast and set it with the proper regard for its virtues. Nevertheless, it remains a verbose and ponderous play, overrun with a pompous air of profundity and bowed down under the weight of its elocutionary excesses.

Nor do I think that its message to the effect that war takes its cruel toll of those who bring it about is as valuable to us as it might be in other quarters.

Zweig's bitterness against the human destruction wrought by his own nation in the two wars eventually destroyed him. In Brazil not long after, and before the Allied forces halted the German offensive, he and his wife committed suicide.

Actually, *Jeremiah* was the Guild's third undertaking that season. In cooperation with Herman Shumlin they had staged Thornton Wilder's *The Merchant of Yonkers,* opening in Boston December 12, 1938, before coming to New York on December 28 for a run of about thirty-nine performances, with Jane Cowl and June Walker in the principal feminine roles. While the rather showy and laggard production by Max Reinhardt isn't significant, the play itself is, in terms of its subsequent history. In 1954, Wilder offered the play again, this time with a new title—*The Matchmaker*—at the Edinburgh Festival, with Ruth Gordon in the title role, and brought it to New York, in 1955, where it became a solid hit and later a successful film. The following decade saw it transformed once again, this time into one of the most successful musicals of all time, *Hello, Dolly!*

Financially, the 1938–1939 season had been disastrous for the Guild to this point, and with the expensive failure of *Jeremiah* they were

$60,000 in debt. So Theresa Helburn listened carefully that spring when playwright Philip Barry phoned to say he'd been chatting with Katharine Hepburn about appearing in a new comedy he was writing. Barry and Miss Hepburn had met when she starred with Cary Grant in a film version of his *Holiday,* and they had talked then about the possibility of his writing a play for her.

Miss Hepburn, for her part, was ready to return to the stage, having managed to offend Hollywood by her blithe irreverence toward its moguls and its strange standards, also having earned the epithet of "box-office poison." She had been crucified repeatedly in interviews, by refusing to take the whole Hollywood posture seriously. As a result, as Douglas Gilbert noted in the *World-Telegram* on her return to New York, she was the victim of some of the most atrocious publicity ever written by man or beast.

> I don't blame them—it's the custom. But I think it is wrong, and I never did cooperate. The publicity people must have loathed my guts. If it's done me in, it's done me in.
>
> I suffered the most idiotic interviews, until I stopped them. They'd ask me the most personal questions, and I'd answer them idiotically, thinking they'd understand. "Was I married and who was my husband, and have I any children?" and I used to say, "Sure, I have had four husbands and I have seven children—all colored." And they would print it.
>
> I went out there on a six-year contract for RKO. It was too long. So I bought my contract back. I still had two pictures to make. I made a lot of money, but in Hollywood you get 9,000,000 times what you are worth. I was never a great draw. I was overpaid.

Her return to the stage was felicitous indeed. Philadelphia, where *The Philadelphia Story* opened prior to its New York engagement, was ecstatic. "To put it in a palindrome," announced Linton Martin of the *Inquirer* the next morning, "it's a WOW!" J. H. Keene in the *Philadelphia Daily News* described the comedy as "one of the smartest and wittiest collections of stage fireworks touched off in or about these parts in too long a time, and abetted by some extraordinarily fruity performances in the principal characterizations, it is destined to become a public riot of no mean proportions."

Set on Philadelphia's socially select Main

The Philadelphia Story—Philip Barry's sophisticated comedy provided a triumphant vehicle for Katharine Hepburn, here with Frank Fenton.

The Philadelphia Story—Katharine Hepburn and Joseph Cotten.

The Philadelphia Story—Shirley Booth and Van Heflin.

Line, the play offered Katy as Tracy Lord, a spoiled and pampered debutante about to launch her second marriage, this time to a social nonentity who had worked himself up from the coal mines to a position where he could guide the Lord family fortunes. Her father is having an affair with a Russian dancer, and her mother is reminded from time to time of her possibly gamey early life in Germantown. A brother, a writer, and a girl photographer for a scandal magazine also enter the domestic scene. Using innuendo and quick thrusts of wit, Barry milked more laughter out of this admixture of characters than anyone else might have with farce. Miss Hepburn was an utter delight, and enjoyed the talents of an able supporting company which included Joseph Cotten as her first husband, Van Heflin as the writer, Frank Fenton as the husband-elect, also Shirley Booth, Forrest Orr, Lenore Lonergan, Dan Tobin, Vera Allen, and Nicholas Joy.

Following the March 28, 1939, opening at the Shubert Theatre in New York, Brooks Atkinson wrote:

> Certainly Mr. Barry has written Miss Hepburn's ideal part. It has whisked away the monotony and reserve that have kept her acting in the past within a very small compass. As the daughter of the rich she plays with grace, jauntiness and warmth—moving across the stage like one who is liberated from self-consciousness and taking a pleasure in acting that the audience can share. . . . For this is an occasion that deserves appreciation. When the Theatre Guild, Miss Hepburn and Mr. Barry are in top form at the same time, all is for the best in the best of all possible Broadways. Although the comedy of manners has almost been lost in the dark whirl of world affairs, it is still a source of unholy delight when experts write, act and produce it.

It would be unfair to praise Barry and Miss Hepburn as well as producers Helburn and Langner without also crediting the deft direction by Robert B. Sinclair, and the appropriately cheery setting of Robert Edmond Jones. *The Philadelphia Story* pulled the Guild out of the hole, paying off its accumulated indebtedness and bankrolling a number of productions to come. It played a total of three years, in New York, then on the road, finally closing after the third production in the Quaker City for which it was named.

VII
1939-1948

SIMPLICITY is an abiding virtue in the theatre, as it is in life, and it had much to do with the appeal of the plays by William Saroyan, with whom the Guild found itself involved in the spring of 1939, and twice more in the season that followed. His *My Heart's in the Highlands* was produced that April by the Group Theatre, then taken over by the Guild, for a total of forty-three performances. It is a blissfully uncomplicated little play, dealing with an old, near-bankrupt storekeeper near Fresno, California, who gives credit to a self-declared poet and his son. They in turn take in a trumpet-playing Shakespearean actor. At the end, the actor dies, the little grocery story fails, and the poet and his son are evicted. While some critics deplored its lack of formal structure, others valued it for the warmth and validity of its human values. The playwright himself said:

> The message of the play is the simplest and earliest message of man to man: For the love of God, be alive; be grateful for the miracle of possessing substance, of being able to draw energy from the great source of energy, and for the instinct to approach danger and death with pride, humor and humbleness. . . . As for the moral of the play, it is the very simplest: It is better to be poor and alive than rich and dead. In short, it is better to be a good human being than a bad one. P.S. The idea is not original with me. It is simply that it got displaced two or three years ago.

The thirty-one-year-old Saroyan made enough of an impression with his first play to have it noted as one of the season's best by several of the New York drama critics.

Following the agreeable association with

My Heart's in the Highlands, Langner was receptive that summer when Eddie Dowling, an ex-hoofer who had prospered in the theatre, showed him a new Saroyan script, *The Time of Your Life,* which Dowling wanted to produce in association with the Guild, and with himself in a starring role and Julie Haydon in the feminine lead. Langner and Theresa Helburn agreed to participate and engaged Bobby Lewis to direct. But the play was elusive, and its New Haven opening was chaotic; neither critics nor audience knew just what was going on. Lewis resigned as director the following day, to be succeeded jointly by Langner, Dowling, and Saroyan, who had just arrived from the West Coast. Three days later they opened in Boston, having built an entire new set in the meantime and decided that eight of the cast were not acceptable in their roles; the company changes continued for the next couple of weeks. To add to their problems, Saroyan never had directed a play before, and didn't know how to tell the actors what he wanted, even though he usually knew himself. To add to the friction, Armenian friends of Saroyan began arriving from the West Coast, to be added to the cast. While all this was going on, drama critic George Jean Nathan, who considers himself the discoverer of Saroyan, wrote a piece blaming all the play's tryout troubles on the Guild and predicting its failure when it opened in New York. In Boston, the critics generally rejected it, except for Elliot Norton. who would drop in at rehearsals and make constructive suggestions. If ever a play was directed by committee, this was the one. Meanwhile, Langner and Miss Helburn were making their own alterations and additions where they could. These included bringing in William

The Time of Your Life—playwright William Saroyan confers with actors Eddie Dowling as Joe, Gene Kelly as Harry. *Vandamm photograph.*

The Time of Your Life—Edward Andrews as Tom, Julie Haydon as Kitty, and Eddie Dowling as Joe. *Vandamm photograph.*

The Time of Your Life—playwright William Saroyan (right) with producers Lawrence Langner and Theresa Helburn. *Vandamm photograph.*

The Time of Your Life—William Bendix as Krupp, Tom Tully as McCarthy.

Bendix as the policeman, and, at the suggestion of Lawrence and Armina Langner, using a young dancer named Gene Kelly who had worked for them in the summer theatre in Westport. Miss Helburn brought in another youngster, Celeste Holm, who also launched a distinguished career with this enterprise.

Rehearsals grew progressively more shattering until Langner told Saroyan to get out of the theatre (a compromise was reached by which the author could sit in the orchestra) and Saroyan, in turn, insisted—correctly, as things turned out—that the play absolutely had to have a pinball machine for its climax. Unable to buy a suitable one, Langner had a modelmaker build the famous one which flashed red, white, and blue lights, made all sorts of noises, and waved an American flag at the climactic moment. Saroyan still didn't know how to end the play; it was Philip Barry, in Boston for a visit with the Langners and Miss Helburn, who suggested that Dowling simply rise from his chair, where he'd been sitting practically all evening, walk across the stage, and wave good-bye.

Despite all these troubles and more, *The Time of Your Life* opened to an admiring press, and became the first play to win both the New York Drama Critics Award and the Pulitzer Prize. The New York premiere on October 25, 1939, launched a run of 185 performances. The play was done in London immediately following World War II. Set in a saloon and "entertainment palace" on the San Francisco waterfront, Saroyan's very casual play sort of mills around the character named Joe (Dowling), who drinks champagne, and who makes a dancing doll to divert his prostitute friend Kitty (Miss Haydon) from depressing thoughts about her profession. Also in the bar are Harry the tap dancer (Kelly), an eternally hopeful pinball-machine player, an Arab who plays harmonica, a Negro pianist, and an old Westerner who tells stories, not all of which he finishes. The play achieves its climax after Blick, of the vice squad, torments Kitty and is shot by the old Westerner. The pinball machine hits the jackpot and lights up with the words "American Destiny," and the play comes to a close.

Even the majority of critics who were favorably impressed admitted that they didn't quite understand all that was happening on the stage of the Booth Theatre; Walter Winchell, in the minority, couldn't stand the play, but gave it good publicity by writing so frequently about how much he hated it. N. Buchwald, writing in the *Jewish Morning Freiheit*, seemed to pinpoint Saroyan's essence better than anyone else:

The Time of Your Life is an extraordinary

play. It is full of drama and comedy from beginning to end, yet isn't a drama or a comedy. In fact, it is not a planned dramatic production, rather a free improvisation of a writer, who doesn't work from a plan and who has no basic idea. Whatever strikes him at the moment of playful inspiration, he rolls out on the stage. He brings out a series of extraordinary, different persons who look for peace in a saloon somewhere in San Francisco. Each person is a world in himself, and altogether they create the impression of thrilling, throbbing life. . . . Through every person and their struggles runs one basic thought: it is good to live. The whole "philosophy" of Saroyan's play could be summed up in the simple Jewish saying: "One could live if he were permitted to."

The season continued with Paul Osborn's *Morning's at Seven,* which did not make an indelible impression on Broadway but eventually became a mainstay of community theatre around the country. Ernest Hemingway's *The Fifth Col-*

umn, in an acting version by Benjamin Glazer, had the virtue of timeliness to commend it, though it does not appear as strong in retrospect. The title refers to the snipers behind the lines who damage every effort for a cause. Franchot Tone portrayed an American newspaper correspondent in Spain during the Civil War, with Lee J. Cobb as a Nazi-hating German who is there to fight Fascism. A romance between Tone and an American girl in the room next door was entertaining enough, with Tone being persuasive and Katherine Locke being less than unwilling, but not everyone felt it should have occupied so much time in a drama dealing with the struggle against Franco and his Fascists. Admitting that *The Fifth Column* was an uneven play, Brooks Atkinson pointed out that:

It manages to make a statement that is always impressive and sometimes poignant or shattering. The callous tone of the writing is merely the neuroticism of an author whose emotions are on edge. Mr. Hemingway has

The Fifth Column—Spain during the Civil War is the setting for Hemingway's story in which Lee J. Cobb portrayed an anti-Nazi German and Franchot Tone an American correspondent.

got under the skin of a living subject, and turned burning indignation into a courageous declaration of principle.

Theoretically, two Pulitzer Prizes for drama cannot be awarded in one season, but the Guild took its second with the April 29, 1940, opening of Robert E. Sherwood's *There Shall Be No Night*. Actually, it earned the prize for the 1940–1941 season, despite its earlier opening; *The Time of Your Life* had won for 1939–1940.

Before they became involved in *There Shall Be No Night,* which is set in Helsinki, Finland, at the time of the Russian invasion of that little nation, Alfred Lunt and Lynn Fontanne had been touring in *The Taming of the Shrew* for Finnish relief, so their participation was nothing less than passionate. Sherwood had originally titled the play *Revelation,* and the present title is from the last book of the New Testament, chapter 22: "And they shall see his face, and his name shall be in their foreheads. And there shall be no night there; and they need

The Fifth Column—Katherine Locke and Franchot Tone. *Vandamm photograph.*

There Shall Be No Night—Alfred Lunt, Richard Whorf, Lynn Fontanne, Elisabeth Fraser, Sydney Greenstreet, and Montgomery Clift. *Vandamm photograph.*

Playwright Robert Sherwood's successes for the Theatre Guild included *Reunion in Vienna, Idiot's Delight,* and *There Shall Be No Night. Pach photograph.*

no candle, neither light of the sun; for the Lord God giveth them light: and they shall reign for ever and ever." Bear in mind that what we think of as history now was actually happening then; a play about Finland's brave attempt to hold on to its independence had an immediacy and urgency that was bound to heighten the reactions of its viewers. "Mr. Sherwood," wrote John Mason Brown, "has succeeded as no other dramatist heard from in this country has succeeded in dealing with the topical alarms and abiding implications of Europe's fever chart."

Alfred Lunt portrayed the Nobel Prize-winning neurologist who believes the Russian people don't want to fight. Only after his son is killed on a patrol does he accept the inevitability of going to war for a cause—a war which he and his compatriots are bound to lose. Miss Fontanne appeared as his wife, with Montgomery Clift as their son. The strong cast also included Richard Whorf (who also designed the settings), Sydney Greenstreet, Maurice Colbourne, Thomas Gomez, Phyllis Thaxter, and Elizabeth Fraser. Lunt directed the production, which was a joint undertaking of the Playwrights' Company and the Theatre Guild.

The season drew toward its close with

another Saroyan play, *Love's Old Sweet Song,* an engaging theatre piece which enjoyed the talents of Walter Huston and Jessie Royce Landis. Again the Guild had Eddie Dowling as its co-producer, with Dowling and Saroyan as directors. The Philadelphia tryouts were not encouraging until Langner suggested that it be changed from three acts to two—a simple expedient which doesn't always work but did in this instance. However, when the company got to New York, Saroyan insisted that it should be in three, and following a long and impassioned debate, he prevailed. That meant it opened with a weak second act, and was attacked accordingly by most of the critics. The next day Saroyan phoned Langner to ask that it be restored to the two-act form, but by that time the unfavorable reviews were in print and the damage was done.

One of the affirmative critical votes came from Joseph T. Shipley writing in *The New Leader* of "Saroyan at his flamboyant best," and adding: *"Love's Old Sweet Song* is the first native American surrealist drama; but it brings an old, a universal message mankind must learn to heed." He approved of Saroyan's stand in the play—that the best way to take life is lying down.

"The Broadway wags are calling Helen Hayes's *Twelfth Night* revival 'all this and Evans too,' " quipped columnist Danton Walker in the New York *Daily News* in the fall of 1940, as the Theatre Guild was preparing its first production of its twenty-third season. The pun was on Rachel Field's current popular novel, *All This and Heaven Too,* and the specific reference was to the fact that Maurice Evans was to play Malvolio to Miss Hayes's Viola in the Shakespearean comedy of mistaken identities.

It was a singularly happy association—these two with each other, both of them with director Margaret Webster, and all with the Bard of Avon. It was Miss Hayes's Broadway debut as a Shakespearean actress, and her audiences—not to mention the critics—were delighted. Stewart Chaney designed the settings and costumes, Paul Bowles added appropriately lilting music, and the cast was well selected in just about all roles. Nevertheless, Brooks Atkinson, after carefully quoting the other critics' praise of Miss Hayes in an article he wrote shortly after the November 19 opening, took a dissenting view, meanwhile admitting that he favored Jane Cowl's less amusing but more beautifully conceived and spoken Viola of ten years before.

Love's Old Sweet Song—Walter Huston was a pitchman and Jessie Royce Landis a small-town old maid in the second Saroyan play of the Guild's twenty-second season.

Twelfth Night—Helen Hayes as Viola, Alex Courtnay as Sebastian.

Twelfth Night—Helen Hayes, director Margaret Webster, and Maurice Evans.

Twelfth Night—an informal shot of Mr. and Mrs. Charles MacArthur (Helen Hayes). *Vandamm photograph.*

Twelfth Night—Gilbert Miller was co-producer with the Theatre Guild. *Vandamm photograph.*

Her [Miss Cowl's] Viola suggested the high breeding to which Shakespeare makes more than one reference in the lines. This is what I miss in the lack-luster acting of Miss Hayes. . . . Her reading of the lines is flat. She speaks them as though she were making a virtue of her conversational prose style.

Gilbert Miller was co-producer with the Guild in *Twelfth Night;* he had been Miss Hayes's manager in the highly successful *Victoria Regina.* The Shakespearean comedy ran for 129 performances in New York, followed by seventeen equally felicitous weeks on tour.

That same season three plays were given tryouts on the road, but were not brought to New York. The most auspicious of these was a first full-length drama by Tennessee Williams, *Battle of Angels.* Williams had been introduced to Langner by John Gassner, who had succeeded Harold Clurman as the Guild's play-reader a decade earlier. He had been studying at the New School play-wrighting seminar, which was supervised by Gassner and Theresa Helburn. The play was flawed, but indicated enough quality to warrant Langner's inviting Williams to stay at his farm while rewriting it. Southern in its setting and candid in its situations, it contrasted the decadence of the old Southern families against the sexual vigor of the Cajuns. Margaret Webster agreed to direct it, and Miriam Hopkins was to interpret its principal

Battle of Angels—Miriam Hopkins starred in this first Tennessee Williams play, which ran into censorship problems in Boston. The play which also needed rewriting was not brought into New York. Fifteen years later it did make it to Broadway, under different management, as *Orpheus Descending.*

role, but the gulf between Miss Hopkins' concept of theatre and Williams' was one not likely to be bridged. Also, Boston, where it opened, laughed at the wrong places, and decided that some of its lines needed censoring. Even the Guild subscribers protested the frankness of speech, which prompted Langner and Miss Helburn to defend their selection on the grounds that it did not violate good taste. In a letter to the Boston members they wrote:

> We chose to produce *Battle of Angels* because we felt the young author has genuine poetic gifts and an interesting insight into a particular American scene. The treatment of the religious obsession of one of the characters, which sprang from frustration, did not justify, in our opinion, the censor's action. It was, we felt, a sincere and honest attempt to present a true psychological picture. . . . *The Battle of Angels* turned out badly but who knows whether the next one by the same author may not prove a success?

Williams, however, elected to continue his career with other managements, which staged his *The Glass Menagerie* and *A Streetcar Named Desire* a few years later. Coincidentally, the other most talented new writer of that decade also had been a protégé of Terry Helburn and John Gassner, but chose to offer his first mature plays to other producers. This was Arthur Miller. The Guild offered to stage his *All My Sons* and was rejected; *Death of a Salesman* was not even submitted to the Theatre Guild.

The other two plays staged out of town that season but not in New York were *Hope for a Harvest,* by Sophie Treadwell, and *Somewhere in France,* by Carl Zuckmayer and Fritz Kortner. Miss Treadwell's play did come into Manhattan the following year, however. The New York series, following *Twelfth Night,* included a Ferenc Molnár play, *Delicate Story,* starring Edna Best; Lynn Riggs's *The Cream in the Well;* and Philip Barry's *Liberty Jones,* a play with music featuring John Beal and Nancy Coleman.

The Guild learned another bitter lesson about the caprices of public taste when they revived their lauded production of Eugene O'Neill's *Ah, Wilderness!* to begin the season of 1941–1942. Film actor Harry Carey played the role which George M. Cohan had originated and did it well; the play, as directed by Eva Le Gallienne, got a good press. Despite this, and despite a "popular

Liberty Jones—Philip Barry's play with music had roles for John Beal, Nancy Coleman, Tom Ewell, and Katherine Squire. *Vandamm photograph.*

Liberty Jones—John Beal and Nancy Coleman. *Vandamm photograph.*

Ah, Wilderness!—in 1941 the Theatre Guild revived this 1933 hit, this time with Tom Tully as Sid Davis and Harry Carey in what had been the George M. Cohan role, as Nat Miller. *Vandamm photograph.*

Ah, Wilderness!—Enid Markey, Tom Tully, and Ann Shoemaker. *Vandamm photograph.*

Candle in the Wind—the Guild co-produced with The Playwrights' Company. Playwright Maxwell Anderson, director Alfred Lunt, and actress Helen Hayes. *Vandamm photograph.*

prices" ticket offering, people just didn't come, and the production failed to make its own expenses.

Equally unprofitable, from the box-office point of view, was Maxwell Anderson's *Candle in the Wind,* produced in concert with the Playwrights' Company, of which Anderson was a member. With Alfred Lunt directing and Helen Hayes starring, it seemed well-omened, but this love story set against Nazi tyranny in occupied France lacked dramatic strength to match the seriousness and timeliness of its message.

It was a shrewd idea to tour Patterson Greene's *Papa Is All* widely before bringing it to New York, because it proved popular in the provinces but crumpled before a barrage of negative comment in Manhattan. Lawrence Langner's feeling about this is indicated in the comprehensive Theatre Guild collection at the Beinecke Rare Book Library at Yale University; the press book on *Papa Is All* is complete with out-of-town notices, which are almost all quite warm and friendly, but contains none of the New York reviews. The comedy about life among the Pennsylvania Dutch was just the wholesome, American family-type entertainment which audiences around the country seemed to enjoy—and, apparently, still do. Jessie Royce Landis, Celeste Holm, and Emmet Rogers drew a generous share of the applause each evening. Subsequently, the play became an enduring favorite for high school and community theatre productions, and it continues to be staged.

Also set in a farmhouse was Sophie Treadwell's *Hope for a Harvest,* which had toured the previous season to good audience and critical response, but which turned off New York critics who seemed to feel that anything "agricultural" was not for them. In indignation, Langner took

Papa Is All—Celeste Holm and Jessie Royce Landis in the comedy which was well received on tour but unfavorably reviewed in New York. *Vandamm photograph.*

Hope for a Harvest—Fredric March and Florence Eldridge. *Vandamm photograph.*

Hope for a Harvest—Alan Reed, Florence Eldridge, and Fredric March. *Vandamm photograph.*

The Rivals—Bobby Clark (right) revealed a new facet of the Sheridan comedy. His antagonist is Donald Burr. *Vandamm photograph.*

ads in the New York newspapers quoting the good comment of out-of-town critics, but this, instead of helping, only hurt the box office more. Miss Treadwell, who had also written *Machinal,* had grown up in a rural area in the San Joaquin Valley of California, where her new play was set, and wrote knowledgeably and sensitively about the problems of mechanization with people who weren't psychologically ready for the machines. Fredric March and Florence Eldridge led the cast.

It was about time for something to bail out the Guild from its accumulated losses of a

fiscally disastrous season, and Richard Brinsley Sheridan's *The Rivals* might have accomplished this if the rest of the production had measured up to Bobby Clark's hilarious performance as Bob Acres; he captured all the reviews, hands down, which didn't set well with Mary Boland who, as Mrs. Malaprop, was generally unfavorably reviewed. Referring to the Guild's concept of *The Rivals,* Louis Kronenberger wrote in *PM:*

> Certainly, it [the Guild] has made decided, not to say strenuous, efforts. It has come up

The Rivals—Bobby Clark, Mary Boland, and Walter Hampden. *Vandamm photograph.*

The Rivals—Helen Ford as Lucy. *Vandamm photograph.*

Yesterday's Magic—Jessica Tandy and Alfred Drake. *Vandamm photograph.*

with a brand-new prologue by Arthur Guiterman. It has larded the play with songs. It has introduced a lot of new business. Indeed, it has made use at one point or another of every style of comedy you can think of—except the right one.

Kronenberger also had harsh things to say about *Yesterday's Magic,* by Emlyn Williams, which concluded that theatre year for the Guild: "Mr. Williams has not only chosen to tell one of the most battered of sentimental stories, but he has shamelessly exploited it right up to the

hilt." Paul Muni played a once-famous actor ruined by drink who attempts a comeback in *King Lear,* of all things. He falls off the wagon on opening night, which prompts his loyal daughter to give up the man she loves in order to spend the rest of her youth taking care of her drunken father. Neither Muni, nor Jessica Tandy as the daughter, nor a youngster named Alfred Drake was able to do much for this sham drama, and it went the way of all too many other Guild shows that lackluster year.

To mark its twenty-fifth birthday, the

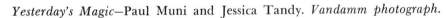

Yesterday's Magic—Paul Muni and Jessica Tandy. *Vandamm photograph.*

Theatre Guild offered two new plays the week of November 8, 1942—*Without Love,* a comedy by Philip Barry starring Katharine Hepburn, and *Mr. Sycamore,* by Ketti Frings, who was to become considerably better known in the theatre a number of years later with her biographical drama about novelist Thomas Wolfe, *Look Homeward, Angel.* Of the first of these, Richard Lockridge noted in the *New York Sun:* "Inadequately explained characters enter and leave as if pulled by strings; about much of it there is a kind of artless abruptness, as if Mr. Barry's political hand did not know what his romantic hand was doing." The playwright's political concern was his belief that Ireland should enter the world conflict on the side of the Allies. Miss Hepburn and Elliott Nugent are the two who, out of earlier unhappiness, decide they don't want love anymore so they marry just for companionship, and you can guess how that turns out. In Miss Frings's *Mr. Sycamore,* a postman (Stuart Erwin) becomes fed up with his human involvement in this world so he turns himself into a tree, which doesn't set entirely well with his wife (Lillian Gish). The play was an adaptation of a short story by Robert Ayre, written in 1907, which in turn was drawn from the Greek legend of Philemon and Baucis, who were granted their wish to die together and were changed into trees. New York could not see Miss Frings's tree for a forest of faults, which, to confuse the metaphor further, the *Journal-American*'s John Anderson found filled with "plenty of corn and plenty of marshmallow." He continued: "Its soggy fantasy becomes a bog, its whimsy turns into a sort of coy idiocy and the whole thing is not only disenchanting but slightly embarrassing."

Around Thanksgiving of 1942 the Guild once again joined forces with the Playwrights' Company to stage S. N. Behrman's *The Pirate,* pairing the delightful and glamorous Lunts. It is interesting to note that this production introduced Lemuel Ayers as a scenic designer and Miles White as a costume designer—a combination which was to show up toward the end of this same season in *Oklahoma!* Alfred Drake, who had come into the Guild circle at the end of the previous year in the ill-fated *Yesterday's Magic,* was to create the role of Curly. Celeste Holm already was well established in the group's productions. Though no one realized it at this particular moment, a

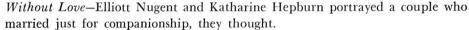

Without Love—Elliott Nugent and Katharine Hepburn portrayed a couple who married just for companionship, they thought.

Without Love—Constance Bennett and Steve Cochran took over the leading roles when the Philip Barry comedy went on tour. *Vandamm photograph.*

Mr. Sycamore—Samuel Leve's setting for Ketti Frings's comedy about a postman who turns into a tree. On stage are Lillian Gish, Russell Collins, Stuart Erwin, and a fourth member of the cast. *Vandamm photograph.*

Without Love—Katharine Hepburn. *Tucker photograph.*

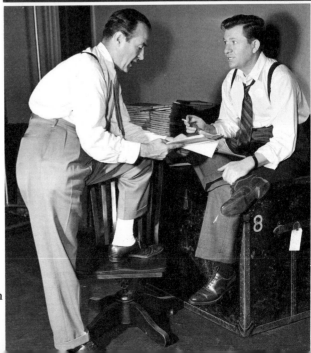

Mr. Sycamore—Stuart Erwin. *Vandamm photograph.*

Mr. Sycamore—director Lester Vail and Stuart Erwin at rehearsal.

The Pirate—once more, the Lunts.

The Pirate—Lemuel Ayers' setting. *Vandamm photograph.*

number of currents, trends, and personalities were converging on a single point in time and in the history of the musical theatre.

Before that moment, however, came the Guild's production of Konstantin Mikhailovich Simonov's staunchly propagandistic drama, *The Russian People,* in an English adaptation by Clifford Odets. Opening at the time when Stalingrad was under siege, the play was performed by more than 200 companies attached to the Red army. It is peopled with almost stock heroic and nonheroic characters who face death without despair, sure that eventually the motherland will triumph over the Nazi invaders—which it did, in fact. The Guild playbill quoted a Russian critic, K. Borisov, on the reaction to the drama of Russian audiences:

> The hearts of the spectators beat faster, and no one is ashamed of his tears. . . . We are not only touched, but intent; we are not only shaken, but filled with hatred of the enemy. . . . "The motherland demands it"—this is the root of all the emotions, deeds, and actions of these people. "The motherland demands it"—this is the law to which their lives, thoughts and feelings are subordinated.

Nevertheless, American critics found it melodramatic and naïve; obviously, the response to a propaganda play depends at least partly on where you stand.

The story of *Oklahoma!* has been told so often that it has become legend in the theatre, yet the facts continue to eclipse any success story which the most fertile imagination might dream up. Its beginnings go back not just to the 1931 Guild production of Lynn Riggs's *Green Grow the Lilacs,* on which it is based, but far beyond—to a tradition of musical theatre which had to be discarded before anything so new and portentous could emerge.

Except on the operatic stage, America had not taken the musical theatre seriously in the twentieth century. It was expected to entertain, which, as a rule, it did in a superficial fashion, and the music was supposed to be singable on your way home. Not even the devotees of that curious though frequently appealing hybrid, the operetta, ever considered that they might be dealing with a legitimate art form or dramatic entity, though they might have surmised—correctly—that some operetta music, as that by Victor Herbert and Franz Lehar, might indeed survive and enjoy an enduring life of its own.

The Russian People—Rudolph Anders is the Nazi officer dining with the mayor (E. A. Krumschmidt) and his wife (Eleonora Mendelssohn) and trying to persuade her to betray three of her friends. *Wide World photograph.*

The Russian People—Clifford Odets, who adapted Simonov's propagandistic drama for the Guild production. *Vandamm photograph.*

So most musicals were in the nature of revues. If there was plot, it was seldom more than enough to lend a sketchy continuity to the proceedings. Characterization was equally offhand, but no one really minded; audiences were not looking for the life force, or subtleties of motivation, or the exploration of human conflict in anything with music. There were a few exceptions—the Guild's production of *Porgy and Bess,* notably, but even this was characterized as "a folk opera" to more or less explain that it was not to be thought of as an ordinary musical. The George Gershwin–Du Bose Heyward–Ira Gershwin work is legitimately opera, of course, but it had enough spoken dialogue to at least suggest a new kind of musical theatre which didn't fit any of the old categories.

Perhaps a more significant event occurred on the night of December 25, 1940, when a "musical comedy" entitled *Pal Joey* opened at the Ethel Barrymore Theatre in New York, produced and directed by George Abbott; the Guild had no connection with this one. It was based on a series of short stories by John O'Hara which had run in *The New Yorker.* It starred young Gene Kelly as a nightclub entertainer who is a thoroughgo-ing heel with women, letting himself be kept by the wealthy Vera (Vivienne Segal) for whom he throws over a sweet, innocent kid (Leila Ernst) who is genuinely in love with him. If any conventional musical had dared to make a hero out of such a character, it at least would have him redeemed by the love of a pure woman at the final curtain. Not *Pal Joey.* He never reforms, and audiences are left to conclude that there are some pretty crummy types around and about. While they might have accepted such an obvious truth in serious drama, they were startled to hear it said with music. The music was mighty good, as written by Richard Rodgers with lyrics by Lorenz Hart; these were the two who had done two editions of *The Garrick Gaieties* for the Guild in 1925 and 1926.

So *Pal Joey* at least put forth the novel idea that musical theatre might be reasonably substantial. Of course, it held to the traditions in a number of ways. With a nightclub setting, it permitted the usual "acts," though even these were better integrated into the story than was customary.

It probably was to the Guild's good fortune that they were relatively inexperienced with musicals, because instead of trying to stick with the established formulas they went ahead on their own, taking what were for the time long, long chances. It was, in bitter truth, a time for gambling: in 1942 they were down to about $30,000 in the bank, following several seasons in which box-office failures outweighed their scattered hits, and perhaps something of an all-or-nothing attitude affected their decisions at this point. It was Theresa Helburn who had the idea of making Lynn Riggs's *Green Grow the Lilacs* into a musical. Some time earlier she and Langner had suggested to Richard Rodgers that he adapt the *Lysistrata* of Aristophanes as a musical, but he didn't care for the idea. He was more receptive, however, to the Riggs play, and discussed it with his long-time collaborator, Lorenz Hart. The lyricist, however, was in poor health and about to leave for Mexico for a rest, but he gave permission to Rodgers to seek another collaborator. Oscar Hammerstein II, who was approached next, was more than agreeable. Not only did he take kindly to working with Rodgers, but he himself had tried to promote a musical version of *Green Grow the Lilacs* some years before, having suggested a collaboration at that time to composer Jerome Kern, who had turned it down.

The play's book and score were completed before the fall of 1942, and the producers set about casting. Alfred Drake, who had appeared in *Yesterday's Magic* the preceding season, had a fine singing voice and the virile good looks to qualify as Curly, the cowboy. Joan Roberts, a clear-voiced soprano who had worked in one of Hammerstein's musicals, became Laurey. These two, with Rodgers and Hammerstein, performed the songs of the show at a number of fund-raising cocktail parties, but investors came into the project only slowly and cautiously. Eventually about $90,-000 was raised—enough to stage a musical then but only a fraction of what the same show would cost today.

While the play was in rehearsal, Miss Helburn and John Gassner, the Guild's play-reader, suggested that a good, rousing ensemble song be added during the second act. The composer and lyricist obligingly came up with "Oklahoma!" The play's opening and its first song ("Oh, What a Beautiful Mornin'!") had come right out of Riggs's stage directions for his play:

> It is a radiant summer morning several years ago, the kind of morning which, en-

Oklahoma!—author and lyricist Oscar Hammerstein II. *Graphic House photograph.*

Oklahoma!—Alfred Drake as Curly, Betty Garde as Aunt Eller, and Joan Roberts as Laurey. *Graphic House photograph.*

Oklahoma!—Howard da Silva as Jud Fry, Alfred Drake as Curly McLain.

veloping the shapes of earth—men, cattle in a meadow, blades of young corn, streams—makes them seem to exist now for the first time, their images giving off a visible golden emanation that is partly true and partly a trick of imagination focusing to keep alive a loveliness that may pass away . . .

The opening ballad and subsequent songs gave the impression that the show was something of a pastorale—"The Surrey with the Fringe on Top," "Many a New Day," "People Will Say We're in Love," spiced with the comic "Kansas City," "I Cain't Say No" and "It's a Scandal." Yet in truth *Oklahoma!* still was, like the original play, a psychological drama. There was Jud, the psychopath who solaced himself with pictures of naked women down in his smokehouse, lusting after Laurey and brooding vengeful murder when she marries Curly. It added the note of menace which the musical needed for contrast, also, and not incidentally, lifting it out of the format of superficial entertainment which had demeaned this kind of theatre in the past. So the truth is that the show had plot, though some reviewers dismissed that aspect of it with the same clichés they

had been applying to musicals over the years.

The staging team was spectacularly talented, though not thought of in terms of musical theatre as much as some of their contemporaries. Rouben Mamoulian, who had shaped *Porgy and Bess,* was brought back to direct. Agnes de Mille prepared the dances; her ballet *Rodeo* had suggested her fitness to do the choreography for *Oklahoma!* Set designer Lemuel Ayers and costumer Miles White also were relatively untrammeled by the standard ways of doing a musical.

One thing these highly individual talents agreed on was that the show, as an entity, should come first. That is, nobody would put in anything which would be competitive with the rest of the production; the idea was not to "stop the show" (though a number of the songs and dances did just that) but to keep it moving. This again was a relatively new concept.

The musical first played to an audience in New Haven, Connecticut, for three nights in mid-March, 1943, with the title *Away We Go!* Eventually that was discarded, as were *Swing Your Lady, Cherokee Strip,* and *Yes-sirree.* The Boston tryout

Oklahoma!—choreographer Agnes de Mille.

went encouragingly, yet not all the seats were sold for the opening performance at the St. James Theatre in New York on March 31, 1943. Even so, it was one of the memorable openings in the history of the American theatre, and the following morning the critics found a variety of ways to say that something quite spectacular had happened. It took a music critic—Olin Downes of the *Times*—to note its deeper significance: "And the thing has style . . . the sum of the piece indicates a direction that American opera of native cast might take in the period before us." While there wasn't much critical dissent, a few of the reviewers were reluctant to give more than condescending approval. "Nothing much in the way of a book," dismissed Louis Kronenberger in *Time* magazine. Stark Young in *The New Republic* observed that it "reminds us at times of a good college show." But they were far outweighed by critics such as Burns Mantle of the New York *Daily News* who, with other superlatives, enthused: "*Oklahoma!* is different—beautifully different."

The show made many reputations and en-

hanced those of the men and women who already were well established in the theatre. Joan McCracken as the girl who falls down, Celeste Holm as Ado Annie, Howard da Silva as the glowering Jud Fry, Joseph Buloff as Ali Hakim the peddler, Katherine Sergava, Marc Platt, and Bambi Linn in The Dream Ballet, and a number of others achieved the brightest and most durable fame in their portrayals.

Oklahoma! proved the most profitable enterprise in the Guild's entire history. It ran for 2,212 performances—five years and nine weeks—at the St. James. Its national company toured for ten and a half years. It was separately produced for USO camp shows overseas. New companies were formed for London, where it broke the Drury Lane Theatre all-time record with 1,548 performances; South Africa, Australia, Denmark, Norway, and France. It became a motion picture in 1955. According to Richard Rodgers, it still is being played somewhere in the world every night. Its earnings were and continue to be prodigious. After about ten years its original investment of

Oklahoma!—Joan McCracken. *Graphic House photograph.*

Oklahoma!—Joseph Buloff as Ali Hakim, Celeste Holm as Ado Annie.

Oklahoma!—The Dream Ballet; the postcard girls.

Oklahoma!—The Dream Ballet; Bambi Linn in the foreground, Katherine Sergava as the bride. *Graphic House photograph.*

Oklahoma!—The Dream Ballet; Marc Platt and Katherine Sergava. *Vandamm photograph.*

Oklahoma!—Katherine Sergava as Laurey in The Dream Ballet. *Graphic House photograph.*

Oklahoma!—the Rodgers and Hammerstein adaptation of Lynn Riggs's *Green Grow the Lilacs* became the greatest box-office success in the Theatre Guild's history. *Vandamm photograph.*

Oklahoma!—Betty Jane Watson and John Raitt, two of the many who succeeded Joan Roberts and Alfred Drake as Laurey and Curly. *Atwell photograph.*

$83,000 had yielded a clear profit of over $5,000,-000; a $1,500 investor had a return of about $50,-000. These sums have since continued to increase. And the Theatre Guild, after years of wondering where the money for the next show was coming from, finally was not only secure but satisfyingly, resoundingly rich.

In the light of today's more—though not ideally—enlightened attitudes toward race, in and out of the theatre, the flap over the casting of Negro singer Paul Robeson in the title role of the Guild's *Othello* in the fall of 1943 seems ridiculous and a trifle sad in retrospect. Actually it shouldn't have been that startling; Margaret Webster, who staged the Shakespearean tragedy, had done it with Robeson in the role thirteen years earlier in London. Fully expecting the barrage of scholarly and not-so-scholarly protest which followed the Guild's production opening at the Shubert Theatre on October 19, 1943, she had done considerable research proving, at least to her own satisfaction, that when Shakespeare wrote "Moor of Venice" he meant "Blackamoor of Venice."

Nevertheless, this became an issue in a number of the articles which were written during its run of 280 performances in New York—a record for a Shakespearean drama—and the subsequent and equally successful tour. An article in the *Cleveland Plain Dealer* by William McDermott

Othello—Uta Hagen as Desdemona, Margaret Webster (who also directed) as Emelia, and James Monks as Cassio. *Vandamm photograph.*

Othello—José Ferrer as Iago, Paul Robeson as Othello, and James Monks as Cassio. *Vandamm photograph.*

Othello—Paul Robeson and José Ferrer.

Othello—the murder of Desdemona (Paul Robeson, Uta Hagen).

quoted Miss Webster as having said: "The black skin is more than a physical requirement for Othello. It implies a great many psychological requirements which the play needs, if it is to be understood. Othello was of a different race from Desdemona. That is what the play is about." Another tack was taken by a columnist, Mike Gold, in the *Daily Worker,* who saw deep ideological meanings not superimposed—he carefully commended Miss Webster for not turning the drama into "a modern morality play on the theme of race equality"—but intrinsic to Shakespeare's words and intended meanings: "The image of Africa shines forth, a great, noble folk striving for love and brotherhood like Othello, but enslaved and betrayed by the malice of an inferior white, Iago." He goes on to note that our Deep South is full of such Iagos—mayors, schoolteachers, and journalists who "hate the Negro and have spent a lifetime doing nothing else." The article also noted that Shakespeare was not only approved but admired in Soviet Russia.

It's interesting to note that a year later

the idea of a Negro Othello still was being weighed, this time in the case of Canada Lee. George Freedley wrote: "I find it difficult to accept the idea of Othello's being played by a Negro when Shakespeare so clearly states that this noble general is a distinguished Moor, which is quite another thing." George Jean Nathan had dismissed the matter bluntly with: "Black or white, the whole question rests on whether the actor can act the role. Robeson acts it poorly."

Did he? You have your choice of an infinite range of opinions. For example, almost everyone admired the sonority and resonance of Robeson's voice, but not everyone agreed that it was an unfailing asset: some believed it got in the way of the drama and of the characterization. Still, two factors showed that this was an exciting *Othello*—one, the fact that it drew capacity audiences for so long; the other, the fact that so much was written about it. To have gone this far and have mentioned only Miss Webster and Robeson is not meant to suggest they were the substance of the production. Even today, which is quite a number of Iagos later, young José Ferrer's concept of the role is fondly recalled as a model of malice. And Uta Hagen's Desdemona was just about universally admired. Opening night was a clear triumph, with ten curtain calls at the conclusion of what the *Herald Tribune*'s Howard Barnes termed "a consummate Shakespearean revival." The effect of that opening night performance was noted by critic Burton Rascoe of the *New York World-Telegram:*

> Never in my life have I seen an audience sit so still, so tense, so under the spell of what was taking place on the stage as did the audience at the Shubert last night. And few times in my life have I witnessed so spontaneous a release of feelings in applause as that which occurred when the tragedy was ended. It was a tribute to something fine, something thrilling, something great.

Rascoe found Robeson's Moor moving and magnificent, but he still accorded the highest acting honors to Ferrer and Miss Hagen. Everyone was affected by Robert Edmond Jones's settings and lighting. Perhaps a further reason why this *Othello* worked so well with its audience was noted in a final sentence of Rascoe's review: "Not incidentally, this is one Shakespearean performance in which every word uttered on the stage is clear and distinct."

A novel by Richard Hughes, published under two titles—*A High Wind in Jamaica* and *The Innocent Voyage*, came to the stage of the Belasco Theatre November 15 under the second of these names to prove that the Guild, even after such triumphs as *Oklahoma!* and *Othello*, still had not lost the ability to miss. Paul Osborn's adaptation of the adventure story presented an appealing cluster of children inadvertently captured by pirates during a voyage from London to Jamaica in the 1860's. Naturally, the kids and the buccaneers get along agreeably, for the most part, even getting through to the captain, played by Oscar Homolka. Abby Bonine was the featured child, and the youngsters included Guy and Dean Stockwell. The Guild originally had announced that Erwin Piscator, the talented German, would direct (newspapers substituted "Continental" for German, the latter being an unpopular word in 1943, though Piscator was Jewish and a refugee from the Nazis). However, he withdrew less than a month before the scheduled opening, and the playwright, Osborn, took over. Two weeks after the change, *The New York Times* reported that, according to members of the cast, Theresa Helburn of the Guild was directing, but the program still carried the line, "staged by the author." Whoever did it, the play was poorly received, for the most part.

The Guild already had staged two plays by the Czech writer Franz Werfel—*Goat Song* and *Juarez and Maximilian*, when it turned to *Jacobowsky and the Colonel* to wind up its twenty-sixth season. A difficulty this time was the fact that there were two authors to deal with, and they differed sharply on their basic concept of the drama. Werfel had gotten his ideas for *Jacobowsky* from a refugee, and embellished it with his own experiences while fleeing from the Nazis. It concerns a Jewish refugee escaping from the invading Nazis in France who teams up with an autocratic Polish colonel with a medieval mind. Viennese actor Oscar Karlweiss and American actor Louis Calhern created the two roles, with the French actress Annabella as the girl who travels across France with them.

Werfel had discussed the theme at a Hollywood dinner party with S. N. Behrman, who also was a Guild playwright, and they agreed to do it together, though it really did work out as a Behrman adaptation of a Werfel play. The friction between them stemmed from Werfel's belief that

The Innocent Voyage—Oscar Homolka and Abby Bonine. *Vandamm photograph.*

The Innocent Voyage—Oscar Homolka and Herbert Berghof. *Vandamm photograph.*

Jacobowsky and the Colonel—Franz Werfel and S. N. Behrman collaborated on this sensitive play about a Polish Jew fleeing the Nazis who pairs up with an old guard colonel. Oscar Karlweiss as Jacobowsky, with Coby Ruskin, as a chauffeur. *Vandamm photograph.*

Jacobowsky and the Colonel—Louis Calhern as the colonel, with Annabella as the girl who joins the two men. *Graphic House photograph.*

Jacobowsky and the Colonel—Louis Calhern. *Vandamm photograph.*

the treatment should be serious, more in the European tradition, while Behrman wanted to make the same points about human nature within the framework of comedy. Eventually Werfel accepted Behrman's concept, but he still published his own version later. It was the first Guild directing assignment for young Elia Kazan, whose maturity of thought—belying his very boyish appearance and manner—quite won over Langner and Miss Helburn, the producing team; the play was staged in association with Jack H. Skirball. It was—and is—a good play; certainly timely during the year's run it earned in New York and subsequent success on the road. The blend of comedy and compassion in a situation fraught with threat and malice proved dramatically effective, and the characterizations were interesting. Critics and audiences liked *Jacobowsky and the Colonel*, though it didn't earn raves; most of the good comment went to Karlweiss and Calhern for their performances.

Annabella, married at the time to Marine lieutenant Tyrone Power, was called decorative, charming, or attractive by most of the reviewers, who apparently felt nothing would be gained by a detailed evaluation of her as an actress, though John Chapman of the *Daily News* did suggest that her passion for the colonel in the play and for France might not be too deep, and Robert Garland of the *Journal-American* decided that her performance was "not more than so-so." The *World-Telegram*'s Burton Rascoe, by contrast, was in no mood to evade his duty even if she was pretty, a fighting man's bride, and an ally:

> In my whole life (I give you my word) I have never seen or heard an actress botch up good lines as badly as Annabella does. Give her a speech which has satirical overtones in it and she will render it like a Brooklyn burlesque queen. . . . Give her a speech (such as she had last night) in which she is supposed to be both pensive and philosophical and, by the living gods, she will deliver it as though she were doing "Mairzy Doats" as a recitative!

He had started his review with the statement that "An incredibly talentless actress named Annabella made me spiritually ill last night." The attack inspired her to send him a large bottle of castor oil, a development duly reported by columnists Leonard Lyons and Earl Wilson, among others; the incident contributed a small measure of publicity to the play, including a newspaper ad allegedly placed by the actress, quoting other critics' favorable comment about her, in rebuttal to Rascoe, who, having had his say, chose to ignore it.

In 1944, the Guild moved from the Guild Theatre building on West 52nd Street to a former private home and gambling club (apparently also a bordello in its earlier days) at 23 West 53rd Street, remaining there until the offices were moved to the present location at 226 West 47th Street in 1967. The first play to be rehearsed in the large ballroom on the second floor of the 52nd Street location was *Embezzled Heaven,* based on Franz Werfel's novel, and adapted for the stage by Ladislaus Bush-Fekete and Mary Helen Fay. Like most Guild productions it enjoyed the services of able people, notably B. Iden Payne as director and Ethel Barrymore in the role of cook to a countess; Albert Basserman was cast as the Pope, with Eduard Franz, Sanford Meisner, and Martin Blaine in other parts. Despite agreement that Miss Barrymore acted more like a countess than a cook, her performance was praised as the staunchest factor of the evening, following the October 31, 1944, opening. The play turned out to be one of those dramatic efforts, sincerely motivated, that was faulted in too many ways to achieve the desired effect on stage. Louis Kronenberger of *PM* noted this, writing:

> Even at its best—during the prologue and the first act—it succeeds in being agreeable at the cost of being too pretty and unreal; it seems like one of those Daudet stories that are part of beginner's French. After that, moreover, the idyllic atmosphere dissolves into pure unreality, into scenes that simply don't come off, and into a final scene at the Vatican that—whatever force it may have possessed in Werfel's novel—seems merely mawkish and dull.

Embezzled Heaven suggests that heaven is achieved through faith and love, and not by plan. Miss Barrymore portrayed a Czech cook who sends money to her nephew to study for the priesthood, assuming she'll then have a "private priest" to pave her way to heaven. Eventually she learns he is a swindler, but discovers the truth about redemption in an interview with the Pope, after which she dies.

Drama critic Walter Kerr was teaching at Catholic University in Washington when he began experimenting with the idea of creating

Embezzled Heaven—B. Iden Payne directed this drama adapted from a Franz Werfel story. In the kitchen scene above are Augusta Rolland, Bettina Cerf, Ethel Barrymore, Graham Velsey, Sanford Meisner, and Madeline Lee. *Vandamm photograph.*

Embezzled Heaven—film actor Albert Basserman made his American stage debut as the Pope. *Vandamm photograph.*

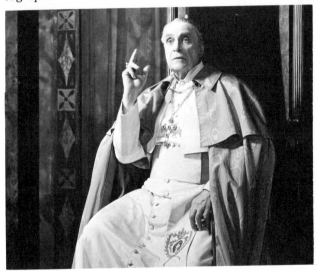

Embezzled Heaven—Sanford Meisner. *Valente photograph.*

189

Embezzled Heaven—Eduard Franz. *Blechman photograph.*

Sing Out, Sweet Land!—Walter Kerr's musical brought Burl Ives to Broadway.

Sing Out, Sweet Land!—Alfred Drake and Viletta Russell. *Vandamm photograph.*

a musical out of American folk music. Genesis of the project, he said, was hearing his mother sing "Polly Wolly Doodle" around the house twenty-five years before. But he knew the danger in merely combining a lot of traditional American songs and adding the appropriate costumes and setting; it would turn into a pageant. This he avoided first by giving the evening a kind of dramatic sequence, then by adding some comic sketches to keep things from getting too ponderously historical. As the show evolved, it became essentially a comedy all the way, which provided the continuity as well as ways for working in the songs, and gave the musical its exuberance. *Sing Out, Sweet Land!* was produced by Langner and Miss Helburn for the Guild two days after Christmas, 1944, at the International Theatre, a large house on Columbus Circle (since razed), with Alfred Drake and Burl Ives heading the cast. Leon Leonidoff, of Radio City Music Hall, staged the production, while author Kerr directed those segments which were essentially dramatic rather than musical. Other talent included Elie Siegmeister who arranged and conducted the music; Doris Humphrey and Charles Weidman, dances; Albert Johnson, sets; and Lucinda Ballard, costumes.

While such critics as Robert Garland and

Sing Out, Sweet Land!—Bibi Osterwald.

Sing Out, Sweet Land!—Michael Fitzmaurice and Alma Kays. *Graphic House photograph.*

John Chapman were thoroughly charmed, others were not quite ready to succumb to the show. Jay Carmody, writing in the *Washington Star,* might have had a good point when he observed: "Walter Kerr's musical cavalcade of America, now given the noblest ministrations of the Theatre Guild, will turn out to be a hit, but to this pair of eyes it missed the fullness of the promise that was in it in its original presentation at Catholic University." He continued: "It is still one of the most delightful things of the season, if not as good as it might have been." Lewis Nichols of *The New York Times* enjoyed the music though not the book: "But Walter Kerr, who provided the connecting links, has written a book that is coy, cute and—to come right out with it—often childish."

If there is any historical significance to the Guild's next undertaking, Philip Barry's comedy, *Foolish Notion,* it is merely that Tallulah Bankhead was making her first and only appearance under the Guild banner, and quite possibly the venture was more entertaining offstage than on. The star blew up on reading a revised third act script in Baltimore because the playwright had not written in the kind of dramatic scene for her she wanted. Later that night in her hotel suite she offended Barry by announcing, in his presence: "You ought to have a great playwright like Noel Coward write you a great play," adding that "the trouble with you Theatre Guild people is— you are just *too* normal!" Barry got angry too; in fact, he was still so upset the next day that his nose began to bleed and he was hospitalized; a small blood vessel had broken. Meanwhile Tallulah calmed down, but began to run a temperature which, she assured producer Langner, would not be a problem. "The thing about me, Darling,"

Foolish Notion—Tallulah Bankhead made her one appearance in a Guild play as the star of Philip Barry's comedy. Her companions, Henry Hull and Donald Cook.

Foolish Notion—Henry Hull and Tallulah Bankhead.

she confided to him, "is that I give my best performance when I am slightly ill, because then my diaphragm is not quite so powerful." At another time, in a blend of modesty and good sense, she observed: "I'm not worried about myself in this play, Darling, but I am worried about what happens to the play when I am not on stage."

Foolish Notion was not welcomed with cheers in New York, but Miss Bankhead got enough loyal comment to create a mild interest in the play, and it did do quite well in its subsequent tour around the country. Quoth *The New Yorker:*

> Miss Bankhead gives another example of her rare accomplishments as an actress. Lines that really aren't especially funny are made to seem so because of the peculiar accent given them by that deep and celebrated voice; scenes that might be painfully whimsical in any other hands are redeemed by her curious, ironic style; confused or incredible situations grow almost plausible just because almost anything is possible when Miss Bankhead is around. I'm afraid that she isn't quite enough to save Mr. Barry's play from its fundamental shapelessness, but I can't think of anybody who could have made a better try at it.

Following the spectacular success of *Oklahoma!,* which was going into its third year in the spring of 1945, it was to be expected that the Guild would want Rodgers and Hammerstein to prepare another musical for them, and that the composer and librettist would be agreeable about resuming what had been so rewarding a relationship. The problem was to find a suitable story, and Langner and Miss Helburn believed that they had one in Ferenc Molnár's *Liliom,* which they had done as a straight play in 1921. Unfortunately, Rodgers and Hammerstein weren't especially enthusiastic about it, and Molnár, now white-haired, didn't like the idea of having his play transformed into a musical. The second obstacle was overcome by having Molnár see *Oklahoma!,* following which he gave his permission on the condition that his *Liliom* be treated as tastefully and charmingly. There still remained the problem of getting the other two to do it, but after nine months, they agreed; a factor in the solution was the decision to change the setting from Budapest to a coastal town in Maine, which meant that Rodgers could write in an American idiom which was more in keeping with his style.

Another asset to the project was the signing of John Raitt, whom Armina Marshall (Mrs. Langner) had heard about through her niece in California. She met him in Hollywood, and suggested him as a replacement for Curly in *Oklahoma!* on the hunch that he could sing. Sing he could indeed, as a New York audition eventually proved, and Rodgers immediately decided Raitt should be Liliom, the carousel barker. Others of the *Oklahoma!* creative team involved included director Rouben Mamoulian, costume designer Miles White, and choreographer Agnes de Mille. Jo Mielziner designed the settings.

There were alterations to be made following the opening in New Haven, but by the time *Carousel* arrived in New York on April 19, 1945, it was, as a great number of its eternal devotees will agree, one of the most melodious, exhilarating, and dramatically valid musicals ever written. Certainly the Rodgers score is among his highest achievements—songs such as "If I Loved You," "The Barker's Soliloquy," "You'll Never Walk Alone," "What's the Use of Wond'rin'" and "June Is Bustin' Out All Over." Benjamin F. Glazer's adaptation not only captured the values of the Molnár original, but provided additional depth of character—enough that Molnár himself was moved to tears when he saw it. No critic captured the feeling of it better or more concisely than John Chapman of the *Daily News,* who wrote: "*Carousel* is one of the finest musical plays I have seen and I shall remember it always. It has everything the professional theatre can give it—and something besides: heart, integrity, an inner glow." The musical did not touch the record of *Oklahoma!,* but it played 890 performances in New York and 650 on tour, plus another 567 a few years later in London. It continues to be revived often; some of its music, such as "You'll Never Walk Alone" and "If I Loved You," seems to have eclipsed in popularity the songs from *Oklahoma!,* and time already seems to be according *Carousel* the higher rating, even though it was the second of the two at the box office. Besides Raitt as Billy Bigelow (the Liliom role), the original company included Jan Clayton as his girl, Julie Jordan, Jean Darling as Carrie Pipperidge, Murvyn Vye as Jigger, and Bambi Linn as Billy and Julie's daughter, Louise.

It was during the mid-1940's that the system of group management, which had prevailed since the Theatre Guild began, finally was aban-

Carousel—another smashing success for Rodgers and Hammerstein was this full-bodied musical derived from Molnár's *Liliom*. Foreground, Jan Clayton as Julie and Jean Darling as Carrie, with girls of the company and (right) Eric Mattson as Mr. Snow.

Carousel—John Raitt as the carousel barker, Billy Bigelow. *Valente photograph.*

Carousel—Jan Clayton as Julie Jordan and Jean Darling as Carrie Pipperidge.

Carousel—Jan Clayton and John Raitt.

Carousel—Jean Darling as Carrie and Murvyn Vye as Jigger Craigin.

doned, though it had in fact been exercised less and less over several preceding years as other members of the board decreased their participation and Langner and Miss Helburn made more of the decisions. The change had been tacitly recognized in 1939 when Philip Barry, who found the system of producing plays with six directors extremely confusing to a playwright, insisted that if the Guild were to produce *The Philadelphia Story,* only Langner and Miss Helburn should do it.

Along with repairing the Guild's finances, Barry's comedy proved a turning point in Guild management, being the first to be produced without the joint services of the board of managers. "Terry and I worked together as producers of the play without friction and with complete sympathy and understanding of each other's point of view, and we in turn were similarly in rapport with the author," recalled Langner in his autobiography, *The Magic Curtain.*

Thus was born the new system of Guild management which has lasted down to today, with Terry and myself usually working as supervisors of the play. At the inception of this new plan any group of two members of the Guild Board were permitted to produce plays in this way, provided the play itself was not vetoed by the Board as being below Guild standards. No other board members availed themselves of this opportunity, however, and from this time on the selection and production of plays became solely the responsibility of Terry and myself

Some time later Philip Moeller, Lee Simonson, and Helen Westley resigned from the Guild, being given pensions and preferred stock in the company. Theresa Helburn and Lawrence Langner were named co-administrative directors with full artistic control. Maurice Wertheim continued as a member of the board, finally resigning in 1946. The group management had worked for a number of years, but had become something of an obstacle as the Guild increased the size and scope of its operation, and as what had been an almost family-type operation became necessarily more complex, requiring, perhaps paradoxically, a less complex directorship.

The season of 1945–1946 would have been

194

In 1939 directorship of the Theatre Guild was formally placed in the hands of Theresa Helburn and Lawrence Langner, who had been two of the Guild's board of six directors. *Kesslere photograph. Vandamm photograph.*

a financial disaster, and a rather sorry experience artistically as well, were it not for Alfred Lunt and Lynn Fontanne, who bailed out the Guild with Terence Rattigan's *O Mistress Mine.* More of that in a moment. It began that fall with a new Sam Behrman comedy, *Dunnigan's Daughter,* in which June Havoc, in the title role, portrayed the girl whose father had died in jail and who then had married a brutally selfish millionaire, in the posture of Dennis King. The two are living in Mexico, where he is exploiting the poor peasants. Also on hand is his daughter (Jan Sterling) and her high-school sweetheart (Richard Widmark) who works for the State Department and is as noble as the old man is base. The question, which takes a long evening to resolve, is whether wife and stepdaughter will compromise their lofty standards to live in comfort with the old tyrant, or align themselves with the idealistic young man. Not only was it a tiresome and obvious play, but the direction by Elia Kazan accomplished nothing to salvage it; he was criticized by one reviewer for never changing pace in a production which badly needed anything possible to liven it up. Another critic noted that Kazan had "endeavored to en-

liven it with varying pace and with broad, sweeping movements, but that he had been defeated by the extremely literary quality of the script." No matter who was blamed, *Dunnigan's Daughter* went down in defeat.

Behrman wasn't the only playwright held responsible for an unsuccessful production that season; William Shakespeare also had to assume some of the blame for the failure of a project, budgeted at the then substantial sum of $100,000, to stage two of his lesser plays. Florence Reed, Jessie Royce Landis, and Henry Daniell were among the players in *The Winter's Tale,* which earned what might be described as a respectful press. After all, nobody wants to knock Shakespeare, but the reviewers were not shy to mention that *The Winter's Tale* posed some problems which the Guild production—variously rated from inadequate to excellent—could not solve. Burton Rascoe of the *New York World-Telegram,* who admitted that he'd never liked the play, discovered it, in the Guild's staging, "a thing of utter magnificence." Samuel T. Wilson, critic of the *Columbus* (Ohio) *Dispatch,* described it as "something that no one seeing it is likely soon to forget."

Dunnigan's Daughter—June Havoc, in the title role, with Richard Widmark.

Dunnigan's Daughter—June Havoc, Dennis King, and Luther Adler. *Graphic House photograph.*

The Winter's Tale—Jessie Royce Landis as Hermione and Geraldine Brooks as her daughter, Perdita. *Vandamm photograph.*

The Winter's Tale—Romney Brent as Autolycus. *Vandamm photograph.*

The Winter's Tale—Henry Daniell as King Leontes. *Vandamm photograph.*

The Winter's Tale—Florence Reed as Paulina. *Vandamm photograph.*

Charles Gentry of the *Detroit Times* called it "an exciting production of one of the last and dullest of the Bard's works." The Shakespearean troupe prepared a second play that season—*The Merry Wives of Windsor*—which was presented in other Guild cities but not in New York. Charles Coburn played Falstaff. Neither play was able to draw an audience, which could have been because a taste for Shakespeare, such as has been nurtured over the past several years by summer festivals of the Elizabethan playwright's works in Connecticut, Ontario, Ohio, Oregon, and other areas, had not yet been developed. But the Guild also erred in beginning what could have been a lasting and quite possibly profitable project with two of the least popular plays. Had they begun with a *Macbeth, Taming of the Shrew,* or *Hamlet,* they might have built enough of a following to have attempted *The Winter's Tale* and *The Merry Wives of Windsor* later. As it was, they dropped the whole enterprise.

The Lunts had appeared in Rattigan's play, *Love in Idleness,* in London before the Guild presented them in it in New York under the new title, *O Mistress Mine,* later taking it on

197

a long, cross-country tour. The prevailing critical feeling was that it was the Lunts' show, a fact which Lewis Nichols of *The New York Times* noted, adding: ". . . and it may be said of Mr. Rattigan that he has politely stepped out of their way." Howard Barnes of the *Herald Tribune* expressed a similar attitude: "Whatever the author had in mind when he wrote *O Mistress Mine* has become strictly the property of the chief players." This might not have been a compliment if applied to anyone else, but in the case of Lunt and Miss Fontanne, it clearly was. They knew what to do with a play, and were sensible enough to realize that on occasion the play might have to serve them, when their contribution was the more substantial, instead of having them serve the play—which they also could do fastidiously, when the drama warranted the dominant position. It was in writing of this particular production that Lawrence Langner dwelt on the attributes of the Lunts which distinguished everything they did on stage:

> Once the play has opened, Alfred and Lynn treat it in a manner which is rare in the theatre. No mother could take care of her babies more conscientiously than the Lunts take care of their plays. Each performance is for them of equal importance. "It's cheating the public to take their money and then let them down," I have always heard Lynn remark. And they demand from their company the same attitude toward their work that they themselves bring to it. Fooling on stage, breaking up other actors, and other devices for relieving the tedium of consecutive performances, are taboo with the Lunts, who work ceaselessly to deepen their parts and to find better ways of playing them. When *The Taming of the Shrew* returned after over a year's tour, it was played infinitely better by the entire company than at the end of the New York run. After playing *O Mistress Mine* for three years, during the last Saturday matinee Alfred said to young Dick Van Patten, playing the juvenile, "I have a new idea for this scene. I think it will improve it. We have one more chance to try it before we close the play." This attitude is so rare in the theatre that it calls for special mention, for usually after playing for a long time, most actors lose all interest and become automatic or indifferent.

Leonid Andreyev's *He Who Gets Slapped,* which the Guild had introduced in America in 1922, was presented in a revival on March 20,

O Mistress Mine—the Theatre Guild and producer John C. Wilson brought Terence Rattigan's comedy and the Lunts from London, where it was titled *Love in Idleness*. It ran for three years there, in New York, and on the road, and saved what would have otherwise been a losing twenty-eighth season for the Guild.

O Mistress Mine—Alfred Lunt, Lynn Fontanne, and Dick Van Patten.

1946, in an attempt to stimulate what had been a lethargic season except for the Lunts' comedy. In the new staging, director Tyrone Guthrie treated the play like the circus which provides its setting, and Judith Guthrie had made some adaptations in the original play book to accommodate this approach. The costumes and settings by Motley and a competent cast helped to achieve the effect Guthrie was seeking, with the result that the newspaper reviews were generally favorable. Still, there were some who wondered if the play really deserved a revival, or if it could be made timely at the dawn of the atomic age. Among the dissenters, Louis Kronenberger of *PM* liked the "tingling, hopped-up excitement" of the first half, then added: "After that, everything started to crumble. The falsity remained without the lure. The speeches got longer and fancier and more foolish." What Guthrie had tried to overcome was the melodramatic aspect of the play which was more apt to be tolerated or even accepted in 1922 than in 1946. To some degree he succeeded. Still, the hint of reservation, or doubt, in even the favorable reviews, coupled with some

He Who Gets Slapped—Dennis King. *Vandamm photograph.*

He Who Gets Slapped—Stella Adler and John Abbott. *Universal photograph.*

He Who Gets Slapped—Judith Guthrie adapted and Tyrone Guthrie staged the Andreyev drama. *Vandamm photograph.*

199

He Who Gets Slapped—Stella Adler. *Blechman photograph.*

He Who Gets Slapped—Dennis King. *Vandamm photograph.*

He Who Gets Slapped—Susan Douglas and Jerome Thor.

elusive mass instinct, sufficed to keep the public away.

Guild audiences had not been treated to a new play by Eugene O'Neill in thirteen years. *Ah, Wilderness!* and *Days Without End* had been done in the season of 1933–1934, and the former had been revived in the fall of 1941. So expectations were high for a twenty-ninth season which promised *The Iceman Cometh* as an opener and *A Moon for the Misbegotten* later on. As things turned out, the second of these was done only on tryout tour, and didn't reach Broadway until a decade later. But *The Iceman Cometh* launched that theatre year, opening at the Martin Beck Theatre on October 9, 1946.

It was obvious that O'Neill had turned back to the time in his youth when he was doing some serious drinking in Jimmy-the-Priest's, a saloon in 1968 discovered by Louis Sheaffer, researching for the first volume of his O'Neill biography (*O'Neill: Son and Playwright*), to have been located at 252 Fulton Street in New York City. Critic Joseph T. Shipley, some time before, had discovered an O'Neill short story, *Tomorrow*, in the June, 1917, issue of *Seven Arts* magazine, which he describes as a detailed summary of *The Iceman Cometh*. O'Neill wrote the play about 1939 and it premiered in 1946, so you could estimate the incubation period of the drama at no less than three decades.

It is set in the saloon of Harry Hope, in the back room of which are sleeping a strange assortment of derelicts. They include a general,

The Iceman Cometh—the happy gathering at Harry Hope's saloon in the O'Neill drama. *Vandamm photograph.*

a former anarchist, a law school graduate, an ex-policeman, and a correspondent. Hope hasn't stepped outside his door in twenty years, and the patrons also view his bar as a refuge from the alien world. Only three hookers and the bartender, who also functions as a procurer for them, show any life. Into this dismal situation comes a young man who confides that he has betrayed his associates in the International Workers of the World, whereupon Slade, the former revolutionary, talks him into suicide. Then in comes Hickey, a salesman, who convinces everybody that it is a bright new day, and time for all these guys, who solace themselves with promises of doing something worthwhile in the future, to go out and do it. They are enchanted by Hickey and by his message, and out they go. But the world is too much with them, to paraphrase Wordsworth, and back they come to the refuge of their liquor and their illusions.

Any play which ran four hours was bound to encounter objections to its length, which this one did. For example, there is a single speech by Hickey—in which he admits that he has killed his wife, but urges the other men to go out and give substance to their dreams—which lasts nineteen minutes. On the other hand, some of the critics not only accepted but cheered every word and every minute of this latest O'Neill drama. Brooks Atkinson began with the straightforward

statement: "Mr. O'Neill has written one of his best plays." He continued:

Writing it for a performance that lasts more than four hours is a sin that rests between Mr. O'Neill and his Maker. Long plays have become nothing more than a bad label with our first dramatist. But if that is the way Mr. O'Neill wants to afflict harmless playgoers, let us accept our fate with nothing more than a polite demurer. For the only thing that matters is that he has plunged again into the black quagmire of man's illusions and composed a rigadoon of death as strange and elemental as his first works. Taking his characters again out of the lower depths, as he did in the "S. S. Glencairn" series, he is looking them over with bleak and mature introspection. And like all his best works, this one is preeminently actable. The Theatre Guild performance, under Eddie Dowling's direction, is a masterpiece of tones, rhythms, and illumination.

All the critics, whether they admired or deplored the play, wrote at enough length about it to indicate they considered either it or its author consequential. It was a memorable production, effectively set and lighted by Robert Edmond Jones and with sensitively detailed performances by such actors as Dudley Digges (Harry Hope), James Barton (Hickey), Carl Benton Reid, and

The Iceman Cometh—Carl Benton Reid as Larry Slade, the ex-anarchist; James Barton as Hickey; Dudley Digges as Harry Hope, proprietor of the saloon; and Nicholas Joy as "The Captain." *Vandamm photograph.*

E. G. Marshall. "I have never seen so many exciting performances in one play," enthused the *Daily News*'s John Chapman, who found the play "magnificent in plan, in size, in scope, and in depth." Richard Watts, Jr., of the *New York Post* shared with the majority some reservations about the play, meanwhile recognizing its stature: "*The Iceman Cometh* goes about its storytelling too slowly and at too great length and it has its share of other faults, too. But it is a drama that gives the entire American theatre dignity and importance."

For the Martin Beck engagement, the play began at 5:30 P.M., with a ninety-minute intermission for dinner, concluding at 11:30. Later the Guild began it at 7:30 and ran it straight through.

Indicative of the quality of stage humor that year is the fact that George Jean Nathan, in his *Theatre Book of the Year, 1946–47,* rated George Kelly's *The Fatal Weakness* the best new comedy, also applauding playwright Kelly as best director and Ina Claire for the season's best performance by an actress. This is not to imply that the play was sharply deficient in amusement; even the critics admitted enjoying it, despite any reservations some of them might have had. However, Louis Kronenberger took its measure fastidiously in his review for *PM,* observing:

> In a well-regulated theatre, there would be half-a-dozen comedies a year at least as good as *The Fatal Weakness,* and several that were better. . . . The right first comment is that it is an entertaining evening for grown-up people. The second, I'm afraid, is that Mr. Kelly has up his sleeve less the ingredients for one particular, highly integrated comedy than certain scenes and characters that might find houseroom in a large assortment of plays. There is something rather haphazard about it all. But if Mr. Kelly's craftsmanship is far from organic, it is all the same sharp.

Refreshingly unsentimental, the play introduced Ina Claire as the wife who discovers that her husband (Howard St. John) is having an affair. The switch is that she lets him marry the other woman, and being an incurable romantic who loves to go to weddings, she attends theirs. Her performance was not brittle—though brittle she could be—but appealingly amiable, adaptable, and effortlessly artful.

If *The Fatal Weakness* was the best new comedy that year, Oscar Wilde's indestructible

The Iceman Cometh—Tom Pedi as Rocky, the night bartender. *Vandamm photograph.*

The Iceman Cometh—Jeanne Cagney and Ruth Gilbert. *Pix photograph.*

The Iceman Cometh—opening day (with a 5:30 P.M. curtain for the four-hour drama), October 9, 1946. *Rice photograph.*

The Fatal Weakness—Howard St. John and Ina Claire.

The Fatal Weakness—Ina Claire, Mary Gildea, Jennifer Howard, and Howard St. John.

The Fatal Weakness—playwright George Kelly.

The Importance of Being Earnest, written in 1894, was the best old one. It became available to the Guild through an arrangement made with Hugh Beaumont in London providing for importation of good English productions and, in return, a means for presenting plays mounted by the Guild for English audiences as well as American. The first importation, in association with John C. Wilson, was John Gielgud's English troupe in the Wilde play, which the author had subtitled "a trivial comedy for serious people." The reviews positively glowed, not only for Gielgud's Jack Worthing ("an ascetic arrogance that is enormously witty," wrote Atkinson of *The New York Times*), but for Pamela Brown's icy condescension as Gwendolyn, Jane Baxter's merriment as Cecily, Jean Cadell's and John Kidd's robust humor as the governess and the rector, respectively, Margaret Rutherford's overbearing Lady Bracknell, Robert Flemyng's well-bred revelry as Algernon, and for the work of the remaining players. It was Miss Brown's American debut; her experience in having played more than seventy-five roles in stock and repertory, though still a very young actress, gave her a polish and assurance which American audiences and critics just weren't used to seeing in an ingenue. Miss Brown later played Angelica in *Love for Love,* opposite Gielgud, and appeared with him again—and memorably—in Christopher Fry's *The Lady's Not for Burning.*

Having succeeded so felicitously with old English comedy, the Guild next went even older and, if possible, more English, with *Love for Love,* which William Congreve had written in 1695. Gielgud had portrayed Valentine, who feigns madness to avoid giving up his inheritance, in a London production four years before the New York opening, and repeated the role for the Guild. However, the 471 performances achieved in England were not matched here, possibly because the play opened almost at the end of the season (May 26, 1947), but largely, perhaps, because there just wasn't that much of a taste for Restoration comedy in these rebellious colonies. While Gielgud was generously praised for his work both as actor and director, it was Miss Pamela Brown who most completely charmed the critics again. Her throaty voice seemed to add intriguing new subtleties to Angelica's lines.

In retrospect, a Theatre Guild opening in Columbus, Ohio, proved far more significant than anything it did that season on Broadway, with

203

The Importance of Being Earnest—Robert Flemyng as Algernon, Jane Baxter as Cecily, Pamela Brown as Gwendolyn, and John Gielgud as Jack (also Ernest). The Oscar Wilde play introduced Miss Brown to the American stage. *Vandamm photograph.*

The Importance of Being Earnest—Jean Cadell as Miss Prism and John Kidd as the Reverend Canon Chasuble. *Vandamm photograph.*

The Importance of Being Earnest—Margaret Rutherford made her American stage debut as Lady Bracknell; with her is Jean Cadell as Miss Prism, right. *Vandamm photograph.*

Love for Love—Cyril Ritchard at Tattle, John Gielgud as Valentine, and Pamela Brown as Angelica. *Vandamm photograph.*

the exception of O'Neill's *The Iceman Cometh.* On Thursday evening, February 20, 1947, the Hartman Theatre's curtain rose on Eugene O'Neill's *A Moon for the Misbegotten* in that midwestern city, to the bewilderment or open distaste of many in the audience. "A ten-year-old boy could write a play like that," observed one theatre professional attending the opening. Actor Louis Calhern, who had starred at the Hartman the previous week in *The Magnificent Yankee,* told a reporter: "O'Neill now is childish. He is surrounded by friends who keep telling him he is a genius and he believes it."

Bud Kissel, of the *Columbus Citizen,* dismissed it as "an unimportant play," subsequently writing that the premiere was most apt to be remembered for the restlessness of the audience and the short intermissions. By contrast, drama critic Samuel T. Wilson of the *Columbus Dispatch* saw *Moon* as "the playwright's present towering achievement as a dramatic craftsman and above all as a poet . . . full of sentiment, music and meaning, warmth of human observation and comment, and vast sorrowfulness." And in the *Ohio State Journal,* Mary McGavran found it "beautiful in its very ugliness."

What might have alienated people was the fact that no one in *Moon* is admirable, attractive, or apt to stir audience sympathy in the usual way. Josie Hogan is a twenty-eight-year-old woman, five feet, eleven inches tall, weighing 180 pounds, and stronger than most men. She is coarse in manner and fairly foul-mouthed in speech, encouraging the impression that she's had her share of men. Her father, Phil Hogan, is a conniving petty thief, and Jim Tyrone, who owns the rocky New England farm on which the Hogans live, is weak-willed and alcoholic. But what the play eventually reveals is the sensitivity and painful vulnerability of this battleship of a woman. O'Neill also probes as deeply into the weaknesses of Tyrone, so that you come to understand the needs of each, and how well each could provide emotionally for the other, if only they were blessed with the adaptability and good sense and self-control that we like to see on the stage and the printed page, even if we do not always expect it in living people.

Like so much of O'Neill, *Moon* is autobiographical, except in this case he was writing about his brother, who also is painstakingly depicted, with O'Neill's parents, in *Long Day's Journey Into Night.* The playwright—never an

easy man to work with—compounded the Guild's casting problem by insisting that the actress and actor to play Josie and her father had to be Irish. Well, finding a girl of the required dimensions, appearance, and sensitivity was difficult enough without adding the qualification of national heritage. The large Irish girls who showed up for—or were enticed into—auditions had very little acting experience. Eventually the part was assigned to Mary Welch, who wasn't really large enough although she obligingly fattened up to 170 pounds, but she was an excellent actress and did have some Irish heritage. James M. Kerrigan was cast as Phil Hogan, with James Dunn as Tyrone. Arthur Shields, also suitably Irish, directed.

A Moon for the Misbegotten is indeed a tragedy, in mood and as it affects the principals, even if it is not so in the classic sense. The tragic hero with a single, fatal flaw hardly describes Jim Tyrone who, frankly, isn't much of a man, despite his forays into brief affairs with assorted females. Rather, like Chekhov's *The Cherry Orchard,* it reveals its tragedy in the subtext—beneath the words rather than explicitly in them. And therein lies its poetry as well. Still, on a few occasions one of the characters will say something so lyrical and revealing that the whole drama is illuminated. Such is Josie's line when she holds the sleeping Jim in her arms through the remainder of the night, in lieu of physical love: "May you have your wish and die in your sleep soon, Jim darling. May you rest forever in forgiveness and peace."

Moon earned negative notices on its brief tour after the Columbus opening. In Pittsburgh the president of the Chamber of Commerce attacked the Theatre Guild for its failure "to give consideration to the public morals." Pittsburgh newspapers attacked it not only in their reviews but in their editorial columns. The play was closed in Detroit the day after it opened, on the charge that it was "dirty and riqué," and deletions were ordered before it could continue there. Of course, much of the feeling against it came from easily offended Irish descendants.

As little as five years later, in 1952, critics were starting to discern the values in the play; it was published that year by Random House. Even then, book reviewer Orville Prescott of *The New York Times* whipped it as "a dull and dreary play about three miserable wretches utterly defeated by life and their own weakness of charac-

A Moon for the Misbegotten—the Theatre Guild premiered this superb O'Neill drama, which ran into considerable trouble, including censorship, on its tryout tour and was closed without coming into New York, though another producer finally did it on Broadway a decade later. James Dunn, J. M. Kerrigan, and director Arthur Shields of the original *Moon*.

ter." In Boston, critic Elliot Norton valued it as "memorable for its beauty, despite its faults."

Moon finally achieved its Broadway premiere in the spring of 1957, produced by Carmen Capalbo and Stanley Chase, with the former directing. Wendy Hiller portrayed Josie, despite the fact that she was not the girl, physically, whom O'Neill had envisioned; Franchot Tone had the role of James Tyrone, with Cyril Cusack, an Irish actor, as Phil Hogan. The critical tide finally seemed to have turned when the play opened off-Broadway, at Circle in the Square, in June of 1968, with Salome Jens, Mitchell Ryan, and W. B. Brydon in the principal roles. Critics who covered the opening approved enthusiastically, with the *Times*'s Clive Barnes deeming it "a most distinguished play, and a most distinguished revival." Theodore Mann directed.

The Guild opened *Oklahoma!* and S. N. Behrman's comedy *Jane* in London during its twenty-ninth season. *Jane* made it to New York about six years later.

Perhaps it was to be expected that a musical entitled *Allegro* would be described, by critics who found it less lively than its musical title, as "andante" (John Chapman, *Daily News*) and "lento" (Robert Garland, *Journal-American*)—both words meaning slowly. This view was countered by professional observers and a whole raft of dilettantes who saw profound artistic worth, not to mention social significance, in the Richard Rodgers–

Oscar Hammerstein II musical play which launched the Guild's thirtieth season on October 10, 1947. Flushed with the spectacular success of *Oklahoma!*, these two uncommonly talented gentlemen had decided to make even more daring a break with the traditional musical by telling a simple narrative in what might have seemed, at first, a straightforward manner. What happens in *Allegro* is that Joseph Taylor, Jr., is born in 1905 in a small town, grows up, goes away to college, returns home to marry and go into general medical practice with his father, but is conned into becoming a big-city specialist by his socially ambitious wife. Eventually he leaves her and his fancy office, to return to small-town doctoring and the lovely, well-motivated nurse who is ready to stand and lie at his side.

The trouble was that simplicity was defeated by an almost ponderous treatment, including the use of a Greek chorus, making its comment musically, with the result that the eventual impression was more one of ostentation. Lacking was the fluidity of staging which would have achieved, to a degree, the desired effect. And other elements, such as Agnes de Mille's choreography, failed to integrate themselves into the purportedly simple narrative as they should have. While Rodgers' score did introduce some musical devices which were not ordinarily encountered in Broadway shows, they were derivative, for the most part, and not particularly daring to the musically

Allegro—playwright-lyricist Oscar Hammerstein II and composer Richard Rodgers tried a new and somewhat novel approach to musical theatre. *Vandamm photograph.*

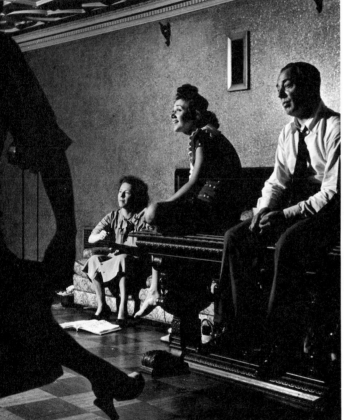

Allegro—Richard Rodgers at rehearsal.

Allegro—take a break. *Cosmo-Sileo photograph.*

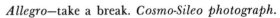

Allegro—Roberta Jonay and John Battles. *Vandamm photograph.*

207

Allegro—Lisa Kirk. *Vandamm photograph.*

Allegro—the wedding scene.

Allegro—John Conte and Katrina Van Oss. *Vandamm photograph.*

Allegro—Kathryn Lee and Harrison Muller. *Vandamm photograph.*

informed. Still, there were zestful performances—Lisa Kirk's singing of "The Gentleman Is a Dope" (shades of "The Lady Is a Tramp" from *Pal Joey*), Annamary Dickey's singing and acting as the young man's mother, John Battles as Joe, Jr., and William Ching as his father. A number of critics singled out Roberta Jonay for special praise for her performance as Joe's sweetheart who turns into a bitchy, adulterous wife. Miss de Mille directed the show, with Hammerstein also serving in that capacity from time to time. Rodgers and Hammerstein and the rest of the creative-producing team did accomplish one objective, which was to shape a show in which the songs and drama were reasonably integrated, rather than separate and alternating. Actually, the composer and lyricist had been moving in this direction for some time; *Oklahoma!* is an example. It became more conspicuous a technique in *Allegro*.

If there is any reason to remember Jan de Hartog's drama *This Time Tomorrow,* other than for the historical record, it would be for a wonderful story which George Jean Nathan recalled in a second column he wrote about the Guild production which had arrived November 3 at the Ethel Barrymore. Nathan hated the play, labeling it:

> One-ounce drama passed off for an intellectual, philosophical and scientific tone by loading it up with solemn bosh about everything

from hypnotism to symbolic astrology, from cancer research to metaphysics, and from psycho-therapeutics to what well may be the most revolutionary theory heard in the world since Genesis, to wit, that if a woman of nymphomaniac tendencies pines for love and gets it, her contentment will be so great it will kill her.

This is what is known in the writing trade as a wrap-up sentence.

Anyway, after belaboring Mr. de Hartog's drama at considerable length, Nathan finally reminisced about a long-gone ritual of opening nights:

Whenever any such play shows up, it induces people who are bored stiff by it nevertheless flatteringly to remark that it took courage to produce it. Which recalls the late Helen Westley, who for many years was a member of this same Theatre Guild's board of directors. On the Guild's opening nights, the grand old girl, begauded as ever like the gypsy queen in an 1890 comic opera, always deposited herself in a seat on the aisle in one of the rear rows of the theatre. On the various occasions when her Guild associates saw fit to put on plays like this de Hartog exhibit, it was her pleasure to hail me on my way out at the first intermission and loudly to assure me that if I didn't think the play was a polecat I was crazy. At the second intermission, she would lean over as I went up the aisle and beamingly yell, "See, I told you! It's getting even lousier." And at the evening's end she would grab me by the arm and gleefully shout, "My God, did you ever see anything like it?"
I miss her.

A popular playwright in his native England, where two of his plays had run up to totals of over 1,000 performances, Terence Rattigan had not made much of an impression on American audiences until the Guild brought over the London production of *The Winslow Boy* in the fall of 1947. Perhaps the theme—a father's dogged campaign to vindicate his son of a false accusation—appealed to the American sense of justice as it had to the English. The play is based on fact. George Archer-Shee was a boy dismissed for petty theft from the Royal Naval Academy. Even though the case was closed, his father eventually was able to reopen it through the parliamentary provision for reviewing a government decision: "Let right

This Time Tomorrow—Ruth Ford and Sam Jaffe.

be done." Archer-Shee was found to be innocent.

In *The Winslow Boy,* Alan Webb portrayed the father of the fourteen-year-old naval cadet (Michael Newell) found guilty of stealing, forging, and cashing a five-shilling postal note. In the course of the long campaign to have the case reopened, the father loses his health and almost sacrifices his wife's loyalty. He spends all his money on the case, even to the point where an older son cannot continue his education. He is so ridiculed that his daughter's fiancé drops her. Perhaps more poignant than any of this is the fact that the lad himself loses interest; when the trial is about to be decided, he's attending a movie. It is a mature, thought-out, and beautifully detailed play, and was praised more for its high morality than for any dramatic excitement, though it does achieve some as it moves toward the final curtain.

Shaw's *You Never Can Tell* represented a considerable financial loss for the Guild, which brought it to the stage of the Martin Beck Theatre on March 16, 1948, with Leo G. Carroll, Patricia Kirkland, Tom Helmore, Nigel Stock, Frieda Inescort, Faith Brook, Ralph Forbes, Walter Hudd, and William Devlin in the cast. The critical consensus was favorable, both to the play and the production, though John Chapman of the New

The Winslow Boy—Madge Compton and Alan Webb as the parents of a lad (Michael Newell) involved in a celebrated English court case. *Vandamm photograph.*

The Winslow Boy—Madge Compton, Michael Newell, and Frank Allenby. *Vandamm photograph.*

York *Daily News* found himself getting sleepy, and Robert Garland in the *Journal-American* decided that it simmered more or less sedately between the occasions when it came to a boil. Almost everyone agreed that Shaw resolutely refused to be dated—an opinion that continues to hold with many of his plays. Peter Ashmore's direction was not to the taste of Brooks Atkinson of the *Times*, and his other negative comments, though relatively mild, added up to a notice hardly apt to start a stampede toward the box office. According to the Guild poll of its 15,000 New York members, most of them enjoyed the Shaw play. But expenses were high and summer was coming on, so it was closed at a loss.

You Never Can Tell—From left, Faith Brook, Tom Helmore, Frieda Inescort, Leo G. Carroll, Patricia Kirkland, Walter Hudd, Nigel Stock, and Ralph Forbes.

You Never Can Tell—Frieda Inescort, Faith Brook, and Tom Helmore. *Vandamm photograph.*

210

VIII

The Theatre Guild on Radio and Television

by Armina Marshall

IN THE spring of 1945 the Theatre Guild began thinking of new areas of activity. During World War II the Guild, like everyone in the entertainment field, had been forced to curtail the production of plays. But with the European phase of World War II ended and the prospect of peace in the Pacific, it seemed the auspicious time to reactivate productions. Before the war the Theatre Guild had made overtures toward the National Broadcasting Company suggesting a series of radio dramas, adapted from plays which we already had produced on Broadway and around the country. NBC, however, did not agree that the country was ready for this caliber of theatre. In fact, an executive of the network told us quite bluntly that "the name of the Theatre Guild is the kiss of death in radio." This man's attitude was fairly typical since the prevalent belief in broadcasting circles at the time was that programming with anything "cultural" about it would not be accepted by the radio audience.

By 1945, however, radio seemed ready for such an experiment, and a second approach proved successful. With William H. Fitelson, our general counsel, as spokesman, and the advertising agency of Batten, Barton, Durstine & Osborn assisting in our campaign, the Theatre Guild entered into a contract with the United States Steel Corporation to produce a weekly series under the name of "The Theatre Guild on the Air." The program was to be designed to bring the living theatre into the homes of millions of radio listeners, especially in those areas where professionally mounted stage plays were not available to the public. We planned to use not only plays which the Theatre Guild

had produced but other interesting properties which could be adapted for radio.

Thus the Guild found itself not only with a new challenge but the opportunity to widen the range of its theatrical activities. Lawrence Langner felt that it was illogical to be concerned with the artistic standards of the living theatre and yet be completely indifferent to what was being done with the plays presented to millions of Americans after they had left the stage. Many of the Theatre Guild dramas and comedies had been made into films, though rarely achieving the artistic quality of the original theatre productions. In many instances they were changed for commercial purposes and often miscast because of the need to use important movie stars. The plays were rewritten for the film medium, leaving the viewing public with a watered-down version of what usually had been a fine, well-written, and well-produced play. By this time subsidiary rights to plays were being zealously sought for radio as well as for films. It was evident that radio would prove a glutton for the many stage properties, and with the Theatre Guild backlog of almost 200 plays, there would shortly be a demand for those which were still available and not already sold to motion-picture companies.

These were the circumstances which had led the Theatre Guild to decide to produce its own plays on the air instead of merely leasing them to radio networks or other producers. We at the Guild felt that the standards of radio were mediocre at best, because they were geared to a public which for the most part never stepped inside a theatre. At that time the plays of Shaw,

O'Neill, and the other leading English and American playwrights were unknown to all but a small fraction of the listening audience. Shakespeare was a subject which had to be studied in school but with which the average person had little identification. Our goal was to attempt to change that.

With our background, a network contract, and a distinguished corporation as our sponsor, we had high hopes for a fine program. We were amateurs in the medium to be sure, but we did not expect to remain so for long. Our plan was to use the stars who had appeared in the plays originally on stage, or substitute others who would be able to equal those performances. We also arranged for rehearsal periods to be longer than those ordinarily allotted to one-hour radio shows, in the hope that a finished performance could be achieved. Homer Fickett, experienced in radio, was chosen to direct the series. He agreed with the Guild's proposals and attitudes, since his first love also was the theatre. He approved of the idea of using plays that had been produced successfully on stage, and of using the legitimate actors who had played in them.

Since the programs were to be broadcast "live" from a theatre, we decided to have an audience there, in the hope that their reactions would help to give the radio listeners the feeling of a theatrical experience. It proved to be an excellent idea. However, there was the problem that actors who were quite at ease on stage became uneasy and self-conscious when they had to perform before microphones, and it was here that Homer proved especially effective. Drawing on his own background in broadcasting, he was able to give them assurance, and for the most part he achieved excellent performances. One of his innovations was to have a soundproof glass booth built in the orchestra pit of the theatre from which we were broadcasting. Homer and his assistant, Doris Quinlan, worked inside the air-conditioned booth in full view of the actors. From this convenient location he was able to direct the play much in the fashion of an operatic conductor, who directs his singers from a pit set in the stage so designed that cannot be seen by the audience. Soundlessly, Homer could signal his cast for timing and movement, as well as every line, sneeze, cough, laugh, or flood of tears. Every gesture from Homer meant something, and they were strange gestures indeed, but the actors understood, and it all gave them confidence.

On September 9, 1945, "The Theatre Guild on the Air" began with *Wings over Europe,* a play by Maurice Browne and Robert Nichols, and adapted by Arthur Arent. It had been one of the outstanding dramas of the Guild's 1928–1929 season. This proved to be an excellent choice for the first program of the series, since the play anticipated the atomic bomb, which had become a reality only a short time before we had opened our program. In spite of the Guild's inexperience in radio, we managed to achieve a superior production, beautifully acted by a fine cast headed by Burgess Meredith. Response from radio critics was highly favorable, and a number of them predicted that the entire series would prove to be outstanding. It was.

Producing on radio, however, was far different from producing in the theatre, as the Guild directors quickly discovered. On stage, a dramatic situation can be presented through the use of voice, body movement, gesture, and facial expression. It can quicken the imagination of the audience through the eye as well as the ear and has the advantage of scenery, costumes, and lighting, as well as sound, to enhance the interest of the public. On radio, sound furnished the only means of communicating ideas, emotions, and the sense of place. At first, this seemed a tremendous limitation, and in terms of usual theatre practice, it was. What we quickly learned, however, was that with radio, the focal point becomes the imagination of the listener. Radio, having only sound as the medium, demands the most in that respect, and thus calls for a kind of dramatic creativity which simply does not exist in the production of a play or on TV, which can be seen as well as heard.

With *Wings over Europe,* the Theatre Guild was launched into what was to become a sixteen-year relationship with our sponsor, United States Steel. We produced eight years of weekly radio programs, and went on to eight years of television.

During those first months on radio the Guild produced many of its previous successes with their original stars, including *Jacobowsky and the Colonel,* with Louis Calhern, Annabella, and Oscar Karlweiss, and *The Guardsman* with Lynn Fontanne and Alfred Lunt, which had been their first success as a starring couple. These were followed by plays by Sidney Howard, Maxwell Anderson, Eugene O'Neill, S. N. Behrman, Arthur Miller, John van Druten, Marc Connolly, Edna

Ferber, and George Kaufman. Casts included Walter Huston, Katharine Hepburn, Shirley Booth, Oscar Homolka, Helen Hayes, Helen Menken, Gertrude Lawrence, Charles Laughton, Gene Kelly, Fredric March, Florence Eldridge, Thornton Wilder, and Dorothy McGuire. The Lunts played in seven programs during the first season.

During this initial season it was decided to do O'Neill's lengthy drama, *Strange Interlude*, in two episodes: the first one week and the second the following week. The network informed the Theatre Guild that they would not allow it to be broadcast. They were concerned after reading the script, about the scene in which Nina, the principal feminine character, is advised by her mother-in-law to have an abortion rather than bear a child. There was a great deal of apprehension from the network but the Theatre Guild had a contract with United States Steel which gave us full autonomy in the selection of plays. The network did not have the legal right to cancel the broadcast. United States Steel resolved the problem by living up to its contract, and the Theatre Guild was able to present the play as written. There were only a few letters of protest about the mention of the abortion, though the advertising agency had expected an avalanche of indignant mail. There also were only a few letters of congratulations on presenting this outstanding drama which was disappointing to all of us.

For the first year on radio, Lawrence Langner served as commentator. Born in Wales, he had a particularly mellow voice and excellent diction. It was thought that this would be an asset to "The Theatre Guild on the Air" by providing a presentation of distinction for each program. Unfortunately, it did not work out that way. Reports came from west of the Mississippi that the plays on the air were all well and good—nothing wrong with them—but why did they have that dude introducing the program? So Lawrence, who wasn't enjoying his job, willingly stepped down. Ironically, a commentator later chosen—Norman Brokenshire—spoke in a manner so colloquial that it seemed almost absurd to us at the Theatre Guild. He made frequent mistakes in grammar, and in introducing the stars often mispronounced their names. We always were relieved when Norman finished his introduction because we had passed that hurdle and could go on with the play. Finally, after one especially disastrous opening, Lawrence and I insisted that he be removed as commentator.

We made an appointment with Irving Olds, chairman of the board of United States Steel, with whom we had been closely associated and who had been most cooperative. The purpose of the meeting was to try to convince him that we should have a new commentator. We felt a bad image was being projected not only for "The Theatre Guild on the Air" but also for United States Steel.

After politely listening to our reasoning, Irving Olds disagreed. "He is much more representative of the large part of our audience than you are, Lawrence," he explained. "His speech is commonplace but the audience identifies with it. He makes mistakes, but so do they. They don't feel that they are being talked down to. In fact, we get more letters about how happy they are to have Norman than they are to have the Lunts."

Our association with United States Steel had been a unique experience for the Guild. There were none of the uncertainties concerning contracts, negotiations, and business dealings which were commonplace in the harassing dealings of the Broadway theatre. Our initial contract was for a year, and at the end of that year, following extensive examination and planning, it was renewed.

By the end of the eighth year of radio, television had advanced to the point where many sponsors were deciding it was a better medium for advancing their advertising and public relations. The Guild had already had some limited experience with TV. After the London opening of *Oklahoma!*, Lawrence and I had visited the British Broadcasting Company, where Denis Johnston, an old friend and author of *The Moon in the Yellow River*, which the Guild had produced, was in charge of the program department. We had seen some television plays given there under his supervision. Though technically imperfect, they gave evidence that the medium would ultimately be capable of bringing the finest works of the theatre into homes even to a greater degree than radio.

Upon our return to New York, Lawrence explained his ideas to Niles Trammel, John Royal, and Warren Wade of NBC. It was agreed that as an experiment the Guild would produce a television play each month for seven months. It was a unique agreement because the Guild and NBC each footed its share of the bill. The Guild formed a new department, headed by Warren Caro. NBC was to furnish the directors; the Guild would supply the plays and the actors. By experimenting with these productions we expected to learn from one play to the next just what the new medium called for. This turned out to be the case.

The first play was *John Ferguson* which had been one of the plays of the first Theatre Guild season in the spring of 1919. It turned out to be a disaster. Jack Gould wrote in his column the next morning, "The Theatre Guild entered into the field of TV last night and fell flat on its art." However, we picked up the pieces and went on to experiment with six more plays.

We were fortunate in procuring from Bernard Shaw the rights to present *Great Catherine*. It was to be done exactly as he had written it, with no cutting allowed. We had approached Shaw during our radio series for permission to do his plays but his answer always was, "Yes, but not one line cut." Since the plays were generally long, even for the theatre, it was impossible to get through them in one hour. *Great Catherine,* a long one-act play, ran less than an hour, and we were able to present it with a fine cast headed by Gertrude Lawrence, Micheál Mac Liammóir, David Wayne, and Joan McCracken. It was the first Shaw play to be performed on television, and it helped to open the first large TV studio of NBC. A kinescope of the show reposes in the Museum of Modern Art in New York. *Great Catherine* was followed by Thornton Wilder's *Our Town,* and of all the plays we did during this experimental period, it probably fitted the television medium best. Raymond Massey starred in the cast as the stage manager, and it proved highly successful. John Gassner, writing in *The Forum,* predicted:

> Unless I greatly miss my guess, the Theatre Guild's telecast of *Our Town* over NBC on Sunday, June 6, 1953, will go down in history as the day when televised drama was really born. It was the first time that a play of quality was televised in the new medium with style and distinction.

Our experiment with TV had proven successful.

Consequently, with this experience behind us and at the end of our eighth year on radio, it seemed obvious that television would follow. Also, with a record of eight years with the same sponsor, it seemed natural that the Guild and United States Steel would unite for a television series. This was agreed, with a contract stipulating a one-hour program every other week.

We realized that running a TV series was in no way easy sailing compared to a radio program. TV would be much more difficult. Producing a TV play every other week demanded almost as much effort as the production of a theatre play. It required the scenery, costumes, properties, and lighting, and keeping the budget balanced withal. We used many more artists: the scene designer, the costumer, the music conductor, the lighting expert, the property men. We selected different directors who seemed most suitable for each play. There were all of the usual problems of writing, editing, and casting that could only be compared to all actual theatre productions. Led by W. H. Fitelson, our producing manager, we assembled a talented group of editors, directors, and writers. Included in our staff over the eight years of TV were Carol Irwin, John Haggott, Marshall Jamison, Anna May Franklin, Arthur Heineman, Dorothy Hechtlinger, Terry Lewis, and Gene Coffin. Also George Kondorf, who acted as producer for the series over a period of six years. One quality that our program engendered in everyone working on it was that of dedication. Each broadcast was like an opening night for the staff and the stars. There was always an air of excitement. If a program turned out badly there was as much depression over it as there would be for a play on Broadway that had bombed and was closing on Saturday. But by and large there was an air of achievement, and it became a way of life for everyone participating.

A number of the writers who adapted stage plays for radio first, then for TV productions, also are distinguished today for their own original dramas. These include Robert Anderson, who adapted thirty-six plays, Paddy Chayefsky, Millard Lampell, John LaTouche, Frank Gilroy, Ira Levin, N. Richard Nash, Kenyon Nicholson, Henry Denker, Arnold Schulman, and Michael Dyne. The busiest adapter over the years was Arthur Arent, who fitted sixty-eight plays to the radio format and six for TV.

Almost every star in the theatre and moving pictures appeared at one time or another on the program, many of them before they became great popular stars. These include Paul Newman, Joanne Woodward, John Cassavetes, Andy Griffith, Johnny Carson, and Cliff Robertson. We also have great satisfaction in following the careers of young directors who helped make the program an important one. Their names are current today in the theatre and moving pictures as well as TV:

Norman Felton, Alex Segal, Sam Wanamaker, Sidney Lumet, Fielder Cook, Dan Petrie, Jack Smythe, Elliot Silverstein, and Paul Bogart, just to mention a few.

We did not limit ourselves to stage plays, but also produced plays written originally for television. Some of these were outstanding programs, such as *P.O.W., The Last Notch, Noon on Doomsday, Bang the Drums Slowly, One Red Rose for Christmas,* and *Shadow of a Pale Horse.*

In a number of instances over the years, our television dramatic material has been developed into plays for the theatre. *No Time for Sergeants,* which Ira Levin adapted from Mac Hyman's story for "The Theatre Guild on the Air," became a Broadway comedy hit soon after. A movie version followed, after which it returned to TV as a long-running comedy series.

By the beginning of the eighth year of our TV series, the listening audience had begun to change. TV material was judged largely on the ratings, and the ratings were most often dependent on the popularity of the stars used on the program. Often the material had to be fashioned for the stars. Also good TV writers were being tempted into the films where the remuneration was greater. There were still talented people writing for TV, but the market was changing. The TV serial in which a single popular star could be seen weekly would invariably attract a large following.

After seven years of TV, United States Steel began to change its policy of advertising. "The Theatre Guild on the Air" and the United States Steel Hour had served as a means of establishing good public relations in the industry and with the viewing public. But the sponsor was now leaning toward advertising in other areas. It was becoming obvious to both the Theatre Guild and United States Steel that our program had served its purpose and that it was time to discontinue.

The United States Steel Hour finally came to an end after eight years of television drama, when the Guild and the sponsor agreed to end the series. We had the good fortune to close our eighth season with Lynn Fontanne and Alfred Lunt in *The Old Lady Shows Her Medals* by James M. Barrie on June 12, 1963. It was a moving and memorable program, and one that we of the Theatre Guild shall always be proud of.

Our program over the sixteen years had been a fruitful one. We had succeeded in a regular program of theatre and had maintained generally a superior quality of production. We had the satisfaction of knowing that for a great many of the plays we produced we had extended the audience far beyond the usual run of a Broadway play. Over the years we had served the purpose we had hoped to do in bringing theatre into the homes of the great public who otherwise would never have had the opportunity to see these plays.

IX

1948-1958

IF THE Guild's excursions into a racially integrated theatre seem tentative by today's standards, they were bold in their time. *Porgy, Porgy and Bess,* and the casting of a genuine black (Paul Robeson) as Othello all broke the tradition of using Negroes only as servants or as comic characters. Today's new appraisal of history's black leaders was foreshadowed by *Set My People Free,* which opened November 3, 1948, at the Hudson Theatre in New York. Dorothy Heyward, co-author of *Porgy,* had taken her title from an old spiritual and her story from an abortive slave revolt in her native Charleston, South Carolina, in 1822.

Denmark Vesey, who might or might not have been an African prince, was brought to America on a slave ship at the age of fourteen. At thirty-three he won his freedom and soon after worked out a careful plan for freeing all the slaves of Charleston, also for killing much of the white population. Because the white men never interfered with Negro church services (unless the slaves stayed out after "drum beat" or curfew), it was possible for Vesey and his followers, who eventually numbered thousands, to plan their insurrection in the churches. Vesey, who had educated himself by reading and copying the Bible, saw himself as Moses, designated by God to lead his children out of bondage. So well-planned was his revolution that he kept his name secret from all but his captains and his six disciples. It was one of the latter, a head slave, or handkerchief-head, as the boss slave was called, who finally put his personal loyalty to his white master ahead of his racial loyalties, and revealed the plot.

This was the story which Miss Heyward brought to the stage, with honesty and occasional

eloquence; the Guild endowed it further with a strong cast, direction by Martin Ritt, and Ralph Alswang's settings. It earned approval for the dignity of its subject, its humane understanding of both blacks and whites, and a few finely wrought characterizations. Juano Hernandez conveyed the revolutionary zeal of the original Vesey, and Canada Lee revealed the anguish that went into George Wilson's decision to give away the plot. Still, it did not achieve the dramatic power it

Set My People Free—Dorothy Heyward's drama told the true story of Denmark Vesey's slave revolt. Blaine Cordner as Captain Wilson and Canada Lee as George, the head slave who betrayed Vesey.

Set My People Free—Juano Hernandez as Denmark Vesey, Muriel Smith, and Canada Lee.

The Silver Whistle—José Ferrer (center) as the con man who brightens life in an old folks' home, with Burton Mallory and William Lynn. *Vandamm photograph.*

The Silver Whistle—José Ferrer and Doro Merande. *Vandamm photograph.*

The Silver Whistle—Frances Brandt, Eleanor Wilson, and Kathleen Comegys. *Vandamm photograph.*

should have, possibly because the playwright's division of the story into ten quite separate scenes tended to diffuse it. Also, it lacked a consistency of style, going from melodrama to violence to character analysis to ritual. Brooks Atkinson suggested that if it had been poetically written, it might have been as "ruefully exalting" as the spiritual which had provided its title. It did re-affirm the dignity of the theatre in dealing with social issues, with history in a realistic rather than a romantic way, and with the inevitable struggle involved in making moral decisions.

Less probing but more popular was Robert E. McEnroe's *The Silver Whistle,* starring José Ferrer, which launched its run at the Biltmore just three weeks after *Set My People Free* had started at the Hudson. The Langners had introduced the comedy, set in a garden adjoining a church and an old people's home, the previous summer at their Westport (Connecticut) Country Playhouse. Ferrer was generally credited with making a somewhat straggling bit of whimsy seem a great deal better than it actually was. He portrayed the wandering pitchman who camps for a time at the old folks' home, inspiring the inmates to a renewed zest for living with cure-alls which are as fraudulent as he is, but also with a personal exuberance which is genuine. William Hawkins, in his *World-Telegram* review, compared the production to the old popular song, "It ain't what you do, it's the way that you do it," finding it "entirely endearing, gay and funny often to the point of being bawdy. . . . There are laughs in this play every few lines. Sometimes they come in bursts, but more often they are tender, deeply sympathetic and satisfying." The critic concluded

The Silver Whistle—George Mathews. *Vandamm photograph.*

William Hawkins in the *World-Telegram* found the same costumes "wonderfully elaborate . . . making the stage a whirl of lush color and elegant line." He and a few other critics found the comedy acceptable and even deft in spots. It seemed that everybody had something to say about Miss Ballard's costumes, which, according to Robert Coleman of the *Mirror*, were "vulgar without being funny." Richard Watts, Jr., in the *New York Post*, thought they added greatly to the humor and charm. To Howard Barnes of the *Herald Tribune*, her settings and costumes gave "scene after scene more bounce than is to be found in the writing."

French actor Jean Pierre Aumont starred

with the statement that *"The Silver Whistle* performs a rare service these days in suggesting that tomorrow may be brighter than today."

Ferrer portrayed Oliver Erwenter, who arrives at the home insisting that he is seventy-seven and that his free living actually has kept him young. The truth is that he is just a middle-aged wanderer with few restrictive moral scruples who wants to find out if living past the age of seventy would be worthwhile. He gets the people to eat outdoors and even promotes a bazaar. At the end, even after one of Oliver's pals has told the truth about him, temporarily putting the oldsters back into their previous stultifying resignation, they still respond to his enthusiasm and discover that they can maintain this new and livelier attitude on their own.

The Theatre Guild's and playwright John Van Druten's taste for E. F. Benson's whimsical novels about life in an English village in 1912 was not universally shared, as became evident when Van Druten's *Make Way for Lucia,* based on one of these stories, came to the Cort Theatre that December. To catch the spirit, they imported English actress Isabel Jeans to play the title role, that of a bitchy interloper who challenges the social leadership of Miss Mapp (Catherine Willard) in the town of Tilling. Cyril Ritchard played her dilettante companion. Hobe Morrison, reviewing for *Variety,* concluded that it didn't add up to much of a show, but he did admit that "Lucinda Ballard's drawing room setting and splendacious costumes have hideous elegance."

Make Way for Lucia—Isabel Jeans (with Cyril Ritchard) was brought from England to appear in John van Druten's stage adaptation of an E. F. Benson novel about English village life. *Golby photograph.*

Make Way for Lucia—Philip Tonge and Catherine Willard. *Golby photograph.*

in his own play, *L'Empereur de Chine,* in Paris and again when it was brought to this country in Philip Barry's translation, first as *Figure of a Girl,* when it opened in New Haven, and as *My Name Is Aquilon* by the time it reached the Lyceum in New York on February 9, 1949. It provided an American debut for actress Lilli Palmer, a native of Vienna who had grown up in England and in France and was married at that time to English actor Rex Harrison. Aumont was not happy with a change made for the American version. He portrayed Pierre, a romantic liar who manages to live by his charm, and rather well at that, attracting so lovely a maiden as Miss Palmer.

My Name Is Aquilon—Jean Pierre Aumont co-starred with Lilli Palmer in Philip Barry's adaptation of Aumont's own play, *L'Empereur de Chine. Vandamm photograph.*

My Name Is Aquilon—Arlene Francis and Lawrence Fletcher. *Vandamm photograph.*

My Name is Aquilon—Jean Pierre Aumont and Lilli Palmer. *Vandamm photograph.*

Eventually he is lying less, and she is lying more. In Aumont's original version, he also fell deeply in love with the girl's mother and had an affair with her. The producers here apparently felt that audiences wouldn't find that acceptable, so they had him making a coarse proposal to the girl's stepmother (transformed from her real mother).

Audiences found Aumont ingratiating, as they have ever since, and everybody flipped over Miss Palmer. The play was a failure. Reviewers were fairly scornful of a playwright who writes himself a role as a devil with women, especially when he had failed to make it entertaining.

Alfred Lunt and Lynn Fontanne, who have been married for a long spell, must love each other—but this is their own affair and I would not pry into it. What concerns me is that they love audiences—not as selfish hams seeking applause, but as a genuinely unselfish pair who will do all they can to make other people happy.

Thus, with his usual directness, did *Daily News* critic John Chapman salute the Lunts on their twenty-fifth anniversary as an acting team, which also was opening night of *I Know My Love,* by S. N. Behrman, based on Marcel Achard's *Auprès de ma blonde,* at the Shubert Theatre on November 2, 1949. The Theatre Guild, which had enjoyed the talented couple's services for twenty-one years, had previously presented them with a silver plaque on which all the plays in which they had appeared were listed. On this opening night, their twenty-fifth play, *I Know My Love,* was added to

I Know My Love—Lynn Fontanne and Alfred Lunt as a couple celebrating their fiftieth wedding anniversary in 1938. *Vandamm photograph.*

I Know My Love—the Lunts as the same couple, much earlier in their turbulent marriage. *Vandamm photograph.* This was the twenty-fifth play in which Lynn and Alfred had appeared together.

the twenty-four others engraved on the plaque.

While it was a rather inconsequential play, it was an ideal vehicle for the Lunts, especially on this anniversary occasion. They portrayed a Back Bay Boston couple married fifty years, with the clan gathered to celebrate the occasion, in the first act. Thereafter, resorting to the motion-picture flashback technique, the playwright presented them as a young couple getting engaged in 1888, again in 1902, at the end of the First World War, and in 1920, when the husband is having an affair with his daughter's best friend. Beset with family troubles as the couple were, the Lunts still exploited the comic richness which Behrman had provided for them, even when he was failing to show much motivation for the other characters. What came through beautifully, thanks to them, were warmth, charm, humor, love, and an unlimited joy of living.

Of all the tributes, perhaps the least effusive and most telling was written by Lawrence Langner for his autobiography, *The Magic Curtain,* with reference to *I Know My Love:*

As I write these lines, the Lunts are just completing a long tour of this play, during which they have encountered blizzards, railroad strikes, and other mishaps, while for the greater part of the tour Lynn played her part with a broken wrist, her left arm in a sling, an example of stoicism that is rarely encountered nowadays. Yet both Alfred and Lynn felt that in touring this play, they were repaying an obligation to their audiences who have enthusiastically supported them all over the country, which is in the great tradition of the great actors of America—a tradition which they have been the foremost to uphold in our time.

It takes a great deal to obscure Shakespeare, but Katharine Hepburn, with the best intent and purest motives, accomplished just that when she opened at the Cort Theatre on January 26, 1950, as Rosalind in *As You Like It.* It was hard to see the Forest of Arden, or most of the characters who tripped through it, for Miss Hepburn, and especially for her long, shapely legs, praised by almost every reviewer. One gathers from her notices that winter morning after the opening that the season hadn't had much to offer in that respect before she showed up in tights, masquerading as a boy.

As You Like It—Katharine Hepburn's legs attracted as much attention as Shakespeare's lines. *Vandamm photograph.*

As You Like It—William Prince as Orlando, Katharine Hepburn as Rosalind, in the wedding scene. *Vandamm photograph.*

As You Like It—Bill Owen, Pat Englund, and Ernest Thesiger. *Vandamm photograph.*

As You Like It—Katharine Hepburn and William Prince. *Vandamm photograph.*

221

While she was almost universally admired as a woman, a personality, and indeed as an actress, there was a sharp division of critical opinion over her Rosalind. Atkinson of the *Times* found too much Yankee in her, adding that she was:

> . . . too sharply defined a personality for such romantic make-believe. Her acting is tight; her voice is a little hard and shallow for Shakespeare's poetry; she has to design the character too meticulously. And is this a New England accent we hear twanging the strings of Shakespeare's lyre? Miss Hepburn's acting lacks the softness and warmth that commend Rosalind so passionately to Orlando.

Representing an opposite point of view, Richard Watts, Jr., of the *Post* asserted that he was proud of her:

> Making no compromises with that bravely individual style which drives people to either enthusiasm or distraction, she plays with such spirit, tenderness, humor, grace, and vitality, and looks so beautiful, that her Rosalind becomes a characterization of sheer loveliness. No actress I have ever seen in this celebrated role has approached her in bringing it to poetic life.

Michael Benthall's direction made the play sumptuous or heavy-accented, depending on where you stood and whom you read the next day. There was prevailingly good comment about William Prince's handsome Orlando, Cloris Leachman's capricious Celia, Bill Owen's Touchstone, and Ernest Thesiger's Jaques.

All the time that Langner was pursuing his profession as a patent attorney, helping to run the Theatre Guild, and operating the Westport Country Playhouse during the summer with his wife, Armina Marshall, he also was writing plays and getting them produced. In the fall of 1933 he was represented as collaborator in three plays on Broadway. One was his version of Strauss's *Die Fledermaus,* with lyrics by Bob Simon, which came to the stage under the title of *Champagne Sec.* The Guild was offering Molière's *School for Husbands* in the adaptation by Langner and Arthur Guiterman. And *The Pursuit of Happiness,* written by Lawrence and Armina and premiered that July at Westport, had been brought into town by Rowland Stebbins; it was good for a year's run. It became known as the bundling play, because of a scene in which a young Hessian

officer and a colonial girl enjoy this kind of a date—in a bed, for warmth, but with a board separating them. The scene was Armina's idea, and it was instrumental in transforming a fairly serious drama about equality in Revolutionary War times into a delightful comedy, making the same points more effectively. It also was played in London and later made into a motion picture. The play for years has been a staple of summer and community theatre.

In February of 1950 it returned to the New York stage as a musical, *Arms and the Girl!,* by Herbert and Dorothy Fields and Rouben Mamoulian, with lyrics by Dorothy, music by Morton Gould, direction by Rouben, and choreography by Michael Kidd. Nanette Fabray and Georges Guétary played the roles originated seventeen years earlier at Westport by Peggy Conklin and Tonio Selwart. The musical turned out to be less than people had been led to expect by the success of the play, but there were compensations, such as Pearl Bailey, portraying an escaped slave from Virginia, singing "There Must Be Something Better Than Love" and "Nothin' for Nothin'."

Also first produced at Westport, William Inge's *Come Back, Little Sheba* was presented as the fourth and final Guild production of the 1949–1950 season, as well as the only original script;

Arms and the Girl!—the musical adaptation of *The Pursuit of Happiness* revived bundling on the Broadway stage. The bundlers above are Nanette Fabray and Georges Guétary. *Vandamm photograph.*

Arms and the Girl!—Nanette Fabray and Pearl Bailey. *Vandamm photograph.*

Arms and the Girl!—Nanette Fabray and Georges Guétary. *Vandamm photograph.*

Come Back, Little Sheba—mercilessly honest was William Inge's portrait of a middle-class marriage, providing exquisite roles for Shirley Booth and Sidney Blackmer. *Vandamm photograph.*

everything else had been an adaptation or a revival. Frank, painful, and pitiful, it is the story of a lower-middle-class couple whose futility changes before your eyes from stultifying to terrifying. Doc (Sidney Blackmer) is a chiropractor who years ago had to quit medical school to marry the girl who is now his frowsy but affectionate wife (Shirley Booth). His sense of failure and the whole circumstance of his dreary life have driven him to drink, though when you meet the couple, he is recovering from his alcoholism under the watchful eye of his wife.

When she takes in an attractive coed, who double-crosses her fiancé by playing around with a stupid athlete, the combination of vicarious sex and vicarious resentment is enough to turn the husband, who is, after all, only a spectator, back to the bottle. Eventually he returns from the hospital to the wife who has finally matured enough to quit living in the past and consider the present. "Come back, little Sheba" is her plaintive search for her lost dog. She finally accepts the fact that the dog is gone for good.

Louis Sheaffer, critic of the *Brooklyn Eagle*, noted both the limitations and the potential of playwright Inge: "Although he hasn't quite mastered his art, there's the breath of life in his play, a quality that some more experienced playwrights have never been able to capture in their works." Atkinson found it "straightforward and unhackneyed and, in its best moments, terrifyingly true." Even those who didn't care for it (Howard Barnes of the *Herald Tribune* dismissed it as "dramatic trivialities") were intrigued enough to discuss and dissect it at some length in their reviews, and to imply they agreed with John Chapman who wrote: "Mr. Inge's play is interesting enough to make me want to see the next one he does."

In the wake of John Patrick's *The Hasty Heart*, which was a warm, compassionate, and touching play, audiences were not at all prepared for what seemed like a tasteless turnaround when the Theatre Guild, in association with Russell Lewis and Howard Young, presented his *The Curious Savage;* it opened the Guild's thirty-third season on October 24, 1950, at the Martin Beck. The new play, though set in the present, hearkened back to the unenlightened past when the mentally ill were considered a fit subject for comedy. In fairness to Patrick, this might not have been quite what he intended, but that is how it came across. His intended comment—hardly

Come Back, Little Sheba—Shirley Booth and Sidney Blackmer. *Vandamm photograph.*

The Curious Savage—George Jenkins designed and lit John Patrick's play. It starred Lillian Gish (holding teddy bear, at right). *Valente photograph.*

original—was that those in mental institutions might be more sane than those outside. And he implemented this theme with his story of an institutionalized Mrs. Savage (Lillian Gish) whose incarceration stems from the fact that she is generous with her money. She has been committed by her stepchildren. At the play's conclusion, the lady returns to the allegedly sane world outside, but you know she's going to miss the more sensible life in the asylum.

Miss Gish was a latecomer in the starring role. Patrick had written the play with Patricia Collinge in mind, but at the close of the tryout engagement in Wilmington, Delaware, she quit, explaining that so many line changes had been made that she no longer felt comfortable. Her understudy, Marie Carroll, took over in Boston, and was soon replaced by Miss Gish, whose appealing performance brought a measure of mildly favorable critical comment, which *The Curious Savage* probably wouldn't have warranted without her. Richard Watts, Jr., of the *New York Post* found it "surprisingly pleasant entertainment," having decided that in his handling of the mentally ill the playwright has managed to "remove the greater part of the embarrassment and substitute an oddly likable charm."

Proficient writers of dramatic verse never have been plentiful, and the mid-twentieth century would not have much of solid value to offer along that line were it not for England's Christopher Fry. He had written *The Lady's Not for Burning* as resident playwright of the London Art Theatre, which produced it in the spring of 1948. A year later it opened in London's West End, to run for 294 performances, with John Gielgud and Pamela Brown in the principal roles. The Guild brought it with its stars to New York in November of 1950 for a gratifying run of 151 performances —considerable, for a play so esoteric in its literary style, considering the usual taste of an American audience.

The play earned its popularity through its admirable sense and sound. The sense is a story of world-weariness, witch-hunting, and love in the fifteenth century, couched in sharply witty terms and styled as bright, intelligent comedy. The sound is the lofty music of poetry—not just facile versifying but a truly lyrical use of words and meanings. Gielgud portrayed a discharged soldier, so disgusted with the world that he wants to be hanged. He has confessed a couple of murders— which he has not committed—in the hope of being executed. Miss Brown appeared as Jennet Jourdemayne, charged with being a witch because she likes to live by herself and speaks French to her poodle. She, by contrast, wants desperately to live. So when she and the soldier are thrown together, almost immediately falling in love, their quite opposite outlooks provide for a richness of acerbic and romantic exchange.

It was a real thrill—as it still is—to hear

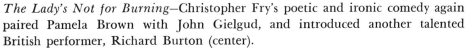

The Lady's Not for Burning—Christopher Fry's poetic and ironic comedy again paired Pamela Brown with John Gielgud, and introduced another talented British performer, Richard Burton (center).

a cast speak the English language as beautifully as this one did. John Chapman of the *Daily News* did not admire Fry's literary style (the *Daily News* rarely resorts to poetry, being rather blunt and basic in its use of words) but admitted he came away from the theatre with "a hot desire to hear Miss Pamela Brown talk the English language as long as breath is left in her." The cast was good across the board; it included Eliot Makeham, David Evans, Richard Leech, Peter Bull, and a promising young actor named Richard Burton. Lawrence Langner, speaking for the Guild and for himself, rated Fry a spiritual descendant of Shakespeare who, he believed, "may turn the English-speaking theatre back to the poetic drama which is its highest expression."

Another London success of two seasons earlier imported by the Guild for an opening also that November was the revival of Sir John Vanbrugh's Restoration comedy, *The Relapse*, with Cyril Ritchard as Lord Foppington and his wife, Madge Elliott, as Berinthia. Generally the Guild was credited for the elegance of the production, and just about everyone admired Ritchard's Foppington, as well as his adept staging of the 254-year-old romp. Worth quoting are the first two

The Relapse—Sir John Vanbrugh's Restoration comedy featured Cyril Ritchard as Lord Foppington and Madge Elliott as the widow Berinthia.

paragraphs of the review by Whitney Bolton of the *Morning Telegraph,* whose nostalgia for Restoration times shines through every sentence:

> If I could buy one theatre ticket in New York—and only one—the money would ride without a second's hesitation on a play that is 254 years old, a rake-helly, swift, bold, brash, and audacious old-time comedy called *The Relapse,* or *Virtue in Danger.* It's the best fun show in all of Broadway.
>
> The Restoration boys wrote with a good bawdy appreciation of the fact that there is more to think about in a bedroom than how to pay for the wall-to-wall rugs. They knew that when the sun goes down the beaux wake up and that a lady's virtue, impregnable in daylight, is gossamer by moonlight. They wore long curls and fancy clothes and swished all over the place, these lads, but in the cool of the evening when the dancing began they were there—as men. Stalwart men, chasing men, boys with a job to do in the parlor and a good strong will to do it. They were a menace to fireside morals, and proud of it.

As has been noted before, a sheaf of good reviews availeth naught if the box office take does not match the cost of the production. *The Relapse* was expensive to import and mount: it lost $77,000 in its American engagement, which is a considerable sum today and was even larger then.

When the Guild's new production of Shaw's *Saint Joan* starring Uta Hagen opened at the Cort Theatre on October 4, 1951, New Yorkers had two earlier stagings to compare it with. One was the premiere American presentation, also by the Guild, in 1923, with Winifred Lenihan as *The Maid,* and the other, the 1936 version, under another management, in which Katharine Cornell had played the role. In addition, critics who ventured off Manhattan were able to—and did—compare it with Miramova's Joan in San Francisco or Mary Newcombe's at the Old Vic in London. Then, too, there was the movie version with Ingrid Bergman; there have been others since.

The comparisons were all made, signifying if not nothing, very little. *Saint Joan,* which is Shaw's greatest play and to some critics, one of the finest dramas to have been written in the twentieth century, can really be measured only against itself; the spirit of the production must match the spirit of the play, in intelligence, in human passion, in dignity, in humor, and even in divine assurance. This is a large order, but the fact is that *Saint Joan* cannot begin to express itself if it is deficient in any of these areas. The focal role itself permits no compromise. Joan must be fairly earthy; she is a farm girl. But she must not be crude, or doltish, or common, because, as Shaw carefully points out, she was exceptional, and she came from a fairly substantial family. Joan had class. She also had perhaps the most supreme and impregnable confidence of any woman in or out of royal ranks; the saints talked to her. This means that an audience must see Joan as she appeared to her doubters, to her inquisitors, to the people who adored and followed her, and to herself; and anyone who looks for just one of these Joans, to the exclusion of the others, is missing one of the very points that Shaw makes: that by being straightforward and essentially uncomplicated, Joan utterly baffled her own contemporaries and was an enigma through the five centuries before Shaw explained her in his play.

There was every evidence that Margaret Webster, who staged the new *Saint Joan*, understood all this implicitly. You could not say that she had taken this or that particular tack. She managed, by examining Joan from all sides, to encompass the reality and the spirituality—which, in the final analysis, might be the most pertinent reality after all—of the girl. And with an actress as pliable, yet resolute, as Uta Hagen, the approach worked beautifully. Miss Hagen's Joan was real, honest, a bit cocky, and, like Joan again, a bit upper class. Her Joan did not retreat into spirituality; she soared into it, tendering compassion to those unfortunates who could not hear her saintly "voices" or refused to believe that she could.

If there was a single prevailing characteristic in the production, it was dignity, which is not to be confused with stiffness or stuffiness. Each actor seemed to bestow uncommon talent on the personality he was to portray, to avoid stereotypes and, collectively, to fill the stage with individuality. James Daly as de Baudricourt, Frederic Worlock as the Archbishop, Paul Ballantyne as La Hire, John Buckmaster as the Dauphin, Alexander Scourby as Couchon, Andrew Cruickshank as Warwick, and Frederick Rolf as the Inquisitor were some of those to counter in their own ways the peculiarly bright and brief fire of Joan. It was this emphasis on individuality which sustained the drama even though some of Shaw's long, philosophical statements—statements of undeniable substance and intelligence—tended to get in the way of the play if they were not handled

Saint Joan—proving that lightning can strike twice, the Guild scored with a revival of Shaw's eloquent dramatic biography, with Uta Hagen as Joan of Arc. Margaret Webster directed.

Saint Joan—Uta Hagen with John Buckmaster as the Dauphin.

Saint Joan—Uta Hagen and Kendall Clark as Brother Martin.

exactly right. Elinor Robbins' costumes, Richard Senie's sets, and the whole tasteful guidance of the production were attuned to just the kind of *Saint Joan* which Shaw seems to have wanted. It is an inspired play as well as an inspiring one, and on this memorable occasion for the Guild, the English theatre, and theatre in America, it lifted up the spirit as few dramatic enterprises have before or since. If there was an artistic high point in the Theatre Guild's first half-century, which is up to the time of the writing of this book, this Margaret Webster–Uta Hagen *Saint Joan* could well be it.

In mid-December of 1951 the Guild offered another John Patrick comedy, *Lo and Behold,* in which the playwright tried with intermittent success to blend farce and fantasy. Leo G. Carroll appeared as a dying author who finishes himself off with one hearty meal, knowing it will kill him, after having made some unusual provisions in his will. For one thing, he wants the house boarded up and never sold, so his ghost can live there comfortably. What he has not expected is that other ghosts should move in—an Indian maiden whose brave had shoved her off a cliff, a concert pianist who had met an untimely end, and a Southern belle who had intercepted a bullet meant for her lover, with Doro Merande, Roy Irving, and Cloris Leachman in these roles. Also staying on in the house are the young doctor

(Jeffrey Lynn) to whom the writer had willed part of his estate, and the housekeeper (Lee Grant) who had innocently served the fatal meal. It is a play funnier in its premise than in its resolution, which is another way of saying that the first act goes better than the second. Burgess Meredith's direction worked in the first half but failed to solve the farce-fantasy problems in the second. Still, audiences were amused.

Richard Burton, who had been introduced to American audiences a year before in *The Lady's Not for Burning,* returned with another London success as a co-star with American actress Dorothy McGuire in Jean Anouilh's *Legend of Lovers.* In England it had been titled *Point of Departure,* and in its native France, *Eurydice.* A couple of thousand years earlier it had taken shape as the story of the musician Orpheus, who descended to the underworld to charm the gods of that region into giving back his beloved Eurydice. This they do, with the provision that he must not look back at her during the return trip. He looks and loses her a second and final time. In the Anouilh treatment, Orpheus (Burton) is an idealistic accordion-player and Eurydice (Miss McGuire) a third-rate actress who holds the country and state record for sleeping around. They meet in a railway station, love, then she is killed. The musician gets her back, but makes the mistake of delving into her past; he wants to know all about those

Lo and Behold—Jeffrey Lynn, Leo G. Carroll, and Lee Grant rehearse a scene from John Patrick's comedy. *Friedman photograph.*

228

Lo and Behold—Doro Merande as Minnetonka Small-flower. *Vandamm photograph.*

Legend of Lovers—Dorothy McGuire and Richard Burton. *Swope photograph.*

Legend of Lovers—Dorothy McGuire and Richard Burton, rehearsing. *Swope photograph.*

affairs. So she dies again and he follows in suicide.

It is a tedious play. Anouilh is pronounced ennui, and the ennui seldom was more pronounced in a theatre that season. Walter Kerr, in the *Herald Tribune,* found Burton an actor of tremendous promise, as did Richard Watts, Jr., in the *New York Post,* and quite a few others. Miss McGuire also earned general critical approval, usually with the accessory note that she was limited by her role. In the *Journal-American,* George Jean Nathan observed that the Orpheus legend always sounds silly when retold in modern dress, and in this case the silliness was compounded by the writing and staging.

When S. N. Behrman's *Jane* finally made it to New York, on February 1, 1952, it already had been playing in England and on the Continent for five years, and had been completely rewritten six times since its original opening night (January 29, 1947, Blackpool, England). In 1946 Behrman had agreed to dramatize a short story by W. Somerset Maugham, of the same title, about a frumpy woman who comes from Liverpool in 1915 to upset social London with her honesty and candor. The problem, as Nathaniel Benchley anal-

Legend of Lovers—Hugh Griffith. *Swope photograph.*

Jane—S. N. Behrman's comedy, based on a W. Somerset Maugham story, cast Edna Best as a drab Liverpool woman who turns into a London dazzler. *Vandamm photograph.*

Jane—Edna Best and Basil Rathbone. *Vandamm photograph.*

yzed it in an article for *Theatre Arts* shortly before the New York opening, was that in a play you can't simply *say* that a person is honest; you have to show it. This was just one of the matters which the playwright approached with the trial-and-error method. He eventually settled on 1939 as the time of the play, and had the lady express a mildly liberal political point of view in order to establish her independence of thought, but it is interesting that nary a critic even mentioned this aspect of the story. What they did notice, and for the most part enjoy, was Jane's free-spirit approach to her own life. She marries a man twenty-seven years younger than she, not out of any romantic delusion that she loves him, but because she thinks marriage would be a nice change.

But what made *Jane* appealing was the transformation—*Pygmalion* revisited. The middle-aged lady from Liverpool was drab as can be. Transformed into a bare-shouldered enchantress with uncommon coolth, she delighted her audiences—and Edna Best was just the actress to do it. Why this sort of sudden alteration continues to work is something of a mystery, but it almost always does. Writing about just this gambit in *Look* magazine, John Lardner mentioned a movie in which Lana Turner was turned from grub to butterfly just by snatching off her glasses, adding that no one was startled: "She should have begun the scene wearing a shroud, or a mainsail." By contrast, he found Jane's transformation effective, comparing her in her Liverpool black dress to the average man's conception of Daniel Boone in his old age. In the second-act evening gown, she knocked the audience cold. Cyril Ritchard staged the play with the appropriate British embellishments, and the talented Miss Best was abetted by Basil Rathbone as a writer (Behrman obviously had Maugham himself in mind) and Philip Friend as the lady's "young man." Rathbone was listed in the program as co-star, which indeed he was; the dialogue between the weary, skeptical writer and Jane is the heart of the comedy. Valentina's costuming of Miss Best was a key factor in the effect achieved by the production, and Elfi von Kantzow's elaborate, slightly decadent drawing room provided quite the right setting.

In *Venus Observed,* which established itself at the Century Theatre on February 13, Christopher Fry again demonstrated his enchantingly elliptical employment of the English language, as he had in *The Lady's Not for Burning,* though with significant difference. The first play soared on its poetry, and the second threatened to become submerged in the very lyricism of its words. Each contrasted the autumnal resignation of a man with the springlike anticipation and life-love of a younger woman, though the conclusions do not follow the same pattern.

Rex Harrison portrayed the aging duke, experienced in astronomy and women, who brings three of his ex-mistresses to his home with the intention of marrying one of them, but falls in love with the daughter of his secretary instead. She was played by Lilli Palmer—Mrs. Harrison at the time. Whitney Bolton appreciated the skill of the director, Laurence Olivier, in staging so insubstantial a drama: "Sir Laurence has directed with full knowledge that he had to teach a cast how to walk a shallow field of blossoming words."

About this time a move was made to increase considerably the strength of the touring theatre with a merger involving the Theatre Guild–American Theatre Society and the Council of the Living Theatre. It was worked out by Warren Caro, executive director of the TG-ATS, in order to provide a wider selection of plays for subscription audiences, as well as to provide a secure touring arrangement in which other managements could participate. Caro, a Cornell graduate, had come to the Guild in 1946 following service as a Coast Guard officer in World War II. An attorney by training, he quickly progressed in the organization, tightening up its business procedures and revitalizing its touring and subscription activities.

By 1957, the twenty-fifth anniversary of the TG-ATS, eighteen cities were on the subscription list and road grosses had risen from $1,039,086 for 122 playing weeks in 1950–1951 to $2,216,368 for 174½ weeks in 1956–1957. A party

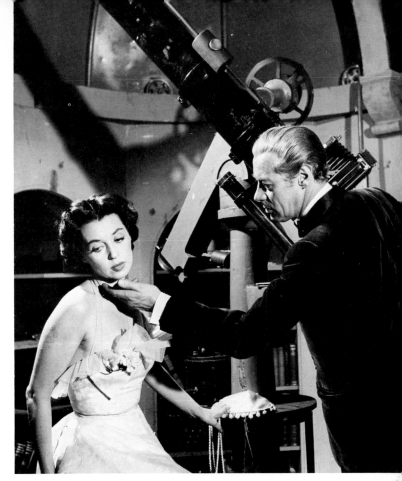

Venus Observed—Rex Harrison was the aging duke and amateur astronomer who falls in love with a young secretary (Lilli Palmer). *Swope photograph.*

Venus Observed—James Westerfield, Stuart Burge, and John Williams. *Swope photograph.*

in New York celebrating the silver anniversary saluted such key people as Addie Williams, the Guild's New York subscription secretary for thirty-five previous years and the ATS consultant since that venture had begun in 1932; Langner, the president, and Caro, as well as all the subscription managers in the "road" cities. In 1956–1957, twenty-eight productions toured, and each city saw a minimum of six and a maximum of ten of them.

Loyalty to G. B. Shaw probably was the prime motivation behind Theresa Helburn and Lawrence Langner's decision to present his *The Millionairess*, first in England, then in New York, in association with the H. M. Tennent Ltd. management of London. They knew the play, having staged its American premiere at the Westport Country Playhouse in 1938, at which time *Variety* judged it not a particularly likely prospect for Broadway. However, they hoped that with the right star, it might have a chance, and Katharine Hepburn, they decided, was the one who could carry it.

She tried, heaven only knows. At the October 17, 1952, opening in New York, her performance inspired at least one reviewer to refer to the event as a track meet, and everyone commended the lady for her energy, endurance, and speed. As a rich woman who destroys whatever she cannot possess, she twice threw a man to the mat, and never moved at anything approximating a normal ladylike walk. It was an exhilarating experience for the audience—enough, in some cases, to compensate for a rather mean-spirited play; Shaw's love for money and his reverence for power were almost too evident, and the writing in *The Millionairess* certainly is not his best.

This same Shavian work already had been done a couple of times in New York. The Dramatic Workshop of the New School offered it in the spring of 1949 with Margrit Wyler, formerly a leading lady of Vienna's Volkstheater, in the title role, and Equity Library Theatre staged it at the end of that season with Terese Hayden doing the part. It continues to find its way to the stage; an off-Broadway production opened March 2, 1969, with Barbara Caruso as the millionairess.

A cogent comment on the play and Miss Hepburn was written by W. Macqueen Pope about the London opening, which preceded her engagement in New York:

The Millionairess—Shaw's play gave Katharine Hepburn a chance to prove her energy, endurance, and speed. *McBean photograph.*

The Millionairess—Robert Helpmann and Katharine Hepburn. *McBean photograph.*

The Millionairess—Cyril Ritchard and Katharine Hepburn.

She raged through the part, she moved like lightning, she was energy incarnate. But she knew what she was doing. She understood full well what Shaw meant, perhaps even a little better than he did himself, for *The Millionairess* is probably the worst play he ever wrote. It has little or no shape, parts of it are already terribly dated—Shaw was over 80 when he wrote it—and is little more than a torrent of words which almost swamp the idea behind them. But in the hands of Katharine Hepburn the play became vital. She compelled attention and all else was forgotten. She knew no restraint, and one marvelled how she got her breath, for she never seemed to take one. It was a night to remember.

Mr. and Mrs. Rex Harrison (Lilli Palmer), who had concluded the Guild's thirty-fourth season in Fry's *Venus Observed*, returned to Manhattan at midpoint of the thirty-fifth as two of the several entertaining players in Peter Ustinov's *The Love of Four Colonels*. A play which managed to be both scintillating and silly needed all the style a cast and director could provide, and Harrison didn't let anyone down, either when he was onstage or in his directorial capacity. As an evil spirit, countered by Leueen MacGrath as the good fairy, he deviously manipulated four officers —all colonels, obviously—who are assembled to

The Love of Four Colonels—at rehearsal: Leueen Mac-Grath, Guild producers Theresa Helburn and Lawrence Langner, Lilli Palmer, and Rex Harrison.. *Erwin photograph.*

The Love of Four Colonels—Lilli Palmer, Rex Harrison, Leueen MacGrath, and Stefan Schnabel. *Erwin photograph.*

solve problems of the Allied Military Administration in Germany following World War II. They were represented by Larry Gates as an American, Robert Coote as an Englishman, George Voskovec as a Frenchman, and Stefan Schnabel as a Russian. While they cannot agree on anything political or military, they do cooperate on a competition to seek the favor of Sleeping Beauty (Miss Palmer), each executing the romance in his own favorite period of national history. Ustinov's dialogue among the colonels was zestfully satirical, perhaps even Shavian. As the play turned into the Sleeping Beauty allegory it sacrificed something of that wit but it did give Miss Palmer the chance to show her enchanting self in four variations of her role (she changed to fit each colonel's ideal of a girl) and also let the four actors do their variations on a theme. The aim of all this was fun—sophisticated fun at that—and people generally had a good time with *The Love of Four Colonels*. A final scene in London, which presented the four colonels' wives, was dropped, with the author's permission, when the play came to New York. The producers felt it would be anticlimactic. Ustinov's comedy did walk off with the New York Drama Critics Award as the best foreign play of that season, which implies that the competition was not remarkable.

Joshua Logan and the Theatre Guild combined their talents to produce *Picnic*, by William Inge, polishing it during a long and expensive tour around the country before bringing it into New York. With Logan directing, a most convincing small-town Kansas setting by Jo Mielziner, and a memorably suitable company, it became not only the season's best play (Pulitzer Prize and New York Drama Critics Award) but easily its most exquisite production as well, and a credit to all concerned. The play had its world premiere in Columbus, Ohio, where Samuel T. Wilson, critic of the *Columbus Dispatch*, found it a fascinating mosaic of small-town life, also crediting Logan's direction as "a superb piece of dramatic orchestration."

Wilson discerningly compared Inge's play to inert chemicals suddenly activated by a catalyst, with Ralph Meeker, in the latter capacity, as the defensively brash young stud who stirs up a nest of volatile women. Originally titled *Front Porch*, it is there, in the heat of a Kansas summer in the 1930's, that a picnic is being planned when young Hal Carter comes along, all muscle and male sexuality. He takes away the breath of Madge Owens (the almost unbearably nubile Janice Rule), awes

The Love of Four Colonels—Rex Harrison and Lilli Palmer. *Swope photograph.*

The Love of Four Colonels—playwright Peter Ustinov.

Picnic—Ralph Meeker and Janice Rule. *Arthur photograph.*

Picnic—Ralph Meeker as Hal, the young vagrant who wanders into a small Kansas town. Janice Rule was Madge, the local girl who falls in love with him, and Paul Newman played her amiable but unexciting steady boyfriend, Alan.

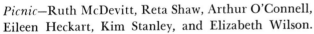

Picnic—Ruth McDevitt, Reta Shaw, Arthur O'Connell, Eileen Heckart, Kim Stanley, and Elizabeth Wilson.

Picnic—Kim Stanley.

Picnic—Janice Rule. *Arthur photograph.*

her sister Flo (Kim Stanley), and alarms their mother (Peggy Conklin) who wants Madge to marry a nice boy with a college education (Paul Newman). Nor is his influence overlooked by an old maid schoolteacher (Eileen Heckart) who exploits the situation to get a commitment, finally, from her long-term beau (Arthur O'Connell).

While Hal and Madge eventually do run off together, Inge really draws no conclusions, and this is part of the beauty of *Picnic*. You are exposed to a moment in the separate and collective lives of these otherwise anonymous people. It is their explosive moment—dramatic in itself, yet even more compelling for what it reveals, or implies, about what they have been and what they might become. Nobody in his right mind believes that Hal and Madge will live happily ever after; there's too much going against them, including their own natures. But an audience can suspect that their irresistible sexual and perhaps romantic appeal for each other will compensate for a lot of unhappiness—for a while, anyway. As for the others, the coming and going of Hal will leave them as they were and change them. They will live substantially the same lives but

with the difference that for that one little while something happened; the world came alive, and they will be nourished by that brief excitement for the rest of their days.

These characters seemed to be people Inge knew; no island-locked New Yorker could have fashioned them, or that midsummer Midwestern lethargy in which they were trapped. Though transplanted to New York, Inge had been born in Independence, Kansas, thirty-nine years before, and after growing up in such an atmosphere had taught drama, then became critic of the *St. Louis Star-Times*. In *Picnic* he had written a sturdier play than his earlier *Come Back, Little Sheba*, and had woven a more complex fabric of personalities without any sacrifice of the clarity of his design. The play became a hit in New York, despite some criticism of Logan's direction as being too conspicuous—too patently Logan trademark—when it might better have remained less obtrusive. Others felt that his staging lent force to the drama and bite to the comedy. In retrospect, both claims seem valid. No matter who staged *Picnic* thereafter (everybody did, and the play continues to be performed from time to time), he couldn't avoid incorporating something of the Logan touch, even if he tried. This was in part because Logan had literally changed the play—he convinced Inge that lines and scenes should be treated differently in the writing—but also because he had indelibly imprinted his style on it. Hobe Morrison, reviewing *Picnic* in *Variety*, predicted that it would "provide a boost for the careers of virtually everyone involved." It did.

By 1953 it was beginning to become evident that television not only could gain from the theatre but could contribute to it. Frederick Knott's long-running suspense drama, *Dial M for Murder*, at the Plymouth Theatre, originally had been presented on British TV. Horton Foote's *The Trip to Bountiful* had been conceived as a stage play, but at the suggestion of Fred Coe, a television producer, he turned his notes into a TV script and it was done on NBC in March with Lillian Gish starred. Reworked into a full-length play, it was tested at the Westport Country Playhouse and on the road before the New York opening at Henry Miller's on November 3.

In *The Trip to Bountiful* the Texas-born Foote offered the gently compassionate portrait of an old woman (Miss Gish) making what would barely pass for a home with a bitchy daughter-in-

The Trip to Bountiful—Frederic Downs, Lillian Gish, and Frank Overton. *Graphic House photograph.*

The Trip to Bountiful—Jo Van Fleet and Gene Lyons. *Graphic House photograph.*

law (Jo Van Fleet) and ineffectual son (Gene Lyons) in a Houston apartment. Miss Gish's Carrie Watts, trying to find self-assurance, dignity, and peace of mind, believes they might be waiting for her in Bountiful, Texas, a tiny town which was quietly disintegrating even when she had left it many years before. So she starts out on the journey, having to hide from her pursuing son and daughter-in-law. Along the way she picks up a war bride (Eva Marie Saint), who becomes her companion.

Eventually, after all sorts of vicissitudes, she gets back to Bountiful—or where it once stood. The town has disappeared; the farm fields have returned to forest. But Carrie Watts still is redeemed by the experience, having found just the qualities she was seeking already within her.

Miss Gish rewarded her audiences with what critic John Beaufort of the *Christian Science Monitor* describes as "one of those rare performances that touch at the heart of human existence." Another to earn excellent notices was Miss Van Fleet as the wife. Wolcott Gibbs in *The New Yorker* wrote:

> Miss Van Fleet's diction is like the twittering of an exhausted bird, intermittently punctuated by screeches of rapture or despair; her little trills of laughter are terribly unnerving, having no remotest connection with amusement; her habitual expression is as vacant as the moon but somehow smoldering; her gestures are profuse, abrupt, and almost completely meaningless; her carriage is languorous but at the same time industrious, in the sense that all the separate parts of her body are deeply involved in getting her slowly from place to place. Altogether, it is one of the funniest and most awe-inspiring comments on Southern womanhood I have ever seen, and I only regret that I wasn't privileged to watch it all night long.

Daily News critic John Chapman, hearkened back to the Guild's 1928 production of *Wings over Europe,* by Robert Nichols and Maurice Browne, when he reviewed *The Burning Glass,* by Charles Morgan, following its March 4, 1954, opening at the Longacre. Roughly speaking, they were the same play, he concluded, with no implication of plagiarism. Each dealt with a young scientist who discovered a power which could control the world. *Wings over Europe* was prophetic, in that its fantasy became the reality of atomic power not many years later. In *The Burning Glass* it was the energy of the sun which was about to come under man's control—and we're not far from that, either. A play which was more apt to stir the mind than the pulse, it debated whether man should be given mastery over nature when he has not yet achieved mastery over himself. Walter Kerr of the *Herald Tribune* deduced the play was intended to be an intellectual thriller, and doubted in his next sentence if there was any

The Burning Glass—Walter Matthau and Maria Riva. *Fehl photograph.*

such thing. He valued the play more for its momentary rewards than for any sustained dramatic power. The cast included Scott Forbes as the scientist, Cedric Hardwicke, Maria Riva (Marlene Dietrich's daughter), and Walter Matthau as a scientific colleague.

Only one new play was presented by the Guild in the season of 1954–1955, though busier ones were to follow. In collaboration with Worthington Miner they did Walter Macken's *Home Is the Hero,* in which the playwright, a former member of the Abbey Theatre in Dublin, played a starring role. Writing about the play in *Saturday Review,* Henry Hewes pointed out that it had set a record when produced by the Abbey and added that it also reads well, but went on to voice the prevailing sentiment that the production in New York was not successful.

Macken was cast as the bullying Irishman who comes home after serving a five-year prison sentence for murder to try to make over the family which has barely come to terms with its poverty during the time he's been away. Each member has adapted to the disgrace in his or her own way, and they refuse to change to fit his old image

of them. Glenda Farrell, Christopher Plummer, Donald Harron, Peggy Ann Garner, J. Pat O'Malley, Loretta Leversee, Art Smith, Frances Fuller, and Ann Thomas were Macken's diligent co-artists in a production which failed to stir critical excitement and closed after twenty-nine performances at a loss of $30,000.

The fates seemed to conspire against the Guild production of *The Heavenly Twins,* which began its activities for the 1955–1956 season in New York following a hazardous road tour. It had been adapted and translated by Louis Kronenberger, drama critic of *Time* magazine, from Albert Husson's French comedy-fantasy, *Les Pavés du Ciel,* and Cyril Ritchard had been signed to direct it. Jean Pierre Aumont, who had created the dual male role in the Paris original, was imported to fill the same two parts here. So many changes in the script and style of the comedy were made during the out-of-town tryouts that Kronenberger, on seeing the result, asked that his name be removed from the program credits, which it was. No one was willing to say who had made the alterations, though Theresa Helburn, speaking for the Guild, implied that more than one person was involved.

Home Is the Hero—Peggy Ann Garner and Donald Harron in Irish playwright Walter Macken's bitter drama in which Macken played the starring role. *Fehl photograph.*

238

The Matchmaker—backstage, Eileen Herlie and Ruth Gordon of the cast visit with director Tyrone Guthrie and playwright Thornton Wilder.

Meanwhile, on October 15, Ritchard had to leave the assignment in order to stage *Tales of Hoffmann* at the Metropolitan Opera, so Windsor Lewis was brought in as replacement; Ritchard's name appeared in the program as director, however. The play finally got to Boston, but not without a twenty-four-hour delay caused by torrential rains and subsequent flooding in New England that held up the two baggage cars which were carrying the scenery from Philadelphia.

Its opening there was not encouraging, as evidenced by the telegram sent that night by *Boston Post* critic Elliot Norton to theatre reporter Sam Zolotow of *The New York Times:* "Guild will be lucky if *Heavenly Twins* lasts through subscription season in New York. It's a clinker." Elinor Hughes of the *Boston Herald* was less bleak: "If the Guild could keep the show out of town it might be a smart idea. Road audiences are eager· for entertainment and don't have as much to choose from as the Broadway crowd and *Heavenly Twins* looks too thin for New York."

Nevertheless, the Guild brought it in for an opening on November 4, 1955, at the Booth. *The New York Times,* which seldom expressed an opinion in the headline over a review, was

moved to label this one: "Sin Made Dull," a thesis which Brooks Atkinson developed in the ensuing story. The critical reception was just about unanimously negative. The play did have some audience appeal, however, which could have been partly due to the casting of Faye Emerson, a television favorite at the time, as the woman who shoots her husband (Aumont), who promptly is reincarnated as a grandfather clock. She then is involved in an attempted affair with her dead husband's illegitimate son (also Aumont) when he and his wife (Gaby Rodgers) move in with her. The comedy did give Miss Emerson the opportunity to appear in a dazzling variety of outfits, designed by Helene Pons.

Farce—which includes slapstick—is a kind of theatrical entertainment which most audiences enjoy and most critics protest. The professional aisle-sitters are quick to point out that they do not disapprove of farce as an entertainment form; they merely feel most farce is not well done. This had gone on so long that the public was at the point of deciding that critics simply don't like broad, broad comedy. Then early, in December *The Matchmaker* arrived, co-produced by The Guild and David Merrick, and the Manhattan scribes, almost to a man, put their approval in print. This, they said, was farce as it should be played. As the public was just as pleased, the box office of the Royale was a busy spot for a long time thereafter.

As plays go, *The Matchmaker* is no spring chicken. (Neither is the title character, for that matter.) Its ancestry goes back to a bit of English nonsense, *A Day Well Spent,* by John Oxenford, first produced in London in 1835. This inspired one Johann Nestroy to prepare a German version, *Einen Jux Will Er Sich Machen,* premiered in Vienna in 1842. That apparently was that, for almost a century. In 1938, the Theatre Guild offered an American version written by Thornton Wilder. As *The Merchant of Yonkers* it enjoyed the talents of Jane Cowl and June Walker, but did not prove popular, folding after thirty-nine performances; the Max Reinhardt staging was not much of an asset.

Playwright Wilder, however, was not ready to abandon the property. He did considerable rewriting, changed the title, and offered it again at the Edinburgh Festival in 1954, with Ruth Gordon as Dolly Levi, the matchmaker of Yonkers. Not only was it enjoyed there, but it went on to

The Matchmaker—Loring Smith as the merchant of Yonkers, Eileen Herlie as the New York milliner he wants to wed, and Ruth Gordon as the self-ordained matchmaker who intends to marry him herself. *Kuhn photograph.*

The Matchmaker—avid eavesdropping in the Harmonia Gardens restaurant. From left, Ruth Gordon as the matchmaker and Loring Smith as the rich merchant; Eileen Herlie as the milliner, Arthur Hill as the merchant's chief clerk, Robert Morse as the assistant clerk, and Rosamund Fuller as the milliner's helper. *Kuhn photograph.*

The Heavenly Twins—Jean Pierre Aumont played a dual role opposite Faye Emerson in a comedy he also had done in Paris. *Friedman-Abeles photograph.*

a successful London run before being imported (or returned) to New York, with still more changes in the script. Tyrone Guthrie's boisterous new treatment was just what it had been needing.

Tanya Moiseiwitsch's settings and costumes did more than mirror New York and Yonkers of 1880—place and time of Wilder's version. They were properly theatrical, garish, and make-believe for farce. And the cast, to a man (or woman) played it in the same merrily reckless mood. They included Ruth Gordon, fabulously funny, as the widow who has picked out the widower she will marry. He was Loring Smith, recently of *The Solid Gold Cadillac,* the rich merchant of Yonkers, who wanted to court a handsome New York milliner, as played by Eileen Herlie. Arthur Hill was the merchant's chief clerk, with Robert Morse as the apprentice. The two run off to New York for an adventure, the clerk and the milliner fall in love, and Mrs. Levi lands her merchant.

The play was, and continues to be, garlanded with charming changes of pace. One occurs in the course of a Mack Sennett-like chase in a restaurant, when the thirty-three-year-old clerk, who has never had a date before, asks the milliner if he can put his arm around her waist, and she lets him. Then the mad action is off and running again. Other revealing pauses include those when Mrs. Levi suspends the farce momentarily to chat with the audience, or to converse with the spirit of her departed husband. And there is the famous aside by the cabman, who explains why he will not keep the wallet he has found. Walter Kerr referred to one of these interludes, in concluding his review in the *Herald Tribune:*

> As Ruth Gordon is turning the tide from knockabout farce to pleasant reminiscence, she says of a faded oak leaf that has fallen out of an album that "it didn't have color and it didn't have life." Mr. Wilder has deliberately fashioned a comedy out of an old oak leaf. But he has given it the color it had the day it sprouted, and he has—by some curious alchemy--given it exhilarating life besides.

Even its success in the mid-1950's was not the end of the road for this play. The next decade it was turned into *Hello, Dolly!*

A television interview in which General William F. Dean described the pressures to which he was subjected in a North Korean prison camp started playwrights Henry Denker and Ralph

Berkey thinking along the lines which led to their searching drama, *Time Limit!* It questioned not only the fairness of decisions made by stateside courts of inquiry or courts-martial in cases of alleged disloyalty by American prisoners of war, but the competence of anyone, who has not been exposed to the circumstance of psychological torture himself, to make such a moral decision.

Richard Kiley offered a politely taciturn portrayal as the major who is about to be charged with treason. Subjected to all the deadly brain-washing procedures of his communist captors, he made propaganda broadcasts for them and did everything else they demanded of him. He admits all this, and offers no defense. But the inquiring judge advocate (Arthur Kennedy) is not satisfied with this, and continues to probe, challenge, and examine until it is revealed that the major had collaborated in order to protect the lives of eighteen other soldiers. Such a synopsis oversimplifies the plot and implies that it is little more than melodrama. While it does lean in that direction from time to time, it is profoundly concerned with the morality of accusation—and this at a time only briefly removed from the worst depths of the Joseph McCarthy era.

The play itself does not resort to McCarthy tactics; the atmosphere of the inquiry is essentially reasonable. But it does make the point that it is difficult to evaluate a man's behavior in one set of circumstances, when you are viewing it from an entirely different set of circumstances. *Time Limit!* suffers from the fact that most of the subordinate characters are one-dimensional or, in a couple of instances, hackneyed. The title refers to the question: at what point is the breakup of a brave and loyal man, subjected to all kinds of torture and pressure, forgivable? Or, when does normal human vulnerability become treason? No one has come up yet with a definitive answer, but the theatre has gained from Denker's and Berkey's posing of the question. It received critical commendation in New York as it had on the road, and added dignity of purpose to a Guild season which already was enjoying the fiscal rewards of *The Matchmaker*.

Since time began, a wartime alternate to rape has been to offer a girl the choice between voluntary deflowering and having her near and dear killed. This was the dilemma faced by wholesome Betsy Palmer when Bill Hoffman's comedy, *Affair of Honor*, lunged into the Ethel Barrymore Theatre on April 6, 1956. Dennis King was the

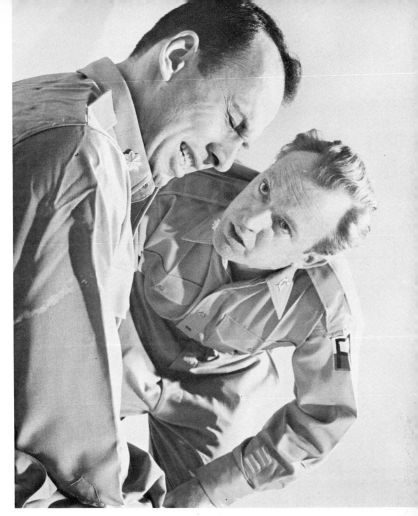

Time Limit!—psychological torture, as used in the Korean War, was the timely topic of this drama which featured Richard Kiley and Arthur Kennedy. *Friedman photograph.*

Time Limit!—Arthur Kennedy, Allyn McLerie, and Harvey Stephens. *Friedman photograph.*

Time Limit!—Frank Aletter, Allyn McLerie, and Richard Kiley. *Friedman-Abeles photograph.*

Time Limit!—Kaie Deei as Colonel Kim overlooks captured Americans in a Korean prison camp. *Friedman photograph.*

Affair of Honor—Dennis King was the British officer who lusted after Betsy Palmer in this Revolutionary drama. *Gigli photograph.*

Affair of Honor—Dennis King wipes away a mock tear as Betsy Palmer pleads for the life of William Prince.

Bells Are Ringing—Judy Holliday portrayed the happily meddlesome answering service operator. *Friedman-Abeles photograph.*

urbane cad, a British army major, putting the question smirkingly to his fair colonial prisoner during the dark days of the American Revolution. For the principals, the several other characters, and the audience, it summed up to a long night of talk, with George Jean Nathan, for one observer, wishing the girl would "shut her big mouth for a moment, take the count, and let everyone go out for a drink," which Nathan thereupon did. King's performance was generally praised, but the play was universally condemned with words such as dull, odious, pornographic, tasteless, and feeble. Hoffman, a television writer, had attempted an epigrammatic style which suggested he was trying to pull off something Shavian.

The Guild's Thanksgiving present to New York the following fall was *Bells Are Ringing,* a singularly happy collaboration which had brought together Jule Styne's music, Betty Comden and Adolph Green's book and lyrics, Jerome Robbins' staging, and Bob Fosse's choreography, along with considerable other talents in production and on stage. Best of all it offered Judy Holliday as the switchboard operator for a tele-

243

Bells Are Ringing—Sidney Chaplin and Judy Holliday.

The Tunnel of Love—Nancy Olson and Tom Ewell are the couple who want to have a baby. *Friedman-Abeles photograph.*

The Tunnel of Love—Nancy Olson, Elizabeth Frazer, and Darren McGavin. *Friedman-Abeles photograph.*

phone answering service who not only takes and delivers messages but is more than ready to make decisions, offer advice, and manipulate romances, including her own. There was a welcome exuberance about it, as in the scene in which she and Sidney Chaplin have just gotten into a subway car. She tells him that people are friendly, but he doesn't believe it, pointing to the glum passengers surrounding them. "If just one person said 'hello' on the subway, everybody would be friends," she insists, and she immediately says hello to a funereal-looking guy in black. And with that, *Bells Are Ringing* sallies into one of those joyous, inspired, and antic ballets that brighten the stage only once in a while. For ten or fifteen minutes the dancing, the helloing, the celebrating, the sheer enthusiasm of all the performers keep the audience in a state of unalloyed delight. With scenes like that, nobody minded that some of the show was clumsy and contrived; it was a real Holliday treat.

The extramarital lark had sung so sweetly at the box office for *The Seven-Year Itch* and its star, Tom Ewell, that a similar theme was employed for *The Tunnel of Love*, by Joseph Fields and Peter De Vries, in which Ewell again played a loving and loyal husband involved in unpremeditated dalliance. Nancy Olson appeared as his wife, who wants a baby, but can't seem to have one. When the shapely investigator (Sylvia Daneel) comes from an adoption agency, he is catapulted into a one-night affair with the girl. So when the couple does get a baby to adopt, it's his own. No one could call it strong theatre—and no one did—but it proved appealing not only on Broadway and in a long Theatre Guild tour, but in every professional or amateur production, in city, town, hamlet, or college drama department, for years after.

To open its fortieth season (1957–1958) the Guild collaborated with the Playwrights Company in a production of Ray Lawler's *The Summer of the Seventeenth Doll*, with the playwright himself in one of the two principal male roles. Arriving at the Coronet on January 22, 1958, it represented a milestone in the history of the Australian theatre, being the first play written and performed by Australians to earn international recognition. Following a good run on its native island-continent, it had moved to London to repeat its success, before coming to New York.

A comedy-drama of disillusionment, *The Summer of the Seventeenth Doll* has to do with antipodean migratory workers who cut sugar cane

for seven months on plantations in the North, and then move South to Melbourne and other big cities to spend their earnings on flings during the hot layoff season. Roo Webber, a boss cutter, and his buddy Barney Ibott return for the seventeenth year to the same boardinghouse, bringing another kewpie doll for the landlady's daughter's collection. On sixteen previous visits the two men have had a ball, shacking up with a couple of barmaids, who were every bit as glad to see summer come.

But the seventeenth summer is different. Barney isn't the lover he still imagines himself to be, and the self-discovery is painful. Roo already has seen a younger man superseding him as king of the cutters. One of their regular girls has slipped off and gotten married. The final moments are slashing and dramatic, as the two men fight, a doll is broken, and all but the immature Olive face the grim fact that the long party's over.

There was a problem of communication; the Australian company spoke a flavor of English that was disconcertingly strange to some in the American audiences (a perennial problem in

The Summer of the Seventeenth Doll—Australian playwright Ray Lawler (on the floor) played one of the leads in his own poignant drama. The other two are June Jago and Kenneth Warren.

The Summer of the Seventeenth Doll—Kenneth Warren, Ray Lawler, June Jago, Madge Ryan, and Ethel Gabriel—all Australians in an Australian play.

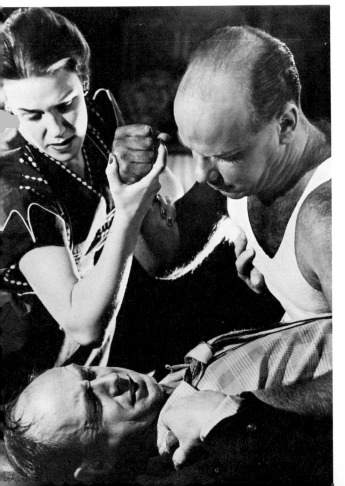

The Summer of the Seventeenth Doll—Kenneth Warren and June Jago.

Sunrise at Campobello—Ralph Bellamy as Franklin
Delano Roosevelt. *Friedman-Abeles photograph.*

Sunrise at Campobello—Mary Fickett as Eleanor
Roosevelt. *Friedman-Abeles photograph.*

theatre; most Americans seem to resent speech in
any dialect other than their own). The critics
mentioned this, sensing that it would become a
barrier, but also were careful to point out the
integrity and honesty of the producers in import-
ing Lawler, his company, and his play. Richard
Watts, Jr., in the *Post* dwelt on this, noting that
while the play is parochial in its setting and
speech, it is universal in what it has to say. He
added: "One immense virtue of the play is that
it always gives the impression of having been out
of the author's heart and soul and because he had
something that he passionately wanted to say." In
1968, with a black cast and setting it was staged
again in New York by the Negro Ensemble Company.

January 30, 1958, was the birthday (it
would have been the seventy-sixth) of the late
President Franklin Delano Roosevelt; months
earlier, playwright Dore Schary decided it would
be the opening night of his new biographical
drama, *Sunrise at Campobello*. Schary, who co-
produced it with the Guild, looked with warm
compassion and insight into three years in the life
of the young Roosevelt, starting in 1921, when
he was stricken with polio while vacationing with
his wife and children on the island of Campobello,
off the coast of Maine, and concluding in 1924,
when he nominated Al Smith for President at

Sunrise at Campobello—Mrs. Roosevelt (center) with Theatre Guild director Theresa Helburn and playwright Dore Schary. *Friedman-Abeles photograph.*

Sunrise at Campobello—at rehearsal: Henry Jones as Louis McHenry Howe and Michaele Myers, who understudied Mary Fickett, as Eleanor Roosevelt. She later replaced Mary Welch as FDR's secretary, Missy LeHand. *Friedman-Abeles photograph.*

Sunrise at Campobello—Mary Fickett and Ralph Bellamy with the Roosevelt children—Perry Skaar, Reni Dengel, James Bonnet, Kenneth Kakos, and Jeffrey Rowland—and James Earl Jones as the Roosevelts' servant. *Friedman-Abeles photograph.*

Sunrise at Campobello—Ralph Bellamy as FDR. *Friedman-Abeles photograph.*

the Democratic National Convention in Madison Square Garden in New York.

It was—and is—a beautifully inspirational play. No one, short of a resolute Roosevelt-hater (and they are dying off), can recall some of the scenes without suddenly finding his eyes damp, and his heart full of pride, admiration, and gladness. Depicted on stage is the truth about Roosevelt and his affliction, told simply, and not only in the factual details but in the spirit. Certainly one of the most stirring curtain scenes in the American theatre is that in which the young politician, wearing braces and aided by crutches, swings to his feet and makes his way to the podium to nominate his friend and political ally for an honor and obligation he himself was to assume eight years later.

Nothing less than masterful was the manner in which actor Ralph Bellamy transformed himself into Roosevelt, not as an imitation of the man but as a total characterization which continued to reveal itself from start to finish of the drama. Director Vincent J. Donehue had guided the rest of the cast as well to individual and total effects of character truth. These included Mary Fickett's Eleanor Roosevelt, Henry Jones as Louis McHenry Howe, Anne Seymour as FDR's mother, Mary Welch as Missy LeHand, and Alan Bunce as Governor Alfred E. Smith, plus many more, including the young actors and actresses who portrayed the Roosevelt children. "Sunrise" was a good word for the title; it lit up the theatre that season in New York and later on tour.

You'd think the Theatre Guild would have had enough of Shaw's nine-hour treatise, *Back to Methuselah,* when it presented the American premiere in 1922, the year after the Irish playwright had completed it. At that time it had been done in segments over three successive weeks, a project which testified to the loyalty and endurance of the subscribers. Shaw himself wasn't even content with the Guild's staging of the play in three parts; he wanted it to be done straight through. Nevertheless, in the fall of 1957 the Guild entered into a deal with Arnold Moss in which he would co-produce *Back to Methuselah* with them, also preparing a much shortened adaptation and acting in it. In beard, knickers, and the familiar belted jacket, Moss portrayed Shaw, tossing in comments on the proceedings culled from the 30,000-word preface to the play. Margaret Webster did the staging and such well-known players as Tyrone Power, Faye Emerson, and Arthur Treacher headed the cast. Quite obviously it was the participation of these three, all familiar through films or television, which made this Shavian road show successful as it hit forty-one United States and Canadian cities, mostly in one-night stands. The Moss adaptation cut the script from 90,000 to about 30,000 words, which meant something close to normal play length.

The producers had shown good sense in touring it this way before scheduling a New York opening, which finally occurred on March 26, 1958, at the Ambassador. On the road, the star names were enough to sell out a house for one night, then the troupe blew town before any of the locals could spread the word that the evening had been less than lustrous. In New York it was different; a platoon of critics descended on the production, bringing a number of points of view but arriving at approximately the same conclusion: that while Shaw uncut was too long, Shaw cut—at least in this instance—wasn't working either. The cast was found to be dutifully earnest rather than wittily iconoclastic, and any number of lines were admired for their trenchant comment on our society. The trouble with cutting Shaw is that you have to leave in whatever is essential to the forward movement of the plot and to characterization. That means you are cutting, in effect, the asides. But there you have the best of Shaw, the cleverest, best-worded, and most intellectually exhilarating aspect of him. The cuts by Moss were the sensible ones—perhaps the inevitable ones; yet the result was a play in which the best evidences of his agile mind had been edited out.

Power, in modestly enveloping tights and sewn-on fig leaves, represented Adam, as well as his descendants from the creation to A.D. 31,958, with the well-curved Miss Emerson, in a similar costume, as Eve and all the women who followed her. The changing times of the play provided them and the rest of the cast with engaging new costumes and personalities every little while. Treacher represented the Establishment, with Valerie Bettis as a serpent, and Richard Easton as Cain. The production, scheduled to run six weeks in New York, closed at a loss after four. However, the tour earnings offset this, and the Guild finally came out about $13,000 ahead, which was much better than their working average with a Shaw play.

X

1958-1968

By autumn of 1958, the Guild had diversified its production talents. Through most of the past forty years, Miss Helburn, Langner, Armina Marshall, and whoever else was part of the team at the time worked ensemble on every production. Now they were spread over several jobs, which, along with other innovations, hinted that the theatre needs of the time were different than they had been. For example, the Guild didn't have anything ready to start the new season, so it had arranged for their subscribers to see *The World of Suzie Wong*, which Joshua Logan was directing for another management (David Merrick, Seven Arts Productions, and Mansfield Productions); it opened October 14.

Langner and Henry T. Weinstein were in charge of *Third Best Sport*, which was undergoing first-act revisions after a summer in Boston. Miss Helburn was involved with a potential Paul Osborn adaptation of Peter De Vries's novel, *Mackerel Plaza*, and considering *The Ostrich and His Egg*, a comedy by André Roussin which was to star Bert Lahr. Miss Marshall was trying to cast the Lonnie Coleman drama, *Jolly's Progress*. The Langners' son, Philip, was preparing *An Inspector Calls* for tour, in association with Laurence Feldman.

Third Best Sport, starring Celeste Holm, did not arrive especially well-omened at the Ambassador on December 30, following a great deal of road time and a lot of corrective work. *The New York Times*'s outrider in Boston the previous August had wired theatre reporter Sam Zolotow:

> The Theatre Guild will be acting wisely if they decide to keep *Third Best Sport* a stock item and not transfer the comedy to Broadway. Another brief stay for Celeste Holm if they go ahead. The Eleanor and Leo Bayer

Third Best Sport—Andrew Duggan and Celeste Holm as a young couple attending a business convention. *Kuhn photograph.*

script is almost completely unrewarding, drawing its humor laboriously from a case of mistaken identity. Nobody in the cast stands out; Celeste has a couple good scenes but otherwise has little opportunity to do her stuff. *Third Best Sport* is a pop foul.

Nevertheless, the Guild brought it in, to earn a blithe commendation from John Chapman of the *Daily News* and lamentations from almost everyone else, though with good words about Celeste. The play—which did indeed become a stock favorite after failing in New York—follows an old formula about the eager wife of a young business-

249

man who tries to be nice to the boss and his impossible wife, but finally offends them by speaking the truth. The denouement always is that the boss decides she has a lot of spunk, whereupon he promotes the peppery little lady's husband. In this instance, Miss Holm and her groom (Andrew Duggan), who would rather be honeymooning, are attending a business convention (that's the third best sport; the other two are sex and baseball). Miss Holm tries to be the perfect Organization Wife, but fails just the way you hope she will, and everything turns out all right anyway. *The New Yorker's* critic wisely spotted the play as a copout by the authors; it starts by satirizing big business and ends by making a safe compromise with that very same Establishment.

William Faulkner's *Requiem for a Nun*, which opened Friday, January 30, 1959, at the Golden, brought audiences a kind of drama far more dark and terrifying than anything they were used to. The dark and terror were not those stock overt qualities of thrillers, but sensations to be felt only by probing deeply into the usually hidden depths of the mind. In his novel *Sanctuary* (1931),

Faulkner had introduced Temple Drake, the teenager kidnapped by a small-time mobster named Popeye and put to work for six weeks in a Memphis whorehouse, where she "loved it." (Nun is a seventeenth-century word for prostitute.) *Requiem for a Nun* (1950) picks up Temple eight years later, married to the man who had failed to come to her aid at the time of her kidnapping, and nostalgic about the Memphis interlude. Her husband isn't much good in bed. Temple has two children, and a maid who had worked with her in the brothel. The maid murders Temple's six-month-old son, whom both women loved, as a punishment for the sin in Temple's past, then goes to her own execution with the assurance that this is the way things must be.

Faulkner's play, adapted from the second novel about Temple Drake, had its world premiere in the fall of 1955 in Zurich, Switzerland, in a translation by Robert Schnorr. The following year Paris was introduced to a French version by Albert Camus; it ran there for two years. A London production also generated considerable interest and critical comment—not all favorable—and all this

Requiem for a Nun—Ruth Ford as William Faulkner's indestructible Temple Drake (Mrs. Stevens at this point in her career), Zachary Scott as her uncle, and John Dorman as her jailer. *Graphic House photograph.*

Requiem for a Nun—Christian Flanders as Pete, with Ruth Ford. *Graphic House photograph.*

Requiem for a Nun—Bertice Reading as Nancy, with Ruth Ford. *Friedman-Abeles photograph.*

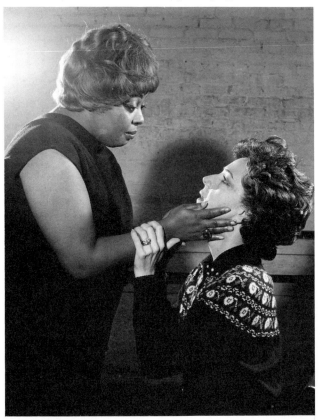

activity stirred curiosity about the play when it reached New York. The reviews noted that a literary style which qualified Faulkner as a novelist did not qualify him as a dramatist. Even the *Herald Tribune*'s Walter Kerr, whose critique was essentially favorable, wrote:

> There are hazards in so much insistence on long, rolling verbal patterns studiously separated from one another. . . . Phrases compound themselves until they seem to be evading and even forestalling the action. . . . The narrative style is insistently spare, monochromatic, indifferent to any kind of variety in this tangled, reluctant confession of sin. Mr. Faulkner sticks to the subject grimly, refusing his audience even the shortest of vacations; our noses are kept to the brimstone all night long.

Kerr concluded: *"Requiem for a Nun* is for those who are willing to risk a calculated, somewhat overwritten, but wholly valid experiment. Measured by the blows it delivers at the top of its strange and erratic rhythm, it is an original and stimulating achievement."

Though Ruth Ford proved a fascinating Temple, not everyone agreed she was the right one. Henry Hewes of *Saturday Review,* who had seen (and preferred) the Camus version in Paris, found Miss Ford too mature, too calculating, and too invulnerable for the role. "In playing each line carefully and knowingly, Miss Ford forbids us and the other characters to become involved in her dilemmas. She turns a Dostoevski protagonist into a Pinero lady. She makes a fight for her soul into a fight for her composure." Zachary Scott as the smug, moralizing lawyer added dimension to the play, and Bertice Reading as Nancy, the ex-prostitute-turned-maid-turned-murderess, was widely admired for her smoldering dignity and rocklike faith. Tony Richardson directed *Requiem for a Nun* with less tautness and vitality than some would have preferred, though there were well-staged moments. One occurred when Scott McKay, as Temple's husband, became so infuriated that he didn't notice the whiskey bottle, held high and threateningly in his hand, was draining down his sleeve.

Whenever old hands—or old fans—talk about particularly felicitous recollections of the theatre, they might begin by recalling individual excellences—a performance, a touch at direction, a set— but eventually they come around to the few examples of especially fine teamwork. You don't have to be old, either as a theatre hand or as an aficionado, to remember *A Majority of One*. Now this, let me hasten to add, is not a milestone play, by any means. It was, for its time (a February opening in 1959) actually sort of old-fashioned; Walter Kerr called it strictly square, but with love in his words. It was the happy result of a singularly agreeable relationship—playwright Leonard Spigelgass, director Dore Schary, and actress Gertrude Berg. They took an old form—the Brooklyn Jewish comedy—and, while restating the same precepts about candor and honesty which are the eventual purpose of most such plays, they freshened it, ever so appealingly.

For Mrs. Berg, Spigelgass wrote the part of a woman, Jewish-Brooklyn and middle-aged, who grieves for her son, lost in the war with Japan. On a ship to that country she meets a distinguished, reserved Japanese industrialist (Sir Cedric Hardwicke), whose son has been killed by Americans in the same conflict. Obviously, there are obstacles to be overcome before the two can find common ground and, in fact, romance. But for what reason are obstacles raised in plays, if not to be overcome? And what obstacle ever failed to fall before an assault of Jewish motherly common sense? The deep pleasure which the play planted in many (not all) of its audiences meant that all parties had managed to teach a fairly familiar lesson in understanding another's point of view without ever pushing

or, for that matter, sentimentalizing beyond a quite acceptable point. It continues to be a good play, within its quite limited aims, but it probably never again will look as charming as when it had Schary and the late Mrs. Berg, not to overlook Sir Cedric, to give voice to Spigelgass' dialogue. Proof of this once-only combination was the subsequent movie version, directed by Mervyn LeRoy, with Rosalind Russell trying to do a Gertrude Berg, and Alec Guinness as the Japanese gentleman. In the *Washington Post,* Richard Coe called the film "merely disastrous."

A springtime enterprise of the Guild bearing the title *Triple Play* struck a note of memory and another of prediction. The name notwithstanding, it consisted of four one-act plays (called *Triple Play* because they were by three authors). The one-act play had been a staple of the Washington Square Players around the time of World War I. But people seemed more willing to put down their money, in the commercial theatre, for one full-length drama or comedy than two or three shorter ones, and only seldom in the ensuing forty years was a one-act bill offered on Broadway. Maybe *Triple Play* suggested something to others; at any event, a few years after its brief but stimulating stay, the one-acter was back several times in a single season, including a musical (*The Apple Tree*).

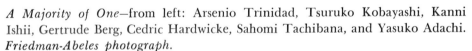

A Majority of One—from left: Arsenio Trinidad, Tsuruko Kobayashi, Kanni Ishii, Gertrude Berg, Cedric Hardwicke, Sahomi Tachibana, and Yasuko Adachi. *Friedman-Abeles photograph.*

A Majority of One—Ina Balin and Michael Tolan. *Friedman-Abeles photograph.*

A Majority of One—Cedric Hardwicke, Gertrude Berg, and Ina Balin. *Friedman-Abeles photograph.*

Hopefully this tiny reawakening will not be ignored. More plays than you'd care to count have been stretched out to an evening's length from a one-act original. The theatre probably would be in a better state if more full-length masterpieces were honed down to a single, compact act, with maybe two or three of them on a single bill. Any critic can, without too much trouble, recall a hundred plays which were not acceptable in two or three acts but which might have worked well enough in one.

The special attraction of *Triple Play* was the acting by Mr. and Mrs. Hume Cronyn (Jessica Tandy); Cronyn also did the staging. Miss Tandy poignantly portrayed a neurotic Southern woman, retreating into her memories for Tennessee Williams' early one-acter, *Portrait of a Madonna*. Cronyn followed as a schoolmaster, demeaned by an overbearing wife, in Chekhov's *On the Harmful Effects of Tobacco*. The two appeared in a pair of O'Casey comedies, *A Pound on Demand* and *Bedtime Story*.

Back in 1938 Betty Comden and Adolph Green started their professional careers as entertainers with an act called The Revuers at the Village Vanguard in Greenwich Village; Judy Holliday was part of the company. From that they graduated to performing in and writing a larger order of songs, sketches, and play book with *On the*

Triple Play—Jessica Tandy and George Mathews in *Portrait of a Madonna,* the first of four one-act plays. *Friedman-Abeles photograph.*

Triple Play—Hume Cronyn and Biff McGuire in *A Pound on Demand. Friedman-Abeles photograph.*

Triple Play—Jessica Tandy in *Bedtime Story. Fehl photograph.*

Town, in which memorable enterprise they were joined by composer Leonard Bernstein and choreographer Jerome Robbins. From then on they were too busy writing for shows to act in them—shows such as *Billion Dollar Baby, Wonderful Town,* the musical version of *Peter Pan* for Mary Martin, *Say, Darling,* and *Bells Are Ringing.*

So *A Party with Betty Comden and Adolph Green* was launched twenty years after their debut, with the avowed purpose of getting them back on stage—with their own material, for the most part. They performed each Monday evening at the Cherry Lane, which did not provide enough seats to accommodate their admirers. Among the latter, happily, were Lawrence Langner and Armina Marshall, who sold them on the idea of a three-week holiday engagement on Broadway; they moved the little revue into the Golden on December 23. So well did this work that the Guild and Frank Perry, who was associate producer, brought it back to the Golden on April 16 for an extended run. A newspaper strike had kept the public from seeing the very cordial reviews following the December opening, but the producers made sure the word got around. "No one else writes satire with

quite so much compactness and precision," commented Brooks Atkinson, who found Miss Comden "elegant and reserved," and Green "affable and ironic." He concluded: "Two brilliant minds are at work on the follies and vulgarities of the world. They observe but they do not participate. For they have style, taste and standards. . . . They also have manners."

As costs were spiraling upward, in theatre and in everything else, failure suddenly was becoming more costly than ever, as the Guild and Dore Schary learned soon after the November 4, 1959, opening of *The Highest Tree,* which Schary wrote and directed. Closed after a three-week run, it represented a loss of over $133,000, of which the Guild and Schary spent about $28,000 and the rest was dropped by backers.

"Rarely has a play had its heart more firmly set in the right place," wrote Richard Watts, Jr., in the *New York Post.*

Its purposes are lofty and serious, its subject matter is of the utmost importance, its voice is clear and frank, and it is well acted by an excellent cast. But unfortunately these are not enough, and Dore Schary's earnest new drama

A Party with Betty Comden and Adolph Green—in person. *Friedman-Abeles photograph.*

The Highest Tree—Kenneth McKenna and Diana Douglas. *Friedman-Abeles photograph.*

The Highest Tree—Miriam Schary, who painted the symbolic picture; playwright-director-producer Dore Schary, and designer Donald Oenslager. *Friedman-Abeles photograph.*

The Highest Tree—Kenneth McKenna and Frank Milan. *Friedman-Abeles photograph.*

has its virtues more than counteracted by its curious failure to come to life on the stage as either a movingly emotional narrative or a stimulating and provocative discussion.

Schary was concerned, as many of us are, with the increase of deadly strontium 90 in the air as the result of nuclear tests. His view was that we should not shrug and accept it, but should ban the testing of nuclear bombs permanently. The crisis this poses takes place in the family of a nuclear physicist, who finally resigns from the government project he'd been working on and joins his son's committee of protest. Most of the critics rejected it, for affectations in the writing particularly, though John McClain in the *Journal-American* found the play worthwhile. The title stemmed from an inspiring idea; if you must climb a tree, climb the highest one you can find.

Another play which proved better in the idea than in the execution was Lonnie Coleman's *Jolly's Progress,* a kind of latter-day *Pygmalion and Galatea,* about an Alabama intellectual (Wendell Corey) who protects an animal-like black teen-ager (Eartha Kitt), then starts to teach her. He quickly discovers that she is a genius, and eventually sends her to Philadelphia for further schooling to save her from the local resentments which have built up against the two of them. Anne Revere as a schoolteacher, on their side against the Ku Klux Klan and the rest of the red-necks, was another strength in a distressingly weak play. The problem was that Coleman could not transfer his sincerity about his theme to the stage. It is an inexpert play; too fragile to carry its own message. Franchot Tone originally had been cast as the man, but quit when the show was in rehearsal. According to one account, he protested the change in emphasis from the man to the girl (the title was changed from *Adam's Way,* referring to his character, to *Jolly's Progress,* referring to hers). However, columnist Dorothy Kilgallen insisted he'd gotten out rather than work with the temperamental and—according to her—undependable Miss Kitt.

To Howard Taubman, who had left his post as music critic for *The New York Times* to replace Brooks Atkinson (who became critic emeritus) as drama critic, *The 49th Cousin* could have and should have been a Jewish *Life with Father.* Instead he found this comedy, which began the Guild's 1960–1961 season, "a series of vaudeville turns connected by a desultory story line," and less a play than a vehicle for Menasha Skulnik.

Florence Lowe and Caroline Francke had written about a German-Jewish patriarch in Syracuse at the turn of the century who believes his three daughters should be protected from predatory males; protection is the last thing the girls want. Martha Scott, Marian Winters, and Evans Evans were the delectable trio, with Gerald Hiken as a peddler who coveted Miss Scott. Despite the comedy's shortcomings, it earned widespread gratitude for providing the opportunity to watch Skulnik in performance. One is inclined to wonder if the authors found their inspiration in the same sort of Jewish father who is so eloquently and pictorially represented in the writings of Sholom Aleichem. Skulnik's Isaac Lowe, among other similarities, talked directly with God, as does Tevye the dairyman, who stepped from the printed page to the stage in 1964 for *Fiddler on the Roof.*

As it had several times before, the Guild went to Columbus, Ohio, in September of 1960 to stage a new play. There were several reasons. The Hartman Theatre, though old (1912) was a good house, and similar in many ways to a number of the Broadway legit theatres. Robert F. Boda, its manager, was a theatre professional in the best sense of the term, who could guarantee them full cooperation and a minimum of problems. Also, Columbus was far enough from New York so that, unlike New Haven or even Boston, it didn't draw the same in-the-know New Yorkers to tryouts. A Columbus audience was, God save it, "typical," neither more nor less sophisticated than the average for a fairly cosmopolitan midwestern city. The idea of being a tryout town appealed to Columbus, and the local press invariably displayed gratifying interest in the new project, which included serious and detailed critical reviews.

Arthur Laurents' *Invitation to a March* was not yet right in Columbus; by New York, details had been better worked out. It is a crisp, honed allegory, or fairy tale about a sleeping beauty (Jane Fonda) whose slumber symbolizes her resistance to a life in which everything is already patterned. The *March* to which we are invited moves to the drumbeat of routine. In a Long Island beachhouse setting by William Pitkin, three mothers attempt to steer the girl's future—a future which apparently will involve one of two sons of the same father, but out of licit and illicit unions. Even in Columbus it was evident that Laurents had written his most cutting dialogue for Eileen Heckart, whose performance was a classically elegant example of

Jolly's Progress—Eartha Kitt as Jolly, before she started to progress. *Kuhn photograph.*

The 49th Cousin—Eli Mintz, Martha Scott, and Menasha Skulnik. *Fehl photograph.*

Invitation to a March—Jane Fonda and Celeste Holm. *Friedman-Abeles photograph.*

Invitation to a March—Tom Hatcher, Jane Fonda, and James MacArthur. *Friedman-Abeles photograph.*

pure bitchery and total candor. This became a problem when Shelley Winters, as a second mother and ostensibly the star, became so upset over the admiration and stage time being gathered in by Miss Heckart that she eventually departed the role, being replaced in Boston by Celeste Holm. Madeleine Sherwood portrayed the third of the mothers—the real parent of the girl. Miss Heckart and Miss Winters (later Holm) had spawned the two lads (Tom Hatcher and James MacArthur).

Laurents staged his own play, which was applauded in New York for having something substantial to say about ourselves, and for saying it with more than ordinary stage wit. ("Mr. Laurents appears close-Shavian," quipped Kerr, who might not be grateful for being reminded. It must have been a night for punning; John McClain, admiring Celeste, referred to Laurents' play as a "Holm run.")

Some (though certainly not all) of the qualities which had made Meredith Willson's *The Music Man* one of the most irresistible musicals ever helped to carry *The Unsinkable Molly Brown* through a 533-performance Broadway run and subsequent tour even though it was not in the same league with the earlier hit. People came away from the theatre tingling with the recollection of Tammy Grimes singing "I Ain't Down Yet," and were willing to shrug off the fact that the story and people, though based on fact, tended to appear one-dimensional. What the show did have, besides Miss Grimes, was the irrepressible rhythm and bounce which Willson's music and lyrics superimposed on Richard Morris' play book. Molly Brown was the girl from the Missouri backwoods who went west, met her man in Leadville, Colorado, got rich with him, and then tried to crash Denver society. She never really made it, but it was (historically and on

The Unsinkable Molly Brown—Tammy Grimes as the girl who set out to conquer Denver society. *Friedman-Abeles photograph.*

The Unsinkable Molly Brown—Theatre Guild producer Lawrence Langner, director and co-producer Dore Schary, composer and lyricist Meredith Willson, and playwright Richard Morris. *Galaxy photograph.*

The Unsinkable Molly Brown—Tammy Grimes and Harve Presnell trying for society. *Friedman-Abeles photograph.*

The Unsinkable Molly Brown—at the table, Tammy Grimes and Mitchell Gregg. *Friedman-Abeles photograph.*

stage) one hell of a try. When Mrs. Brown wasn't invited to a social affair, she would stand outside the host's mansion hollering insults at the guests as they arrived. The show follows her fortunes from her hillbilly beginnings to her survival of the *Titanic* sinking.

Sharing the good critical comment with the gamin Miss Grimes was Harve Presnell as the easy-going Westerner who makes a pile in Leadville. His rich baritone singing voice was especially welcome on a musical stage which frequently is not as musical as it might be. Critical comment about Miss Grimes emphasized the difference between her and the usual leading lady. Wrote George Oppenheimer in *Newsday:*

> She is a wonder, this uninhibited, sprightly, comic and endearing Miss Grimes. . . . She is not beautiful, nor shapely, nor Callas, nor Markova, but she's seductive, buxom, melodious and graceful and when she tries for the first time to play a piano to keep a job (and hold a tune) she is clowning in the great tradition of a Marie Dressler or Fanny Brice.

Love and Libel, which wound up the Guild's activities for that season, is Robertson Davies' play based on his own novel, *Leaven of Malice,* in which a cultural feud between two families in a Canadian town explodes into combat as the result of a prank. Someone has run a newspaper item announcing the engagement of the daughter of one clan to the son of the other. Its bright spots—including Dennis King's performance as a cathedral organist—were not sufficient to carry the play, for which the best word Richard Watts, Jr., could find was "genial." Most praised was David Hays's setting, with its newspaper motif. *Love and Libel* employed that old wheeze of having characters speak directly to the audience, as did *Invitation to a March* and *The*

Love and Libel—Charmion King and Dennis King. *Friedman-Abeles photograph.*

Love and Libel—Amelia Hall and Leo Leyden. *Friedman-Abeles photograph.*

Love and Libel—director Tyrone Guthrie, with actor Dennis King. *Gray photograph.*

Hostage in the same season. There's nothing wrong with it, except that the device should be used only sparingly. In the first half of the 1968–1969 season, it happened on about four opening nights out of every five over a two-month stretch.

Conspicuous in the long list of Theatre Guild productions is the gap of a year between the Broadway openings of *Love and Libel* on December 7, 1960, and *The Captains and the Kings* on January 2, 1962. That year of 1961, however, was particularly well used: the Guild, which always had been international in its selection of plays, went international with its touring as well. The preceding summer the directors of the Guild had been asked to prepare a touring program of plays for the President's special international program for cultural presentations, which in this instance was administered by the American National Theatre and Academy for the United States State Department. So a major activity in the fall of 1960 for Guild directors Lawrence Langner and Armina Marshall was assembling a company and rehearsing the three plays which had been selected as representative of this nation in its writing for the stage. The Langners were assisted by Warren Caro as production executive, Philip Langner as associate producer, and Robert C. Schnitzer as general manager.

The plays and the roster of players were both impressive. Marcella Cisney was selected to direct Thornton Wilder's fantasy, *The Skin of Our Teeth,* in which Leif Erickson and Helen Hayes were Mr. and Mrs. Antrobus, June Havoc portrayed Sabrina, and the announcer was James Broderick. Tennessee Williams' *The Glass Menagerie* was directed by George Keathley, with Miss Hayes as the mother, Broderick as her son, Nancy Coleman as her daughter, and Erickson as the gentleman caller. *The Miracle Worker,* by William Gibson, featured Barbara Barrie as Annie Sullivan and little Rona Gale as her blind, deaf, and mute pupil, Helen Keller. Porter Van Zandt directed. Also appearing in one or more of the three plays were such capable players as Romney Brent, who had worked with the Guild almost since its beginning; Helen Menken, who played the fortune-teller in the Wilder comedy, and Dorothy Sands. The full acting company numbered about two dozen.

Each of the plays was produced under the direct supervision of the playwright, a detail characteristic of the artistic integrity which was evident throughout the project. During 1961, the Theatre

Guild American Repertory Company performed in the capital cities of Europe, the Middle East, and Latin America, proving one of the most universally applauded cultural programs in the State Department undertaking.

Current events frequently invite dramatic treatment on the stage but, for a variety of sometimes nebulous reasons, they seldom produce a great play. The Guild ran into this problem a great number of times; witness Dore Schary's ill-fated *The Highest Tree,* to name just one example. The situation came up again with Leo Lieberman's *The Captains and the Kings,* which opened the 1961–1962 season, though not until the beginning of January of the latter year. The program at The Playhouse carried a line familiar to readers of fiction: "No identification with actual persons, living or dead, is intended or should be inferred." Nevertheless, everybody identified Captain Richard Kohner in the cast with Admiral Hyman G. Rickover, which seemed to be what the playwright really intended.

Prince Juan Carlos of Bourbon (left), the future king of Spain and head of the Spanish government following Franco's retirement, with Helen Hayes and Romney Brent, of the Theatre Guild American Repertory Company, at a United States Embassy reception in Madrid. This was during the United States State Department sponsored tour of Europe, the Far East, and Latin America with three plays.

The Captains and the Kings—Dana Andrews, Conrad Nagel, and Peter Graves.
Friedman-Abeles photograph.

Both were pioneers of nuclear-propelled submarines in the United States Navy. Each had to wage his personal war against flag officers antagonistic to a vessel which could render obsolete their own tradition and experience of fighting ships. Both were Jewish and both were denied promotion to flag rank when such promotion was well-earned. Each man—the fictional and the real—was scrupulously honest, self-disciplined, and inspiring. The best thing about *The Captains and the Kings* was the way it communicated this inspiration.

Generally, however, the play was marred by too sustained a level of crisis, with little relief or contrast. The firmly set jaw, the shouted defiance, the cold ultimatum, the unveiled threat, the monstrous betrayal, the pulsating nobility of self-sacrifice—these all but crowded out the human quality. However, a profound respect for Admiral Rickover was evident in the way Lieberman had written the role and in the way Dana Andrews played it. The cast also included Conrad Nagel as an admiral out to scuttle Captain Kohner's pet project; Charles Ruggles as a double-dealing senator; and Lee Grant as the captain's secretary in love with the skipper (Peter Graves) of a nuclear sub. Flawed as drama, the play still offered cause to be grateful for its inspiration, and for the luster it added to an enduring concept of patriotism.

Having looked to the Navy at a January 2 opening, the Guild turned its attention to the Army two nights later with the New York premiere of Ernest Kinoy's comedy, *Something About a Soldier,* based on a novel by Mark Harris, with direction by Dore Schary, who was co-producer. It was hardly on top of the news, dealing with Army basic training in 1942, a subject which had been worked over a great deal at the time and during the twenty years since.

Like all too many modern stage projects, it attempted to keep the customers laughing and yet punch a message home. Audiences which shy away from genuinely thoughtful drama are to blame for that. Whatever the reason, the hybrid comedy-drama is often with us. Sal Mineo portrayed a seventeen-year-old intellectual who baffles his training sergeant (Ralph Meeker) but is understood and even respected by the company commander (Kevin McCarthy). Both the private and the captain covet the same beautiful counter girl in the PX (Gretchen Walther). She loves the youngster, even when the captain is taking her through basic training in hotel-room lovemaking. If the officer were an or-

Something About a Soldier—Sal Mineo. Friedman-Abeles photograph.

dinary man, that would be it, but out of a sense of obligation to the girl, he takes on responsibility for the boy's life. Only in the final act does the play grasp this issue firmly.

Where belief encountered the most difficult obstacle was in the captain's extremely sensitive concern for one of his trainees. The philosophical approach to a twenty-year-old event (the play is one long flashback) revealed subtleties which had been less evident then. Unfortunately, this technique also screened out the sense of reality. *Something About a Soldier* was directed expertly, and praise was due the trio of Mineo, Meeker, and McCarthy, each evolving a highly individual character yet interrelating beautifully. Miss Walther evoked a blend of naïveté and feminine wisdom in her role.

For *A Passage to India,* Santha Rama Rau's dramatization based on the novel by E. M. Forster, Edgard Varèse, the composer of "organized sound," reproduced the echo of the Marabar Caves, not far from Chandrapore in eastern India, as it was in the early 1920's. "It undermines one's hold on life," explained an Indian philosopher to two visiting English ladies. "Speak truth or falsehood, filth or poetry, the echo is the same heavy, booming sound. It erases the moral differences in anything man utters."

A Passage to India—playwright Santha Rama Rau (center) with Gladys Cooper and Eric Portman. *Friedman-Abeles photograph.*

A Passage to India—Gladys Cooper and Eric Portman. *Friedman-Abeles photograph.*

A Passage to India—Zia Mohyeddin. *Friedman-Abeles photograph.*

Small wonder, then, that the two ladies, each hypersensitive in an alien world, react violently when they visit the caves and hear the echo. The elder (Gladys Cooper) hears in it a denial of all the values by which she has lived. The younger (Anne Meacham)—already unnerved by the strangeness of India, the morning heat, and the prospect of a marriage she is reluctant to embark upon—imagines she is being attacked by the warmhearted, outgoing young Indian doctor (Zia Mohyeddin) who has escorted them to the caves. Out of this comes a trial of the doctor, which actually is a contest between English colonial authority and the emerging national identity of India.

It earned quite good notices, for the most part. George Oppenheimer in *Newsday* admired Miss Rama Rau's fidelity to the Forster original, and preferred the New York production to an earlier one in London. Wrote Walter Kerr: "How much you like the play will depend upon your willingness to pursue several provocative portraits across attenuated terrain. I found the journey interesting." If it did not attract enough people to qualify it as a hit, it could have been, because the author and director Donald McWhinnie presented an austere and arid play, not always in sharp focus, and alternately acted and postured. The vigor of its dialogue, and its perceptions, were consistently admirable.

In June of 1962, *The New York Times* writer Milton Esterow was able to report that the Theatre Guild was planning one of its busiest sea-

A Passage to India—Indian playwright Santha Rama Rau with Adlai Stevenson, United States ambassador to the U.N.

sons in years, with seven productions scheduled. Only two of them were brought to fruition in the following season, although one planned off-Broadway staging of Langston Hughes's *Tambourines to Glory* finally was accomplished a year later under a different management. With Joel Schenker and Michael Kanin as co-producers, the Guild opened its season with *Seidman and Son,* by Elick Moll and based on his own novel of that name. Its principal attractions were Sam Levene as a successful dress manufacturer, plus a line of dresses, gowns, and suits designed by M. Jacques Tiffeau (Monte-Sano & Pruzan, Ltd.), which not only were high fashion but which looked beautiful on the models —and that is a rare combination. Furthermore, *Seidman and Son* is a friendly play, a funny play, and there is tenderness at the heart of it. No matter

that it also looks suspiciously like a formula play; when it is done with the right people (and it was) it can work.

John Chapman of the *Daily News* clobbered it in three ruthless paragraphs, calling it "a pointless and lifeless little cloak-and-suit comedy," but the six other New York daily reviewers were either pleased or amiably forgiving, and, more important, the audiences had a good time. It ran for twenty-seven weeks in New York, then toured, closing in San Francisco in February, 1964. Even so, it was not profitable—this being a frequent circumstance with plays that have the look of success. A large cast made it expensive to tour (about $26,000 a week during the season, though for a stock tour the cost was cut to $19,000).

The combination of actress Gertrude Berg

Seidman and Son—Sam Levene portrayed a dress manufacturer surrounded at each performance by an ever-changing assortment of professional models. *Friedman-Abeles photograph.*

Seidman and Son—Sam Levene in the title role with Frances Chaney as his wife. *Friedman-Abeles photograph.*

Dear Me, the Sky Is Falling—playwright Leonard Spigelgass with Gertrude Berg, star of the comedy. *Friedman-Abeles photograph.*

and playwright Leonard Spigelgass, so felicitous in *A Majority of One*, inspired a box-office advance sale of $400,000 worth of tickets prior to the March 2, 1963, opening of *Dear Me, the Sky Is Falling*, which the playwright fashioned from a story by Mrs. Berg and James Yaffe. Good people were involved in addition to those already named—Howard da Silva, Tresa Hughes, Ron Leibman, Minerva Pious, and William Daniels in the cast, Herman Shumlin as director, and Will Steven Armstrong as designer.

What came forth was the kind of play which should be reviewed not by critics but by mothers. There were about six million people within artillery range of the new comedy at the Music Box who ask no more of the theatre than that it offer Gertrude Berg in comedies in which she is the mother who mixes in everybody's business—and who makes everything turn out all right at the end. Along with the stock ingredients of such a comedy, this one added a confrontation between Mrs. Berg and a psychiatrist, which provided the liveliest skirmish of the evening. Actually, the reviews weren't bad; nobody considered the comedy of much consequence but the majority had a good time.

For the first time in its forty-five years, the Guild was not represented by a Broadway pro-

Dear Me, the Sky Is Falling—Gertrude Berg was the housewife whose foray into psychoanalysis baffles her sister (Tresa Hughes) and husband (Howard da Silva). *Friedman-Abeles photograph.*

duction in the 1963–1964 season. Scheduled was *Conversations in the Dark,* by thirty-one-year-old William Hanley, whose two one-acters, *Mrs. Dally Has a Lover* and *Whisper in My Good Ear,* had attracted interest off-Broadway (he later was to write *Slow Dance on the Killing Ground*). The play was abandoned following its second tryout week in Philadelphia. The play examines two couples and an infidelity affecting both marriages. Jack Warden, Sandra Church, Jon Cypher, and Barbara Barrie made up the cast.

For its forty-seventh season (1964–1965), the Theatre Guild went off-Broadway, and in so doing, gave tacit recognition to the changing facts of theatre life. Almost a half-century before, they had introduced experimentation into the commercial theatre; that was the raison d'être of the new organization—to bring new life to the stage and to break away from the restrictions imposed by the commercial formula. They succeeded so well that within a decade that which had been experimental had become accepted not only by the Guild audiences but by those of other commercial managements as well.

But by the 1960's production costs were too high to permit a great deal of experimentation on Broadway. Off-Broadway, however, you could try the sort of thing that would constitute too much of an economic risk uptown. It was with this in mind that the Guild decided that off-Broadway was the place to try a couple of plays which did not appear to be good commercial possibilities in the Broadway sense. The motivation was excellent, though the selection of plays was not. Better of the two was *The Child Buyer,* which Paul Shyre had adapted from the John Hersey novel of the same name, and which was staged by Richard Altman at the Garrick, in Greenwich Village. It ran for thirty-two performances. An exceptionally well-cast production of an engrossing play, it probably would have been more successful were it not for an uneasy mixture of believable and unbelievable or overdrawn characters.

The Child Buyer is the strange and chilling story of a corporation vice-president (Lester Rawlins) who comes to a New England town to purchase a lively, likable ten-year-old boy genius. He explains that the boy will be washed clean of all memories, his five senses will be figuratively if not literally tied off, and he will be transformed into a thought machine, for which the company is pre-

pared to pay a substantial sum of money. The boy's parents and the whole town are shocked and horrified at such an idea, but the executive knows human nature too well to be put off, and he persists in his carefully thought-out plan to get the boy.

The Child Buyer has much in common with Friedrich Dürrenmatt's *The Visit,* in which a wealthy woman returns to the town of her childhood to bribe the community into murdering the man who had betrayed her many years before. In each play pretentions of morality crumple before human avarice and self-deception. With *The Child Buyer,* author Hersey, adapter Shyre, and director Altman shared the blame for stereotyped secondary characters. The role of the lad was filled capably by nine-year-old Brian Chapin.

Ben Kerner's *All Women Are One,* which the Guild produced in league with movie magnate Joseph E. Levine, managed to survive for six performances at the Gate, also off-Broadway, before it bowed to the inevitable. All it had to offer was an idea; even a cursory reading would reveal the script as contrived, lacking in verbal grace, and clumsy in its symbolism. The playwright's idea was to strand a wrestler and his manager on a mountaintop in Italy. They have been led there by a widow, one of 3,000 women in a town with no men. To raise money, the manager decides on a lottery, with the wrestler as the prize. Obviously, the widow wants the wrestler and, equally obviously, she is going to get him. Director Peter Kass compounded the play's faults by grasping at effects which neither he nor his cast could achieve. The intentional grotesques were labored, the satire soggy, the caricatures blurred. Only Marian Seldes, as the widow, was able to impart some life to the evening, and even her frenetic gaiety eventually wore thin.

It would be almost impossible to admire Peter Shaffer's *The Royal Hunt of the Sun* for the wrong reasons, because the shining drama which opened on October 26, 1965, at the ANTA (originally the Guild Theatre) on West 52nd Street excels in so many areas. As visual spectacle, acting, religious disputation, philosophical discourse, high adventure, history, intensely personal conflict, or as a bouquet of the assorted theatre arts, it was, in that American debut, dazzling. Its prose has the soaring flight of poetry and, at moments, the grandeur of Scripture.

Yet reading what others wrote about that drama, which re-creates the conquest of Peru by

Francisco Pizarro in 1532–1533, one notes perhaps too much attention to *The Royal Hunt of the Sun* as visual theatre and not sufficient appreciation of its remarkable intelligence as a play. This second excellence should stand first. All that you see on stage, no matter how impressive, merely adds dramatic emphasis to that which is said. In subsequent productions the visual element was consistently overemphasized, at the expense of the text. The fact that the play has been referred to as spectacle, pageant, or "a stately and most studied oratorio" (Kerr) would seem to indicate that everybody looked, but not everybody listened.

Shaffer found in this segment of history one of man's most shameful hypocrisies—that of committing his crimes in God's name. Early in the play Pizarro's mission is explained—and "justified"—by the Dominican chaplain: "We'll take from them [the Incas] what they don't value [their gold] and give them instead the priceless mercy of Heaven." The conquerors have the gall to invoke God's help in a plot to murder the 3,000 generals and ministers of Peru's twenty-four million people, after promising that they would meet unarmed. Even Pizarro cannot stomach that. By contrast the Peruvians honor their moral integrity at the cost of their lives. Atahualpa, sovereign Inca of Peru, believes himself to be a god, and for a while accepts Pizarro as one. But when he learns the Spanish leader has broken his word, he concludes: "He lied to me. He is not a god."

The language of this play stirs like music. Describing the Spaniards' climb over the Andes, the narrator, Martin (George Rose), recalls: "The rocks began to whine with cold." Speaking of the violated nation after the Spaniards were through, he says: "The air in Peru is sour and cold, as in a vault." Later he adds, succinctly: "We gave her greed, hunger, and the Cross."

For all this textual richness, there was a visual glory to *The Royal Hunt of the Sun,* as it came to Broadway from London, which transcended all ordinary theatre. Michael Annals had designed a tilted oval platform embraced by a rust-red cyclorama and supporting an upthrust shaft on which hung a great shield emblazoned with a cross. Some time later in the play, the shield divided itself into a dozen wedge-shaped pieces, opening like a sunburst to reveal the muscular, dramatically noble, and brilliantly costumed figure of the god, the Inca, the thirty-three-year-old divine ruler of Peru. Annals' royal Peruvian costumes of feathers, masks, and commanding colors, Mme. Claude Chagrin's pantomime, Martin Aronstein's lighting, and Marc Wilkinson's sound effects all were turned, as were the talents of the players, to the high purpose of the story. This was achieved by the deft hand of director John Dexter. Performances included two of the season's best—Christopher Plummer as the flinty Pizarro and David Carradine as the majestic, trusting Inca god, Atahualpa.

The London stage also was the source of the Guild's two ventures during the 1966–1967 season, which worked out as one miss and one resounding hit. A success across the water had been a little marital (extramarital, really) comedy, *Say Who You Are.* The title comes from an admonition in the London telephone directories. Over there, when you call from a pay phone you do not put your money in the slot until the person you are calling has identified himself. So the phone book advises: "Don't say 'hello'; say who you are."

Well, this wouldn't make much sense to an American audience, so the name was changed to *Help Stamp Out Marriage,* though that doesn't make much sense either. At any event, it had to do with two couples, who, in a conventional farce, would have been running in and out of bedrooms. These kept running in and out of an apartment and using the telephones a great deal. The English telephone procedure became a gim-

The Royal Hunt of the Sun—Michael Annals' setting and royal Peruvian costumes on the god-king Atahualpa and his priests. *Friedman-Abeles photograph.*

The Royal Hunt of the Sun—Pizarro (Christopher Plummer) speaks with Atahualpa (David Carradine), while the boy, Martin Ruiz (Paul Collins), translates. *Friedman-Abeles photograph.*

Help Stamp Out Marriage—director George Abbott added his distinctive touch to this English marital comedy, whose cast included Roddy Maude-Roxby and Valerie French. *Friedman-Abeles photograph.*

Help Stamp Out Marriage—Valerie French, Ann Bell, Roddy Maude-Roxby, and Francis Matthews. *Friedman-Abeles photograph.*

mick, but it was an amusing and sturdy gimmick. It held up all evening, which was more than could be said of the play. It might have been a mistake to assign an American director—even one so adept at comedy as George Abbott—to do an English comedy; one sensed a conflict of styles somewhere along the line. Yet the cast of four was charming and ever so diligent—Roddy Maude-Roxby, Valerie French, Ann Bell, and Francis Matthews. The playwrights—Keith Waterhouse and Willis Hall—occasionally rose above the ordinary in their dialogue, as when Miss French described her husband's unsullied girl friend (who never appears) as "a mimsy little celibate slut."

England's Harold Pinter has one of the most original minds in the theatre today, and *The Homecoming* bears this out as well as anything he has written. He is never trammeled either by neat logic or by what are considered the rules of reasonable and expected behavior. He employs theatre not as an abnormal art form —abnormal in relation to life, that is—but as a supranormal kind of communication—and therein lies its fascination. *The Homecoming* is an adventure in the unfamiliar, and as such was an award-winning and unique asset to the Broadway season when it arrived from London at the Music Box on January 5, 1967. Alexander H. Cohen and Gerry Geraldo brought it over, in association with the Theatre Guild, in the Royal Shakespeare Company's production, staged by Peter Hall.

The play appears deceptively simple in its outline. An English professor of philosophy living in the United States brings his American wife to visit his father, uncle, and two brothers in London. But from the start, the questions take shape. Why is the living room so big, so gray, and why does it look like a room you'd dream of rather than see? Why is the father (Paul Rogers) so furious, and his son Lenny (Ian Holm) so coldly contemptuous? Why do they abruptly change mood and speak as friends? What is the root of the father's black hatred of his brother (John Normington)? What kind of creature is the son Lenny, whose smirk seems to contain all the malice in the world?

When Teddy (Michael Craig) arrives with Ruth, his wife (Vivien Merchant), why do they address each other from separate glass-enclosed worlds? How can she withstand, without batting an eye, the blistering greeting of her father-in-law, who calls her a whore as the least of his insults?

What sensuous meanings are carried by her reverie about the way her underwear moves when her legs move, and her remark that the movement of her lips might be more important than the words which come from those lips? And as the play develops, are we to believe she is a lady or a whore?

The answers to these questions—if there are answers—simply are not as vital as the play which poses them, and the manner in which it does this. What matters is the experience, compounded of brilliant and startling dialogue, shockingly candid statements, abrupt changes of topic (we seem to be forever turning corners as we listen), and pauses as suggestive—or frightening—as anything that is said.

The play drew a divided press—essentially favorable from Richard Watts, Jr., of the *New York Post*, Martin Gottfried of *Women's Wear Daily* and from me, writing for the *World Journal Tribune*. More no than yes were John Chapman of the *Daily News*, Walter Kerr of the *Times*, and George Oppenheimer of *Newsday*. But the comment it occasioned was more significant than the precise degree of approval in the reviews, because all the critics approached it seriously and thoughtfully. And in May it earned the New York Drama Critics Award. *The Homecoming* has been attempted a number of times since, though more

The Homecoming—Vivien Merchant as Ruth and Michael Craig as Teddy, the professor who comes from America to visit his bitterly vindictive father and his two brothers in England. *Levack photograph.*

The Homecoming—Michael Craig as Teddy and Ian Holm as Lenny, with Teddy's wife, Ruth (Vivien Merchant). *Levack photograph.*

The Homecoming—the father, Max (Paul Rogers, second from left), with his three sons—Teddy (Michael Craig), Joey (Terence Rigby), and Lenny (Ian Holm). *Levack photograph.*

often than not to the bewilderment or distaste of its audiences. The problem is that it needs the discerning direction of a Peter Hall and the talent of the Royal Shakespeare Company if its subtleties of mood and mystery are to be articulated adequately. It was not popular on tour; Midwesterners found it shocking. Yet it has, at times, found the skills needed for a proper production, such as the lucid and taut staging of *The Homecoming* by the Hartford Stage Company, in Connecticut.

For its golden anniversary season, the Guild, in association with Joel Schenker, who had been a director of the Theatre Guild for several years, devoted its full forces to the preparation of a musical which seemed to promise a good measure of entertainment as well as a busy box office. Twenty-one years earlier, one of "The Theatre Guild on the Air" radio programs starred Alfred Lunt and Lynn Fontanne in a dramatic adaptation by Erik Barnouw of Arnold Bennett's novel, *Buried Alive,* under the new title of *The Great Adventure.* In the story, a noted English painter is returning home on a ship following long years of exile on a Pacific isle, when his butler dies. The physician mistakenly assumes the butler is the painter, and issues the death certificate in the latter's name. The artist, who welcomes the idea of anonymity, assumes the identity of the butler and watches, with proper grief, as the servant is buried under the master's distinguished name in Westminster Abbey. The artist marries a pleasant and happy woman, finding contentment in his new life, except that he paints on the sly. Eventually his canvases are discovered by his former dealer, and in time his identity is revealed.

The radio play was well received in the 1946–1947 season and again when the Lunts repeated it three years later. Naturally, the Guild envisioned a production on Broadway. They immediately tried to buy the rights from the Bennett estate, but encountered what was, at the time, an insurmountable obstacle. The writer had willed the novel's rights to his wife and the stage and movie rights to a lady of his intimate acquaintance who also called herself Mrs. Bennett. The two ladies wouldn't agree on anything, including what to do with *Buried Alive.* However, television rights were not specified in the will, so the Guild televised the play for the United States Steel program with Hume Cronyn and Jessica Tandy in the leading roles.

Some years later the Bennett estate again was approached about dramatic rights, and as one of the Mrs. Bennetts had died, leaving the other in sole control, the Guild was given permission to do the play. Leonard Spigelgass (*A Majority of One, Dear Me, the Sky Is Falling*) agreed to adapt it, but became ill before it was finished; also, the Lunts, for whom it was intended, did not care for his approach. The next course was to adapt it as a musical. Jule Styne agreed to write the music (he had done *Bells Are Ringing* for the Guild) and E. Y. Harburg joined the team as lyricist. Nunnally Johnson, who had written *Holy Matrimony,* the movie version of the Bennett novel, agreed to prepare the play book. Vincent Price was signed to play the artist—apt, considering the actor's knowledge of painting—with Patricia Routledge, an English actress and singer who had charmed New York the previous season in *How's the World Treating You?,* as the woman he marries.

The opening, on a Saturday night in late January, 1968, proved once and for all not just the power of the critics (if anything, what subsequently happened confused that belief even more than usual) but the influence of the opening-night review in *The New York Times,* regardless of the man who writes it or of what might eventually appear in the drama criticism of the same paper. For the record, *Darling of the Day* was received unfavorably by the network television reviewers, whose influence at the box office was becoming considerable (though more in the case of a musical, which might be more apt to interest a television audience, than a serious drama). They did, however, admire Miss Routledge; her acclaim turned out to be virtually unanimous. Richard Watts, Jr., of the *New York Post* credited the show with "charm, tunefulness, humor, imagination, a good book, impeccable taste and a handsome production." John Chapman of the *Daily News* was delighted with it, though Martin Gottfried of *Women's Wear Daily,* after exempting Miss Routledge, Harburg's lyrics, and the acting of Peter Woodthorpe as the art dealer, destroyed what was left, in his review.

That left *The New York Times,* unquestionably the most influential review of a Broadway or off-Broadway opening. The versatile critic Clive Barnes preferred to attend a dance recital that night, so *Darling of the Day* was reviewed by the *Times*'s second-string drama critic, Dan Sul-

Darling of the Day—Patricia Routledge and Vincent Price recording the songs.

livan (who has since left to become critic of the *Los Angeles Times*). Sullivan, a capable, serious, no-nonsense critic, probably a bit less susceptible to nostalgic charm than Barnes or the *Times*'s Sunday critic, Walter Kerr, did not find the new musical to his taste. Not only that, but for some reason his departmental editor decided to break the *Times*'s tradition of always running a Broadway opening review at the top of the page, and

ran *Darling of the Day* farther down, below Barnes's dance piece. The public, of course, doesn't consciously notice newspaper makeup, but *Times*'s readers know that when a review is dropped down on the page—especially when it is of a Broadway event—the word is no.

A few days later Barnes looked at the show and gave it a generally agreeable mention; certainly more favorable than Sullivan's. This doesn't prove anything—least of all that one was right and the other wrong. There isn't any measurable right and wrong in drama criticism, as far as negative and positive opinions are concerned. But a good notice by the first-string critic could not overcome the effect of a bad notice, the Monday morning immediately after the Saturday opening.

Meanwhile, over in the Sunday department, Kerr was knocking out a paean of praise for Miss Routledge in stunning imagery such as only Kerr can write. He also enjoyed the show, concluding his piece: "In the end, the show wins, and is winning." This did not get into print until February 11, which was two weeks after the opening and after the original reviews had appeared. It was too late; *Darling of the Day* was not going to make it. All this inspired the reasonable conjecture that IF Barnes had gone to the musical instead of the dance recital, or IF Kerr had still been writing opening-night reviews, as he had his first year on the *Times* after the *Herald Tribune* ceased publication, *Darling of the Day* would have made it. To unearth a cliché, no one will ever know.

The main trouble with *Darling of the Day* lay deep in its origins. The leading character—the artist—wants to erase himself from society, and he succeeds. He is a self-effacing man. Now, how can you have, as the hero of a dramatic piece, a man whose aim is to make himself unnoticeable? It can work in a book, but not as easily on stage. Also, Vincent Price did not have the singing voice required for the role.

XI

The Guild in Films: 1968-1969

OVER THE years, the Theatre Guild had shown very little interest in motion pictures, which perhaps can be taken as a measure of its devotion to the living stage. From time to time it was involved with Hollywood, as when Theresa Helburn went there briefly in the 1930's as a studio executive, or when one of its plays was made into a movie. The Guild did participate actively in radio and television for a total of sixteen years, and just as readily might have made the transition to cinema, but always seemed busy enough with theatrical production.

It did, some years ago, agree to sponsor a few notable films that invited the prestige treatment which the Theatre Guild presentation could give. Shakespeare's *Henry V,* in color and starring Laurence Olivier, was one of these. It was presented in Guild cities and Guild theatres on a road-show, reserved-seat basis, with the Guild arranging press screenings and invitational social events to draw attention to it. Later *Hamlet,* also starring Sir Laurence, was circulated in America under Guild auspices, as were Jean Renoir's *The River* and *The Bridge on the River Kwai.*

If the Guild did not see a future for itself in films, Philip Langner, the son of Lawrence and Armina, did. Working as associate producer with Hollywood veteran Stanley Kramer, he helped in making *A Child Is Waiting,* with the Guild owning an interest in the film. The film tactfully and honestly illuminated the delicate problem of retarded children who have been institutionalized, but who poignantly need some evidence of continuing parental affection. Burt Lancaster and Judy Garland played the principal adult roles, and about 100 retarded children were used in the cast. Langner was also associate producer of the film, *Judgment at Nuremberg,* which Philip originally had bought as a play, and which had been done as a television drama. Then Katharine Hepburn asked to see the TV kinescope, showed it to Spencer Tracy, and he too decided to do it as a film. It was an outstanding one.

The Pawnbroker, by Edward Wallant, also was first offered as a stage script, this time to the Guild management, which turned it down. Warren Caro, then general manager of the Theatre Guild–American Theatre Society, had found it and brought it to the Guild's attention. The objection was that it was too somber a story, and quite apart from its apparent dramatic value, it was not the sort of play with which you could raise money for production or earn at the box office. Six months later, Roger Lewis showed it to Philip Langner, with the suggestion that they make it into a film, which they did.

Without consciously realizing the fact at the time, Philip Langner was moving in a direction which would turn the Guild back toward one of its original precepts, which was to present on stage (change to "screen" at this point) those dramas which throw light on pertinent and controversial problems. "I am fascinated by history and I am fascinated by social problems," he explained in discussing this. "And except for *The Pawnbroker,* which was essentially psychological and personal, my films have been either historical or social. Today you just cannot do much of this on stage and survive; theatre audiences are not receptive. On film it is easier to do these things, and to find an audience for them."

At the time of this interview, *In the Matter*

of J. Robert Oppenheimer, dealing with the controversial "father of the atomic bomb," was having trouble attracting audiences to the production by the Lincoln Center Repertory Company which had earned almost universal critical praise. It was a case in point.

This was the attitude which sparked Philip's interest in February of 1967 when he was shown a film script titled *The Slaves* (later shortened to *Slaves*) written by Herbert Biberman (he had directed plays for the Guild in the 1930's and had later worked in Hollywood), John O. Killens, a Negro novelist, and Alida Sherman. It was possibly the first totally realistic film story dealing with slavery in the United States. It was a drama rather than a documentary, yet all but the fictional plot could be documented, and even it had solid precedent.

Langner, as producer, and Biberman, as director, set about finding a locale, finally selecting a plantation near Shreveport, Louisiana, where they got, for the most part, good cooperation. One of the most readable and revealing articles ever carried in *The New York Times* Sunday drama section (January 19, 1969) following the filming was Biberman's account of their experiences in Louisiana. Some attitudes dismayed them, as that of the woman who wouldn't allow them to film scenes with blacks in her parlor, explaining: "There is one condition. You can see that I am an upholder of the old traditions. I mean, I can't allow any niggers in my house. And I am not prejudiced, I want you to un'erstan' that clearly. I am not at all prejudiced. It's only that I got to stand with the old traditions." It was explained that the scene would show the master giving orders to his slaves. "Oh," she beamed, "you can have as many slaves in here as you like."

For the most part, however, the town cooperated. It was not a story to make southerners feel comfortable. A slave withdraws from his dependence on a "good master" to lead a band of runaway blacks. The plantation owner in the story keeps a black mistress and rapes her after she has had enough of him. A slave is hung by his feet and spread, and threatened with having his genitals burned away. Another slave is shot, then whipped to death. A planter sees his whole cotton crop burned by his blacks.

Yet there seemed to be an unspoken agreement that the film was honest, and that it had to be made. Biberman wrote:

On our sets, black and white, plantation owners and field workers, Northern film craftsmen and Southern film craftsmen, actors who earn a million dollars a year and old illiterate people who earn $1.60 an hour, Northern liberals and Southern conservatives, Wallace supporters (and undoubtedly, among the 150 to 200 persons working on our sets, several members of the Ku Klux Klan), met and worked together. All were cooperating in the heat of the South in making a film attacking the institution of slavery and projecting the dignity, the talent, and the intellectual and moral stature of the blacks, even in slavery.

Stephen Boyd portrays the white plantation owner in *Slaves,* with singer Dionne Warwick in a nonsinging role as his mistress, and Ossie Davis

Slaves—singer Dionne Warwick portrayed a white master's black mistress in the Theatre Guild's film dealing with slavery in America.

as the slave who leads the escape at the end.

"To me, *Slaves* seems to be in the center of a trilogy," said Langner shortly before the film's release in the spring of 1969.

There should be at least one comparable film to precede it, dealing with the slave ships which brought the blacks to America, and another, possibly dealing with The Underground, to tell what happened to these people after they escaped.

Questions dealing with the blacks in America are going to be concerning us for many years to come, and I certainly want to do more films that explain the background, or seek to find answers. There have been almost no films delving into Negro history. Only *Slaves* and *Nat Turner* [based on William Styron's novel, *The Confessions of Nat Turner*], about the leader of a slave rebellion in 1831 really look into the Negro past.

Slaves—Ossie Davis and Robert Kya-Hill work for an oppressive master, Stephen Boyd.

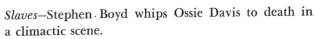

Slaves—Stephen. Boyd whips Ossie Davis to death in a climactic scene.

XII

Today and Tomorrow

In 1958, the first forty years of the Theatre Guild were examined and appraised in an essay by John Gassner, who had been its play-reader from 1929 to 1944 and who was, at the time, Sterling Professor of playwrighting and dramatic literature at Yale University. He pointed out that the organization of the Guild in December of 1918, and its activities thereafter, marked the culmination of a revolution which had begun with the "little theatre" movement about 1912. That was the year when Professor George Pierce Baker's '47 Workshop theatre was established at Harvard University, as well as when the Chicago Little Theatre and the Boston Toy Theatre were founded. He drew attention to the three noteworthy off-Broadway groups after 1914—the Neighborhood Playhouse sponsored by Alice and Irene Lewisohn; the Provincetown Players, guided by George Cram Cook, Susan Glaspell, Robert Edmond Jones, and Eugene O'Neill; and the Washington Square Players, whose leadership included Helen Westley, Lee Simonson, Philip Moeller, and Lawrence Langner. The revolution was against the prevailing commercialism and lack of taste in the American theatre; the Guild's function—or one of its functions—was to carry the revolution out of the limited little theatre arena and into the main battleground of Broadway. Gassner went on to conclude:

A correct estimate of the Guild's position after its first decade (1929) would have included the realization that the revolution was over. The Guild ceased to be revolutionary because its cause had triumphed. Largely as a result of the example set by the Theatre

Guild, Broadway managements became hospitable to plays of intellectual caliber and unconventional dramaturgy. It became possible to produce any kind of drama in New York. In time, the gap between a typical "Guild play" and a typical "Broadway play" became narrower, and in the case of literate and sophisticated comedy, often imperceptible. In the 1930's in fact, it became customary among the young to regard the Theatre Guild as a bastion of conservatism.

This was in spite of the fact that the Group Theatre, which began to make a strong impression as an acting company soon after 1931, was in fact an offshoot of the Guild. Also, the now-secure producing company was continuing to provide opportunities for playwrights—Maxwell Anderson, Robert Sherwood, S. N. Behrman—who were emerging in the 1930's, as it had provided an American audience for Shaw and had produced the ascending O'Neill in the 1920's.

Still the revolution was indeed over by the start of the Guild's second decade. But to assume that the Guild's function had ended then would be as reckless as to conclude that the end of any revolution is the end of the purpose for which it was set in motion. Nor did the Guild then settle for "safe" plays, as it well might have done. It might be hard for young persons to realize the fact from today's point of view, but it took courage then to put yourself economically on the line—as any producer does when the box office opens—with ideological material such as Maxwell Anderson's political satire *Both Your Houses*, Behrman's anti-fascist *Rain from Heaven*, Sherwood's prophetic anti-war *Idiot's Delight,* or John Wexley's drama about the Scottsboro case, *They Shall Not Die.*

The Guild's devotion to Shaw over the years is much to its credit, considering that the production of the witty Irishman's plays represented a cumulative loss of $350,000—which is about the same amount as his own earnings from the Guild productions. Oft-quoted is the Guild's dictum: "When in doubt, play Shaw." Which they did indeed. Less well known is the fact that it usually cost them; but they were loyal, not just to Shaw but to their own standards for the American stage.

Theresa Helburn had stated the organization's principles well in the first years of its relative affluence, at the laying of the cornerstone for the Guild Theatre:

The Guild knew, and still knows, that the function of the theatre is to entertain, that its greatest sin is to be dull, that its greatest commercial asset is to leave its audiences happy and contented. But the Guild knew also that the function of our theatre is not only to entertain but to stimulate, not only to make you feel but to make you think, that its greatest sin is to be superficial, and that while it may leave its audience thrilled by the intensity of life, it must never cheat them by denying its underlying tragedy. The thought of the world comes from the minds that are unsatisfied, suffering, questioning. The greatest advance in the thinking public is brought about by plays that crash the barriers, that leave their audiences quivering, uncomfortable, sometimes disgusted, but always asking "why?" These plays are the Guild's most precious failures, they are its realest successes, even though their success is only apparent in the seasons that come after, for the theatre moves rapidly and the dynamite of one decade is the building stone of the next.

As the years went on, there was less dynamite in the Guild's stage fare. The economy, as much as anything, had sent experimentation back to the off-Broadway scene, in the 1950's, from which it had come thirty or forty years before. Commercial success, coupled with a large, loyal, and somewhat less than daring subscription membership, dictated staying in the Broadway area. (Though in the mid-1960's the Guild did try a couple of off-Broadway projects.) Gassner wrote of the Guild that:

. . . its existence has paralleled decade after decade of American life marked by conflict, crisis, and achievement. The organization's shortcomings and faults have reflected limitations and flaws in the so-called pragmatism of our culture. The very flexibility that has kept the enterprise alive has carried with it the onus of opportunism, and it is especially true that the Guild has been unable to pursue a steady course of artistic development. The Guild's achievements, too, have reflected the American cultural scene—chiefly its independent individuality. From the very beginning the directors refused to rely on private or public subsidy. They preferred a self-sustaining business that would take its chances in the market, in order that the Guild might escape arid academicism and dictation by patrons and government.

Today, the six directors of the Theatre Guild in those first and succeeding years are no longer alive. The organization is in the hands of Lawrence Langner's widow, Armina Marshall, and his son, Philip. Philip Langner is exploring new directions as in cinema, which seems to him a more free and flexible medium. He has introduced a magazine, *Critic's Choice,* in the tradition of *Theatre Guild Magazine,* published between 1925 and 1932, which then was renamed *Stage Magazine,* and continued until 1939. The Theatre Guild–American Theatre Society tours the best plays of each Broadway season in sixteen cities across the country. It also maintains a subscription plan in the New York area, which offers a wide selection of plays, from the Guild and other managements, to members each season. Recently it began inviting its subscription members, including those of the TG-ATS across the country, to join international theatre tours which include a stimulating variety of plays, with opera and ballet, in European countries.

And as always, the Guild office, now just off Times Square on West 47th Street, is in the market for new scripts, new talents, new ideas. For a half-century, the most exciting conversations at the Theatre Guild have begun with "Next season . . ." and the organizational eye always has been on the next enterprise, the next play, the new day.

It still is.

Appendixes

I

List of Theatre Guild Plays

The following plays were presented in New York City, and most of them also on tour throughout the United States, by the Theatre Guild, either alone or in association with others. Some of the plays listed, such as O'Neill's *A Moon for the Misbegotten* and Helen Jerome's adaptation of the Brontë novel *Jane Eyre*, were done on the road but not brought into Manhattan. These two, for example, are included because of the importance of the play in the first instance, and of the principal player (Katharine Hepburn) in the second. Several others were tried out on tour, but were found unsatisfactory for New York presentation and were closed out of town; they are not listed.

This listing of 220 plays probably constitutes the greatest number of hitherto unproduced stage works, importations, and new productions of classics given full-scale professional production by a single management in this country.

Name of Play	Author	New York Opening Date
FIRST SEASON		
The Bonds of Interest	Jacinto Benavente	April 14, 1919
John Ferguson	St. John Ervine	May 12, 1919
SECOND SEASON		
The Faithful	John Masefield	October 13, 1919
The Rise of Silas Lapham	Lillian Sabine	November 25, 1919
The Power of Darkness	Leo Tolstoy	January 19, 1920
Jane Clegg	St. John Ervine	February 23, 1920
The Dance of Death	August Strindberg	May 9, 1920
THIRD SEASON		
The Treasure	David Pinski	October 4, 1920
Heartbreak House	Bernard Shaw *	November 10, 1920
John Hawthorne	David Liebovitz	January 23, 1921
Mr. Pim Passes By	A. A. Milne	February 28, 1921
Liliom	Ferenc Molnár	April 20, 1921
The Cloister	Emile Verhaeren	June 5, 1921
FOURTH SEASON		
Ambush	Arthur Richman	October 10, 1921
Bourbouroche	Georges Courteline	November 28, 1921
The Wife with a Smile	Denys Amiel and André Obey	November 28, 1921
He Who Gets Slapped	Leonid Andreyev	January 9, 1922

* Shaw directed that, after his death, he be referred to only as Bernard Shaw. In his lifetime he was customarily identified by his full name, George Bernard Shaw.

Back to Methuselah	Bernard Shaw	February 27, 1922
What the Public Wants	Arnold Bennett	May 1, 1922
From Morn to Midnight	Georg Kaiser	May 21, 1922

FIFTH SEASON

R.U.R.	Karel Čapek	October 9, 1922
The Lucky One	A. A. Milne	November 20, 1922
The Tidings Brought to Mary	Paul Claudel	December 25, 1922
Peer Gynt	Henrik Ibsen	February 5, 1923
The Adding Machine	Elmer Rice	March 18, 1923
The Devil's Disciple	Bernard Shaw	April 23, 1923

SIXTH SEASON

Windows	John Galsworthy	October 8, 1923
The Failures	H. R. Lenormand	November 19, 1923
The Race with the Shadow	Wilhelm von Scholz	December 14, 1923
Saint Joan	Bernard Shaw	December 28, 1923
Fata Morgana	Ernest Vajda	March 3, 1924
Man and the Masses	Ernst Toller	April 14, 1924

SEVENTH SEASON

The Guardsman	Ferenc Molnár	October 13, 1924
They Knew What They Wanted	Sidney Howard	November 24, 1924
Processional	John Howard Lawson	January 12, 1925
Ariadne	A. A. Milne	February 23, 1925
Caesar and Cleopatra	Bernard Shaw	April 13, 1925
The Garrick Gaieties	Richard Rodgers and Lorenz Hart	June 8, 1925
Arms and the Man	Bernard Shaw	September 14, 1925

EIGHTH SEASON

The Glass Slipper	Ferenc Molnár	October 19, 1925
The Man of Destiny	Bernard Shaw	November 23, 1925
Androcles and the Lion	Bernard Shaw	November 23, 1925
Merchants of Glory	Marcel Pagnol and Paul Nivoix	December 14, 1925
Goat Song	Franz Werfel	January 25, 1926
The Chief Thing	Nikolai Evreinov	March 22, 1926
At Mrs. Beam's	C. K. Munro	April 26, 1926
The Garrick Gaieties (2nd edition)	Richard Rodgers and Lorenz Hart	May 10, 1926

NINTH SEASON

Juarez and Maximilian	Franz Werfel	October 11, 1926
Pygmalion	Bernard Shaw	November 15, 1926
Ned McCobb's Daughter	Sidney Howard	November 29, 1926
The Silver Cord	Sidney Howard	December 20, 1926
The Brothers Karamazov	Jacques Copeau; based on Dostoevski's novel	January 3, 1927

Right You Are If You Think You Are	Luigi Pirandello	February 23, 1927
The Second Man	S. N. Behrman	April 11, 1927

TENTH SEASON

Porgy	Du Bose and Dorothy Heyward	October 10, 1927
The Doctor's Dilemma	Bernard Shaw	November 21, 1927
Marco Millions	Eugene O'Neill	January 9, 1928
Strange Interlude	Eugene O'Neill	January 30, 1928
Volpone	Stefan Zweig's version of Ben Jonson's play	April 9, 1928

ELEVENTH SEASON

Faust	Goethe; Graham and Tristan Rawson version	October 8, 1928
Major Barbara	Bernard Shaw	November 20, 1928
Wings over Europe	Robert Nichols and Maurice Browne	December 10, 1928
Caprice	G. Sil-Vara	December 31, 1928
Dynamo	Eugene O'Neill	February 11, 1929
Man's Estate	Beatrice Blackmar and Bruce Gould	April 1, 1929
The Camel Through the Needle's Eye	Francis Langer	April 15, 1929

TWELFTH SEASON

Karl and Anna	Leonhard Frank; translated from the German by Ruth Langner	October 7, 1929
The Game of Love and Death	Romain Rolland	November 25, 1929
Red Rust	V. Kirchon and A. Ouspensky	December 17, 1929
Meteor	S. N. Behrman	December 23, 1929
The Apple Cart	Bernard Shaw	February 24, 1930
A Month in the Country	Ivan Turgenev	March 17, 1930
Hotel Universe	Philip Barry	April 14, 1930
The Garrick Gaieties (3rd edition)	Various authors and composers	June 4, 1930

THIRTEENTH SEASON

Roar China	S. M. Tretyakov	October 27, 1930
Elizabeth the Queen	Maxwell Anderson	November 3, 1930
Midnight	Claire and Paul Sifton	December 29, 1930
Green Grow the Lilacs	Lynn Riggs	January 26, 1931
Miracle at Verdun	Hans Chlumberg	March 16, 1931
Getting Married	Bernard Shaw	March 30, 1931

FOURTEENTH SEASON

He	Alfred Savoir	September 21, 1931
Mourning Becomes Electra	Eugene O'Neill	October 26, 1931

Reunion in Vienna	Robert E. Sherwood	November 16, 1931
The Moon in the Yellow River	Denis Johnston	February 29, 1932
Too True to Be Good	Bernard Shaw	April 4, 1932

FIFTEENTH SEASON

The Good Earth	Dramatized by Owen and Donald Davis from Pearl Buck's novel	October 22, 1932
Biography	S. N. Behrman	December 12, 1932
American Dream	George O'Neil	February 20, 1933
Both Your Houses	Maxwell Anderson	March 6, 1933
The Mask and the Face	Luigi Chiarelli; translated by Somerset Maugham	May 1, 1933

SIXTEENTH SEASON

Ah, Wilderness!	Eugene O'Neill	October 2, 1933
The School for Husbands	Molière; adapted in rhyme by Arthur Guiterman and Lawrence Langner	October 16, 1933
Mary of Scotland	Maxwell Anderson	November 27, 1933
Days Without End	Eugene O'Neill	January 8, 1934
They Shall Not Die	John Wexley	February 21, 1934
Jig Saw	Dawn Powell	April 30, 1934

SEVENTEENTH SEASON

A Sleeping Clergyman	James Bridie	October 8, 1934
Valley Forge	Maxwell Anderson	December 10, 1934
Rain from Heaven	S. N. Behrman	December 24, 1934
Escape Me Never	Margaret Kennedy	January 21, 1935
The Simpleton of the Unexpected Isles	Bernard Shaw	February 18; 1935
Parade	George Sklar, Paul Peters, and Jerome Moross	May 20, 1935

EIGHTEENTH SEASON

If This Be Treason	Reverend John Haynes Holmes and Reginald Lawrence	September 23, 1935
The Taming of the Shrew	William Shakespeare	September 30, 1935
Porgy and Bess	George Gershwin, Ira Gershwin, Du Bose and Dorothy Heyward	October 10, 1935
Call It a Day	Dodie Smith	January 28, 1936
End of Summer	S. N. Behrman	February 17, 1936
Idiot's Delight	Robert Sherwood	March 24, 1936 On tour

NINETEENTH SEASON

And Stars Remain	Julius J. and Philip G. Epstein	October 12, 1936

281

Prelude to Exile	William McNally	November 30, 1936
But for the Grace of God	Leopold Atlas	January 12, 1937
The Masque of Kings	Maxwell Anderson	February 8, 1937
Storm over Patsy	Bruno Frank	March 8, 1937
Jane Eyre	Helen Jerome	On tour

TWENTIETH SEASON

To Quito and Back	Ben Hecht	October 4, 1937
Madame Bovary	Gaston Baty; from the novel of Gustave Flaubert	November 16, 1937
Amphitryon 38	S. N. Behrman; from the French of Jean Giraudoux	November 1, 1937
The Ghost of Yankee Doodle	Sidney Howard	November 22, 1937
Wine of Choice	S. N. Behrman	February 21, 1938
The Sea Gull	Anton Chekhov; adapted by Stark Young from the Russian	March 28, 1938
Washington Jitters	John Boruff and Walter Hart	May 2, 1938

TWENTY-FIRST SEASON

Dame Nature	André Birabeau	September 26, 1938
The Merchant of Yonkers	Thornton Wilder	December 28, 1938
Jeremiah	Stefan Zweig	February 3, 1939
The Philadelphia Story	Philip Barry	March 28, 1939

TWENTY-SECOND SEASON

My Heart's in the Highlands (with the Group Theatre)	William Saroyan	April 13, 1939
The Time of Your Life (with Eddie Dowling)	William Saroyan	October 25, 1939
The Fifth Column	Ernest Hemingway; acting version by Benjamin Glazer	March 6, 1940
There Shall Be No Night (with the Playwrights' Company)	Robert Sherwood	April 29, 1940
Love's Old Sweet Song	William Saroyan	May 2, 1940

TWENTY-THIRD SEASON

Twelfth Night	William Shakespeare	November 19, 1940
Liberty Jones	Philip Barry	February 5, 1941
Battle of Angels	Tennessee Williams	On tour
Somewhere in France	Carl Zuckmayer and Fritz Kortner	On tour

282

	TWENTY-FOURTH SEASON	
Ah, Wilderness! (revival)	Eugene O'Neill	October 2, 1941
Candle in the Wind (with the Playwrights' Company)	Maxwell Anderson	October 22, 1941
Papa Is All	Patterson Greene	January 6, 1942
Hope for a Harvest	Sophie Treadwell	November 26, 1941
The Rivals	Richard B. Sheridan	January 14, 1942
Yesterday's Magic	Emlyn Williams	April 14, 1942

	TWENTY-FIFTH SEASON	
Without Love	Philip Barry	November 10, 1942
Mr. Sycamore	Ketti Frings	November 13, 1942
The Pirate (with the Playwrights' Company)	S. N. Behrman	November 27, 1942
The Russian People	Konstantin Simonov; American acting version by Clifford Odets	December 29, 1942
Oklahoma!	Richard Rodgers, Oscar Hammerstein II	March 31, 1943

	TWENTY-SIXTH SEASON	
Othello	William Shakespeare	October 19, 1943
The Innocent Voyage	Paul Osborn; based on a novel by Richard Hughes	November 15, 1943
Jacobowsky and the Colonel	Franz Werfel	March 14, 1944

	TWENTY-SEVENTH SEASON	
Embezzled Heaven	L. Bush-Fekete and Mary Helen Fay; based on a novel by Franz Werfel	October 31, 1944
Sing Out, Sweet Land!	Walter Kerr	December 27, 1944
Foolish Notion	Philip Barry	March 31, 1945
Carousel	Richard Rodgers and Oscar Hammerstein II; based on Molnár's *Liliom*	April 19, 1945

	TWENTY-EIGHTH SEASON	
Dunnigan's Daughter	S. N. Behrman	December 26, 1945
The Winter's Tale	William Shakespeare	January 15, 1946
O Mistress Mine (with John C. Wilson)	Terence Rattigan	January 23, 1946
He Who Gets Slapped	Leonid Andreyev; adapted by Judith Guthrie	March 20, 1946
The Merry Wives of Windsor	William Shakespeare	On tour

	TWENTY-NINTH SEASON	
The Iceman Cometh	Eugene O'Neill	October 9, 1946
The Fatal Weakness	George Kelly	November 19, 1946
The Importance of Being Earnest (with John C. Wilson)	Oscar Wilde	March 3, 1947
Love for Love (with John C. Wilson)	William Congreve	May 26, 1947
A Moon for the Misbegotten	Eugene O'Neill	On tour

	THIRTIETH SEASON	
Allegro	Richard Rodgers and Oscar Hammerstein II	October 10, 1947
The Winslow Boy (with Atlantis)	Terence Rattigan	October 29, 1947
This Time Tomorrow	Jan de Hartog	November 3, 1947
You Never Can Tell	Bernard Shaw	March 16, 1948

	THIRTY-FIRST SEASON	
Set My People Free	Dorothy Heyward	November 3, 1948
The Silver Whistle	Robert E. McEnroe	November 24, 1948
Make Way for Lucia	John van Druten	December 22, 1948
My Name Is Aquilon	Jean Pierre Aumont; adapted by Philip Barry	February 9, 1949

	THIRTY-SECOND SEASON	
I Know My Love (with John C. Wilson)	S. N. Behrman; adapted from the French of Marcel Achard	November 2, 1949
As You Like It	William Shakespeare	January 26, 1950
Arms and the Girl!	Book by Herbert and Dorothy Fields and Rouben Mamoulian, music by Morton Gould, lyrics by Dorothy Fields	February 2, 1950
Come Back, Little Sheba	William Inge	February 15, 1950

	THIRTY-THIRD SEASON	
The Curious Savage (with Lewis & Young)	John Patrick	October 24, 1950
The Lady's Not for Burning (with Atlantis)	Christopher Fry	November 8, 1950
The Relapse	Sir John Vanbrugh	November 22, 1950

	THIRTY-FOURTH SEASON	
Saint Joan	Bernard Shaw	October 4, 1951
Lo and Behold	John Patrick	December 12, 1951
Legend of Lovers	Jean Anouilh	December 26, 1951
Jane	S. N. Behrman	February 1, 1952
Venus Observed	Christopher Fry	February 13, 1952

284

The Millionairess	Bernard Shaw	October 17, 1952
The Love of Four Colo-	Peter Ustinov	January 15, 1953
nels		
Picnic (with Joshua	William Inge	February 19, 1953
Logan)		
	THIRTY-SIXTH SEASON	
The Trip to Bountiful	Horton Foote	November 3, 1953
The Burning Glass	Charles Morgan	March 4, 1954
	THIRTY-SEVENTH SEASON	
Home Is the Hero	Walter Macken	September 22, 1954
	THIRTY-EIGHTH SEASON	
The Heavenly Twins	Albert Husson; translated by Louis Kronen-berger	November 4, 1955
The Matchmaker (with David Merrick)	Thornton Wilder	December 5, 1955
Time Limit!	Henry Denker, Ralph Berkey	January 24, 1956
Affair of Honor	Bill Hoffman	April 6, 1956
	THIRTY-NINTH SEASON	
Bells Are Ringing	Betty Comden, Adolph Green; music by Jule Styne	November 29, 1956
The Tunnel of Love	Joseph Fields, Peter De Vries	February 13, 1957
	FORTIETH SEASON	
The Summer of the Sev-enteenth Doll	Ray Lawler	January 22, 1958
Sunrise at Campobello	Dore Schary	January 30, 1958
Back to Methuselah	Bernard Shaw; shortened and adapted by Arnold Moss	March 26, 1958
	FORTY-FIRST SEASON	
A Party with Betty Com-den and Adolph Green (with Town Produc-tions, Inc.)	Betty Comden, Adolph Green	December 23, 1958
Third Best Sport	Eleanor and Leo Bayer	December 30, 1958
Requiem for a Nun (with Myers and Fleisch-mann)	William Faulkner	January 30, 1959
A Majority of One (with Dore Schary)	Leonard Spigelgass	February 16, 1959
Triple Play, four short plays by three authors (with Dore Schary):		April 15, 1959

285

Portrait of a Madonna	Tennessee Williams	
On the Harmful Effects of Tobacco	Anton Chekhov	
A Pound on Demand	Sean O'Casey	
Bedtime Story	Sean O'Casey	

FORTY-SECOND SEASON

The Highest Tree (with Dore Schary)	Dore Schary	November 4, 1959
Jolly's Progress	Lonnie Coleman	December 5, 1959

FORTY-THIRD SEASON

The 49th Cousin	Florence Lowe, Caroline Francke	October 27, 1960
Invitation to a March	Arthur Laurents	October 29, 1960
The Unsinkable Molly Brown (with Dore Schary)	Richard Morris (book), Meredith Willson (music and lyrics)	November 3, 1960
Love and Libel	Robertson Davies	December 7, 1960

FORTY-FOURTH SEASON

The Captains and the Kings (with Joel Schenker)	Leo Lieberman	January 2, 1962
Something About a Soldier (with Dore Schary)	Ernest Kinoy	January 4, 1962
A Passage to India (with Robert Fryer, Lawrence Carr, John Herman)	Santha Rama Rau	January 31, 1962

FORTY-FIFTH SEASON

Seidman and Son (with Joel Schenker and Michael Kanin)	Elick Moll	October 15, 1962
Dear Me, the Sky Is Falling	Leonard Spigelgass	March 2, 1963

FORTY-SIXTH SEASON

No new Theatre Guild productions came into New York.

FORTY-SEVENTH SEASON

The Child Buyer	Paul Shyre; adapted from John Hersey's novel	December 21, 1964 (Off-Broadway)
All Women Are One	Ben Kerner	January 7, 1965

FORTY-EIGHTH SEASON

The Royal Hunt of the Sun (with Theodore Mann, Gerard Oestreicher, Hope Abelson)	Peter Shaffer	October 26, 1965

FORTY-NINTH SEASON

Help Stamp Out Marriage (with Peter Bridge, Don Herbert)	Keith Waterhouse, Willis Hall	September 29, 1966
The Homecoming (with Alexander Cohen)	Harold Pinter	January 5, 1967

FIFTIETH SEASON

Darling of the Day	Nunnally Johnson (book) Jule Styne (music) E. Y. Harburg (lyrics)	January 27, 1968

II

List of Theatre Guild Productions on Radio

Wings over Europe by Robert Nichols and Maurice Browne (September 9, 1945); Burgess Meredith.

Jacobowsky and the Colonel by Franz Werfel and S. N. Behrman (September 16, 1945); Louis Calhern, Oscar Karlweiss, Annabella.

John Ferguson by St. John Ervine (September 23, 1945); Martha Scott.

The Guardsman by Ferenc Molnár (September 30, 1945); Alfred Lunt, Lynn Fontanne.

Ah, Wilderness! by Eugene O'Neill (October 7, 1945); Walter Huston.

Mr. Pim Passes By by A. A. Milne (October 14, 1945); Arlene Francis, Leo G. Carroll.

Sing Out, Sweet Land by Walter Kerr (October 21, 1945); Burl Ives, Arthur Godfrey.

At Mrs. Beam's by C. K. Munro (October 28, 1945); Paulette Goddard, Burgess Meredith.

Storm over Patsy by James Bridie (November 4, 1945); Martha Scott, Aline MacMahon.

The Emperor Jones and *Where the Cross Is Made* by Eugene O'Neill (November 11, 1945); Canada Lee, Boris Karloff.

Pride and Prejudice, adapted by Helen Jerome from Jane Austen's novel (November 18, 1945); Joan Fontaine.

Morning's at Seven by Paul Osborn (November 25, 1945); Stuart Erwin, Shirley Booth, Aline MacMahon, Ralph Morgan.

Elizabeth the Queen by Maxwell Anderson (December 2, 1945); Alfred Lunt, Lynn Fontanne.

Ned McCobb's Daughter by Sidney Howard (December 9, 1945); Alfred Lunt.

The Royal Family by Edna Ferber and George S. Kaufman (December 16, 1945); Fredric March.

Little Women by Louisa May Alcott (December 23, 1945); Katharine Hepburn.

Knickerbocker Holiday by Maxwell Anderson (December 30, 1945); Walter Huston.

Three Men on a Horse by John Cecil Holm and George Abbott (January 6, 1946); Stuart Erwin, Shirley Booth, Sam Levene.

The Silver Cord by Sidney Howard (January 13, 1946); Ralph Bellamy, Ruth Hussey, Estelle Winwood.

Yellow Jack by Sidney Howard and Paul de Kruif (January 20, 1946); Walter Abel, Alan Baxter, Luther Adler.

The Front Page by Ben Hecht and Charles MacArthur (January 27, 1946); Melvyn Douglas, Michael O'Shea.

The Second Man by S. N. Behrman (February 3, 1946); Alfred Lunt.

Prologue to Glory by E. P. Conkle (February 10, 1946); Zachary Scott.

On Borrowed Time by Paul Osborn (February 17, 1946); Walter Huston.

Dead End by Sidney Kingsley (February 24, 1946); Richard Conte, Alan Baxter, Joan Tetzel.

The Show-Off by George Kelly (March 3, 1946); Alfred Lunt.

The Barker by Kenyon Nicholson (March 10, 1946); Pat O'Brien.

The Masque of Kings by Maxwell Anderson (March 17, 1946); Ray Milland.

I Remember Mama by John van Druten (March 24, 1946); Mady Christians, Oscar Homolka.

Strange Interlude (part 1) by Eugene O'Neill (March 31, 1946); Lynn Fontanne.

Strange Interlude (part 2) by Eugene O'Neill (April 7, 1946); Lynn Fontanne.

Seven Keys to Baldpate by George M. Cohan (April 14, 1946); Walter Pidgeon, Martha Scott.

The Green Pastures by Marc Connelly (April 21, 1946); Juano Hernandez, Richard Huey.

Mary of Scotland by Maxwell Anderson (April 28, 1946); Helen Hayes, Helen Menken.

Mary, Mary, Quite Contrary by St. John Ervine (May 5, 1946); Gertrude Lawrence.

Payment Deferred by Jeffrey Dell (May 12, 1946); Charles Laughton, Elsa Lanchester.

They Knew What They Wanted by Sidney Howard (May 19, 1946); John Garfield, June Havoc, Leo Carrillo.

Boy Meets Girl by Bella and Samuel Spewak (May 26, 1946); Gene Kelly.

Call It a Day by Dodie Smith (June 2, 1946); Alfred Lunt, Lynn Fontanne.

Angel Street by Patrick Hamilton (September 8, 1946); Helen Hayes, Victor Jory, Leo G. Carroll.

You Can't Take It with You by George S. Kaufman and Moss Hart (September 15, 1946); Josephine Hull, Kenny Delmar.

Craig's Wife by George Kelly (September 22, 1946); Fredric March, Florence Eldridge.

Our Town by Thornton Wilder (September 29, 1946); Dorothy McGuire, Thornton Wilder.

Dodsworth by Sinclair Lewis (October 6, 1946); Walter Huston, Jessie Royce Landis.

Berkeley Square by John Balderston (October 13, 1946); Rex Harrison.

The Green Goddess by William Archer (October 20, 1946); Ronald Colman.

Accent on Youth by Samson Raphaelson (October 27, 1946); Basil Rathbone, Jane Wyatt.

The Last of Mrs. Cheyney by Frederick Lonsdale (November 3, 1946); Gertrude Lawrence.

The Man Who Came to Dinner by George S. Kaufman and Moss Hart (November 7, 1946); Fred Allen.

Kind Lady by Edward Chodorov (November 10, 1946); Lillian Gish, John Loder.

Burlesque by George M. Watters and Arthur Hopkins (November 24, 1946); Bert Lahr, June Havoc.

A Bill of Divorcement by Clemence Dane (December 1, 1946); James Mason.

Golden Boy by Clifford Odets (December 8, 1946); Dana Andrews, June Havoc, Sam Levene.

The Old Maid by Zoë Akins (December 15, 1946); Judith Anderson, Helen Menken.

Papa Is All by Patterson Greene (December 22, 1946); Oscar Homolka, Aline MacMahon.

Broadway by Philip Dunning and George Abbott (December 29, 1946); James Dunn, Shirley Booth.

The Great Adventure by Arnold Bennett (January 5, 1947); Alfred Lunt, Lynn Fontanne.

The Male Animal by James Thurber and Elliott Nugent (January 12, 1947); Elliott Nugent, Peggy Conklin, Paul Douglas.

A Doll's House by Henrik Ibsen (January 19, 1947); Dorothy McGuire, Basil Rathbone.

Men in White by Sidney Kingsley (January 26, 1947); Burgess Meredith, Marsha Hunt.

The Farmer Takes a Wife by Frank Elser and Marc Connelly (February 2, 1947); William Holden, Claire Trevor, Kenny Delmar.

Abe Lincoln in Illinois by Robert E. Sherwood (February 9, 1947); Raymond Massey, Helen Menken, Alan Baxter.

The Time of Your Life by William Saroyan (February 16, 1947); Dane Clark, Mary Anderson, John Lund.

Blithe Spirit by Noel Coward (February 23, 1947); Clifton Webb, Peggy Wood, Leonora Corbett, Mildred Natwick.

What Every Woman Knows by James M. Barrie (March 2, 1947); Helen Hayes.

No Time for Comedy by S. N. Behrman (March 9, 1947); Fredric March, Florence Eldridge.

Gold by Eugene O'Neill (March 16, 1947); Raymond Massey.

The First Year by Frank Craven (March 23, 1947); Gene Tierney.

Ladies in Retirement by Edward Percy and Reginald Denham (March 30, 1947); Fay Bainter.

Still Life by Noel Coward (April 6, 1947); Ingrid Bergman.

The Importance of Being Earnest by Oscar Wilde (April 13, 1947); John Gielgud.

The Age of Innocence by Margaret Ayer Barnes (April 20, 1947); Gene Tierney.

Escape by John Galsworthy (April 27, 1947); George Sanders, Penelope Ward.

The Animal Kingdom by Philip Barry (May 4, 1947); Fred Astaire.

Macbeth by William Shakespeare (May 11, 1947); Judith Anderson, Maurice Evans.

Uncle Harry by Thomas Job (May 18, 1947); Paul Henreid, Geraldine Fitzgerald.

Ethan Frome by Owen and Donald Davis, adapted from a novel by Edith Wharton (May 25, 1947); Raymond Massey, Pauline Lord, Mary Anderson.

Three Men on a Horse by John Cecil Holm and George Abbott (June 1, 1947); Sam Levene, Shirley Booth, David Wayne.

A Church Mouse by Ladislaus Fodor (June 8, 1947); Basil Rathbone, Pamela Brown, Martha Sleeper.

Clarence by Booth Tarkington (June 15, 1947); Robert Walker.

Old Acquaintance by John van Druten (June 22, 1947); Ilka Chase, Dorothy Gish.

Alice Sit-by-the-Fire by James M. Barrie (June 29, 1947); Helen Hayes.

One Sunday Afternoon by James Hagan (September 7, 1947); James Stewart.

Kiss and Tell by F. Hugh Herbert (September 14, 1947); Elizabeth Taylor.

Guest in the House by Hagar Wilde and Dale Eunson (September 21, 1947); Mary Anderson, Walter Abel, Wendy Barrie, Lucile Watson.

Saturday's Children by Maxwell Anderson (September 28, 1947); John Garfield.

The Admirable Crichton by James M. Barrie (October 5, 1947); Basil Rathbone.

Cyrano de Bergerac by Edmond Rostand (October 12, 1947); Fredric March, Florence Eldridge.

Lady in the Dark by Moss Hart (October 19, 1947); Gertrude Lawrence.

Apple of His Eye by Kenyon Nicholson and Charles Robinson (October 26, 1947); Walter Huston.

The Petrified Forest by Robert E. Sherwood (November 2, 1947); Robert Montgomery.

Victoria Regina by Laurence Housman (November 9, 1947); Helen Hayes.

The Shining Hour by Keith Winter (November 16, 1947); Joan Fontaine.

The Straw by Eugene O'Neill (November 23, 1947); Robert Mitchum, Mary Anderson.

Old English by John Galsworthy (November 30, 1947); Charles Laughton.

The Wisdom Tooth by Marc Connelly (December 7, 1947); Gene Kelly.

The Corn Is Green by Emlyn Williams (December 21, 1947); Helen Hayes.

Little Women by Louisa May Alcott (December 21, 1947); Katharine Hepburn, Paul Lukas.

Her Master's Voice by Clare Kummer (December 28, 1947); Alfred Drake, Arlene Francis, Betty Garde.

The Little Foxes by Lillian Hellman (January 4, 1948); Agnes Moorehead, Thomas Mitchell, Zachary Scott.

Holiday by Philip Barry (January 11, 1948); Margaret Sullavan, Kent Smith.

Three-Cornered Moon by Gertrude Tonkonogy (January 18, 1948); Joan Caulfield, Eddie Albert.

Is Zat So? by James Gleason and Richard Taber (January 25, 1948); Pat O'Brien, Arlene Francis.

Missouri Legend by E. B. Ginty (February 1, 1948); Raymond Massey, Alfred Drake, Mary Anderson.

Romeo and Juliet by William Shakespeare (February 8, 1948); Dorothy McGuire, Maurice Evans, Florence Reed.

Dark Victory by George Brewer, Jr., and Bertram Bloch (February 15, 1948); Madeleine Carroll, Walter Abel.

The Far-Off Hills by Lennox Robinson (February 22, 1948); Jessica Tandy, Hume Cronyn, Mildred Natwick, Whitford Kane.

The Barretts of Wimpole Street by Rudolf Besier (February 29, 1948); Madeleine Carroll, Brian Aherne, Frank Allenby.

Anna Christie by Eugene O'Neill (March 7, 1948); Dorothy McGuire, Burgess Meredith, Oscar Homolka.

She Loves Me Not by Howard Lindsay (March 14, 1948); Eddie Albert, Judy Holliday, Paul Douglas, Kim Hunter.

Grand Hotel by Vicki Baum (March 21, 1948); Marlene Dietrich, Ray Milland.

Remember the Day by Philo Higley and Philip Dunning (March 28, 1948); Deborah Kerr, John Conte.

The Philadelphia Story by Philip Barry (April 4, 1948); James Stewart, John Conte, Joan Tetzel.

Libel by Edward Wooll (April 11, 1948); Michael Redgrave, Walter Hampden, June Duprez.

Anna Karenina by Leo Tolstoy (April 18, 1948); Ingrid Bergman.

Laburnum Grove by J. B. Priestley (April 25, 1948); Charles Laughton.

Rebecca by Daphne du Maurier (May 2, 1948); Michael Redgrave, Flora Robson, June Duprez.

The White-Headed Boy by Lennox Robinson (May 9, 1948); Sara Allgood, Kenny Delmar, Albert Sharpe, Una O'Connor.

Daisy Mayme by George Kelly (May 16, 1948); Ethel Merman, Dean Jagger.

Wednesday's Child by Leopold Atlas (May 23, 1948); Ona Munson, Walter Abel, Arlene Francis, Richard Waring.

Reflected Glory by George Kelly (May 30, 1948); Irene Dunne.

A Bell for Adano by Paul Osborn (September 12, 1948); Robert Montgomery.

For Love or Money by F. Hugh Herbert (September 19, 1948); Joan Caulfield, John Loder.

That's Gratitude! by Frank Craven (September 26, 1948); James Stewart.

The Letter by W. Somerset Maugham (October 3, 1948); Marlene Dietrich, Walter Pidgeon.

Music in the Air by Jerome Kern and Oscar Hammerstein II (October 10, 1948); Mary Martin, Peter Lawford, John Conte.

Laura by Vera Caspary and George Sklar (October 17, 1948); Burt Lancaster, June Duprez, George Coulouris.

The Wind and the Rain by Merton Hodge (October 24, 1948); Celeste Holm, John Dall, Otto Kruger.

Morning Star by Sylvia Regan (October 31, 1948); Fay Bainter, Kenny Delmar, Meg Mundy, Karl Malden.

The Criminal Code by Martin Flavin (November 7, 1948); Pat O'Brien, Joseph Calleia, Joan Chandler.

Valley Forge by Maxwell Anderson (November 14, 1948); Claude Rains, June Duprez, George Coulouris, Dean Jagger.

The Winslow Boy by Terence Rattigan (November 21, 1948); Frank Allenby, Alan Webb, Valerie White, Michael Newell.

The Two Mrs. Carrolls by Martin Vale (November 28, 1948); Lilli Palmer, Macdonald Carey, Eddie Albert.

Lovers and Friends by Dodie Smith (December 5, 1948); Walter Pidgeon, Madeleine Carroll.

Spring Again by Isabel Leighton and Bertram Bloch (December 12, 1948); Monty Woolley, Elizabeth Patterson.

Miss Lulu Bett by Zona Gale (December 19, 1948); Jean Arthur.

Rip Van Winkle by Washington Irving (December 26, 1948); Fred Allen.

The Game of Love and Death by Romain Rolland (January 2, 1949); Katharine Hepburn, Paul Henreid, Claude Rains.

O Mistress Mine by Terence Rattigan (January 9, 1949); Alfred Lunt, Lynn Fontanne.

The Late George Apley by John P. Marquand and George S. Kaufman (January 16, 1949); Robert Morley, William Eythe, Irene Rich, Margaret Phillips.

Journey's End by R. C. Sherriff (January 23, 1949); Rex Harrison.

The Late Christopher Bean by Sidney Howard (January 30, 1949); Irene Dunne, Thomas Mitchell.

Beyond the Horizon by Eugene O'Neill (February 6, 1949); John Lund, Richard Widmark, Beatrice Pearson.

Ah, Wilderness! by Eugene O'Neill (February 13, 1949); Walter Huston.

Mary of Scotland by Maxwell Anderson (February 20, 1949); Deborah Kerr, Martita Hunt.

Payment Deferred by Jeffrey Dell from a novel by C. S. Forester (February 27, 1949); Charles Laughton, Jessica Tandy.

Interference by Roland Pertwee and Harold Dearden (March 6, 1949); Raymond Massey, Zachary Scott, June Duprez.

The Gioconda Smile by Aldous Huxley (March 13, 1949); Charles Boyer.

Yesterday's Magic by Emlyn Williams (March 20, 1949); Jean Arthur, Robert Morley.

June Moon by Ring Lardner and George S. Kaufman (March 27, 1949); June Havoc, Eddie Albert, Kenny Delmar, Sam Levene.

Camille by Alexandre Dumas (April 3, 1949); Joan Fontaine, Louis Jourdan.

The Taming of the Shrew by William Shakespeare (April 10, 1949); Burgess Meredith, Joyce Redman.

Summer and Smoke by Tennessee Williams (April 17, 1949); Dorothy McGuire, Tod Andrews.

Alien Corn by Sidney Howard (April 24, 1949); Bette Davis, Kirk Douglas.

The Skin Game by John Galsworthy (May 1, 1949); Charles Laughton, Cedric Hardwicke.

Of Mice and Men by John Steinbeck (May 8, 1949); Burgess Meredith, June Havoc.

Ladies and Gentlemen by Charles MacArthur and Ben Hecht (May 15, 1949); Van Heflin, Ida Lupino.

Flare Path by Terence Rattigan (May 22, 1949); Deborah Kerr, Peter Lawford, Ian Hunter.

The Perfect Alibi by A. A. Milne (May 29, 1949); Boris Karloff, Joan Lorring.

John Loves Mary by Norman Krasna (June 5, 1949); Robert Cummings, Ann Blyth.

Dream Girl by Elmer Rice (September 11, 1949); John Lund, Betty Field.

Libel by Edward Wooll (September 18, 1949); Rex Harrison, June Duprez, Henry Daniell.

The Gentle People by Irwin Shaw (September 25, 1949); Dan Duryea, Sam Levene, Kenny Delmar, Joan Lorring.

Counsellor-At-Law by Elmer Rice (October 2, 1949); James Cagney.

Burlesque by George M. Watters and Arthur Hopkins (October 9, 1949); Bert Lahr, Ann Sothern.

Coquette by George Abbott and Ann Preston Bridgers (October 16, 1949); Dorothy McGuire, Cornel Wilde.

The Thunderbolt by Arthur Wing Pinero (October 23, 1949); Van Heflin, Celeste Holm.

Justice by John Galsworthy (October 30, 1949); Robert Donat, Jessica Tandy, Hume Cronyn.

The Traitor by Herman Wouk (November 6, 1949); Tyrone Power, William Eythe, Nina Foch.

Still Life by Noel Coward (November 13, 1949); Helen Hayes, David Niven.

The Great Adventure by Arnold Bennett (November 20, 1949); Alfred Lunt, Lynn Fontanne.

The Enchanted Cottage by Arthur Wing Pinero (November 27, 1949); Ray Milland.

The Amazing Dr. Clitterhouse by Barre Lyndon (December 4, 1949); Madeleine Carroll, Basil Rathbone.

Street Scene by Elmer Rice (December 11, 1949); Richard Conte, Diana Lynn, Shirley Booth.

The Browning Version by Terence Rattigan (December 18, 1949); Maurice Evans, Edna Best.

The Passing of the Third Floor Back by Jerome K. Jerome (December 25, 1949); Paulette Goddard, Cedric Hardwicke.

While the Sun Shines by Terence Rattigan (January 1, 1950); Peter Lawford, Arthur Margetson.

The Scarlet Pimpernel by Baroness Orcy and Montague Barstow (January 8, 1950); Rex Harrison, Lilli Palmer, Francis L. Sullivan.

Another Language by Rose Franken (January 15, 1950); Helen Hayes, Richard Basehart, Walter Abel.

The Willow and I by John Patrick (January 22, 1950); Jane Wyman, Beatrice Pearson, Mel Ferrer.

Dulcy by George S. Kaufman and Marc Connelly (January 29, 1950); Celeste Holm, Franchot Tone, Lee Bowman.

Autumn Crocus by C. L. Anthony (February 5, 1950); Dorothy McGuire, Charles Boyer.

Goodbye Again by Allan Scott and George Haight (February 12, 1950); Ezio Pinza, Madeleine Carroll, Linda Darnell.

The Druid Circle by John van Druten (February 19, 1950); Charles Laughton, Burgess Meredith.

Heaven Can Wait by Harry Segall (February 26, 1950); Kirk Douglas, Walter Huston.

Lady in the Dark by Moss Hart (March 5, 1950); Gertrude Lawrence, Macdonald Carey, Hume Cronyn.

Our Town by Thornton Wilder (March 12, 1950); Elizabeth Taylor, Walter Huston.

There's Always Juliet by John van Druten (March, 19, 1950); Teresa Wright, Richard Widmark.

The Milky Way by Lunn Root and Harry Clork (March 26, 1950); Danny Kaye, Shirley Booth.

All That Money Can Buy by Stephen Vincent Benét (April 2, 1950); Cornel Wilde, Walter Huston, Martha Scott.

Seventh Heaven by Austin Strong (April 9, 1950); Joan Fontaine, Robert Cummings.

Great Expectations by Charles Dickens (April 16, 1950); Joan Fontaine, Richard Todd, Francis L. Sullivan.

National Velvet by Enid Bagnold (April 23, 1950); Peggy Ann Garner, Mickey Rooney.

Double Door by Elizabeth McFadden (April 30, 1950); Douglas Fairbanks, Jr., Geraldine Fitzgerald, Florence Reed.

Petticoat Fever by Mark Reed (May 7, 1950); Gertrude Lawrence, Walter Pidgeon, Arthur Treacher.

The Trial of Mary Dugan by Bayard Veiller (May 14, 1950); Paulette Goddard, Pat O'Brien, Tom Drake.

Page Miss Glory by Philip Dunning and Joseph Schrank (May 21, 1950); Betty Hutton, Ronald Reagan, Jack Carson.

Minick by George S. Kaufman and Edna Ferber (May 28, 1950); Lee Bowman, Sterling Holloway, Arlene Francis, Nina Foch.

Call It a Day by Dodie Smith (June 4, 1950); Gertrude Lawrence, Franchot Tone.

Edward, My Son by Robert Morley and Noel Langley (September 10, 1950); Rosalind Russell, Charles Laughton.

The Barker by Kenyon Nicholson (September 17, 1950); Ginger Rogers, Paul Douglas.

There Shall Be No Night by Robert E. Sherwood (September 24, 1950); Alfred Lunt, Lynn Fontanne.

Brigadoon by Alan Jay Lerner and Frederick Loewe (October 1, 1950); Dennis Morgan, Patrice Munsel.

Blow ye Winds by Valentine Davies (October 8, 1950); William Holden, Celeste Holm.

I Know Where I'm Going by Michael Powell and Emeric Pressburger (October 15, 1950); David Niven, Geraldine Fitzgerald, Bonita Granville.

A Farewell to Arms by Ernest Hemingway (October 22, 1950); Joan Fontaine, Humphrey Bogart.

Michael and Mary by A. A. Milne (October 29, 1950); Joan Fontaine, Herbert Marshall.

Alice Adams by Booth Tarkington (November 5, 1950); Judy Garland, Thomas Mitchell.

The Voysey Inheritance by Harley Granville-Barker (November 12, 1950); Douglas Fairbanks, Jr., Angela Lansbury, Cecil Parker.

Dr. Jekyll and Mr. Hyde by Robert Louis Stevenson (November 19, 1950); Fredric March, Barbara Bel Geddes, Hugh Williams.

Theatre by Guy Bolton and W. Somerset Maugham (November 26, 1950); Gloria Swanson, Melvyn Douglas, Tom Helmore.

Carousel by Richard Rodgers and Oscar Hammerstein II (December 3, 1950); Cornel Wilde, Patrice Munsel.

Lottie Dundass by Enid Bagnold (December 10, 1950); Dorothy McGuire, Jessica Tandy.

Boomerang! by Richard Murphy (December 17, 1950); Kirk Douglas.

David Copperfield by Charles Dickens (December 24, 1950); Boris Karloff, Flora Robson, Cyril Ritchard, Hugh Williams, Richard Burton.

State Fair by Phil Stong (December 31, 1950); Van Heflin, Gene Lockhart, Kathleen Lockhart, June Lockhart.

The Third Man by Graham Greene (January 7, 1951); Joseph Cotten, Signe Hasso.

Trilby by George du Maurier (January 14, 1951); Teresa Wright, Rex Harrison.

The Fortune Hunter by Winchell Smith (January 21, 1951); John Lund, Jeanne Crain.

The Morning Glory by Zoë Akins (January 28, 1951); Anne Baxter, John Hodiak.

Come Back, Little Sheba by William Inge (February 4, 1951); Gary Cooper, Shirley Booth.

Within the Law by Bayard Veiller (February 11, 1951); Ginger Rogers, Lee Tracy.

Promise by Henry Bernstein (February 18, 1951); Gloria Swanson, Hume Cronyn, Margaret Phillips.

Father of the Bride by Edward Streeter (February 25, 1951); Spencer Tracy, Joan Bennett, Elizabeth Taylor.

Hamlet by William Shakespeare (March 4, 1951); John Gielgud, Dorothy McGuire, Pamela Brown.

The Hasty Heart by John Patrick (March 11, 1951); John Lund, Jane Wyatt, Richard Greene.

Jeannie by Aimée Stuart (March 18, 1951); Barry Sullivan, Margaret Phillips, Signe Hasso, Una O'Connor.

A Tale of Two Cities by Charles Dickens (March 25, 1951); Douglas Fairbanks, Jr.

The Fallen Idol by Graham Greene (April 1, 1951); Walter Pidgeon, Signe Hasso, Jack Hawkins.

This Side of Paradise by F. Scott Fitzgerald (April 8, 1951); Richard Widmark, Nina Foch.

Light Up the Sky by Moss Hart (April 15, 1951); Joan Bennett, Sam Levene, Thelma Ritter.

The First Year by Frank Craven (April 22, 1951); Richard Widmark, Kathryn Grayson.

Man in Possession by H. M. Harwood (April 29, 1951); Rex Harrison, Lilli Palmer.

Candida by George Bernard Shaw (May 6, 1951); Katharine Cornell.

Craig's Wife by George Kelly (May 13, 1951); Rosalind Russell, Melvyn Douglas.

Ethan Frome adapted by Owen and Donald Davis from a novel by Edith Wharton (May 20, 1951); Shirley Booth, Raymond Massey, Margaret Phillips.

Elmer the Great by Ring Lardner (May 27, 1951); Paul Douglas.

Biography by S. N. Behrman (June 3, 1951); Rosalind Russell, Burgess Meredith.

The Heiress by Ruth and Augustus Goetz from a novel by Henry James (September 9, 1951); Betty Field, Cornel Wilde, Basil Rathbone.

The Glass Menagerie by Tennessee Williams (September 16, 1951); Helen Hayes, Montgomery Clift.

This Woman Business by Benn W. Levy (September 23, 1951); David Niven, Margaret Phillips, Nigel Bruce.

Main Street by Sinclair Lewis (September 30, 1951); Joseph Cotten, Joan Fontaine.

Casanova Brown by Nunnally Johnson (October 7, 1951); Dan Dailey, Diana Lynn, Kenny Delmar.

The Major and the Minor, adapted from the screenplay by Edward Childs Carpenter (October 14, 1951); Ray Milland, Joan Fontaine.

Pygmalion by George Bernard Shaw (October 21, 1951); Alfred Lunt, Lynn Fontanne.

Skylark by Samson Raphaelson (October 28, 1951); Rosalind Russell, Macdonald Carey.

A Foreign Affair by George Fox and George Tilton (November 4, 1951); Marlene Dietrich, Richard Widmark.

Age of Innocence by Margaret Ayer Barnes (November 11, 1951); Claudette Colbert, Macdonald Carey.

Twentieth Century by Ben Hecht and Charles MacArthur (November 18, 1951); Claudette Colbert, Gregory Ratoff.

Allegro by Richard Rodgers and Oscar Hammerstein II (November 25, 1951); Jane Powell, John Lund, Kenny Delmar.

Good Housekeeping by William McCleery (December 2, 1951); Rosalind Russell, Walter Abel.

The Lost Weekend by Charles Jackson (December 9, 1951); William Holden, Brenda Marshall.

Arrowsmith by Sinclair Lewis (December 16, 1951); Tyrone Power, Loretta Young.

The Beloved Vagabond by William J. Locke (December 23, 1951); Rex Harrison, Beatrice Pearson.

Goodbye, Mr. Chips by James Hilton (December 30, 1951); Alan Webb, Margaret Phillips.

I Know My Love by S. N. Behrman (January 6, 1952); Alfred Lunt, Lynn Fontanne.

Look to the Mountain by LeGrand Cannon, Jr. (January 13, 1952); Dorothy McGuire, John Ireland.

Daisy Mayme by George Kelly (January 20, 1952); Betty Hutton.

The Thief by Henry Bernstein (January 27, 1952); Dorothy McGuire, David Niven, Roddy McDowall.

The Old Lady Shows Her Medals by James M. Barrie (February 3, 1952); Alfred Lunt, Lynn Fontanne.

The Meanest Man in the World by Augustin MacHugh (February 17, 1952); James Stewart, Josephine Hull, Coleen Gray.

The Traitor by Herman Wouk (February 19, 1952); Humphrey Bogart, Lauren Bacall.

Oliver Twist by Charles Dickens (February 24, 1952); Basil Rathbone, Boris Karloff, Leueen McGrath, Melville Cooper.

Portrait in Black by Ivan Goff and Ben Roberts (March 2, 1952); Barbara Stanwyck and Richard Widmark.

The Search by Richard Schweizer and David Wechsler (March 9, 1952); Montgomery Clift, Fay Bainter.

Love From a Stranger by Agatha Christie (March 16, 1952); Ray Milland, Edna Best.

Second Threshold by Philip Barry (March 23, 1952); Fredric March, Dorothy McGuire.

An Ideal Husband by Oscar Wilde (March 30, 1952); Rex Harrison, Lilli Palmer.

The Silver Whistle by Robert E. McEnroe (April 6, 1952); James Stewart, Diana Lynn.

Florence Nightingale by Cecil Woodham-Smith (April 13, 1952); Katharine Cornell, Brian Aherne.

The Truth About Blayds by A. A. Milne (April 20, 1952); Madeleine Carroll.

The Sea Wolf by Jack London (April 27, 1952); Burgess Meredith, Boris Karloff, Margaret Phillips.

Dear Brutus by James M. Barrie (May 4, 1952); David Niven, Angela Lansbury, Madeleine Carroll.

Prologue to Glory by E. P. Conkle (May 11, 1952); John Lund, Wanda Hendrix.

Over 21 by Ruth Gordon (May 18, 1952); Van Heflin, Ruth Gordon.

The Bishop Misbehaves by Frederick Jackson (May 25, 1952); Charles Laughton, Josephine Hull, Vanessa Brown.

Remember the Day by Philo Higley and Philip Dunning (June 1, 1952); Helen Hayes, Macdonald Carey.

The Wisteria Trees by Joshua Logan (September 14, 1952); Helen Hayes, Joseph Cotten.

George Washington Slept Here by George Kaufman and Moss Hart (September 21, 1952); Van Heflin, Ann Rutherford, Kenny Delmar.

Elmer the Great by Ring Lardner (September 28, 1952); Eddie Bracken, Wanda Hendrix.

Morning Star by Sylvia Regan (October 5, 1952); Gertrude Berg, Sylvia Sidney.

Tommy by Howard Lindsay and Bertrand Robinson (October 12, 1952); Wanda Hendrix, Wally Cox, Kenny Delmar.

The Sea Gull by Robert Nathan (October 19, 1952); John Lund, Viveca Lindfors.

Hobson's Choice by Harold Brighouse (October 26, 1952); Madeleine Carroll, Burgess Meredith, Melville Cooper.

Lo and Behold by John Patrick (November 2, 1952); Ann Blyth, Basil Rathbone, Jeffrey Lynn.

Magnificent Obsession by Lloyd Douglas (November 9, 1952); Rosalind Russell, Mel Ferrer.

All About Eve by Mary Orr (November 16, 1952); Tallulah Bankhead.

The Winslow Boy by Terence Rattigan (November 23, 1952); Basil Rathbone, Alan Webb, Margaret Phillips.

Liliom by Ferenc Molnár (November 30, 1952); Richard Widmark, Karl Malden, Geraldine Page.

The Damask Cheek by John van Druten and Lloyd Morris (December 7, 1952); Rosalind Russell, Kevin McCarthy.

The House of Mirth by Edith Wharton (December 14, 1952); Joan Fontaine, Franchot Tone.

The Pickwick Papers by Charles Dickens (December 21, 1952); Alan Webb, Cyril Ritchard, Melville Cooper, John Williams.

The Unguarded Hour by Bernard Merivale (December 28, 1952); Michael Redgrave, Nina Foch.

State Fair by Phil Stong (January 4, 1953); Van Johnson, Nancy Olson.

Jane by S. N. Behrman (January 11, 1953); Michael Redgrave, Edna Best.

Trial by Forgery by Bernard C. Schoenfeld (January 18, 1953); Joseph Cotten, Anne Baxter.

The Scarlet Letter by Nathaniel Hawthorne (January 25, 1953); Dorothy McGuire, Cedric Hardwicke.

Reflected Glory by George Kelly (February 1, 1953); Bette Davis, Macdonald Carey.

Man and Superman by George Bernard Shaw (February 8, 1953); Maurice Evans, Deborah Kerr.

Cass Timberlane by Sinclair Lewis (February 15, 1953); Fredric March, Nina Foch.

The Show-Off by George Kelly (February 22, 1953); Paul Douglas, Jan Sterling.

O'Halloran's Luck by Stephen Vincent Benét (March 1, 1953); James Stewart, John Lund, Gloria De Haven.

Vanity Fair by William Makepeace Thackeray (March 8, 1953); Joan Fontaine.

A Square Peg by Lewis Beach (March 15, 1953); Thomas Mitchell, Thelma Ritter, Jane Wyatt.

The Old Maid by Zoë Akins (March 22, 1953); Betty Field, Nina Foch.

The Brass Ring by Irving Elman (March 29, 1953); Melvyn Douglas, Gloria De Haven.

Great Expectations by Charles Dickens (April 5, 1953); Boris Karloff, Melville Cooper, Margaret Phillips, Tom Helmore, Estelle Winwood.

The Glass Menagerie by Tennessee Williams (April 12, 1953); Shirley Booth.

The Petrified Forest by Robert E. Sherwood (April 19, 1953); Tyrone Power.

1984 by George Orwell (April 26, 1953); Richard Widmark.

Quiet Wedding by Esther McCracken (May 3, 1953); Diana Lynn, John Dall, Jessie Royce Landis.

Black Chiffon by Lesley Storm (May 10, 1953); Judith Anderson, Burgess Meredith.

The Importance of Being Earnest by Oscar Wilde (May 17, 1953); Rex Harrison, Lilli Palmer.

Kate Fennigate by Booth Tarkington (May 24, 1953); Wendell Corey, Martha Scott.

The Grand Tour by Elmer Rice (May 31, 1953); Jean Arthur.

Julius Caesar by William Shakespeare (June 7, 1953); Maurice Evans, Basil Rathbone.

III

List of Theatre Guild Productions on Television

UNITED STATES STEEL HOUR

P.O.W. by David Davidson (October 27, 1953); Gary Merrill, Phyllis Kirk, Richard Kiley, Brian Keith, Johnny Stewart.

Hope for a Harvest by Sophie Treadwell, adapted by Norman Lessing (November 10, 1953); Faye Emerson, Robert Preston.

Tin Wedding by Hagar Wilde and Judson O'Donnell, adapted by Hagar Wilde (November 24, 1953); Eddie Albert, Phyllis Thaxter.

Man in Possession by H. M. Harwood, adapted by Arthur Arent (December 8, 1953); Rex Harrison, Lilli Palmer.

The Vanishing Point by A. E. Hotchner, adapted by Hotchner and Norman Lessing (December 22, 1953); Claude Dauphin, Peter Lorre, Viveca Lindfors.

Hedda Gabler by Henrik Ibsen, adapted by Erik Barnouw (January 5, 1954); Tallulah Bankhead, Luther Adler.

The Rise of Carthage by Lawrence Williams, adapted by Raphael Hayes and Arthur Arent (January 19, 1954); Paul Douglas, Nina Foch.

Papa Is All by Patterson Greene, adapted by Erik Barnouw (February 2, 1954); Walter Slezak, Jessie Royce Landis.

Highway by Sophie Treadwell, adapted by Earl Hamner (February 16, 1954); Diana Lynn.

Morning Star by Sylvia Regan, adapted by Arthur Arent (March 2, 1954); Gertrude Berg.

Welcome Home by N. Richard Nash (March 16, 1954); Helen Hayes, Charles Ruggles.

The Last Notch by Frank D. Gilroy (March 30, 1954); Jeff Morrow, Richard Jaeckel, Louisa Horton.

Late Date by William Kendall Clarke (April 13, 1954); Jessie Royce Landis.

The Laphams of Boston by William Dean Howells, adapted by Robert Walsten (April 27, 1954); Thomas Mitchell, Dorothy Gish.

The End of Paul Dane by Morton Wishengrad and Virginia Mazer (May 11, 1954); Teresa Wright, Robert Preston.

The Great Chair by Leo Lieberman (May 25, 1954); Gary Merrill, Walter Hampden.

Good for You by Robert McMenamin (June 8, 1954); Diana Lynn, Orson Bean, Kenny Delmar.

Fearful Decision by Richard Maibaum and Cyril Hume (June 22, 1954); Ralph Bellamy.

Haven's End by John P. Marquand, adapted by David Davidson (July 6, 1954); Howard Lindsay.

A Garden in the Sea by Michael Dyne (July 20, 1954); Dorothy McGuire.

Oberstrasse 49 by Eileen and Robert Mason Pollack (August 3, 1954); Dan O'Herlihy, Margaret Phillips.

The Grand Tour by Elmer Rice, adapted by Arthur Arent (August 17, 1954); Zachary Scott, Julie Haydon.

Two by Morton Wishengrad and Virginia Mazer (August 31, 1954); Pat Crowley, Jerome Courtland.

The Notebook Warrior by Ira Levin (September 14, 1954); Richard Kiley, Sidney Blackmer, Ben Gazzara.

Baseball Blues by Steven Gethers (September 28, 1954); Frank Lovejoy.

The Man with the Gun by W. E. C. Fairchild, adapted by Arthur Arent (October 12, 1954); Gary Merrill.

The Fifth Wheel by William McCleery, adapted by Irving Gaynor Neiman (October 26, 1954); Faye Emerson, Franchot Tone, Orson Bean.

Goodbye . . . But It Doesn't Go Away by Raphael Hayes (November 9, 1954); Jack Carson, June Lockhart.

King's Pawn by Irving Gaynor Neiman, based on "The Man in the Goldfish Bowl" by Walter C. Brown (November 23, 1954); John Forsythe, Janet Blair, Neil Hamilton.

One for the Road by Ellis St. Joseph (December 7, 1954); Charles Coburn, Jeff Donnell.

Presento by Joseph Julian (December 21, 1954); Don Taylor, Pat Crowley, Hans Conried, Shirley Yamaguchi.

The Thief by Henry Bernstein, adapted by Arthur Arent (January 4, 1955); Diana Lynn, Paul Lukas, Mary Astor, Patric Knowles.

The Bogeyman by Francis Rosenwald (January 18, 1955); Celeste Holm, Robert Preston.

Six O'Clock Call by James Yaffe (February 1, 1955); Gertrude Berg.

Freighter by George Lowther (February 15, 1955); Thomas Mitchell, James Daly, Henry Hull.

Man in the Corner by Ernest Pendrell (March 1, 1955); Jack Carson.

No Time for Sergeants by Mac Hyman, adapted by Ira Levin (March 15, 1955); Andy Griffith.

Scandal at Peppernut by Kate and Howard Phillips, adapted by Kay Arthur (March 29, 1955); Terry Moore.

The Rack by Rod Serling (April 12, 1955); Wendell Corey, Keenan Wynn, Marshall Thompson.

Roads to Home by Horton Foote (April 26, 1955); James Daly, Beatrice Straight.

Fearful Decision by Cyril Hume and Richard Maibaum (May 10, 1955); Ralph Bellamy.

Big Winner by Richard Bimonte (May 24, 1955); Frank Puglia, Marita Reid.

Hung for a Sheep by Frank D. Gilroy (June 7, 1955); Hugh Marlowe, Jerome Thor, George McCready.

Red Gulch by Arthur Arent (June 21, 1955); Teresa Wright, Franchot Tone.

The Meanest Man in the World by Augustin Mac-Hugh, adapted by Joseph Julian (July 6, 1955); Wally Cox, Josephine Hull, Betsy Palmer, Kenny Delmar.

The Gambler by Irving Richin (July 20, 1955); Jack Carson.

The Seven Veils by Muriel and Sidney Box, adapted by Arthur Arent (August 3, 1955); Dan O'Herlihy, Diana Lynn.

The Bride Cried by Mae Cooper and Grace Klein (August 17, 1955); Janice Rule.

Counterfeit by J. B. Priestley, adapted by Ellen Violett (August 31, 1955); Boris Karloff, Edna Best.

A Wind from the South by James Costigan (September 14, 1955); Julie Harris.

Ashton Buys a Horse by Norman Lessing (September 28, 1955); Menasha Skulnik.

Obsession by Ernest Pendrell (October 12, 1955); Phyllis Thaxter.

Shoot It Again by Claude Binyon, adapted by Robert Emmett (October 26, 1955); Geraldine Page.

Outcast by Turner Bullock (November 9, 1955); Lillian Roth.

Incident in an Alley by Rod Serling (November 23, 1955); Farley Granger.

Edward, My Son by Robert Morley and Noel Langley (December 7, 1955); Robert Morley.

White Gloves by James Costigan (December 21, 1955); Joan Blondell, Joanne Woodward.

Bring Me a Dream by John Vlahos (January 4, 1956); John Cassavetes, Lois Smith.

The Great Adventure by Arnold Bennett, adapted by Kay Arthur (January 18, 1956); Jessica Tandy, Hume Cronyn.

A Fair Shake by Caleb Gray (February 1, 1956); John Kerr.

Command by Christopher La Farge, adapted by Paul Monash (February 15, 1956); Cameron Mitchell, James Gregory, Marshall Thompson, Biff McGuire.

The Candidate by S. S. Schweitzer (March 14, 1956); Ralph Bellamy.

Thirty-Year Man by Edward Breen (March 28, 1956); Pat O'Brien.

Funny Heart by Mel Goldberg (April 11, 1956); Imogene Coca.

Noon on Doomsday by Rod Serling (April 25, 1956); Everett Sloane, Jack Warden, Lois Smith, Albert Salmi, Philip Abbott.

Honest in the Rain by Mort Thaw (May 9, 1956); Ethel Merman.

The Old Lady Shows Her Medals by James M. Barrie, adapted by Robert Anderson (May 23, 1956); Gracie Fields, Jackie Cooper.

The Boarding House by James Joyce, adapted by Will Lorin (June 6, 1956); Evelyn Varden.

Moment of Courage by Henry Misrock (June 20, 1956); Macdonald Carey, Kim Hunter.

Operation 3R's by Helen Cotton (July 4, 1956); Robert Culp, Sallie Brophy, Frank Milan, Gerald Price.

The Partners by Bernard C. Schoenfeld (July 18, 1956); Luther Adler, Virginia Vincent, Mark Richman.

Stopover at Sublimity by Lucille Duffy (August 1, 1956); Lisa Daniels, John Napier, Efrem Zimbalist, Jr.

The Five Fathers of Pepi by Ira and Jane Avery (August 29, 1956); Paul Newman.

We Must Kill Toni by Leslie Duncan (September 12, 1956); Norman Lloyd, Fritz Weaver, Lisa Daniels.

Bang the Drum Slowly by Arnold Schulman from the novel by Mark Harris (September 26, 1956); Paul Newman, Albert Salmi, Georgann Johnson.

Sauce for the Goose by Robert Emmett (October 10, 1956); Gypsy Rose Lee, Gig Young, Leora Dana.

Wetback Run by Ted Apstein (October 24, 1956); Rip Torn.

Survival by Alfred Brenner (November 7, 1956); Franchot Tone, Albert Salmi, Arnold Moss.

Tom Sawyer adapted by Frank Luther (November 21, 1956); John Sharpe, Bennye Gatteys, Jimmy Boyd.

Hunted by Morton Wishengrad (December 5, 1956); Ann Sheridan, Theodore Bikel.

The Old Lady Shows Her Medals by James M. Barrie, adapted by Robert Anderson (December 19, 1956); Gracie Fields, Biff McGuire, William LeMassena.

The Human Pattern by Irving H. Cooper (January 2, 1957); Thelma Ritter.

To Die Alone by Robert and Wanda Duncan (January 16, 1957); Burl Ives, Jane Pickens.

They Never Forgot by Norman A. Brooks (January 30, 1957); Lloyd Bridges, Viveca Lindfors.

Inspired Alibi by Gertrude Schweitzer, adapted by S. S. Schweitzer (February 13, 1957); Shelley Winters, Pat Hingle, Edward Andrews.

Shadow of Evil by Curtis Kenyon (February 27, 1957); Lee Marvin, Jack Cassidy, Shirley Jones.

The Bottle Imp by Robert Louis Stevenson, adapted by Arthur Steuer (March 13, 1957); Farley Granger.

Hidden Fury by George Bellak (March 27, 1957); James Gregory.

The Hill Wife by Alfred Brenner, based on several poems by Robert Frost (April 10, 1957); Melvyn Douglas, Geraldine Page, Albert Salmi.

A Matter of Pride (Blue Serge Suit) by John Langdon, adapted for TV by Frank Gilroy (April 24, 1957); Philip Abbott, Robert Simon, Joseph Sweeney, Burt Brinckerhoff.

A Drum Is a Woman by Will Lorin, from a Duke Ellington recording (May 8, 1957); Duke Ellington.

Shadow in the Sky, adapted by S. S. Schweitzer, based on a screenplay by Deska (May 22, 1957); Richard Kiley, Peter Cookson, Bonita Granville.

The Little Bullfighter by Juarez Roberts (June 5, 1957); Nehemiah Persoff, Rip Torn. Olga Bellin, Miko Oscard.

Upbeat by James Elward (June 19, 1957); Patti Page, Biff McGuire, Kathleen Maguire, Jon Cypher.

Side Show (Outside Man) by Shelby Gordon (July 3, 1957); Abe Simon, Lisa Daniels, Reed Morgan.

Victim by James Elward (July 17, 1957); Walter Matthau, Dean Stockwell.

The Change in Chester by Arthur Hailey (July 31, 1957); John McGiver, Tom Poston, Mary Sinclair, Alan Hewitt.

A Loud Laugh by Harberd Hogan (August 14, 1957); June Lockhart, Louis Jean Heydt, Dick Davalos.

Up Above the World So High by Mort Thaw (August 28, 1957); Jack Warden, Dennis Kohler, Carmen Mathews.

Windfall by Bob and Wanda Duncan (September 11, 1957); Ed Begley, Philip Abbott, Andrew Duggan, Frances Fuller.

Haunted Harbor (Legend of St. Croix) by Henry Misrock (September 25, 1957); Burgess Meredith, Gaby Rodgers.

Who's Earnest?, based on *The Importance of Being Earnest* by Oscar Wilde, adapted by Anne Croswell and Lee Pockriss (October 9, 1957); Dorothy Collins, Edward Mulhare, David Atkinson, Martyn Green.

Crisis in Coroma by Elliott Baker (October 23, 1957); Charles Ruggles, Elliott Nugent.

The Locked Door by Gertrude Schweitzer (November 6, 1957); Ralph Bellamy, June Lockhart, Brandon DeWilde.

Huck Finn by Lee Pockriss and Anne Croswell, music by Frank Luther (November 20, 1957); Jack Carson, Basil Rathbone, Jimmy Boyd, Florence Henderson, Earle Hyman.

You Can't Win by Robert Emmett (December 4, 1957); Bert Lahr.

Little Charlie Don't Want a Saddle by Juarez Roberts (December 18, 1957); June Lockhart, John Beal, Dennis Kohler.

The Charmer by Douglas Taylor (January 1, 1958); Gypsy Rose Lee, Rip Torn, Edmon Ryan.

The Bromley Touch, adapted by Kay Arthur from a *New Yorker* story by Edward Newhouse (January 15, 1958); Cameron Mitchell, Leora Dana, Biff McGuire.

Never Know the End by Irving Gaynor Neiman (January 29, 1958); Andy Griffith, Nehemiah Persoff, Larry Blyden, Patricia Benoit.

The Reward by Laura Z. Hobson, adapted by Mort Thaw (February 12, 1958); Cathleen Nesbitt, Nancy Coleman.

Walk with a Stranger by H. N. Clauss (February 26, 1958); Ed Begley, William Shatner.

Give Me My Son by Anne Wormser and Jess Oppenheimer, adapted by Abby Mann (March 12, 1958); Richard Kiley, Betsy Palmer, Alexander Scourby, Lori March, Dennis Kohler.

Top Secret Mission by Irving Gaynor Neiman from a novel by Madeleine Duke (March 26, 1958); Beatrice Straight, Robert Wright, Josef Yadin.

Beaver Patrol by John Vlahos (April 9, 1958); Walter Slezak.

The Public Prosecutor by Fritz Hochwalder, adapted by Theodore Apstein (April 23, 1958); Walter Slezak, Dolores Del Rio, John Baragrey, Frank Conroy.

A Man in Hiding (The Gift of Harbor) by Leonard Moran (May 7, 1958); William Shatner, Michael Higgins, John Sutton, Ian Wolfe.

Hour of the Rat by Jon Manchip White, adapted by Arthur Hailey (May 21, 1958); Dan Duryea.

A Family Alliance, adapted by Kay Arthur from a short story by Dorothy Canfield (June 4, 1958); Bill Hayes, Florence Henderson, Roberta Haynes.

The Littlest Enemy, adapted by Lois Jacoby from a play by Nigel Kneale (June 18, 1958); Mary Astor, Frank Conroy, Lili Darvas.

Hidden River by Ruth Goetz and Storm Jameson, adapted by Ted Apstein (July 2, 1958); Richard Kiley, Erin O'Brien-Moore, Farley Granger.

Flint and Fire by Dorothy Canfield, adapted by H. N. Clauss (July 16, 1958); Robert Culp, Gloria Vanderbilt, Edward Andrews, Una Merkel.

The Climate of Marriage by Helen Cotton (July 30, 1958); James Daly, Leora Dana, Betsy Palmer.

Old Marshals Never Die, from a story by John H. Holland and adapted by John Vlahos (August 13, 1958); William Shatner, Cameron Prud'homme, Joanne Linville, Robert Emhardt, Crahan Denton.

The Guest Cottage by John Whedon (August 27, 1958); Elliott Nugent, Larry Blyden, Joanna Moore.

The Wound Within by Henry Denker (September 10, 1958); Farley Granger, Mary Sinclair, Frank Conroy.

Death Minus One by Arthur Hailey (September 24, 1958); Alexander Scourby, Meg Mundy.

Midsummer by Viña Delmar, adapted by Arthur Heinemann (October 8, 1958); Barbara Bel Geddes, Jackie Cooper.

Secret in the Family by Helen Hull, adapted by Louis Pelletier (October 22, 1958); Faye Emerson, Edward Andrews.

Second Chance by Steven Gethers (November 5, 1958); Melvyn Douglas, Nancy Olson, Meg Mundy, Martin Rudy.

This Day in Fear by Malcolm Hulke and Eric Paice, adapted by Arthur Heinemann (November 19, 1958); Barry Sullivan, Geraldine Brooks, Philip Bourneuf.

The Enemies by Stephen Vincent Benét, adapted by Robert Van Scoyk (December 3, 1958); Ed Begley, Betsy Palmer.

One Red Rose for Christmas by Paul Horgan, adapted by Leonard Moran (December 17, 1958); Helen Hayes.

Goodbye . . . But It Doesn't Go Away by Raphael Hayes (December 31, 1958); Neville Brand, Jeff Donnell, George Voskovec, Inga Swenson.

Dangerous Interlude by F. Wyndham Mallock, adapted by Robert Van Scoyk (January 14, 1959); Viveca Lindfors, Torin Thatcher.

Family Happiness by Leo Tolstoy, adapted by Morton Wishengrad (February 11, 1959); Jean Pierre Aumont, Gloria Vanderbilt.

Trap for a Stranger by Betty Ulius (February 25, 1959); Teresa Wright, George C. Scott.

The Square Egghead by Louis Pelletier (March 11, 1959); Tom Ewell, June Lockhart.

Night of Betrayal by James Lipton (March 25, 1959); Roddy McDowall, Victor Jory, Carol Lawrence.

Trouble-in-Law by Danny Simon (April 8, 1959); Gertrude Berg, Betsy von Furstenberg.

Little Tin God by Joe Palmer, Jr. (April 22, 1959); Richard Boone, Jeff Donnell, Paul McGrath.

The Wayward Widow, based on a story by Thomas Hardy, "The Distracted Preacher," adapted by Michael Dyne (May 6, 1959); Betsy Palmer, Richard Greene.

Call It a Day by Dodie Smith, adapted by Robert Van Scoyk (May 20, 1959); Faye Emerson, Edward Andrews.

Whisper of Evil by Lesley Storm, adapted by Morton Wishengrad (June 3, 1959); Nina Foch, John Beal, Chester Morris.

No Leave for the Captain, from a novel by Gerhard Rasmussen, adapted by Robert Van Scoyk (June 17, 1959); Maurice Evans, Diana van der Vlis, Geraldine Brooks.

Apple of His Eye, adapted by Helene Hanff from a play by Charles Robinson and Kenyon Nicholson (July 1, 1959); Eddie Albert, Carol Lawrence, Frank McHugh.

The Pink Burro, adapted by Kay Arthur from a play by Jean Riley (July 15, 1959); June Havoc, Edward Andrews, Jane Withers.

Wish on the Moon by Sumner Locke Elliott (July 29, 1959); Peggy Ann Garner, Erin O'Brien-Moore, Biff McGuire, William Gaxton.

Seed of Guilt by Barbara Chain (August 12, 1959); Peggy Wood, Gloria Vanderbilt, Patty Duke.

A Taste of Champagne, adapted by Robert Van Scoyk from a short story by Alan Seager (August 26, 1959); Hans Conried, Monique Van Vooren, Scott McKay.

The Case of Julia Walton, adapted by Harold Gast from a screenplay by Jay Ingram (September 9, 1959); Nina Foch, Alan Baxter, Jeffrey Lynn.

The Hours Before Dawn, adapted by Philip C. Lewis from a novel by Celia Fremlin (September 23, 1959); Teresa Wright, Mark Richman, Colleen Dewhurst, Jack Carter.

Rachel's Summer, adapted by Ron Sproat from a story by Charles Jackson (October 7, 1959); Martha Scott, Burt Brinckerhoff, Patty McCormack.

Holiday on Wheels by Mel Tolkin, Mel Brooks, and Sydney Zelinka (October 21, 1959); Sid Caesar, Audrey Meadows, Peter Gennaro, Wisa D'Orso, Paul Weston and Orchestra, Gisele Mackenzie, Tony Randall.

Big Doc's Girl, adapted by Leonard Moran from a novel by Mary Maderia (November 4, 1959); Margaret O'Brien, Gene Raymond, Robert Lansing, Gene Hackman.

The Last Autumn, adapted by Arthur Heinemann from a novel by Herbert Gutterson (November 18, 1959); Pat Hingle, Alexis Smith.

One Red Rose for Christmas by Paul Horgan (2nd version) adapted by Leonard Moran (December 16, 1959); Helen Hayes, Patty Duke.

Act of Terror by Thomas Weitzner (December 30, 1959); Mark Richman, George Grizzard, Frank Conroy, Nancy Berg.

Queen of the Orange Bowl, adapted by Robert Van Scoyk from a TV play by Roger Squire (January 13, 1960); Anne Francis, Johnny Carson, Glenda Farrell, Frank McHugh.

You Can't Have Everything, adapted by James Yaffe from a TV play by Jack Pulman (January 27, 1960); Piper Laurie, Donald Moffat, Florence Reed.

The American Cowboy by Joe Stein, Lucille Kallin, Norman Barasch, and Carol Moore (February 10, 1960); Fred MacMurray, Edie Adams, Carol Burnett, Hans Conried, Wally Cox.

The Women of Hadley (First part), adapted by Erik Barnouw from the novel by Roger Eddy (February 24, 1960); Richard Kiley, Mona Freeman, Mary Astor, Rita Gam, Cedric Hardwicke.

Revolt in Hadley (Second part) (March 9, 1960); same cast as above.

The Charlie and the Kid by James Lipton (March 23, 1960); Richard Boone, Geraldine Brooks.

How to Make a Killing by Alan Caillou (April 6, 1960); Eva Gabor, Robert Loggia, Claude Dauphin.

The Girl Who Knew Too Much, adapted by Harold Gast from a story by Murray Teigh Bloom (April 20, 1960); Mona Freeman, Arthur Hill, Alan Baxter.

Girl in the Gold Bathtub, adapted by Robert Van Scoyk from a novelette by Victor Canning (May 4, 1960); Marisa Pavan, Jessie Royce Landis, Edward Andrews, Johnny Carson.

Game of Hearts, adapted by Philip C. Lewis from a TV play by Douglas Rae (June 1, 1960); Jeff Donnell, Arthur Hill, Robert Webber, Betsy Palmer.

The Impostor, adapted by James Yaffe from a story by Michael Dyne (June 15, 1960); Ann Sheridan, Liliane Montevecchi, Jean Pierre Aumont.

The Great Gold Mountain, adapted by Ron Sproat from a novel by James McCague (June 29, 1960); Polly Bergen, Burt Brinckerhoff, Robert Lansing, Ed Begley.

Shadow of a Pale Horse by Bruce Stewart, adapted by Joe Palmer, Jr. (July 20, 1960); Dan Duryea, Frank Lovejoy.

The Case of the Missing Wife by Orin Borsten (August 10, 1960); Red Buttons, Nancy Wickwire, John Colicos.

Bride of the Fox, adapted by Kay Arthur from a teleplay by Budd Fishel and Barry Hyams (August 24, 1960); Richard Kiley, Ina Balin, Alan Baxter.

When in Rome, adapted by Robert Van Scoyk from a TV play by George Barraud (September 7, 1960); Arlene Francis, Hans Conried, Howard Morris.

The Man Who Knew Tomorrow, adapted by Harold Gast from a TV play by Paul Lee (September 21, 1960); Jeanne Crain, Cliff Robertson.

Revolt of Judge Lloyd by Paul Manning and Joe Graham (October 5, 1960); Claire Trevor, Jeff Morrow.

Step on the Gas: A Musical Comedy Ride with the American Motorist by Will Glickman, Sydney Zelinka, Lucille Kallen, and Bill Brown (October 19, 1960); Jackie Cooper, Hans Conried, Pat Carroll, Shari Lewis, Shirley Jones.

A Time to Decide by Sidney Carroll from a novel by Edward Newhouse (formerly *The Temptation*) (November 2, 1960); Barry Nelson, Cathleen Nesbitt, Nina Foch.

The Yum-Yum Girl adapted by Robert Van Scoyk from a short story by John Latham Toohey (November 30, 1960); Anne Francis, Robert Sterling.

Shame the Devil by Louis Pelletier and Jack Anson Finke (December 14, 1960); Betsy Palmer, Vincent Price.

The Coming of Christ—Project 20 by Richard Hanser (December 21, 1960).

Operation Northstar by Donald Bull (December 28, 1960); Barry Sullivan, Mona Freeman.

The Mating Machine by Bernard Slade (January 11, 1961); Diana Lynn, George Grizzard, Geraldine Brooks, John Ericson.

The Devil Makes Sunday by Bruce Stewart (January 25, 1961); Dane Clark, Martyn Green, Brooke Hayward, Fritz Weaver.

The Big Splash by Harold Gast (February 8, 1961); Jack Carson, Arlene Francis.

The Two Worlds of Charlie Gordon (formerly *Flowers for Algernon*) by James Yaffe from a story by Daniel Keyes (February 22, 1961); Cliff Robertson, Mona Freeman.

Private Eye, Private Eye by Will Glickman, Sydney Zelinka, Lucille Kallen, and William Brown (March 8, 1961); Ernie Kovacs, Edie Adams, Hans Conried, Pat Carroll.

Welcome Home by N. Richard Nash (March 22, 1961); Shirley Booth.

The Oddball by Bernard Slade (April 5, 1961); Hans Conried, Faye Emerson.

The Shame of Paula Marsten (formerly *The Litter of Flowers*) by Richard F. Stockton (April 19, 1961); Anne Baxter, Gene Raymond.

Summer Rhapsody (formerly *A Special Kind of Summer*) by John Holt (May 3, 1961); Tom Tully, Glenda Farrell.

The Leonardi Code by Donald Bull (May 17, 1961); Sally Ann Howes, Barry Morse.

Famous, adapted by Robert Van Scoyk from a story by Stephen Vincent Benét (May 31, 1961); Eddie Albert, Dolores Gray.

Trial Without Jury by Harold Gast (June 14, 1961); Richard Kiley, Mary Fickett.

The Haven by Tad Mosel (June 28, 1961); Helen Hayes, Gene Raymond.

Watching Out for Dulie, adapted by Arthur Heinemann from a novel by David Westheimer (July 12, 1961); Larry Blyden, Shari Lewis, Patricia Cutts, Lloyd Bochner.

Double-Edge Sword (originally *The Colonel*) by Jon Manchip White (July 26, 1961); Leo G. Carroll, Sarah Marshall, Lloyd Bochner, Cathleen Nesbitt.

The Golden Thirty by Larry Cohn (August 9, 1961); Henny Youngman, Keir Dullea, Nancy Kovack.

Woman Across the Hall by Robert Wallsten (August 23, 1961); Glenda Farrell, Alan Bunce, Ruth Ford.

Delayed Honeymoon (formerly *Reservations*), adapted by Robert Van Scoyk from a story by Peter Taylor (September 6, 1961); Larry Blyden, Elinor Donahue, Nancy Carroll, James Broderick.

Street of Love, adapted by Harold Gast from a play by Max Ehrlich (September 20, 1961); Millie Perkins, Douglas McClure.

Brandenburg Gate by John Vlahos (October 4, 1961); Richard Kiley, Barry Morse, Anne Meacham, Dina Merrill.

Bury Me Twice (formerly *Full Circle*), adapted by Charles Robinson from a play by Brian Clemens (October 18, 1961); Dan O'Herlihy, Phyllis Thaxter, Leo G. Carroll.

Little Lost Sheep by Ernest Kinoy (November 1, 1961); Hans Conried, Jane Wyatt.

Man on the Mountaintop by Robert Alan Aurthur (November 15, 1961); Cliff Robertson, Paul McGrath, Salome Jens.

Tangle of Truth, adapted by Jerome Coopersmith from a novelette by Paul Ernst (November 29, 1961); Macdonald Carey, Jeff Donnell, Darryl Hickman, Carolyn Groves.

My Wife's Best Friend by Robert Van Scoyk (December 13, 1961); Larry Blyden, Joanna Moore, Doris Dalton.

The Bitter Sex, adapted by Richard F. Stockton from a play by Donald Wilson (December 28, 1961); Mona Freeman, Barry Morse, Lloyd Bochner.

Far From the Shade Tree by Joe Palmer, Jr. (January 10, 1962); Jack Carson, Anita Louise, Keir Dullea.

The Big Laugh by Bernard Slade (January 24, 1962); Teresa Wright, Arthur Hill, Murray Hamilton.

Nightmare at Bleak Hill, adapted by Lois Landauer from a story, "Romney" by A. L. Barker (February 7, 1962); Douglas Fairbanks, Jr., Leora Dana, Donald Madden.

The Perfect Accident (formerly *Scene of the Accident*), adapted by Michael Gast from a play by Michael Gilbert (February 21, 1962); Robert Horton, Carolyn Groves, Alan Bunce, Shepperd Strudwick.

Who Is This Woman? (formerly *Eva? Caroline?*) adapted by Thomas W. Phipps from a story by Allan Vaughn Elston (March 7, 1962); Gloria De Haven, Arthur Hill, Donald Davis.

Two Black Kings by Sidney Carroll (March 21, 1962); Eva Gabor, Kevin McCarthy, James Broderick.

The Loves of Claire Ambler (formerly *Claire Ambler*), adapted by Sidney Carroll from the novel by Booth Tarkington (April 4, 1962); Maurice Evans, Janice Rule, Nancy Carroll.

The Go-Between, adapted by Robert Van Scoyk from a play by Lois Hire (April 18, 1962); Barbara Cook, John Lupton, Keefe Brasselle, Cely Carrillo.

A Man for Oona (formerly *Two Ducks in a Pond*) by Michael Dyne (May 2, 1962); Tallulah Bankhead, Nancy Carroll, Murray Matheson.

The Other Woman (formerly *Alias Mrs. Fiske*) by Richard F. Stockton (May 16, 1962); Jeanne Crain, Lloyd Bochner, Hugh Reilly.

You Can't Escape, adapted by Harold Gast from a play by Jacques Gillies (June 13, 1962); Mark Richman, Shirley Knight, Simon Oakland, Michael Tolan, Alice Ghostley.

Scene of the Crime, adapted by Sidney Carroll from a play by Brian Clemens (June 27, 1962); Harry Townes, Betty White, Patricia Collinge.

Night of the Fourth, adapted by Richard F. Stockton from a play by Jack Roffery and Gordon Harbord (July 11, 1962); Barry Sullivan, Zia Mohyeddin, Nan Martin.

Honor in Love, adapted by Irving Gaynor Neiman from *Immortality Becomes Allard* by John P. Marquand (July 25, 1962); Carol Lawrence, Biff McGuire.

Male Call by Daniel Rudsten (August 8, 1962); Larry Blyden, Gary Crosby, Mindy Carson, Fred Clark, Zohra Lampert.

Murder on the Agenda, adapted by Joe Palmer, Jr., from a play by Eynon Evans (August 22, 1962); James Daly, Mona Freeman, Ralph Meeker, Simon Oakland, Harry Townes.

Dry Rain by Harold Gast (September 5, 1962); John Kerr, Phyllis Newman, Johnny Desmond.

The Inner Panic by Al Meglin (September 12, 1962); Cynthia Pepper, Tommy Sands, Glenda Farrell, Simon Oakland.

The White Lie by John Hess (October 3, 1962); David Wayne, Neva Patterson, Sallie Brophy, Adam Kennedy.

Wanted: Someone Innocent, adapted by Michael Dyne from a novelette by Margery Allingham (October 17, 1962); Kim Hunter, Diana Hyland, Robert Lansing, Werner Klemperer, Bibi Osterwald.

A Break in the Weather, adapted by Sam Hall from a novel by Florence Jane Soman (October 31, 1962); Eddie Albert, Augusta Dabney, Lawrence Weber.

Marriage Marks the Spot, adapted by Ted Berkman from a story by Libbie Block (November 14, 1962); Darren McGavin, Julius La Rosa, Pippa Scott.

Farewell to Innocence by Jack Pulman (November 28, 1962); John Beal, Vicki Cummings, Thomas Chalmers, Royston Thomas, Jeff Donnell.

Big Day for a Scrambler by Richard F. Stockton (December 12, 1962); James Whitmore, Priscilla Gillette, Whitfield Connor, Peter Palmer.

The Duchess and the Smugs, adapted by Ellen Violett from a story by Pamela Frankau (December 26, 1962); Patty Duke, Fritz Weaver, Scott Forbes, Eugenie Leontovich.

The Young Avengers (formerly *The Enemy*), adapted by Robert Crean from a story by Charlotte Armstrong (January 9, 1963); Keir Dullea, Elizabeth Ashley, Cameron Prud'homme.

Fair Young Ghost, adapted by Leonard Moran from a story by Kenneth Kay (January 23, 1963); Robert Lansing, Cathleen Nesbitt, Dolores Dorn, Shirley Knight.

The Troubled Heart by Arthur Hailey (February 6, 1963); John Colicos, Toby Robins, Corinne Conley, Ted Fellows.

Night Run to the West, adapted by Morton Wishengrad from a novella by H. E. Bates (February 20, 1963); Colleen Dewhurst, Ralph Meeker.

Moment of Rage, adapted by Arthur Heinemann from *A Question of Fact,* a play by Wynyard Browne (March 6, 1963); Charles Aidman, Marc Connelly, Kathryn Hays, Glenda Farrell.

The Secrets of Stella Crozier, adapted by Sam Hall from a story by Booth Tarkington (March 20, 1963); Diana Millay, Elinor Donahue, Patricia Morrison, Frank Overton.

Mission of Fear, adapted by Richard F. Stockton from a novel by George Harmon Coxe (April 3, 1963); Robert Horton, Salome Jens, Roy Poole.

The Soldier Ran Away by Nicholas E. Baehr, adapted from a story by Kay Boyle (April 17, 1963); John Beal, Royston Thomas, Audra Lindley, Martin Sheen.

The Many Ways of Heaven, adapted by Ellen Violett from a story by George Loveridge (May 1, 1963); Dan Duryea, Cathleen Nesbitt, Nancy Wickwire, Casey Peters.

Don't Shake the Family Tree by Leslie McFarlane (May 15, 1963); Jim Backus, Orson Bean, Ethel Griffies, Frank McHugh, Fred Gwynne, Paul Reed, Ruth White.

A Taste of Champagne, adapted by Robert Van Scoyk from a story by Alan Seager (May 29, 1963); Hans Conried, Monique Van Vooren, Scott McKay.

The Old Lady Shows Her Medals, adapted by Robert Anderson from a play by James M. Barrie (June 12, 1963); Alfred Lunt, Lynn Fontanne, Donald Madden, Cathleen Nesbitt.

Index

Italic numbers refer to illustrations.

Abbey Theatre (Dublin), 238
Abbott, George, *33,* 179, *268,* 269
Abbott, John, *199*
Abel, Walter, 61, *115*
Accent on Youth, 152
Achard, Marcel, 219
Actors Equity Association, 7, 19, 150, 151
Actors Theatre (N.Y.), 55
Adachi, Yasuko, *252*
Adam's Way, 256
Adding Machine, The, 18, 23, *23,* 24, *24*
Adler, Luther, *196*
Adler, Stella, *199, 200*
Affair of Honor, 241, 243, *243*
Agate, James, 146
Ah, Wilderness!, 91, 92, 93, 126, *127,* 128, *128,* 172, *172, 173,* 200
Albee, Edward, 1, 9, 124
Aleichem, Sholom, 256
Aletter, Frank, *242*
Alexander, Katherine, *104, 105*
Alison's House, 110
All God's Chillun, 89
All My Sons, 159, 172
All Women Are One, 266
Allegro, 206, *207,* 208, *208*
Allen, Kelcey, 68
Allen, Martha-Bryan, 16
Allen, Vera, 163
Allenby, Frank, *210*
Allgood, Sara, 151, *151*
Alswang, Ralph, 216
Altman, Richard, 266
Alvin Theatre (N.Y.), 129
Ambassador Theatre (N.Y.), 248, 249
Ambush, 14, *14*
America, 133
American Academy of Dramatic Arts, 2
American Dream, 124, *124, 125*
American Dream, The, 124
American National Theatre and Academy, 260
American Theatre Society, 119, 231, 232
Amiel, Denys, 14
Amphitryon 38, 152, *153,* 154, *154*
And Stars Remain, 148, *148*
Anders, Glenn, 31, *32,* 63, *76,* 81, *81, 82,* 89, *104, 105,* 108, 136
Anders, Rudolph, *179*
Anderson, John, 138, 151, 176
Anderson, Judith, 90, *115,* 126, *127*
Anderson, Maxwell, 107, 125, *126,* 129, 131, 136, 146, 149, 150, 173, *173,* 176, 212
Anderson, Phyllis, 85
Anderson, Robert, 107, 108, 214
Andrews, Dana, *261,* 262
Andrews, Edward, *165*
Andreyev, Leonid, 14, 199
Androcles and the Lion, 39, 40, *40*
Anglin, Margaret, 31
Anna Christie, 86, 87, 88, 89, 96
Annabella, 187, 188, *188,* 212
Annals, Michael, 267, *267* (sets and costumes)
Anouilh, Jean, 228, 229
ANTA Theatre (N.Y.), 34, 266
Antony and Cleopatra, 35
Apple Cart, The, 101, 102, *102*
Apple Tree, The, 252

Archer, William, 21, 22
Archer-Shee, George, 209
Arent, Arthur, 212, 214
Ariadne, 33, *33*
Arms and the Girl, 222, *222*
Arms and the Man, 36, *37, 38,* 60, 62
Armstrong, Will Steven, 265
As You Like It, 58, 220, *221,* 222
Ashmore, Peter, 60, 210
Astor, Lady, 58
At Mrs. Beam's, 40, *43*
Atkinson, Brooks, 35, 64, 75, 108, 111, 112, 114, 115, 129, 134, 145, 163, 167, 169, 201, 203, 210, 217, 222, 224, 239, 254, 256
Atlas, Leopold, 148
Attic Nights, 40
Atwill, Lionel, 34, *34, 35*
Aumont, Jean Pierre, 218, 219, *219,* 238, 239, *240*
Auprès de ma blonde, 219
Away We Go!, 181
Ayers, Lemuel, 176, *178* (setting), 181
Ayre, Robert, 176

Back to Methuselah, 16, *16,* 17, *17,* 47, 48, 50, 51, 52, 53, 248
Bailey, Pearl, 222, *223*
Bailie, Earle, 119
Baker, George Pierce, 2, 4, 276
Baker, Lee, *33, 39, 114*
Balin, Ina, *253*
Ballantyne, Paul, 227
Ballard, Lucinda, 190, 218
Ballet Theatre, 62
Bang the Drum Slowly, 215
Bankhead, Tallulah, 4, 191, *191,* 192
Banks, Leslie, *151,* 152, 154, *155, 156*
Barker, Margaret, *117*
Barnes, Clive, 206, 271, 272
Barnes, Djuna, 85
Barnes, Howard, 186, 198, 218, 224
Barnouw, Eric, 271
Barrie, Barbara, 260, 266
Barrie, James M., 215
Barry, Philip, 104, *104,* 161, 163, 166, 172, 176, 191, 192, 194
Barrymore, Ethel, 154, *155,* 189, *189*
Barton, James, 97, 98, 201, *201*
Basserman, Albert, 189, *189*
Batten, Barton, Durstine & Osborn, 211
Battle of Angels, 171, *171,* 172
Battles, John, *207,* 208
Baty, Gaston, 152
Baxter, Jane, 203, *204*
Bayer, Eleanor, 249
Bayer, Leo, 249
Beal, John, 172, *172*
Beaufort, John, 237
Bedtime Story, 253, *254*
Before Breakfast, 86
Behrman, S. N., 58, 70, *71,* 100, 122, 124, 136, 137, 145, 146, 148, 152, 154, 156, 176, 187, 188, 195, 206, 212, 219, 220, 229, 230, 276
Beinecke Rare Book Library (Yale), 85, 173
Belasco Theatre (N.Y.), 187
Belinda, 11
Bell, Ann, *268,* 269
Bell, James, *149*
Bellamy, Ralph, *246,* 247, *247*
Bells Are Ringing, 243, *243,* 244, *244,*

254, 271
Ben-Ami, Jacob, 26, *26,* 40, *41*
Benavente, Jacinto, 6
Benchley, Nathaniel, 229, 230
Bendix, William, 166, *166*
Bennett, Arnold, 18, 271
Bennett, Constance, 177
Bennett, Richard, *15,* 16, 31, *32*
Benthall, Michael, 222
Berg, Gertrude, 252, *252, 253,* 264, 265, *265*
Berghof, Herbert, *187*
Bergman, Ingrid, 226
Bergner, Elisabeth, 137, 138, *138*
Berkey, Ralph, 240, 241
Bernstein, Leonard, 254
Best, Edna, 172, 230, *230*
Bettis, Valerie, 248
Beyond the Horizon, 86, 87, 89
Biberman, Herbert, 107, 111, 136, 274
Billion Dollar Baby, 254
Biltmore Theatre (N.Y.), 82, 217
Biography, 122, *123,* 124
Birabeau, André, 158
Blackmar, Beatrice, 82
Blackmer, Sidney, *223,* 224, *224*
Blaine, Martin, 189
Blair, Mary, 86
Block, Anita, 85
Bluebeard's Eighth Wife, 112
Boda, Robert F., 256
Bogart, Humphrey, 126, *127*
Bogart, Paul, 215
Boland, Mary, 174, *174*
Bolton, Whitney, 226, 231
Bonds of Interest, The, 6, *6,* 7
Bonine, Abby, 187, *187*
Bonnet, James, *247*
Booth, Shirley, 126, *162,* 163, 213, *223,* 224, *224*
Booth Theatre (N.Y.), 166, 239
Borned in Texas, 106
Boruff, John, 156
Boston Advertiser, 108–9
Boston Herald, 239
Boston Post, 239
Boston Toy Theatre, 276
Boston Transcript, 11
Both Your Houses, 125, *125, 126,* 146, 276
Bourbouroche, 14
Bowles, Paul, 169
Boyd, Stephen, 274, *275*
Brady, Alice, 92, 100, *100, 101,* 112, *114*
Brand, 21
Brandt, Frances, *217*
Brent, Romney, 36, 37, 40, *40,* 57, 139, *139, 197,* 260, *261*
Bridie, James, 135, 150
British Broadcasting Company, 213
Broadhurst Theatre (N.Y.), 152
Broderick, James, 260
Brokenshire, Norman, 213
Brontë, Charlotte, 149
Brook, Faith, 209, *210*
Brooklyn Eagle, 145, 224
Brooks, Geraldine, *196*
Brothers Karamazov, The, 68, *68,* 102
Broun, Heywood, 9, 10, 19
Brown, Ann, 142, *143*
Brown, John Mason, 107, 108, 129, 148, 169
Brown, Pamela, 203, *204,* 225, *225,* 226

Browne, Maurice, 80, 212, 237
Bruckner, Ferdinand, 134, 135
Bruning, Albert, *41, 49*
Brydon, W. B., 206
Bubbles, John W., 142
Buchwald, N., 166
Buck, Pearl, 120
Buckmaster, John, *144,* 227, *227*
Bull, Peter, 226
Buloff, Joseph, 182, *182*
Bunce, Alan, 247
Buoyant Billions, 58
Burge, Stuart, 231
Buried Alive, 271
Burning Glass, The, 237, 238, *238*
Burr, Donald, 174
Burton, Richard, *225,* 226, 228, 229, *229*
Bush-Fekete, Ladislaus, 189
But for the Grace of God, 148, *149*
By Way of Obit, 96
Byington, Spring, 134, *135*
Byron, Arthur, *160*

Cabot, Eliot, *67, 79*
Cadell, Jean, 40, *43,* 203, *204*
Caesar and Cleopatra, 34, *34,* 35, *35*
Cagney, Jeanne, *202*
Cahill, Lily, 81, *81,* 137
Calhern, Louis, 187, 188, *188,* 205, 212
Call It a Day, 139, 142, *144,* 145, *145*
Call Me Mister, 137
Calvert, Louis, 21
Camel Through the Needle's Eye, The, 82, *83*
Campbell, Mrs. Pat, 8, 64
Camus, Albert, 250, 251
Candida, 55, 61
Candle in the Wind, 173, *173*
Capalbo, Carmen, 206
Čapek, Karel, 19
Caprice, 62, 80, *81*
Captain Brassbound's Conversion, 57
Captains and the Kings, The, 260, 261, *261,* 262
Carey, Harry, 172, *172*
Carmody, Jay, 191
Carnovsky, Morris, 63, *68, 69,* 73, *104, 126*
Caro, Warren, 213, 231, 232, 260, 273
Carousel, 13, 60, 172, *193*
Carradine, David, 267, *268*
Carroll, Leo G., 60, 118, *119, 120,* 209, *210,* 228, *228*
Carroll, Marie, 225
Carroll, Raymond G., 19
Carson, Johnny, 214
Carter, Jack, 72, *72*
Caruso, Barbara, 232
Cass Theatre (Detroit), 99
Cassavetes, John, 214
Cassidy, Claudia, 142
Castle Square Theatre (Boston), 31
Cavanaugh, Slim, *110*
Century Theatre (N.Y.), 231
Cerf, Bennett, 95
Cerf, Bettina, *189*
Chagrin, Mme. Claude, 267
Chaliapin, Feodor Ivanovich, 45
Champagne Sec, 222
Chaney, Frances, *265*
Chaney, Stewart, 169
Chapin, Brian, 266
Chaplin, Sydney, 244, *244*
Chapman, John, 188, 191, 192, 202, 206, 209, 219, 224, 226, 237, 249, 264, 269, 271
Chase, Ilka, 124, 131

Chase, Lucia, 62
Chase, Stanley, 206
Chayefsky, Paddy, 214
Chekhov, Anton, 10, 156, 205, 253
Cherry Lane Theatre (N.Y.), 254
Cherry Orchard, The, 10, 205
Chiarelli, Luigi, 126
Chicago Journal of Commerce, 142
Chicago Little Theatre, 276
Chicago Tribune, 142
Chief Thing, The, 40, *43*
Child Buyer, The, 266
Child Is Waiting, A, 273
Ching, William, 208
Chlumberg, Hans, 110
Chocolate Soldier, The, 36
Christian Science Monitor, 8, 237
Church, Sandra, 266
Circle-in-the-Square (N.Y.), 206
Cisney, Marcella, 260
Claire, Ina, 3, 122, *123,* 124, *145,* 146, 202, *203*
Clarence, 31
Clark, Alexander, 119, *123*
Clark, Bobby, 174, *174*
Clark, Kendall, 146, *228*
Claudel, Paul, 21
Clayton, Jan, 192, *193, 194*
Cleveland Plain Dealer, 184
Clifford, William, 142
Clift, Montgomery, 158, *159, 168,* 169
Cloister, The, 14, *14*
Clurman, Harold, 36, 63, 68, 85, 118, 171
Cobb, Lee J., 167, *167*
Coca, Imogene, *106*
Cochran, Charles B., 137
Cochran, Steve, *177*
Cochrane, June, *36*
Coe, Fred, 236
Coe, Richard, 252
Coffin, Gene, 214
Cohan, George M., 93, 128, *128*
Cohen, Alexander H., 269
Cohen, Harold, 141
Colbert, Claudette, 81, *82*
Colbourne, Maurice, *53,* 57, 169
Coleman, Lonnie, 249, 256
Coleman, Nancy, 172, *172,* 260
Coleman, Robert, 218
Coleman, Warren, 142, *143*
Collinge, Patricia, 158, 224
Collins, Paul, *268*
Collins, Russel, *177*
Columbus (Ohio) *Citizen,* 205
Columbus (Ohio) *Dispatch,* 197, 205, 234
Comden, Betty, 242, 253, 254, *255*
Come Back, Little Sheba, 222, *223,* 224, *224,* 236
Comegys, Kathleen, *217*
Commonweal, The, 39, 110
Compton, Madge, *210*
Congreve, William, 203
Conklin, Peggy, 222, 236
Connelly, Marc, 212
Conroy, Frank, *100*
Constant Nymph, The, 138
Conte, John, 208
Conversations in the Dark, 266
Conway, Peggy, 36
Cook, Donald, *191*
Cook, Elisha, Jr., *127*
Cook, Fielder, 215
Cook, George Cram, 3, 86, 276
Coolidge, Calvin, 34
Cooper, Gladys, *144,* 145, *145,* 263, *263*
Coote, Robert, 234

Copeau, Jacques, 68, *69*
Cordner, Blaine, *216*
Corey, Wendell, 256
Cornell, Katharine, 61, 150, 226, 245
Cort Theatre (N.Y.), 218, 220, 226
Cossart, Ernest, *37,* 63, *73, 78,* 112, 119, *119, 120, 152*
Cotten, Joseph, *161,* 163
Council of the Living Theatre, 231
Country Cousin, The, 31
Courteline, Georges, 14
Courtnay, Alex, *170*
Covarrubias, Miguel, 39
Coward, Noel, 141, 191
Cowl, Jane, *137,* 160, 169, 171, 239
Crabtree, Paul, 97
Craig, Gordon, 51
Craig, Michael, 269, *269, 270*
Crawford, Cheryl, 62, 63, 118
Cream in the Well, The, 172
Creative Art, 4
Crews, Laura Hope, 11, *12,* 31, *33,* 67, 68
Critics' Choice (magazine), 277
Cromwell, John, 68
Cronyn, Hume, 253, *254,* 271
Croué, Jean, 68
Crouse, Russel, 94
Cruickshank, Andrew, 227
Cummings, Constance, 152, *152*
Curious Savage, The, 224, *224,* 225
Cusack, Cyril, 206

da Silva, Howard, *181,* 182, 265, *265*
Daily Worker (N.Y.), 186
Daly, Arnold, 46
Daly, James, 227
Daly, Orlando, 33
Dame Nature, 158, *159*
Dance of Death, The, 9, *9*
Dane, Clemence, 107
Daneel, Sylvia, 244, 245
Daniell, Henry, 195, *197*
Daniels, William, 265
Dante, Jean, *145*
Darling, Jean, 192, *193, 194*
Darling of the Day, 271, *272, 272*
Darnton, Charles, 108
Davies, Robertson, 259
Davis, Donald, 120
Davis, Ossie, 274, *275*
Davis, Owen, 120
Days Without End, 45, 91, 92, 93, 94, 126, 131, *131, 132,* 133, *133,* 200
de Casalis, Jeanne, 21
de Cordoba, Pedro, *37, 38*
de Ghelderode, Michel, 9
de Hartog, Jan, 208, 209
de Mille, Agnes, 181, *181,* 192, 206, 208
De Vries, Peter, 244, 245, 249
Dean, Alexander, 14
Dean, Basil, 36
Dean, Gen. William F., 240
Dear Me, the Sky Is Falling, 265, *265*
Death of a Salesman, 159, 172
Deei, Kaie, 242
Dekker, Albert, *20*
Delicate Story, 172
Dengel, Reni, *247*
Denker, Henry, 214, 240, 241
Design for Living, 141
Desire Under the Elms, 89, 126
Detroit Times, 197
Devil's Disciple, The, 24, *25,* 46, 60
Devlin, William, 209
Dexter, John, 267
Dial M for Murder, 236
Dickey, Annamary, 208

Digges, Dudley, 5, 6, *9*, 10, 11, *12, 20, 23, 24,* 29, 63, *63, 69,* 73, 77, *78, 79,* 81, 149, 154, *155,* 201, *201*
Doctor's Dilemma, The, 61, 72, 73, *74*
Dodge, Mable, 87
Donehue, Vincent J., 247
Donnelly, Gerard B., 133
Dorman, John, *250*
Dostoevski, Fyodor, 68
Douglas, Diana, *255*
Douglas, Melvyn, 148
Douglas, Susan, *200*
Dowling, Eddie, 97, 164, *165,* 166, 169, 201
Downes, Olin, 182
Downs, Frederic, *237*
Drake, Alfred, 175, *175,* 176, 180, *180,* 181, 190
Drury Lane Theatre (London), 182
Dudley, Doris, 146
Duggan, Andrew, *249,* 250
Dulcy, 31
Duncan, Augustin, 5, 6, 7, *41*
Duncan, Todd, 142, *143*
Dunn, James, 98, 99, 205, *206*
Dunnigan's Daughter, 195, *196*
Dürrenmatt, Friedrich, 266
Dynamo, 45, 81, *81, 82,* 90, 91
Dyne, Michael, 214

Eames, Clare, *3, 39,* 63, *63, 66, 67*
Easiest Way, The, 86
Eastman, Max, *3*
Easton, Richard, 248
Eaton, Walter Prichard, 4, 19
Edinburgh Festival (1954), 160, 239
Edwards, Osborne, 14
Eldridge, Florence, 14, *14,* 62, *173,* 174, *174,* 213
Eliot, Sam, *3*
Elizabeth and Essex, 107
Elizabeth the Queen, 107, 108
Elliott, Madge, 226, *226*
Ellis, Evelyn, 72, *72*
Ellis, Mary, 90
Elzy, Ruby, 142
Embezzled Heaven, 189, *189, 190*
Emerson, Faye, 239, *240,* 248
Emperor Jones, The, 86, 87, 88
Empire Theatre (N.Y.), 129
End of Days, An, 92, 131
End of Summer, 139, 145, *145,* 146, *146*
Englund, Pat, *221*
Enrico IV, 70
Epstein, Julius, 148
Epstein, Philip, 148
Equity Library Theatre, 232
Eric, Fred, *10, 11*
Erickson, Leif, 260
Ernst, Leila, 179
Erskin, Chester, 112
Ervine, Nora, 51
Ervine, St. John, 6, 7, 8, 9, 10, 46, 50, 51, 55
Erwin, Stuart, 176, *177*
Escape Me Never, 137, 138, *138*
Esterow, Milton, 263
Ethel Barrymore Theatre (N.Y.), 179, 208, 241
Eurydice, 228
Evans, David, 226
Evans, Evans, 256
Evans, Julius, 119, *119*
Evans, Maurice, 169, *170*
Evreinov, Nikolai Nikolayeivich, 40
Ewell, Tom, *172,* 244, *244, 245*

Fabian Society, 45
Fabray, Nanette, 222, *222, 223*
Failures, The, 26, *26*
Fairweather, Wallace Cranston, 45
Faithful, The, 7, *7,* 8
Fanny's First Play, 57
Farley, Morgan, *29*
Farrell, Glenda, 238
Fata Morgana, 28, 29, *29, 30,* 35
Fatal Weakness, The, 202, *203*
Faulkner, William, 250, 251
Faust, 50, 77, *78*
Faversham, William, 46
Fay, Mary Helen, 189
Feldman, Laurence, 249
Felton, Norman, 215
Fenton, Frank, *161, 163*
Ferber, Edna, 212, 213
Fernald, Chester B., 126
Ferrer, José, *185,* 186, 217, *217,* 218
Fickett, Homer, 212
Fickett, Mary, *246,* 247
Fiddler on the Roof, 256
Field, Sylvia, *20*
Fields, Dorothy, 222
Fields, Herbert, 222
Fields, Joseph, 244, 245
Fifth Column, The, 167, *167,* 168
Figure of a Girl, 219
Fischer, Alfred, 60
Fiske, Minnie Maddern, 122
Fitelson, William H., 211, 214
Fitzgerald, Barry, 96, 98
Fitzmaurice, Michael, *191*
Five Kings, 149
Flanders, Christian, *251*
Flaubert, Gustave, 152
Flemyng, Robert, 203, *204*
Fletcher, Lawrence, *219*
Flynn, Gertrude, *118, 125*
Fonda, Jane, 256, *257*
Fontanne, Lynn, 3, 8, 29, *30,* 31, *31,* 36, *37, 38,* 40, *41, 43,* 51, 62, 63, 64, *65,* 70, *71,* 72, *73, 74, 76,* 77, *77, 78,* 81, *81,* 89, *101,* 107, 108, *108,* 116, 117, 141, *141,* 142, *142,* 146, *147,* 152, *153,* 154, 156, *157,* 168, *168,* 169, *178,* 195, 197, 198, *198,* 199, 212, 213, 215, 219, 220, *220,* 271
Foolish Notion, 191, *191*
Foote, Horton, 236
Forbes, Ralph, 209, *210*
Forbes, Scott, 238
Ford, Helen, *175*
Ford, Ruth, *209, 250,* 251, *251*
Forster, E. M., 262
Forsyte Saga, The, 94
Forty-ninth Cousin, The, 256, 257
'47 Workshop Theatre (Harvard), 2, 4, 276
Forum, The, 214
Fosse, Bob, 243
Fourteenth of July, The, 100
Fowler, Mary, *21*
Fox, Dorothy, *140*
Francis, Arlene, 62, *219*
Francke, Caroline, 256
Frank, Bruno, 150
Frank, Leonhard, 100
Frank, Waldo, 2
Franklin, Anna May, 214
Franz, Eduard, 189, 190
Fraser, Elizabeth, *168,* 169, *244*
Frazee Theatre (N.Y.), 19
Frederick, Pauline, 149

Freedley, George, 186
Freel, Aleta, *126*
Freeman, Helen, 5
French, Valerie, *268,* 269
Friel, Brian, 133
Friend, Philip, 230, 231
Frings, Ketti, 176
From Morn to Midnight, 18, 19
Front Porch, 234
Fry, Christopher, 203, 225, 231, 233
Frye, Dwight, *41*
Fuller, Frances, 238
Fuller, Rosamund, *240*
Fulton Theatre (N.Y.), 7, 16
Funny Thing Happened on the Way to the Forum, A, 154

Gabriel, Ethel, *245*
Gabriel, Gilbert W., 64, 82, 117, 124, 133, 145
Gaffney, Leo, 109
Gahagan, Helen, 148, *148*
Gale, Rona, 260
Galsworthy, John, 24, 94
Game of Love and Death, The, 100, *101*
Garde, Betty, *180*
Garland, Judy, 273
Garland, Robert, 139, 140, 188, 190, 206, 210
Garner, Peggy Ann, *238*
Garrick Gaieties, The, 36, *36,* 37, 104, *106,* 179
Garrick Theatre (N.Y.), 5, 6, 7, 11, 16, 18, 26, 31, 35, 48, 50, 51, 87
Garrick Theatre (N.Y.—Off-Broadway), 266
Gassner, John, 84, 85, *85,* 160, 171, 172, 180, 214, 276, 277
Gassner, Mollie, 85
Gate Theatre (N.Y.), 266
Gates, Larry, 234
Gaul, George, *16, 17, 41,* 48, 62, 63, 68, *69, 78,* 81
GBS and the Lunatic, 16
Gellius, Aulus, 40
Genet, Jean, 9
Gentry, Charles, 197
Geraldo, Gerry, 269
Gershwin, George, 70, 142, *144,* 179
Gershwin, Ira, 142, *144,* 179
Getting Married, 46, 112, *112*
Ghost of Yankee Doodle, The, 154, *155*
Gibbs, Wolcott, 156, 237
Gibson, William, 260
Gielgud, John, 61, 203, *204,* 225, *225*
Gilbert, Douglas, 161
Gilbert, Ruth, *202*
Gildea, Mary, *203*
Gillmore, Frank, 150
Gillmore, Margalo, *15,* 16, 63, *66,* 70, *71, 75, 75, 78, 83,* 137
Gilpin, Charles S., 86
Gilroy, Frank, 214
Giraudoux, Jean, 152, 154
Gish, Dorothy, 112
Gish, Lillian, 176, *177,* 224, *224,* 225, 236, 237, *237*
Glaspell, Susan, 3, 110, 276
Glass Managerie, The, 172, 260
Glass Slipper, The, 39, *39*
Glazer, Benjamin, 167, 192
Gleason, Jackie, 128
"Glencairn," cycle, 89
Goat Song, 40, *41, 42, 43,* 187
Gobelin tapestries, 34

Goethe, Johann Wolfgang von, 50, 77
Gogol [Nikolai], 156
Gold, Mike, 186
Gomez, Thomas, 169
Good Earth, The, 120, *121, 122*
Goode, Reginald, *25*
Goodman, Edward, 2, *3*
Gordon, Ruth, *104,* 134, *134,* 136, *136,* 160, 239, *239,* 240, *240*
"Gospel of Creation," 16
Gottfried, Martin, 269, 271
Gould, Bruce, 82
Gould, Jack, 214
Gould, Morton, 222
Grant, Cary, 161
Grant, Lee, *228,* 262
Grauer, Ben, *33*
Graves, Peter, *261,* 262
Great Adventure, The, 271
Great Catherine, 214
Great God Brown, The, 45, 87, 89
Greaza, Walter N., *151*
Green, Adolph, 243, 253, 254, *255*
Green, Paul, 117
Green Grow the Lilacs, 4, 106, 109, *109,* 110, *110,* 178, 180
Greene, Patterson, 173
Greenstreet, Sidney, *121,* 142, *142, 153, 168,* 169
Gregg, Mitchell, *259*
Grieg, Edvard, 22
Griffith, Andy, 214
Griffith, Hugh, *230*
Grimes, Tammy, 258, *258,* 259, *259*
Grossmith, Lawrence, 57, *139*
Group Theatre, 117, 118, 164, 276
Guardsman, The, 29, *30,* 31, *31,* 62, 64, 212
Guétary, Georges, 222, *222, 223*
Guild Theatre (N.Y.), 34, 61, 93, 107, 136, 154, 189, 277
Guinness, Alec, 252
Guiterman, Arthur, 128, 129, 175, 222
Guthrie, Judith, 199, *199*
Guthrie, Tyrone, 199, *199,* 239, 240, *260*

Hackett, Francis, 14
Hackett, James K., 8, *8*
Hagen, Uta, 26, 156, *157, 184,* 186, *186,* 226, 227, *227,* 228, *228*
Haggott, John, 214
Hairy Ape, The, 86
Hale, Louise Closser, *21*
Hale, Richard, *110*
Hall, Amelia, *260*
Hall, Lois, 158, *159*
Hall, Peter, 169
Hall, Thurston, *137*
Hall, Willis, 269
Halliday, John, *137*
Hamlet, 60, 273
Hammerstein, Oscar II, 13, 60, 180, *180,* 192, 206, *207,* 208
Hammond, Percy, 26, 77, 104, 108, 138
Hampden, Walter, *174*
Hanley, William, 266
Hanrahan, John, 62
Happiness, 31
Harburg, E. Y., 271
Hardwicke, Cedric (Sir), 60, 238, 252, *252, 253*
Harp of Life, The, 31
Harrigan, William, *118*
Harris, Mark, 262

Harrison, Rex, 219, 231, *231,* 233, *233, 234*
Harron, Donald, 238, *238*
Hart, Lorenz, 35, *36,* 179, 180
Hart, Walter, 156
Hartford Stage Company, 271
Hartman Theatre (Columbus), 205, 256
Hasty Heart, The, 224
Hatcher, Tom, *257,* 258
Haunted, The, 115
Havoc, June, 195, *196,* 260
Hawkins, William, 217, 218
Hayden, Terese, 232
Haydon, Julie, 164, *165,* 166
Hayes, Cardinal [Patrick Joseph], 55
Hayes, Helen, 34, *34,* 35, 129, *130,* 169, *170, 171,* 173, *173,* 213, 260, *261*
Hays, David, 259
He, 112, *113*
He Who Gets Slapped, 14, *15,* 16, 199, *199, 200*
Heartbreak House, 10, 11, *11,* 44, 45, 46, 52, 55
Heavenly Twins, The, 238, 239, *240*
Hecht, Ben, 151
Hechtlinger, Dorothy, 214
Heckart, Eileen, *235,* 236, 256, 258
Heflin, Van, 146, *162,* 163
Heiman, Marcus, 119
Heineman, Arthur, 214
Helburn, Theresa, 1, *1,* 2, 4, 5, 11, 28, 31, 35, 49, 54, 55, 57, 58, 59, 62, 70, 84, 89, 95, 97, 98, 99, 129, 130, 139, 161, 163, 164, *166,* 171, 172, 180, 187, 188, 190, 192, 194, *195,* 232, *233,* 238, *247,* 249, 273, 277
Hello, Dolly!, 160, 240
Helmore, Tom, 209, *210*
Help Stamp Out Marriage, 267, *268,* 269
Helpmann, Robert, *232*
Heming, Violet, 21
Hemingway, Ernest, 167
Henri, Robert, 2
Henry V, 273
Henry VIII, 60
Henry Miller's Theatre (N.Y.), 11, 93, 131, 236
Henry Street Settlement, 17, 48
Hepburn, Katharine, 60, 61, 104, 149, *150,* 161, *161,* 163, 176, *176,* 213, 220, *221,* 222, 232, *232,* 233, 273
Herbert, Henry, 5
Herbert, Victor, 178
Herlie, Eileen, *239,* 240, *240*
Herman, William, 85
Hernandez, Juano, 216, 217
Herne, James A., 86
Hersey, John, 266
Hewes, Henry, 238, 251
Heyward, Dorothy, 70, 142, 216
Heyward, Du Bose, 70, 142, *144,* 179
High Tor, 150
High Wind in Jamaica, A, 187
Highest Tree, The, 254, *255,* 256, 261
Hiken, Gerald, 256
Hill, Arthur, 240, *240*
Hiller, Wendy, 206
Hoffman, Bill, 241–243
Holiday, 161
Holl, Friedrich, 77
Holliday, Judy, 243, *243,* 244, *244,* 253
Holloway, Baliol, *74, 75*
Holloway, Sterling, *30,* 36, *36,* 106

Holm, Celeste, 166, 173, *173,* 176, 182, *182,* 249, *249,* 250, *257,* 258
Holm, Ian, 269, *270*
Holmes, John Haynes, 139
Holy Matrimony, 271
Home Is the Hero, 238, *238*
Homecoming, 115
Homecoming, The, 269, *269,* 270, 271
Homolka, Oscar, 187, *187,* 213
Hoover, Herbert, 125
Hope for a Harvest, 172, 173, *173, 174*
Hopkins, Arthur, 86, 89, 106
Hopkins, Miriam, 154, 156, 171, *171,* 172
Hostage, The, 259, 260
Hotel Universe, 104, *104, 105*
Houghton, Norris, 158
House of Connelly, The, 117, *117,* 118
Houseman, John, 136
Howard, Jennifer, *203*
Howard, Sidney, 31, 64, 154, 212
Howells, William Dean, 8
How's the World Treating You?, 271
Hudd, Walter, 209, *210*
Hudson Theatre (N.Y.), 216, 217
Huffaker, Lucy, *3*
Hughes, Elinor, 239
Hughes, Langston, 264
Hughes, Richard, 187
Hughes, Tresa, 265, *265*
Hughie, 96, 97
Hull, Henry, *118,* 149, *150, 191*
Hull, Josephine, *29*
Humphrey, Doris, 129, *129,* 190
Hunted, The, 115
Husson, Albert, 238
Huston, Walter, 93, 128, 169, *170,* 213
Hyman, Mac, 215

I Know My Love, 219, 220, *220*
Ibsen, Henrik, 21, 22, 44
Ibsen Club, 44
Iceman Cometh, The, 95, 96, 97, 98, 200, *200, 201,* 202, *202,* 205
Idiot's Delight, 139, 146, *147,* 277
If This Be Treason, 139, *140,* 141
Ile, 86
Importance of Being Earnest, The, 203, *204*
In the Beginning, 48
In the Matter of J. Robert Oppenheimer, 273, 274
In the Meantime, 108
In the Zone, 74, 86, 87
Inescort, Frieda, *25, 79,* 209, *210*
Inge, William, 222, 224, 234–236
Innocent Voyage, The, 187, *187*
Inspector Calls, An, 249
Inspector General, The, 156
Insull, Samuel, 62
International Theatre (N.Y.), 190
Invitation to a March, 256, *257,* 258, 259
Ionesco, Eugene, 9
Irving, Henry, 29
Irving, Roy, 228
Irwin, Carol, 214
Ishii, Kanni, *252*
Ives, Burl, 190, *190*

Jackson, Sir Barry, 50
Jacobowsky and the Colonel, 187, 188, *188,* 212
Jaffe, Sam, *209*
Jago, June, *245, 246*
James, Morgan, *159*

Jameson, House, 36
Jamison, Marshall, 214
Jane, 58, 206, 229, 230, *230*
Jane Clegg, 8, 9, *9*, 10
Jane Eyre, 149, *150*
J.B., 116
Jeans, Isabel, 218, *218*
Jens, Salome, 206
Jeremiah, 159, 160, *160*
Jerome, Helen, 149
Jewish Morning Freiheit (N.Y.), 166
Jig Saw, 134, *135*
Jitta's Atonement, 50, 55, 56
John Bull's Other Island, 44
John Ferguson, 6, 7, *7*, 8, 13, 214
John Golden Theatre, 64, 76, 90, 250, 254
John Hawthorne, 11
Johnson, Albert, 190
Johnson, Howard, 76
Johnson, Nunnally, 271
Johnston, Denis, 118, 213
Jolly's Progress, 249, 256, *257*
Jonay, Roberta, *207*, 208
Jones, Henry, 247, *247*
Jones, James Earl, *247*
Jones, Robert Edmond, 2, 3, 4, 74, 87, 89, 92, 112, *114* (set), *115*, 131, 163, 186, 201, 276
Jonson, Ben, 54, 77
Jorgulesco, Jonel, *119* (costume), *120* (set)
Joy, Nicholas, 163, *201*
Juan Carlos, Prince of Bourbon, *261*
Juarez and Maximilian, 63, *63*, *64*, 187
Judgment at Nuremburg, 273
Judson Concert Bureau, 62
Julius Caesar, 35

Kahn, Otto, 5
Kaiser, Georg, 18, 19
Kakos, Kenneth, *247*
Kanin, Michael, 264
Karl and Anna, 100, *100*
Karlweiss, Oscar, 187, 188, *188*, 212
Kass, Peter, 266
Kauffman, George, 213
Kaye, Ben, 35
Kays, Alma, *191*
Kazan, Elia, 99, 188, 195
Keathley, George, 260
Keene, J. H., 161
Kelly, Gene, *165*, 166, 179, 213
Kelly, George, 202, *203*
Kelly, Walter C., *125*, *126*
Kemble-Cooper, Violet, *102*
Kennedy, Arthur, 241, *241*
Kennedy, Margaret, 137, 138
Kenton, Edna, 5
Kern, Jerome, 180
Kerner, Ben, 266
Kerr, Alfred, 136
Kerr, Walter, 189, 190, 191, 229, 237–238, 240, 251, 252, 258, 263, 267, 269, 272
Kerrigan, James M., 98, 205, *206*
Kettering, Charles F., 2
Kidd, John, 203, *204*
Kidd, Michael, 222
Kiley, Richard, 241, *241*, *242*
Kilgallen, Dorothy, 256
Killens, John O., 274
King, Charmion, *260*
King, Dennis, *16*, 21, 195, *196*, 199, *200*, 241, 243, *243*, 259, *260*
King Lear, 175

Kingston, Gertrude, 59
Kinoy, Ernest, 262
Kirchon, V., 104
Kirk, Lisa, 208, *208*
Kirkland, Alexander, *80*
Kirkland, Patricia, 209, *210*
Kissel, Bud, 205
Kitt, Eartha, 256, *257*
Klaw and Erlanger, 2, 119
Klaw Theatre (N.Y.), 39
Knott, Frederick, 236
Kobayashi, Tsuruko, *252*
Komisarjevsky, Theodore, 21
Kondorf, George, 214
Korff, Arnold, *123*
Kortner, Fritz, 172
Kramer, Stanley, 273
Kronenberger, Louis, 174, 175, 182, 189, 199, 202, 238
Kruger, Otto, *100*, *101*
Krumschmidt, E. A., *179*
Krutch, Joseph Wood, 114, 154
Kya-Hill, Robert, 275

Lady from the Provinces, 102
Lady's Not for Burning, The, 203, 225, *225*, 228, 231
Lahr, Bert, 249
Lampell, Millard, 214
Lancaster, Burt, 273
Landis, Jessie Royce, 57, 158, *159*, 169, *170*, *173*, *173*, 195, *196*
Langer, Francis, 82
Langner, Lawrence, 1, *1*, 2, 4, 5, 6, 10, 16, 17, 28, 40, 44–61, 62, 63, 64, 70, 74, 84, 86–99, 100, 102, 122, 129, 133, 139, 141, 146, 156, 163, 164, 166, *166*, 169, 171, 172, 173, 188, 190, 191, 192, 194, *195*, 198, 211, 213, 220, 222, 226, 232, *233*, 249, 254, *259*, 260, 276
Langner, Philip, 249, 260, 273, 274, 277
Langtry, Mrs. (Edward [Lily]), 31
Lardner, John, 230
Larimore, Earle, 63, *66*, *67*, 70, 76, *83*, 89, 92, *103*, *105*, 112, *131*, *132*, 133, *133*
Lascelles, Ernita, 16, *17*, 48
Last Notch, The, 215
Lathrop, Cynthia, 85
LaTouche, John, 214
Laughton, Charles, 213
Laurents, Arthur, 256, 258
Lawford, Ernest, *80*
Lawler, Ray, 245, *245*, 246
Lawrence, Bea, 85
Lawrence, Gertrude, 213, 214
Lawrence, Reginald, 139
Lawson, John Howard, 18, 19, 31, 33
Lawson, Wilfred, 148, 149
Lazarus Laughed, 45
Leachman, Cloris, 222, 228
Leaven of Malice, 259
Lee, Canada, 186, 216, *216*, 217
Lee, Kathryn, *208*
Lee, Madeline, *189*
Leech, Richard, 226
Le Gallienne, Eva, 11, *13*, 51, 148, *149*, 172
Legend of Lovers, 228, 229, *229*, 230
Lehar, Franz, 178
Leibman, Ron, 265
Leigh, Philip, *28*, *66*
Lemon, Courtenay, 70, 85
Lenihan, Winifred, 26, *26*, 27, 28, *28*, 52, 53, 62, 77, *79*, 226

Lenormand, H. R., 26, 107
Leonard-Boyne, Era, *102*
Leonidoff, Leon, 190
Lerner, Alan Jay, 64
LeRoy, Mervyn, 252
Leve, Samuel, *177* (set)
Levene, Sam, 264, *264*, 265
Leversee, Loretta, 238
Levin, Ira, 214, 215
Levine, Joseph E., 266
Levy, Benn W., 152
Lewis, Bobby, 164
Lewis, Roger, 273
Lewis, Russell, 224
Lewis, Terry, 214
Lewis, Windsor, 239
Lewisohn, Alice, 17, 48, 276
Lewisohn, Irene, 276
Lewisohn, Ludwig, 24
Lewys, Gladys Adelina, 91
Leyden, Leo, *260*
Liberal Club, 3
Liberty Jones, 172, *172*
Lieberman, Leo, 261, 262
Liebert, Gaston, *28*
Liebovitz, David, 11
Life with Father, 94, 256
Light, James, 86
Liliom, 11, 13, *13*, 22, 51, 192
Lillie, Beatrice, 118, *119*, *120*
L'Illustration, 158
Lincoln Center Repertory Company, 274
Linley, Betty, *41*
Linn, Bambi, 182, *183*, 192
Lion Tamer, The, 112
Lippmann, Walter, 2
Littell, Robert, 81, 107, 108
Livesey, Roger, 150, 151
Living Mask, The, 70
Lo and Behold, 228, *228*, 229
Locke, Katherine, 167, *168*
Lockhart, Gene, *128*
Lockridge, Richard, 176
Loeb, Philip, 29, 63
Loewe, Frederick, 64
Logan, Joshua, 234, 236, 249
London Art Theatre, 225
Lonely Heart, The, 149
Lonergan, Lenore, 163
Long Day's Journey Into Night, 205
Longacre Theatre (N.Y.), 237
Look Homeward, Angel, 176
Look Magazine, 230
Loraine, Robert, *132*
Lord, Pauline, *31*, 32, 90
Los Angeles Times, 272
Love and Libel, 259, 260, *260*
Love for Love, 203, *204*
Love in Idleness, 197
Love Is Not So Simple, 149
Love of Four Colonels, The, 233, *233*, 234, *234*
Love's Old Sweet Song, 169, *170*
Lowe, Florence, 256
Lucky One, The, 21
Lumet, Sidney, 215
Lunt, Alfred, 3, 8, 29, *30*, *31*, *31*, 36, *38*, 40, *41*, *43*, 51, 62, *63*, *63*, *64*, *66*, *68*, *69*, 70, 71, 72, *73*, *74*, *75*, *78*, *81*, *81*, 89, *101*, 107, 108, *108*, 116, 117, *117*, 141, *141*, 142, *142*, 146, *147*, 152, *153*, 154, 156, *157*, 168, *168*, 169, 173, *178*, 195, 197, 198, *198*, 199, 212, 213, 215, 219, 220, *220*, 271

Lunt and Fontanne Acting Company, 152
Lyceum Theatre (N.Y.), 219
Lynn, Jeffrey, 228, *228*
Lynn, William, *217*
Lyons, Gene, 237, *237*
Lyons, Leonard, 188
Lysistrata, 180

MacArthur, Charles, *171*
MacArthur, James, *257*, 258
Macgowan, Kenneth, 24, 89
MacGrath, Leueen, 233, *233*
Machinal, 174
Macken, Walter, 238
Mackerel Plaza, 249
MacLeish, Archibald, 116
MacLiammoir, Micheál, 214
Madame Bovary, 152, *152*
Magic Curtain, The, 102, 220
Magnificent Yankee, The, 205
Maid of the Ozarks, 99
Major Barbara, 77, *78, 79*
Majority of One, A, 252, *252, 253,* 265
Make Way for Lucia, 218, *218*
Makeham, Eliot, 226
Mallory, Burton, *217*
Malvern Festival, 58
Mamoulian, Rouben, 72, *73,* 102, *103,* 107, 142, 181, 192, 222
Man and Superman, 44, 59
Man and the Masses, 28, 29, *30*
Man of Destiny, The, 39, *39*
Mann, Theodore, 206
Man's Estate, 82, *83*
Mansfield, Richard, 22, 36, 46
Mansfield Productions, 249
Mantle, Burns, 33, 40, 126, 129, 159, 182
March, Fredric, 62, *173,* 174, *174,* 213
Marco Millions, 74, *75,* 88, 89, 107
Margaret Fleming, 86
Margo, 149, *150*
Markey, Enid, *173*
Marquis, Marjorie, *128*
Marshall, Armina, 3, 19, 40, *41,* 56, 57, 60, 61, 62, 70, *70,* 94, 96, 97, 98, *140,* 211–215, 222, 249, 254, 260, 277
Marshall, E. G., 202
Marshe, Vera, *140*
Martin, Linton, 161
Martin, Mary, 254
Martin Beck Theatre (N.Y.), 91, 97, 104, 107, 110, 200, 202, *202,* 209, 224
Mary of Scotland, 129, *130,* 131
Masefield, John, 7, 8
Mask and the Face, The, 126, *127*
Mason, Reginald, 64, *65,* 112
Masque of Kings, The, 149, 150, *150*
Masses, The, 3
Massey, Raymond, 214
Matchmaker, The, 160, 239, *239,* 240, *240*
Mathews, George, *218, 253*
Matthau, Walter, 238, *238*
Matthews, Brander, 2
Matthews, Francis, *268,* 269
Mattson, Eric, *193*
Maude-Roxby, Roddy, *268,* 269
Maugham, Somerset W., 126, *127,* 229
Mavor, Dr. Osborn Henry, 135
Maxine Elliot Theatre (N.Y.), 46
Mayors, Robert, *149*
McCallion, James, *149*

McCarthy, Kevin, 262
McCarthy, Lillah, 36
McClain, John, 256, 258
McCollum, Barry, 7
McCracken, Joan, 182, *182,* 214
McDermott, William, 184
McDevitt, Ruth, *235*
McEnroe, Robert E., 217
McGavin, Darren, *244*
McGavran, Mary, 205
McGuire, Biff, *254*
McGuire, Dorothy, 213, 228, 229, *229*
McKay, Scott, 251
McKenna, Kenneth, 25, *255*
McLerie, Allyn, *241, 242*
McNally, William, 148
McWhinnie, Donald, 263
Meacham, Anne, 263
Meeker, Ralph, 234, 235, *235,* 262
Meiser, Edith, 29, *30,* 113
Meisner, Sanford, 36, 63, 189, *189*
Mendelssohn, Eleonora, *179*
Menken, Helen, 129, *130, 131,* 213, 260
Merande, Doro, 217, 228, *229*
Mercer, Beryl, 70
Merchant, Vivien, 269, *269, 270*
Merchant of Yonkers, The, 160, 239
Merchants of Glory, 40, *41*
Meredith, Burgess, 61, 150, 212, 228
Merivale, Philip, 129, *130,* 136, *137, 144,* 145, *145*
Merrick, David, 249
Merry Wives of Windsor, The, 197
Meteor, 100, 101, *101*
Metropolitan Opera, 239
Meyer, Josephine A., 1, 2, 3, 5
Midnight, 108, *109*
Mielziner, Jo, 64, *70* (set), 192, 234
Milady's Dress, 31
Milan, Frank, *255*
Milestones, 31
Millay, Edna St. Vincent, 5, 6, *6*
Miller, Arthur, 159, 172, 212
Miller, Gilbert, 57, *171, 171*
Miller, Jackie, *110*
Millionairess, The, 57, 61, 232, *232, 233*
Milne, A. A., 11, 21, 33
Milton, Robert, 156
Mineo, Sal, 262, *262*
Miner, Worthington, 117, *117,* 158, 160, 238
Mintz, Eli, 257
Miracle at Verdun, 110, 111, *111*
Miracle Worker, The, 260
Miramova, 226
Mr. Pim Passes By, 11, *12,* 62
Mr. Sycamore, 176, *177*
Mrs. Dally Has a Lover, 266
Mrs. Warren's Profession, 44
Moeller, Philip, 1, *1,* 2, 3, 4, 5, 17, 24, 28, 29, 33, 39, 48, 51, 62, 70, 80, 84, 104, 107, 108, 112, 124, 139, 146, *148,* 151, 152, 156, 194, 276
Mohyeddin, Zia, 263
Moiseiwitsch, Tanya, 240
Molière, 128, 129, 222
Moll, Elick, 264
Molnár, Ferenc, 11, 29, 39, 172, 192
Monks, James, *184, 185*
Montgomery, Douglass, *81, 101, 124, 125*
Month in the Country, A, 102, *103*
Moon for the Misbegotten, A, 96, 97, 98, 99, 200, 205, 206, *206*
Moon in the Yellow River, The, 118, *118,* 213

Moon of the Caribbees, 86
Morgan, Agnes, 17, 48
Morgan, Charles, 237
Morgan, Claudia, *155,* 156
Morning's at Seven, 167
Morris, McKay, *43, 57, 140*
Morris, Richard, *259*
Morrison, Hobe, 218, 236
Morse, Robert, 128, 240, *240*
Moscow Art Theatre, 22, 68, 102
Moss, Arnold, 248
Moss, Paul, 35
Motley, 199
Mourning Becomes Electra, 91, 92, 93, 112, 114, *114,* 115, *115, 116,* 126
Muller, Harrison, *208*
Muni, Paul, 112, 175, *175*
Munro, C. K., 40
Munsell, Warren P., 19, 62, 142
Museum of Modern Art, (N.Y.), 214
Music Box Theatre (N.Y.), 265, 269
Music Man, The, 258
My Fair Lady, 64
My Heart's in the Highlands, 164
My Life in Art, 102
My Name Is Aquilon, 219, *219*
Myers, Michele, *247*

Nagel, Conrad, *261,* 262
Nash, N. Richard, 214
Nat Turner, 274
Nathan, George Jean, 9, 28, 68, 69, 70, 93, 120, 154, 156, 164, 186, 202, 208, 209, 229, 243
Nation, The, 4, 24, 114, 154
National Broadcasting Company, 211, 213, 214, 236
Natwick, Mildred, 146
Nazimova, Alla, 51, 57, 92, 102, *103,* 104, 112, *114,* 115, *115,* 120, *121, 122,* 139, *139*
Ned McCobb's Daughter, 64, *66*
Negro Ensemble Company, 246
Neighborhood Playhouse, 17, 48, 89, 276
Nestroy, Johann, 239
New Leader, 169
New Republic, 14, 151, 182
New School Dramatic Workshop, 232
New York American, 82, 133
New York Daily News, 126, 129, 159, 169, 182, 188, 192, 202, 206, 209, 210, 219, 226, 237, 249, 264, 269, 271
New York Drama Critics Circle Award, 146, 166, 234, 269
New York Herald, 8
New York Herald Tribune, 74, 78, 104, 148, 160, 186, 198, 218, 224, 229, 237, 240, 251, 272
New York Journal, 138
New York Journal-American, 151, 176, 188, 206, 210, 229, 256
New York Mirror, 218
New York Morning Telegraph, 226
New York Post, 68, 81, 202, 218, 222, 225, 229, 246, 254, 269, 271
New York Sun, 19, 64, 176
New York Times, 23, 35, 54, 75, 134, 136, 145, 158, 182, 187, 191, 198, 203, 205, 206, 210, 222, 239, 249, 256, 263, 269, 271, 272, 274
New York Tribune, 8, 9, 26, 77
New York World, 64, 107
New York World Journal Tribune, 269

New York World-Telegram and Sun, 139, 140, 156, 161, 186, 188, 195, 217, 218
New Yorker, The, 62, 145, 156, 179, 192, 237, 250
Newcombe, Mary, 226
Newell, Michael, 209, *210*
Newman, Paul, 214, *235,* 236
Newsday (L.I.), 259, 263, 269
Newton, Theodore, *136*
Nichols, Lewis, 191, 198
Nichols, Robert, 80, 212, 237
Nicholson, Kenyon, 214
Nightshade, 10
Nivoix, Paul, 40
No Time for Sergeants, 215
Nobel Prize, 6, 94, 99, 169
Noon on Doomsday, 215
Normington, John, 269
Norton, Elliot, 164, 206, 239
Nugent, Elliott, 176, *176*

O Mistress Mine, 195, 198, *198*
Obey, André, 14
O'Casey, Sean, 253
O'Connell, Arthur, *235,* 236
Odets, Clifford, 178, *179*
Oenslager, Donald, *255*
O'Hara, John, 179
Ohio State Journal, 205
Oklahoma!, 59, 106, 109, 176, 178, 180, *180,* 181, *181,* 182, *182, 183, 184,* 187, 192, 206, 208, 213
Old Lady Shows Her Medals, The, 215
Old Maid, The, 148
Olds, Irving, 213
Olivier, Laurence, 124, 231, 273
Olson, Nancy, 244, *244,* 245
O'Malley, J. Pat, 238
O'Malley, Rex, 57
On the Harmfulness of Tobacco, 253
On the Town, 253, 254
One Red Rose for Christmas, 215
O'Neil, George, 124
O'Neill, Carlotta (Mrs. Eugene), 94, 95, 97, 99, 131, 133
O'Neill, Eugene, 3, 28, 45, 73, 74, 75, 76, 81, 84, 86–99, *86,* 112, 114, 115, 116, 124, 126, 128, 131, 133, 137, 172, 200, 201, 205, 206, 212, 213, 276
O'Neill: Son and Playwright, 200
O'Neill's Cycle, 94, 95
Oppenheimer, George, 259, 263, 269
Orpheus Descending, 171
Orr, Forrest, 163
Osborn, Paul, 167, 187, 249
Osterwald, Bibi, *190*
Ostrich and His Egg, The, 249
Othello, 184, *184, 185,* 186, *186,* 187
Our Town, 214
Ouspensky, A., 104
Out of This World, 154
Out There, 31
Overton, Frank, *237*
Owen, Bill, *221,* 222
Oxenford, John, 239
Oxford, Earl, *140*

Pagnol, Marcel, 40
Pal Joey, 179, 208
Palmer, Betsy, 241, 243, *243*
Palmer, Lilli, 219, *219,* 231, *231,* 233, *233,* 234, *234*
Papa Is All, 173, *173*
Parade, 139, *139,* 140

Parry, Albert, *9, 10*
Party with Betty Comden and Adolph Green, A, 254, *255*
Pascal, André, 61
Passage to India, A, 262, 263, *263*
Patch, Miss (Shaw's secretary), 58
Patrick, John, 224, 228
Paul, Cedal, 160
Paul, Eden, 160
Pawnbroker, The, 273
Payne, B. Iden, 189
Pedi, Tom, *202*
Peer Gynt, 21, *21,* 22
Pemberton, Brock, 126
Perkins, Osgood, 129, *129, 145,* 146
Perry, Frank, 254
Perry, Frederick, 108, *109*
Peter Pan, 254
Peters, Rollo, 5, 6, *6, 7*
Petrie, Dan, 215
Philadelphia, Here I Come, 133
Philadelphia Daily News, 161
Philadelphia Inquirer, 161
Philadelphia Public Ledger, 19
Philadelphia Story, The, 149, 161, *161, 162, 163,* 194
Philanderer, The, 44
Phillips, Mary, *125, 126*
Phillips, Minna, 119, *120*
Picnic, 234, *235,* 236, *236*
Pidgeon, Walter, 128
Pins and Needles, 139
Pinski, David, 10
Pinter, Harold, 269
Pious, Minerva, 265
Pirandello, Luigi, 54, 68, 70
Pirate, The, 176, *178*
Piscator, Erwin, 187
Pitkin, William, 256
Platt, Marc, 182, *183*
Plautus, Titus Maccius, 152
Playhouse Theatre (N.Y.), 261
Playwrights' Company, 169, 173, 176, 245
Plummer, Christopher, 238, 267, *268*
Plymouth Theatre (N.Y.), 236
PM (N.Y.), 174, 189, 199, 202
Point of Departure, 228
Point Valaine, 141
Pollock, Arthur, 145
Pons, Helene, 239
Pope, W. Macqueen, 232–233
Porgy, 70, 72, *74,* 107, 142, 216
Porgy and Bess, 70, 139, 142, *143, 144,* 179, 181, 216
Portman, Eric, 152, 263
Portrait of a Madonna, 253, *253*
Pound on Demand, A, 253, 254
Povah, Phyllis, 25
P.O.W., 215
Powell, Dawn, 134
Power, Tyrone, 188, 248
Power of Darkness, The, 8, *9*
Powers, Tom, 39, *39,* 40, 63, 76, 89, 101, *102,* 112, 146
Prelude to Exile, 148, *149*
Prescott, Orville, 205
Presnell, Harve, 259, *259*
Price, Vincent, 271, 272, *272*
Prince, William, *221,* 222, 243
Processional, 19, 31, *33*
Proctor, Catherine, *33*
Provincetown Players, 1, 3, 5, 73, 84, 86, 89, 276
Puccini, Giacomo, 13
Pulitzer Prize, 31, 64, 76, 110, 120, 125, 146, 166, 168, 234

Pure in Heart, The, 149
Pursuit of Happiness, The, 57, 222
Pygmalion, 63, 64, *65,* 230
Pygmalion and Galatea, 256
Pyne, Mary, 86

Quinlan, Doris, 212
Quintessence of Ibsenism, 45

Race with the Shadow, The, 26
Races, 134, 135, 136
Radio City Music Hall, 190
Rain from Heaven, 136, *137,* 276
Rains, Claude, 63, 101, *102,* 112, *113,* 119, *120, 121, 122,* 134
Raitt, John, *184,* 192, *193, 194*
Rama Rau, Santha, 262, *263*
Random House, 95, 205
Raphael, Alice and Claire, 2
Rascoe, Burton, 186, 188, 189, 195
Ratés, Les, 26, *26*
Rathbone, Basil, 230, *230,* 231
Rattigan, Terence, 195, 198, 209
Rauh, Ida (Mrs. Max Eastman), 3
Rawlins, Lester, 266
Reading, Bertice, 251, *251*
Red Rust, 104, 105, *105*
Reed, Alan, *174*
Reed, Florence, 195, *197*
Reicher, Emmanuel, 8, 10
Reicher, Frank, 14, *14, 18*
Reid, Carl Benton, 201, *201*
Reinhardt, Max, 19, 107, 160, 239
Relapse, The, 226, *226*
Renoir, Jean, 273
Requiem for a Nun, 250, *250,* 251, *251*
Reunion in Vienna, 116, *116,* 117, *117,* 141
Revelation, 168
Revere, Anne, 256
Rice, Elmer, 18, 23
Richardson, Tony, 251
Richman, Arthur, 14
Ricketts, Charles, 54, 55
Rickover, Hyman G. (Admiral), 261, 262
Ridges, Stanley, *124,* 126, *131, 132,* 133
Rigby, Terence, *270*
Riggs, Lynn, 4, 106, 109, 110, 172, 178, 180
Right You Are, If You Think You Are, 68, *70*
Risdon, Elizabeth, *11, 67*
Rise of Silas Lapham, The, 8, *8*
Ritchard, Cyril, *204,* 218, *218,* 226, 230, *232,* 238, 239
Ritt, Martin, 216
Riva, Maria, 238, *238*
Rivals, The, 174, *174*
River, The, 273
Roar China, 106, 107, *107*
Robb, Lotus, 25
Robbins, Elinor, 228
Robbins, Jerome, 243, 254
Roberts, Joan, 180, *180*
Robertson, Cliff, 214
Robeson, Paul, 184, *185,* 186, *186,* 216
Robinson, Edward G., 22, *22,* 41, *43,* 63, *63, 68, 69,* 70
Rodeo, 181
Rodgers, Gaby, 239
Rodgers, Richard, 13, 35, *36,* 60, 179, 180, 182, 192, 206, *207,* 208
Roeder, Ralph, 3, *11*
Roege, Estelle, 3
Roger Bloomer, 23
Rogers, Emmet, 173

Rogers, Paul, 269, *270*
Rogers, Will, 93, 128
Rolf, Frederick, 227
Rolland, Auguste, *189*
Rolland, Romain, 100
Romeo and Juliet, 125
Rooche, Viola, 57
Roosevelt, Franklin Delano, 119, 125, 246, 247, 248
Rose, George, 267
Roussin, André, 249
Routledge, Patricia, 271, 272, *272*
Rowe, Kenneth, 85
Rowland, Jeffrey, *247*
Royal, John, 213
Royal Hunt of the Sun, The, 266, 267, *267, 268*
Royal Shakespeare Company, 269, 271
Royale Theatre (N.Y.), 134
Royle, Selena, *22, 132*
Ruben, José, *137*
Ruggles, Charles, 262
Rule, Janice, 234, *235, 236*
R.U.R., 19, *20*
Ruskin, Coby, *188*
Russell, Rosalind, *106*, 252
Russell, Viletta, *190*
Russian People, The, 178, *179*
Ruth, Babe, 97
Rutherford, Margaret, 203, *204*
Ryan, Madge, *245*
Ryan, Mitchell, 206

Sabine, Lillian, 8
Sacco-Vanzetti, 56
Saint, Eva Marie, 237
St. James's Theatre (London), 81
St. James Theatre (N.Y.), 182
Saint Joan, 26, 27, *28*, 50, 51, 52, 53, 54, 55, 61, 98, 110, 137, 226, 227, *227*, 228, *228*
St. John, Howard, 202, *203*
St. Louis Star-Times, 236
Sanctuary, 250
Sands, Dorothy, 260
Sanford, Erskine, 11, *11, 12*, 63
Sardou, Victorien, 45
Saroyan, William, 164, *165, 166, 166, 169*
Saturday Review, 238, 251
Savior, Alfred, 112
Savo, Jimmy, 139, *139, 140*
Say, Darling, 254
Say Who You Are, 267
Schary, Dore, 246, *247*, 252, 254, *255, 256, 259*, 261, 262
Schary, Miriam, *255*
Schenker, Joel, 264, 271
Schildkraut, Joseph, 11, *13, 21*, 22, *22*
Schnabel, Stefan, *233*, 234
Schnitzer, Robert C., 260
Schnorr, Robert, 250
School for Husbands, The, 128, 129, *129*, 222
Schulman, Arnold, 214
Scott, Martha, 256, *257*
Scott, Zachary, *250*, 251
Scottsboro case, 134
Scourby, Alexander, 227
Sea Gull, The, 156, *157*
Second Man, The, 70, *71*
Segal, Alex, 215
Segal, Vivienne, 179
Seidman and Son, 264, *264, 265*
Seldes, Gilbert, 11, 112
Seldes, Marian, 266
Selwart, Tonio, 222

Senie, Richard, 228
Sentimental Journey of an Exile, The, 136
Sergava, Katherine, 182, *183*
Set My People Free, 216, *216*, 217, *217*
Seven Arts Magazine, 200
Seven Arts Productions, 249
Seven Year Itch, The, 244, 245
Seymour, Anne, 247
Shadow of a Pale Horse, 215
Shaffer, Peter, 266, 267
Shakespeare, William, 34, 35, 44, 54, 58, 61, 125, 129, 141, 149, 169, 171, 184, 186, 195, 212, 220, 222, 226, 273
Shannon, Effie, 46, 47, *160*
Shannon, Frank, 120
Shaw, Charlotte (Mrs. G. B.), 17, 49, 50, 51, 54, 56, 57, 58, 92
Shaw, George Bernard, 8, 10, 16, 17, 24, 26, 28, 34, 36, 39, 40, 44–61, *53*, 63, 72, 88, 90, 101, 110, 112, 118, 137, 138, 192, 209, 210, 211, 214, 226, 228, 232, 248, 276
Shaw, Reta, *235*
Sheaffer, Louis, 200, 224
Sheffield, Justus, 5
Sheridan, Richard Brinsley, 174
Sherman, Alida, 274
Sherwood, Madeleine, 258
Sherwood, Robert E., 116, 117, 146, 168, 169, *169*, 276, 277
Shields, Arthur, 98, 205, *206*
Shields, Helen, *158*
Shipley, Joseph T., 8, 17, 101, 115, 116, 136, 169, 200
Shoemaker, Ann, *173*
Shubert, Lee, 50, 119
Shubert brothers, 2, 19, 119
Shubert Theatre (N.Y.), 163, 184, 186, 219
Shumlin, Herman, 156, 160, 265
Shyre, Paul, 266
Sidney, Sylvia, *151*, 152
Siegmeister, Elie, 190
Sifton, Claire, 108
Sifton, Paul, 108
Sil-Vara, G., 81
Silver Cord, The, 62, 64, 67
Silver Whistle, The, 217, *217*, 218, *218*
Silverstein, Elliot, 215
Simon, Bob, 222
Simonov, Konstantin Mikhailovich, 178
Simonson, Lee, 1, *1*, 4, 5, 7, *7* (set), 8, *11* (set), 13, *13*, 16, 19, 21, *23* (set), *24* (set), 26, 28, *42* (set), 46, 48, 51, 54, 63, *75* (set), *83* (set), 84, 108, 139, *139* (set), 142, 152, 194, 276
Simpleton of the Unexpected Isles, The, 57, 138, 139, *139*
Sinclair, Hugh, 119, *120, 138*
Sinclair, Robert B., 163
Sing Out, Sweet Land!, 190, *190*, 191, *191*
Skaar, Perry, *247*
Skin of Our Teeth, The, 260
Skinner, Richard Dana, 39, 110
Skirball, Jack H., 188
Skulnik, Menasha, 256, *257*
Slaves, 274, *274, 275*
Sleeping Clergyman, A, 135, 136, *136*
Slow Dance on the Killing Ground, 266
Smallens, Alexander, 142
Smith, Art, 238
Smith, Dodie, 142, 145

Smith, Kent, 160, *160*
Smith, Loring, 239, *240*
Smith, Muriel, 217
Smythe, Jack, 215
Solid Gold Cadillac, The, 240
Something About a Soldier, 262, *262*
Somewhere in France, 172
Sondergaard, Gale, *124*, 125
Soudeikine, Sergei, 142, *143* (set)
Spigelgass, Leonard, 252, 265, *265*, 271
Squire, Katherine, *172*
Stage Magazine, 62, 277
Stanislavsky, Constantin, 22, 45, 102
Stanley, Kim, *235*, 236
Starbuck, Betty, 37
Stebbins, Rowland, 222
Stehli, Edgar, 63
Steinach, Dr. E., 47
Stephens, Harvey, *241*
Sterling, Jan, 195
Stern, Benjamin, 46
Stevens, Ashton, 141
Stevens, Emily, *29*
Stevens, Onslow, 158, *159*
Stevenson, Adlai, *263*
Stewart, Fred, *158*
Stillman, Henry, 10
Stock, Nigel, 209, *210*
Stockwell, Dean, 187
Stockwell, Guy, 187
Stopes, Al, *134*
Storm in a Teacup, 150,
Storm over Patsy, 150, 151, *151*
Strachey, Lytton, 107
Strange Interlude, 45, 74, *74*, 75, *75*, 76, *76*, 77, 86, 88, 89, 90, 91, 115, 126, 137, 146, 213
Strasberg, Lee, 36, 118
Straus, Oscar, 36
Streetcar Named Desire, A, 172
Strindberg, August, 9, 10, 45
Strudwick, Shepperd, *125, 135*, 146
Studebaker Theatre (Chicago), 62
Styne, Jule, 243, 271
Styron, William, 274
Sullivan, Dan, 272
Summer of the Seventeenth Doll, 245, *245, 246, 246*
Sunrise at Campobello, 246, *246*, 247, *247*, 248
Suzanna and the Elders, 57
Swope, Gerard, 19
Sydney, Basil, 21, 24, *25*, 90

Tachibana, Sahomi, *252*
Take Me Along, 128
Tambourines to Glory, 264
Taming of the Shrew, The, 40, 139, 141, *141*, 142, 168, 198
Tandy, Jessica, 175, *175*, 253, *253*, 254, 271
Tarkington, Booth, 31
Taubman, Howard, 256
Taylor, Laurette, 31
Tempest, Marie, 122
Tennent, H. M. Ltd., 232
Terry, Ellen, 29, 31
Thaxter, Phyllis, 169
Theadore, Ralph, *134*
Theatre Arts Magazine, 229–230
Theatre Book of the Year 1946–47, 202
Theatre Guild Acting Company, 62, 63
Theatre Guild American Repertory Company, 260, 261
Theatre Guild–American Theatre Society, 120, 231, 273, 277

Theatre Guild Magazine, 62, 277
Theatre Guild Quarterly, 62
Theatre Guild School of the Theatre, 62, 72
Theatre Guild: The First Ten Years, The, 4
Theatre Magazine, 36
There Shall Be No Night, 168, 168
Thesiger, Ernest, 136, 221, 222
They Knew What They Wanted, 31, 32, 64, 146
They Shall Not Die, 134, 134, 277
Third Best Sport, 249, 249, 250
This Time Tomorrow, 208, 209
Thomas, Ann, 238
Thompson, Daisy, 3
Thor, Jerome, 200
Thorndike, Sybil, 50, 52, 55
Three Plays for Puritans, 24, 34
Tidings Brought to Mary, 21, 21
Tiffeau, M. Jacques, 264
Time Limit!, 240–241, 241, 242
Time Magazine, 182, 238
Time of Your Life, The, 164, 165, 166, 166, 168
Times (London), 146
To Quito and Back, 151, 151
Tobin, Dan, 163
Tolan, Michael, 253
Toller, Ernst, 28, 29
Tolstoy, Leo, 8
"Tomorrow," 200
Tone, Franchot, 70, 103, 105, 109, 110, 110, 117, 167, 167, 168, 206, 256
Tonge, Philip, 218
Too True to Be Good, 57, 118, 119, 120, 139
Torres, H. L., 23
Touch of the Poet, A, 94, 97, 99
Tracy, Spencer, 273
Tragedy of the Elderly Gentleman, The, 49
Trammel, Niles, 213
Trask, C. Hooper, 6
Travers, Henry, 40, 40, 63, 64, 65, 103, 112, 112, 121, 122
Treadwell, Sophie, 172, 173, 174
Treasure, The, 10, 10
Trebitsch (Shaw's translation), 55, 56
Tretyakov, S. M., 106
Trinidad, Arsenio, 252
Trip to Bountiful, The, 236, 237, 237
Triple Play, 252, 253, 253, 254
Triumph of Reason, The, 100
Truex, Ernest, 134, 135
Trumbo, Dalton, 156
Tucker, Dudley, 3
Tully, Tom, 166, 172, 173
Tunnel of Love, The, 244, 244, 245
Turgenev, Ivan, 102
Turner, Eva, 138
Turner, Lana, 230
Twelfth Night, 169, 170, 170, 171, 172
Tyler, George, 86

Unfinished Comedy, The, 58
United States State Department, 260, 261
United States Steel Corporation, 211, 212, 213, 214, 215, 271
Unsinkable Molly Brown, The, 258, 258, 259, 259
Ustinov, Peter, 233, 234, 234

Vail, Lester, 177
Vajda, Ernest, 28

Vale, Rita, 78
Valentina, 231
Valley Forge, 136, 136, 137
van Druten, John, 212, 218
Van Fleet, Jo, 237, 237
Van Oss, Katrina, 208
Van Patten, Dick, 198, 198
Van Zandt, Porter, 260
Vanbrugh, Sir John, 226
Varèse, Edgar, 262
Variety, 141, 218, 232, 236
Velsey, Graham, 189
Vendrenne and Barker, 59
Venus Observed, 231, 231, 233
Verhaeren, Emile, 14
Verwayne, Percy, 72
Vesey, Denmark, 216
Victoria Regina, 171
Viele, Sheldon K., 14
Village Vanguard, 253
Visit, The, 266
Volpone, 77, 78
von Kantzow, Elfi, 231
von Scholz, Wilhelm, 26
Voskovec, George, 234
Vreeland, Frank, 64
Vye, Murvyn, 192, 194

Wade, Warren, 213
Walker, Danton, 169
Walker, June, 33, 33, 39, 39, 109, 110, 129, 129, 160, 239
Wall Street Journal, 23, 24
Wallace, Henry, 59
Wallant, Edward, 273
Walter, Eugene, 86
Walters, Charles, 140
Walther, Gretchen, 262
Wanamaker, Sam, 215
Waram, Percy, 21, 78, 108
Warden, Jack, 266
Warren, Kenneth, 245, 246
Warwick, Dionne, 274, 274
Washington Jitters, 156, 158
Washington Post, 252
Washington Square Players, 1, 2, 3, 4, 5, 44, 74, 84, 86, 87, 156, 252, 257
Washington Star, 191
Waterhouse, Keith, 269
Watkins, Linda, 62, 108, 109, 134, 134
Watson, Betty Jane, 184
Watson, Douglas, 138
Watson, Lucile, 11
Watson, Minor, 146, 146
Watts, Richard, Jr., 74, 75, 148, 160, 202, 218, 222, 225, 229, 246, 254, 259, 269, 271
Wayne, David, 214
Webb, Alan, 209, 210
Webb, Clifton, 148, 148
Webster, Margaret, 156, 169, 170, 171, 184, 184, 186, 227, 228, 248
Wednesday's Child, 148
Weidman, Charles, 129, 129, 190
Weinstein, Henry T., 249
Welch, Mary, 98, 205, 247
Werfel, Franz, 40, 63, 187, 188, 189
Wertheim, Maurice, 1, 1, 4, 5, 6, 74, 84, 87, 89, 194
West, Rebecca, 55
Westerfield, James, 231
Westley, Helen, 1, 1, 3, 3, 4, 4, 5, 5, 6, 6, 7, 10, 11, 13, 20, 29, 29, 35, 35, 41, 63, 72, 77, 78, 81, 84, 109, 117, 135, 139, 141, 194, 209, 276
Westport (Conn.) Country Playhouse,

3, 57, 60, 158, 166, 217, 222, 232, 236
Wexley, John, 133, 134, 277
What Price Glory?, 40
What the Public Wants, 18
Wheatley, Jane, 14, 37
Whipple, Sidney B., 156
Whisper in My Good Ear, 266
White, Miles, 176, 181, 192
White, Paul, 149
Whorf, Richard, 141, 142, 153, 154, 154, 156, 157, 168, 169
Who's Afraid of Virginia Woolf?, 1
Widmark, Richard, 195, 196
Wife with a Smile, The, 14
Wilde, Oscar, 202, 203
Wilder, Thornton, 160, 212, 214, 239, 239, 240, 260
Wilkinson, Marc, 267
Willard, Catherine, 218, 218
Williams, Addie, 232
Williams, Emlyn, 175
Williams, Hope, 118, 119, 120
Williams, John, 86, 231
Williams, Tennessee, 171, 172, 253, 260
Willson, Meredith, 258, 259
Wilson, Earl, 188
Wilson, Eleanor, 217
Wilson, Elizabeth, 235
Wilson, Frank, 72, 72
Wilson, John C., 203
Wilson, Kathryn, 29
Wilson, Samuel T., 197, 205, 234
Winchell, Walter, 110, 166
Windows, 24, 25
Windust, Bretaigne, 152
Wine of Choice, 154, 155, 156
Wingless Victory, 150
Wings over Europe, 77, 80, 91, 212, 237
Winslow Boy, The, 209, 210
Winters, Marian, 256
Winters, Shelley, 258
Winter's Tale, The, 195, 196, 197
Winterset, 146
Winwood, Estelle, 43
Witherspoon, Cora, 135
Without Love, 176, 176, 177
Wolfe, Thomas, 176
Wolheim, Louis, 86
Women's Wear Daily, 68, 269, 271
Wonderful Town, 254
Wood, Peggy, 61
Woodbury, Clare, 110
Woodthorpe, Peter, 271
Woodward, Joanne, 214
Woollcott, Alexander, 19, 34, 64, 150, 154, 155, 156
World of Suzie Wong, The, 249
Worlock, Frederic, 227
Wycherly, Margaret, 9, 9, 48, 49, 112
Wyler, Margrit, 232

Yaffe, James, 265
Yesterday's Magic, 175, 175, 176, 180
Yost, Herbert, 41, 146
You Never Can Tell, 57, 60, 209, 210
Young, Howard, 224
Young, Roland, 24
Young, Stark, 26, 151, 156, 182
Young Belgium Group, 14
Yurka, Blanche, 14, 30, 41, 42, 43

Zola, Emile, 8
Zolotow, Sam, 239, 249
Zuckmayer, Carl, 172
Zweig, Stefan, 77, 159, 160